R.J. MITCHELL **Schooldays to**
SPITFIRE

R.J. MITCHELL Schooldays to SPITFIRE

GORDON MITCHELL

TEMPUS

This edition first published 2006

Tempus Publishing Limited
The Mill, Brimscombe Port,
Stroud, Gloucestershire, GL5 2QG
www.tempus-publishing.com

© Gordon Mitchell, 1986, 1997, 2002, 2006

British Library Cataloguing in Publication Data.
A catalogue record for this book is available from the British Library.

ISBN 0 7524 3727 5

Typesetting and origination by Tempus Publishing Limited
Printed and bound in Great Britain

Contents

About the Author

Dr Gordon Mitchell PhD CBiol FIBiol is the son of R.J. Mitchell, and was until his retirement a biologist at the University of Reading. He is still, aged 85, an active member of the Spitfire Society. He lives in Cheltenham.

Appendices

Abbreviations Used

AC – Air Commodore
ACM – Air Chief Marshal
AM – Air Marshal
AVM – Air Vice-Marshal
CO – Commanding Officer
MRF – Marshal of the Royal Air Force

The book is an absolutely first-class effort, and I hope very much that it achieves the success it deserves.
Sir George Edwards, OM, CBE, FRS, FEng (April 1986)

Your book relates the sad and poignant story about the life of not only the most outstanding aircraft designer of my time but also of a man of incredible moral and physical courage. I think that it will be recognised as the classic narrative on the birth of the Spitfire and will put all other publications in the shade.
Alex Henshaw, MBE (April 1986)

You are to be much congratulated on your book about R.J. A very thorough job and I feel R.J. would have been pleased with it. It fills a much-needed gap in the literature of aviation.
The late Jeffrey Quill, OBE, AFC, FRAeS (March 1986)

The Spitfire fighter – the most renowned of all fighter aircraft in the war of 1939–45. Mitchell wedded good engineering to aerodynamic grace and made science his guide. The Spitfire exemplified Mitchell's special quality of combining fine lines with great structural strength.
Colston Shepherd (Oxford Dictionary of National Biography 1949 Edition. By permission of Oxford University Press)

Your dad was one of the greatest men of the twentieth century and provided the free world with a superb weapon.
Dr Derek Armstrong, Ontario, Canada (July 2000)

Dear Dr Mitchell, The Prime Minister fully understands your wish to see that your father's services to aircraft design are recognised with a posthumous high honour.
Letter received from 10 Downing Street (December 1999)

I have no doubt that your father's design will still be flying a hundred years after the aircraft's first flight, and giving pilots and aviation lovers the same pleasure as it has for the past sixty-four years.
ACM Sir Peter Squire KCB, DFC, AFC, ADC, FRAeS, RAF (September 2000)

Unlike some men who achieve considerable success when young, it was quite obvious that R.J.'s success had not gone to his head and it never did. A man in a million.
From Never a Dull Moment *by Denis Le P. Webb – at Supermarine for forty-four years from 1926 (May 2001)*

For Gordon with best wishes and a salute for your father without whose genius we could not have won the Malta battle of 1942. Ask those who were there.

The late Wg Cdr P.B. 'Laddie' Lucas, CBE, DSO (and Bar) (c.1995)

Your book has been a useful source for this work (*Swift Justice*) and is essential reading for Supermarine watchers.

Grp Capt. Nigel Walpole, OBE, BA, RAF (Author of Swift Justice, *May 2000)*

Website (2006) www.rjmitchell–spitfire.co.uk

Foreword

*by The Right Honourable The Lord Balfour of Inchrye, PC, MC,
Under Secretary of State for Air, 1938–1944*

I know I fell in love with her the moment I was introduced that summer day in 1938. I was captivated by her sheer beauty; she was slimly built with a beautifully proportioned body and graceful curves just where they should be. In every way to every young man – or, in my case, middle-aged man – she looked the dream of what one sought. Mind you, some of her admirers warned me that she was what mother called 'a fast girl', and advised that no liberties should be taken with her until you got better acquainted.

I was warned to approach her gently but once safely embraced in her arms I found myself reaching heights of delight I had never before experienced.

Thus was my introduction to that early Spitfire, the consummation of R.J. Mitchell's design work of sixteen years, supported by a team of colleagues without whom, as he was always at pains to stress, he could never have achieved all that he did.

Success could only have been won by hard work, knowledge and intense determination during those pre-Spitfire years of development.

Not everyone connects Mitchell's ultimate success with the creations of his earlier work. Back in 1922, there was the Sea Lion II, winner of that year's Schneider Trophy race; later came his work producing the Royal Air Force (RAF) twin-engined flying boats such as the Southampton, four of which carried out the famous 23,000-mile Far East Flight to India, Australia and Singapore in 1927–28; these were followed by further, ever-improving types such as the Stranraer flying boat, the 'S' series of racing seaplanes which won the Schneider Trophy outright for Britain, and last but not least the dear old Walrus amphibian of last war fame.

In truth, one can say that, in those pre-war years, the RAF was building up the nation's debt to Mitchell, for, as is related within the pages of this book, he designed no less than twenty-four different types of aircraft during his life.

Then came the war, and the culmination of effort and achievement for R.J. Mitchell. The Spitfire came into its own. It would be presumptuous of me to dwell on how this short-range fighter of 1940 became the most versatile aircraft of the RAF. I cite some of the tasks it was used for, and always with great success: low and high offensive operation; ground force attack; high-altitude photo-reconnaissance; a range extended by the jettisonable slipper tank.

This book is a worthy tribute to R.J. Mitchell, to whom our country owes so much, for his work in a life sadly shortened while still full of promise. Within its pages I have read of the experiences of those men who 'did the job', and in admiration of their feats of bravery against the enemy. Sadly we remember those who paid the price with their lives.

I like to think that, somewhere, somehow, R.J. and they are once more in companionship.

Lord Balfour died on 21 September 1988.

Introduction

The leading role in this book is played by the man who has been rightly called one of the outstanding designers of all time, R.J. Mitchell (1895–1937).

The aircraft that he designed do, of course, figure in the narrative but they play a secondary role. Accordingly, this publication is different from all of the many others that have been written about one or other of these aircraft, in particular the Spitfire fighter, about which there appears to be a never-ending urge to write more and more. This book is not just about the Spitfire, laudable though it might be if it were, as within these pages the Spitfire takes its place alongside the twenty-three other aircraft that Mitchell designed in the sixteen years of his brief working life. In turn, these aircraft all take their rightful place a respectful distance behind their creator. Until now, relatively little has been written about Mitchell himself and certainly nothing in such detail as will be discovered within these pages. These are the true facts about the man who achieved so much in so short a time, the man who has been widely acclaimed to have been a genius and whose contribution to the survival of his country was of such magnitude that its debt to him can never be repaid. Mitchell's story is part of the history of Britain and, within this book, it has at last been told in full.

What was my father really like; what training did he have that formed the foundation for such an outstandingly successful career; what did his colleagues who worked with him (probably the most exacting critics) and his test pilots really think of the man? How advanced were his creative ideas in aircraft design; did he have failures as well as successes; was Mitchell an artist in the true sense of the word as well as an engineering genius? Was he a born leader, actively directing and guiding his team of specialists, or was he perhaps really only a figurehead, doing very little and taking all the glory? How did the leaders of the aviation world assess him?

Answers to all these questions and many more personal observations will be found in these pages, including what my father was like to live with; whether he was a good and caring father; whether he was all work and no play, and what, if any, his interests were outside work; what his relationship was with my mother and myself and with his other relatives, and how his success in his career affected these relationships. Last, but by no means least, how did he face up to the severe physical and mental adversity that he had to suffer during the last four years of his life, which has never before been described in such detail?

Sufficient detail is given about all the important aircraft he designed to enable the non-specialist reader to assess his creative genius; also insights into how he learnt from the hard school of failure to turn failures into outstanding successes – how, for example, the first 'Spitfire' was a near disaster; and how he always proclaimed that he was 'just one member of a team of experts'.

In addition to detailing the life story of R.J. Mitchell, this book contains many fine tributes from eminent people who either have a particular knowledge of Mitchell's work, had a special association with his aircraft or who worked with him at Supermarine. I invited a number of people to contribute and all generously accepted; this is in itself a magnificent tribute to my father and my very grateful thanks are due to them all. I am also deeply conscious of the honour that the Rt Hon. The Lord Balfour of Inchrye accorded my father by readily agreeing to write the Foreword and I owe him my very sincere gratitude. As under secretary of state for air, Lord Balfour signed the first order for 310 Spitfires on 3 June 1936 and then later, in 1938, he himself flew half of the RAF's complement, at that time, of two Spitfires!

I am greatly indebted to the late Marian Blackburn, who had the original idea for producing a book about my father, albeit aimed at schoolchildren. She had carried out much research for her proposed booklet, which proved to be of great value to me in the production of this book. I indeed owe Marian Blackburn a great debt of gratitude for sowing the seed which eventually germinated into the present volume.

One further person I wish to mention here is Jeffrey Quill, who gave valued help and advice with the book and, most importantly, rewrote large sections of Chapters 15, 16 and 17, since he felt that the first drafts did not do full justice to the subjects covered. There is no one better qualified to have done this, since Jeffrey's long and distinguished association with the Spitfire is unique, and I am most grateful to him for so willingly undertaking this task.

I carried out as little editing as possible of the invited contributions; likewise no attempt was made to achieve a common style of writing, or to delete similar material being considered in different chapters, provided it was done from differing viewpoints.

Few books published are completely free of mistakes and doubtless this one will be no exception despite the attempt to make it so. Consolation may be obtained from the words of Winston Churchill, who suggested that the presence of mistakes, deliberate or otherwise, in published work could serve a useful purpose by leaving room for criticism, as a result of which the author and the work become better known! Nevertheless, any mistakes found herein are unintentional. In the event, relatively few mistakes were found and have been corrected in this revised Fourth Edition of the book.

My objectives in producing this book have been to achieve a publication that would be seen as the definitive life of R.J. Mitchell, that it would be interesting, informative, readable and authentic, and would be accepted as a worthy tribute to him. I became involved in the project because I was the son of that man, and was, as a result, in a unique position to help the achievement of these objectives. What I have done has been entirely on behalf of my father, for whom no son could have greater affection and pride, and I seek no recognition for myself. If my father had been alive today and his verdict after reading this book had been favourable, then I would have been well satisfied and would have wished for nothing more.

Gordon Mitchell
December 2005

Acknowledgements

It is impossible to produce a book such as this without being able to enlist the help of many people and I am very conscious of how much I owe to so many who so willingly gave this assistance.

Many of these have received mention in the Introduction; equally I am very indebted to Eric Mitchell, R.J.'s brother, and his wife, Ada, for providing material relating to R.J.'s early family life; to the following ex-colleagues of R.J. who talked about the years they had worked with him – Eric Lovell-Cooper, Jack Rasmussen, Arthur Shirvall and Harold Smith; to Mrs Vera Cherry who, as Miss Cross, was R.J.'s secretary for many years and spoke about her memories of those happy times; to Gladys Pickering, wife of the great test pilot George, both of whom knew R.J. and my mother for many years; to Bishop Reeve who recalled the visits he made to R.J. during the last months of his life; and to Mrs Eva Pitman who lived with the Mitchell family in their home in Southampton for a large number of years. Two others who likewise spoke to me about R.J. were Sir Stanley Hooker of Rolls-Royce and AVM 'Webby' Webster, winner of the 1927 Schneider Trophy.

Two people who must receive special mention are Alan Clifton, ex-colleague of R.J.'s, and Hugh Scrope, previously company secretary of Vickers plc. Alan is one of the contributors to the book but, in addition, he helped in several other ways over matters in which he was in a unique position to do so. Hugh seemed to thrive on answering questions, giving permission to use various material and providing invaluable information. I am most grateful to them both for their patience and guidance.

In addition, there is a very large number of people who gave help in a variety of ways, such as providing information, supplying photographs or other material, or giving valuable introductions to other people. Their names are given below in alphabetical order and I am very conscious of the debt of gratitude I owe to them all. Some have received acknowledgement in the text of the book but for completeness are included again here.

Michael Baylis (photographs), Wg Cdr David Bennett (information on memorials), Pat Bennett (son of Alec), Mrs M. Cecil (1927 letter of R.J.'s), Peter Cooke (Spitfire model photograph), Christopher Cornwell (bishop's chaplain, Lichfield), A.E. Crew (Stoke-on-Trent Association of Engineers), H.J. Deakin (Reginald Mitchell CP School), Professor Robin East (University of Southampton), Christopher Elliott (RAF Museum – photographs of many of R.J.'s personal items held by the museum), Richard Falconer (R.J.'s old wrist-watch), Keith Fordyce (curator, Torbay Aircraft Museum), Campbell Gunston (Battle of Britain Memorial Flight), Ronald Howard (son of Leslie), Sqn Ldr Alan Jones (Southampton Hall of Aviation), Howard Jones (director of the British Colostomy Association), Professor Geoffrey Lilley (University of Southampton), the Hon. Patrick Lindsay (Christie's Ltd), Peter March (Air Extra), David Mondey (author), S.S. Miles (sculptor), Eric Morgan (British Aerospace plc), Rosemary Mourant (Mitchell Junior School), A.W.L. Nayler (Royal Aeronautical Society), David Plastow (managing director and chief executive, Vickers plc), David Preston (public relations manager, Rolls-Royce Motors Ltd), RAF Museum, R.A. Randall (editor, *Evening Sentinel*), Richard Riding (editor, *Aeroplane Monthly*), Michael Ridley (curator of museums, Weymouth), David Roscoe (director, public relations, Vickers plc), Martin Snaith (son of Leonard), Southampton Reference Library staff, Cdr Dennis White (director, Fleet Air Arm Museum), Wg Cdr Bill Wood (RAF Museum).

Finally, I wish to record my sincere thanks to my wife, Alison, for her support and patience and for her invaluable assistance, prior to her death in April 2005, in the production of the book.

Gordon Mitchell

Reference Sources

Many references in various publications were consulted in the preparation of this book, but the following should be mentioned as being of particular value and importance:

J. Smith, JRAeS (1954) *The First Mitchell Memorial Lecture*, 58, 311–328.
David Mondey (1975) *The Schneider Trophy*.
C.F. Andrews & E.B. Morgan (1981) *Supermarine Aircraft since 1914*.
J.D. Scott (1962) *Vickers: A History*.

Appreciation

The Late R.J. Mitchell

This appreciation by Sir Robert McLean, chairman of Vickers Aviation Ltd, and of The Supermarine Aviation Works (Vickers) Ltd, was published in *Vickers News* in July 1937. It is reproduced in full by kind permission of Vickers plc.

By the death of Mr R.J. Mitchell at Southampton on 11 June, the world of aviation has lost one who has long been one of its outstanding figures.

After serving an apprenticeship with Messrs Kerr, Stuart & Co. Ltd, of Stoke-on-Trent, he joined the Supermarine company at the age of twenty-two in 1917, was appointed chief engineer and chief designer by 1920, and became a director of the company in 1928.

In 1927 he was awarded the silver medal of the Royal Aeronautical Society in recognition of his share in the British Schneider Cup victory at Venice, and in 1932 the CBE was conferred upon him in recognition of his services to aviation.

In the public mind his name will always be associated with the history of the Schneider Trophy, which, by virtue of the backing given to competing teams by their respective governments, became a grim technical competition with national prestige deeply involved.

In 1922, the Supermarine company had its first victory in the Schneider Trophy at Venice with a flying boat designed by Mitchell; and again in 1927, 1929 and 1931, the series of machines, which finally brought the trophy to Britain for all time, were products of his mind. All these contests and the demand for ever-increasing speed set the designer on each occasion a set of new and difficult problems, the wrong answers to which might end in disaster and loss of life. Those connected with Mitchell during these contests and their attendant anxieties will always remember how he seemed to have anticipated, and to be ready for, any doubts or difficulties which might arise in the execution of the task. It is significant that while other nations applied their best design brains to the production of seaplanes to compete in the Schneider Trophy, it was only Mitchell who, on each occasion, was ready with his machines in time to come over the starting line on the appointed day.

Not the least of his services to the country was the stimulus that these victories gave to British aeronautical technique and the realisation by the public that, in this new adventure of flying, British technique was supreme.

How well he succeeded in combining superb aeronautical design with an adventurous, but always sound, structural technique, is witnessed by the firm's record of service types. There have been the early 'Seagull', an amphibian of which many went into service in Spain and Australia; the 'Southampton', long the standard twin-engined flying boat in the RAF; followed quickly by the 'Scapa' and the 'Stranraer'; all bearing upon them the 'Mitchell' mark of originality, coupled with thoroughly sound execution. With the revival of the amphibian idea in the 'Seagull V', there became available for the Naval Air Service, under the naval name of 'Walrus', a new amphibian for use with the Fleet Air Arm. Of the machines most recently completed by Mitchell, the 'Spitfire', a single-seater fighter, reflects more closely the immense knowledge gained in high-speed work in his Schneider Trophy days. When the achievements of this aircraft come to be made public, it will be recognised that once again he stood head and shoulders above competitors in his solution of a difficult problem.

The impression left on the mind of one who had been in the closest contact with Mitchell for many years in his plans for the future, and in his views on these new problems that arise from day to day in the evolution of flying, was that of a critical mind, not prepared to jump to conclusions or take decisions except on grounds of whose soundness he had satisfied himself. At the same time, no idea was too daring or adventurous to be considered, never from the academic point of view, but always from that of practical application.

Mitchell leaves a record of almost continuous achievement which has not been equalled by any other individual designer in the short history of aviation, and his death at the early age of forty-two is indeed a tragedy. His colleagues and friends can but express to his widow and son their deep sympathy in the sorrow which has overtaken them.

Sir Robert McLean

The Author

Dr Gordon Mitchell, PhD, CBiol, FIBiol

Gordon Mitchell was born on 6 November 1920, the only offspring of
the family. After leaving school, he worked on a farm in Dorset as a pupil
for one year and then entered the University of Reading in September
1940 as an undergraduate. After two years, he voluntarily gave up his
university studies to join the RAFVR in which he served for five years.
First he served on Air-Sea Rescue High Speed Launches, and then in
September 1944 he was commissioned in the Meteorological Branch.
On demobilisation in February 1947, Gordon returned to Reading
University to complete his degree course, and obtained his degree in
1948. Shortly afterwards, he secured a post at the University of Reading's
National Institute for Research in Dairying, where he remained until he
retired in March 1985. He conducted research studies on the nutrition
of farm animals, specialising in the pig, which has a close similarity to
man in many nutritional and physiological features. He was the author
or co-author of many papers published in scientific journals.

He became a member of the academic staff of the University of
Reading in 1952 and the following year obtained his PhD degree. He
served for three years on the senate of the university from 1969, and

as technical secretary on a number of committees and working parties concerned with animal nutrition and allied subjects. He was a member of the executive committee of the Institute of Biology, Agricultural Sciences Division, for a number of years, and later became chairman of this committee. Likewise, he served for several years on the council of the British Society of Animal Production; he was also an elected member of the John Hammond Pig Group and served for a year as chairman of this influential group of advisory, genetic, producer, research, university and veterinary specialists.

Gordon was elected a fellow of the Institute of Biology in October 1979 and for the final six years of his appointment at the NIRD he was head of his department. On retirement, the title of honorary fellow of the University of Reading was conferred upon him, which he was very proud to have been granted. He was also granted the status of honorary research associate of the university's associated institution, the Animal and Grassland Research Institute.

Gordon Mitchell has been a vice-president of the James Butcher Housing Association Ltd in Reading since 1969; in November 1985 he and his wife opened a new specialised nursing unit, bearing the name Mitchell Lodge in recognition of their long connection with the association. He is an active member of the Spitfire Society and of the Bourton-on-the-Water Probus Club.

Following his retirement, he devoted much of his time to the production of this book, its Second Edition in 1997, its Third Edition in 2002, and now, in 2006, this current Fourth Edition, but does not, he says, have plans to write any more! In 1993, Gordon started a campaign to persuade the Royal Mail and the Royal Mint to honour his father, on the occasion of the centenary of his birth on 20 May 1995, in some appropriate way. The success of this long campaign is detailed in Chapter 19.

Since 1989, Gordon has been giving lectures about his father to raise funds for Cancer Research UK (R.J. Mitchell Fund). As at January 2006, he has given 136 lectures and raised a total of £28,232 for the fund. All the money he raises for this designated fund is used for research in colorectal cancer, the form of cancer from which his father died in 1937. His mother died from bladder cancer on 3 January 1946. Gordon is a life governor of Cancer Research UK.

He had been happily married to Alison, whom he describes as a super wife, for fifty-five years when sadly she died on 30 April 2005. He has a family of three, David, Adrian and Penny. In October 1985 he became a proud grandfather for the first time, and in October 1988 for the second time – Nicky and Emma.

Shortly after the publication of the Third Edition of this book in 2002, Gordon had the misfortune of being diagnosed with Parkinson's Disease.

1

R.J. Mitchell

'He's mad about aeroplanes.' That is what the Hanley High School boys said about their friend, Reg Mitchell. Yet, when Reg was born, the aeroplane had not been invented. There had been many experiments with balloons and gliders as men struggled to launch themselves into the air. In 1783 the first successful manned flight was made over Paris in a Montgolfier hot air balloon, and just over 100 years later a German, Otto Lilienthal, flew in a hang-glider. In England, most Victorians laughed at the idea of a flying machine. They said: 'If God had meant men to fly he would have given them wings.' It is all the more surprising that a boy born in such an age would one day design an aircraft able to fly at more than 400 mph.

Reg Mitchell was born on 20 May 1895, at 115 Congleton Road, Butt Lane, Stoke-on-Trent, where his father, Herbert Mitchell, was a headmaster in Longton. Within a few months of his birth the family moved to 87 Chaplin Road, Normacot, near Longton, not far from the centre of Stoke-on-Trent. Later they settled down in nearby Victoria Cottage, a comfortable house well outside the industrial smoke and clatter of the Pottery Towns.

Herbert Mitchell, a Yorkshire man from Holmfirth, had trained as a teacher at York College. After obtaining a headship in Longton, he married Elizabeth Jane, daughter of William Brain, a Master Cooper of Longton. During this time he established printing classes in the Potteries. Soon after moving to Normacot, Herbert Mitchell gave up teaching and became a Master Printer at the firm of Wood, Mitchell & Co. Ltd of Hanley. By hard work and use of his artistic ability he became managing director and eventually the sole owner of the printing works until his death in 1933 at the age of sixty-eight. He played a very active part in Freemasonry and achieved high office in the fraternity.

In the early years of this century, school teachers, and even head-masters, were very poorly paid, so it was probably his high position at Hanley printing works which enabled Herbert Mitchell to live at Victoria Cottage and support his rapidly growing family. Before long there were five children, Hilda the eldest, and then Reg, Eric, Doris and Billy, all born fairly close to each other, so that Mrs Mitchell had her hands full looking after her family and home.

Victoria Cottage in no way resembled a cottage; it was in fact a very pleasant residence, and provided the sort of comfortable surroundings in which the Mitchell children grew up. The house was quite large, with a dining room and drawing room facing the garden. At the back, there was a large kitchen with a black-leaded cooking range and an even larger scullery used for the rougher kind of domestic work. In common with most houses built at that time, Victoria Cottage had both front and back stairs. Mrs Mitchell always kept a maid to assist her with the housework and care of the children, and the back stairs were reserved for the use of the maid. In the Edwardian period, maids were not allowed to retire to bed by way of the carpeted front stairs used by their employers.

The house stood in its own grounds, with a lawn and garden which gave the children plenty of space to romp and play, free from too much adult supervision. Beyond the garden was a coachhouse and stables; but since no coach or horses were kept, these outbuildings were given over to the children for use as playrooms. Mr Mitchell senior was a firm believer in keeping boys out of mischief by providing them with plenty to keep them occupied. He was also very anxious that they should all learn to use their hands. Reg, Eric and Billy were given tools and simple materials, and encouraged to follow their own hobbies and make things for themselves. But whatever task they started it had to be done properly, since their father was a stickler for perfection. Even a menial job, such as sweeping the floor, had to be done thoroughly before it would pass his inspection.

Although their father demanded certain standards of work and behaviour, the Mitchell family enjoyed a happy and secure childhood. Being close to each other in age, there was always someone to play with, and they had the care and devotion of both parents. As so often happens, Mrs Mitchell had a soft spot in her heart for Billy, the youngest. She was a very beautiful woman, adored by all her children, but she also had a very determined streak in her character, a quality inherited by her eldest son.

At the age of eight, Reg Mitchell went to the Queensberry Road Higher Elementary School in Normacot. He had a lively, quick brain, and from an early age he was good at mathematics. His class teacher in this subject was Mr Jolly, a close family friend who lived just across the road from Victoria Cottage. Reg was also inventive and artistic, two gifts which were to play an important part in his career.

A few years ago, Gordon Mitchell received a letter from an ex-pupil at the Queensberry Road School, Beatrice Goulding, saying that she was in the same class as Reg.

> Reg was always a very clever boy but we did not realise we had a genius in our class. As we read later about his wonderful achievements, we were so proud that we knew him. It seems dreadful that such a genius should die so young. A lot of us in the school with Reg were angry that more often than not little mention was made of the fact that he spent most of his young days in Normacot.

Beatrice Goulding sadly died in June 1985.

After finishing his elementary education, Reg moved on to the Hanley High School in Old Street, Hanley. Its use as a school ended in 1939 when it was commandeered by the Army. Subsidence damage subsequently condemned it as being unsafe for further use. It was while he was at this school that Reg first showed an interest in what was later to become his life's work. In late 1908, 'Colonel' S.F. Cody became the first man to fly an aeroplane in England, achieving a flight in Farnborough of 496 yards at a height of up to 60 ft, and in the following year the Short brothers established an aircraft factory on the Isle of Sheppey. Reg was so excited by this new and wonderful idea of flying that he and his brother Eric began to make their own model aeroplanes.

The two Mitchell brothers had no kit or printed instructions to follow; they simply made up shapes of their own designs. As their pocket money was restricted to a few coppers a week, they could not afford to buy much. They used fine strips of bamboo cane to make the wings and fuselage and then glued on a layer of paper to 'keep out the wind'. The parts of the model were held together by a covering of elastic material like stockinette. The propeller, carved out of wood, was turned by a twisted rubber loop. What fun they had as their fragile aircraft swooped and dipped over the lawns at Victoria Cottage.

As well as having a vivid imagination and an easy mastery of mathematics, Reg was also good at games. He was a sturdy, well-built lad, with broad shoulders and, as a capable batsman, he could always be relied upon to get the school cricket team out of trouble and this earned him a good deal of popularity.

At home in Victoria Cottage, there was never a dull moment when Reg was about. He was always inventing something new to amuse his brothers and sisters. He even made a small-sized billiards table, using stretched webbing fabric as cushions, and it gave the boys hours of entertainment. Reg played the game so often that his father, anxious for his son to do well at school, was heard to complain: 'Reg will never pass his examinations if he spends so much time playing billiards.' In spite of his father's gloomy prophecy, he passed all his examinations, taking them in his stride as easily as he fashioned his model aeroplanes. His interest in flying increased when he started to keep racing pigeons and to send them over to France to compete in 'homing' races.

Though he sometimes seemed aloof and occupied with his own interests, Reg was always the leader and instigator of every youthful escapade. He was fond of his brothers and sisters, and his affection for his mother made him feel especially protective towards her favourite, young Billy. This was shown in an incident which occurred when Reg was twelve and Billy only a little lad. One evening, when Billy had been put to bed, the rest of the family sat in the room below enjoying a game of cards. Suddenly they heard a terrific bang overhead, followed by Billy's frightened screams. Reg leapt to his feet and was upstairs in a flash, urged to greater speed by the sight of smoke coming out from under the bedroom door. Without a second's hesitation he plunged into the smoke-filled room and, gathering up the sobbing little boy in his arms, he carried him out to safety. The gaslight was always left on until Billy was asleep, and on this particular evening a sudden gust of wind from the open window had flung the curtains against the gas mantle and they had immediately gone up in flames. The flames spread to a picture cord, and it had been the banging of the picture as it crashed to the floor which had alerted the family. Reg's quick reaction probably saved his young brother's life.

Reg enjoyed his school days, and in his spare time he devoured every scrap of information he could about aeroplanes. In the days when Reg was at school, flying as a mode of travel was only in the experimental stage, and the appearance of any aircraft was likely to make headline news. Reg was not a particularly studious lad – it would seem that he did not have to be from his exam record – he preferred making things to reading books, particularly fiction. He was very persistent. If he set himself a task he would finish it, no matter how boring and tiresome it turned out to be. Once, while still at school, he decided to read the entire works of Sir Walter Scott, though why he chose that particular author, no one knew. Hour after hour he sat on a stool by the kitchen range, ploughing through *Ivanhoe, Kenilworth, Rob Roy* and the rest, until his self-imposed task was completed. Anyone who has struggled through the duller pages of Scott's narrative will have some idea how it must have been for a young and very active lad. But this gift of perseverance, of never giving up a task once he had started it, was one of the reasons for his future success as an aircraft designer.

In 1911, at the age of sixteen, Reg left Hanley High School and his father entered him as an apprentice at the locomotive engineering firm of Kerr, Stuart & Co. The works, situated in Fenton in the centre of Stoke-on-Trent, stood between the railway line and the river, and the firm provided a sound basic training in engineering. Reg, however, found this new life not entirely to his liking. All apprentices had to start work in the engine sheds, and this meant that he had to get up very early and travel down to Stoke on the workmen's tramcar. It wasn't the early rising that he objected to, but the fact that he had to wear overalls and carry his own lunch, which included the detested tea-can – a white enamel can with a handle and a lid serving as a cup – the sort of thing carried by all workmen at that time. Reg had just left school, where he had been a popular member of the first eleven cricket team, and he simply did not enjoy having to travel into town dressed in his overalls with his tea-can. At night he had to return home with grimy hands and with his overalls plastered with oil and dirt. He began to rebel against this daily ordeal, and when he could stand it no longer he openly protested to his father. But Mitchell senior, who was determined that his son's training should be practical as well as theoretical, gave him a brief but emphatic reply: 'You will go, my lad, and you will like it!'

One of his first jobs at Kerr Stuart's was to make the mid-morning tea for his group of fellow-apprentices and for his foreman. It would seem that Reg and the foreman did not exactly hit it off right from the start. One day not long after he started his apprenticeship, having duly made the tea, Reg gave the foreman his mug, whereupon he took one mouthful and promptly spat it out saying, 'It tastes like piss!' Reg said nothing, but thought that if that was what he wanted, he would damn well get it. So next day he went off to the wash-room as usual to fill the kettle with water, but this time instead of tap water, he peed into the kettle. Having boiled it he made the tea and handed the mugs round having first warned his fellow apprentices not to drink any. The foreman took one sip, then another larger one and said, 'Bloody good mug of tea, Mitchell, why can't you make it like this every day?' Honours about even on that episode, it would seem!

When Reg completed his training in the workshops, he moved on to the drawing office. Things now became much better as the hated blue overalls were a thing of the past. During his five-year apprenticeship at Kerr Stuart he attended night school, taking classes in engineering drawing, higher mathematics and mechanics, since he had already decided to make a career in basic engineering. He did so well in mathematics that, while he was attending the Wedgewood Burslem Technical School, he was awarded a special prize, one of three presented by the Midland Counties Union. Also, in 1913, he was awarded the second prize by the Union of Educational Institutions for his success in their examination in Practical Mathematics in the Advanced Stage. For his prize, R.J. selected *Applied Mechanics* by D.A. Low (1910), a textbook for engineering students.

While he was working at Kerr Stuart, Reg made a lathe which he was allowed to erect in one of the downstairs rooms at Victoria Cottage. Because he was so fond of making things, the lathe was in constant use, and it was Eric's job to work the treadle with his foot. If he forgot what he was doing and let his foot slow down, he was quickly roused into vigorous action by a storm of protest from Reg.

His father, Herbert, was a very keen chess player and in due course introduced it to Reg, who found it interesting and soon became quite good at it, so that he quite often had a game with his father. The trouble, however, was that Herbert studied each move very carefully and hence took a long time before deciding what his next move should be. In marked contrast, Reg could usually decide on his next move (and that of his father) quite quickly. Understandably, Reg became more and more frustrated by what he considered to be the unnecessarily slow way in which his father played, while at the same time feeling that it would only upset him if he said anything about it!

As his work at Kerr Stuart progressed, Reg constructed a dynamo, making nearly all the parts himself, either at work or on his home-made lathe. A dynamo is not exactly a simple piece of apparatus, and the fact that he could make one entirely by himself showed his early abilities as a designer and engineer. Undoubtedly, these special gifts helped to bring him success later in his life.

Not content with his dynamo, Reg wanted to set up an electric light circuit. Victoria Cottage, like most houses at that time, was lit by gas and Reg was fond of reading in bed. He resented having to drag himself out from under the blankets to put out the gaslight hanging from a central point in the ceiling. To solve the problem he used a simple Leclanche cell battery and connected up the wires via a switch to an electric bulb hanging at the head of the bed. After that it was quite easy to put out the light when he had finished his book.

In all the various things he made, Reg showed an outstanding creative ability. He had tremendous energy and enjoyed hard work. Whatever he was doing, whether working or playing, he did it wholeheartedly. His gift for making things was encouraged by his father, who wanted all his children to develop their own interests.

In 1916, Reg left Kerr Stuart and began to look round for work. He was now twenty-one, and the First World War was in its second year. He made two attempts to join the forces, but each time he was told that his engineering skills would be of more use in civilian life. While he was looking for a job he did some part-time teaching in Fenton Technical School. In 1917, he applied for a job as personal assistant to Hubert Scott-Paine, the owner, at the Supermarine Aviation Works, Woolston, Southampton. One morning soon afterwards he rushed in to see his former teacher, Mr Jolly, waving a letter in his hand.

'Just look at this!' he cried. 'It's a letter from Supermarines inviting me to go for an interview.'

After a lengthy discussion, Mr Jolly and Reg's father both agreed that it was a splendid opportunity. Reg was torn in two. He was attracted to the idea of working in an aircraft factory, but was reluctant to move so far from home, particularly because he was then courting Miss Florence Dayson, headmistress of Dresden Infants' School. In the end he was persuaded to go. A few days later he travelled down to Southampton and so began a lifelong association with Supermarine.

2

Supermarine

All of Mitchell's work as an aircraft designer was done at the Supermarine factory in Woolston, Southampton. This factory was started in 1912 by a remarkable man named Noel Pemberton-Billing. As a young man he had led an adventurous life in South Africa, and when he returned to England he was caught up in the new craze for 'flying machines'.

While living on a boat, moored on the River Itchen in Southampton, Pemberton-Billing decided to set up his own aircraft factory. Looking round for a possible site he chose a disused coal wharf at Woolston. This piece of wasteland lay on the east bank of the river, just above the old Floating Bridge which for many years ferried people across the Itchen. As J.D. Scott states in his book, *Vickers: A History*, published in 1962 by Weidenfeld and Nicolson, who have given their permission to quote from it, Pemberton-Billing coined the name 'Supermarine', being the logical opposite of 'submarine', since he intended to specialise in machines which would fly over the sea.

The construction work at Woolston attracted the attention of the press. In November 1913 an article appeared in the *Southampton Times and Hampshire Express* under the heading:

Flying Factory at Itchen Ferry

Workmen are engaged on a stretch of river frontage between the Floating
Bridge Hard and the old ferry yard, preparing premises for the construction of Supermarine. There is already on the site one large shed, once
used as a coal wharf, which has been converted into an engine building.
A second shed, 200 ft by 60 ft, is now being constructed. Cottages in Elm
Road, facing the site, are to be altered into offices. The river frontage
up to the Floating Bridge Company's premises has been secured for the
building of 'Water Planes'. Mr Pemberton-Billing, who boasted he would
be given a flying certificate after twelve hours flying, actually gained it
after three hours. He is the proprietor of the venture, which is expected
to be working by Christmas.

In this motley collection of buildings – one shed, a disused coalhouse and
a few empty cottages – Pemberton-Billing began to build flying boats.
As the name suggests, a flying boat had a boat-like hull which enabled
it to operate from water.

Pemberton-Billing's first flying boat, the PB 1, was a biplane with the
pilot's seat placed well forward in the hull. The factory had a slipway
leading into the river, down which the flying boats were launched ready
for take-off. The PB 1 was shown at the Aero and Motor Boat Show at
Olympia in March 1914, where it aroused considerable interest, but as
an aircraft it was not a great success and never flew.

In 1916, Pemberton-Billing disposed of his control of Supermarine,
having previously turned it into a limited company. Subsequently it
came under the management of Hubert Scott-Paine. Known as 'Ginger'
because of his bristling red hair, Scott-Paine was a large jolly man with
a tremendous enthusiasm for flying. He liked anything that went fast
and he had his own motor boat in which he roared up and down
Southampton Water.

In 1923, Scott-Paine in turn sold the Supermarine company to a colleague, Sqn Cdr James Bird, who had joined the company in 1919.

The outbreak of war in 1914 had roused Pemberton-Billing into
action. He asked his draughtsmen to draw up a machine to be used
for reconnaissance work, and he wanted it made quickly. On Monday
morning he set his team to work and within a week the PB 9 was
designed, built and ready to fly. Nicknamed the 'Seven Day Bus' it was
used as a trainer with the Royal Naval Air Service for a short period.

One of the Supermarine designs was a little more successful. This
was the PB 25, a single-seater scout, twenty of which were ordered by
the government.

During the First World War, Britain suffered aerial bombardment
from German Zeppelins. A daylight raid over London, which caused

much loss of life and destruction, shocked the whole nation. In 1916, in a spirit of retaliation, Pemberton-Billing designed a quadruplane which he imagined hopefully would bring the Zeppelins down in flames. This peculiar-looking aircraft, the Night Hawk, had a top speed of 70 mph, while the faster Zeppelin could do 75 mph. In some ways Night Hawk was in advance of its time, for it carried a searchlight and a 1½-pounder gun, but it failed to be accepted for service.

Pemberton-Billing was deeply concerned about the poor quality of the aircraft used by the Royal Flying Corps (RFC). The observer was usually armed with a rifle and a revolver with which he was expected to defend his aircraft. Not surprisingly, the casualty rate was very high.

With the intention of arousing public indignation over the loss of so many young airmen, Pemberton-Billing got himself elected to parliament. In his maiden speech in the House of Commons he violently attacked the government by declaring that the RFC crews were being 'murdered' by lack of efficient machines. Fearing that he might be accused of promoting his own interest in the manufacture of aircraft had caused him previously to dispose of his control of Supermarine.

Under the new ownership of Hubert Scott-Paine, the works became known as The Supermarine Aviation Works Ltd. It remained under government control for the rest of the war and continued to build aircraft. They also produced the first British flying boat fighter, the Baby.

This was the state of affairs at Supermarine when Mitchell arrived at Woolston for his interview with Scott-Paine. This proved to be successful. No doubt his quiet manner, combined with an aggressive jaw which gave his face a determined expression, persuaded Scott-Paine to give the eager young man from Stoke-on-Trent a chance. Mitchell was so delighted at the outcome that he did not even consider returning home; he merely wired his father asking for his belongings to be sent down to Southampton.

Mitchell's first job at Supermarine was acting as personal assistant to Scott-Paine, and in this capacity he soon became familiar with all the work going on in the factory. As we have seen, he had always been interested in flying, and the sight of the flying boats under construction in the sheds excited his interest and introduced thoughts of designing one himself. His practical basic training in engineering stood him in good stead during those first months at Supermarine when he had to make a quick adjustment from locomotives to aeroplanes.

It was not only the work that was new to him; living in Southampton brought Mitchell into fresh surroundings. He was now in his early twenties and all his previous life had been spent in Stoke-on-Trent. There he had grown accustomed to the crowded conditions of an industrial town. Dust and smoke shrouded the Trent Valley, while lines of workers' cottages sprawled across the surrounding hillsides. The drabness of the scene was enlivened by the cheerful friendliness of the people, and that same kindly concern for others was an integral part of Mitchell's nature.

Working at Supermarine, Mitchell looked out on a different world. There in front of him was the River Itchen, widening as it flowed into Southampton Water, and over which the seagulls continually dipped and soared, replacing the homing pigeons of his earlier days.

Scott-Paine quickly recognised the capabilities of his new man, and in 1918, at the end of Mitchell's first year at Supermarine, he made him assistant to the works manager, Mr Leach. Having earned his first promotion, Mitchell decided it was time to marry the girl he had left behind in Staffordshire. It was 1918, and the First World War was not yet over when he paid a hurried visit to his family and told them of his plans. During his brief stay, he and Florence Dayson were married at Meir Church in the village just beyond Normacot. The newly wedded pair returned to Southampton, and for the first months of their marriage they rented a house in Bullar Road, Bitterne Park. To make the journey to Supermarine easier Mitchell bought a motorcycle and sidecar, which was the first vehicle he owned and of which he was extremely proud.

Flo, a girl with thick brown hair and dark eyes, made Mitchell an excellent wife. She shared his love of sport, and over the years she became a very good tennis player. She also had great strength of character and courage, which enabled her to face the loneliness when she had to take second place to Mitchell's work. With him, work was always of major importance, and when he was concentrating on a particular task everything else was forgotten and time was of no importance. But fortunately for Mitchell, Flo understood the ambitions of the man she had married, and was always there, waiting at home, ready to look after him and entertain his friends.

Mitchell was never a good correspondent and hated writing letters. However, he did send one to his brother Eric, who had missed the Meir wedding because he was serving with the British Army stationed in Egypt:

1 October 1918

Dear Eric,

Thank you very much for your letter of 19 August. I like your remarks about my making a page in history, young fellow! Flo joins me in thanking you for your kind wishes, and we must congratulate you on promotion to corporal. We feel quite proud of having a real live corporal in the family.

The war news has been exceedingly good around your quarter of the globe lately, and we are looking forward to seeing you on Southampton quay before so very long.

I am still very busy and have little spare time. We are building Short seaplanes now, and are turning out about six a month. We have got to increase this to nine a month before Christmas, so we shall have plenty to do. I suppose your weather is now at its best. We have had nothing but rain lately. Everyone is busy saving match stalks and cinders to supplement the coal ration!

Flo wishes me to say that you must address your letter to both of us when you write, and don't let the interval be so long this time.

Very affectionately,
Yours,
Reg

Working with seaplanes and flying boats gave Mitchell great satisfaction, because it gave him a chance to use his creative ability. When faced with a problem, he would stick at it until he found the answer. He had an intuitive eye for a good design and he could usually tell merely from looking at a drawing whether it had possibilities. His competence in mathematics was a great help and enabled him to calculate such complicated factors as the stresses in aircraft structures. As J.D. Scott comments, his mind lived with the shapes that would move most effectively through the air. His intuitive understanding of aerodynamic problems impressed most deeply those whose formal training in aerodynamics had gone much further than his own.

But his devotion to work did not prevent Mitchell enjoying himself in his spare time. Being strong and well-built, he played games with the same energetic enthusiasm he showed for work. He and his wife joined the Woolston Tennis Club and soon became amongst the leading players. At the opening of one season, Mitchell and Lady Apsley played a demonstration match against Lord Apsley and his partner. Lord Apsley was MP for the Itchen division of Southampton.

Mitchell was a handsome man. His most striking feature, and the one which attracted everyone's attention, was his fair blond hair, the sort of colour seen on pictures of Plantagenet kings. He had bright, cornflower-blue eyes and a magical smile, of which not everyone received the benefit! Local people in Woolston soon began to recognise him in the streets, and he would sometimes give ladies from the tennis club a lift in the car which by now had replaced his old motorcycle and sidecar.

When Mitchell became assistant works manager in 1918, the Supermarine factory had altered very little from Pemberton-Billing's days. It was still a small firm, its premises consisting of one large hangar where the aircraft were built and smaller buildings on either side used as boat-building sheds and offices. The design team was limited to six draughtsmen and a secretary, and, since there was no money to spare, everything had to be done on a shoestring. But there was a very friendly atmosphere. Any apprentice lending a hand at launching time might be offered a free flight. At such times the lad merely turned his cap back to front and climbed in. Even the girl secretary enjoyed a quick flip round the Isle of Wight.

Like other aircraft firms, Supermarine trained apprentices. One hopeful young lad of sixteen, named Harold Smith, was passing the workshop on his way to an interview at Thornycroft's Shipyard when he caught sight of a flying boat. He was so fascinated that all thoughts of becoming a shipbuilder soon went out of his head. He applied for an apprenticeship at Supermarine and, after an interview with Mitchell, he was taken on. Mitchell was a fairly shrewd judge of character, and on this occasion he chose wisely, for eventually Harold Smith became chief structural engineer at Supermarine. It is of interest that in the early days at Supermarine, apprentices were called to work by the wailing of the six o'clock siren at Thornycroft's Shipyard. Harold spent the whole of his working life at Supermarine; he died on 6 November 1994, aged ninety-two.

It was around this time that Mitchell first learnt to drive a car, being taught by Charles Labette, a junior draughtsman at Supermarine.

When Mr Hargreaves left Supermarine in 1919, Mitchell was appointed chief designer in his place and the following year, just three years after he had joined the firm, he was also made chief engineer when he was still only twenty-five years of age. He remained in this position until 1928, when Supermarine was taken over by Vickers Ltd, and he was then appointed director and chief designer, a position he held until his death in 1937.

As time went on, Mitchell's skills as a designer and engineer established his position in the firm. From the early 1920s onwards he played a decisive part in every new aircraft produced at Supermarine.

3

The Schneider Trophy

When the First World War ended on 11 November 1918, Supermarine was released from government control, leaving Scott-Paine free to build civilian flying boats. His greatest ambition was to win the Schneider Trophy, an international award presented to the nation having the fastest seaplane over a measured course.

The Schneider Trophy, mounted on a marble plinth, shows a female figure, sculpted in silver and bronze, diving to kiss a cresting wave. It was presented in 1913 by Jacques Schneider, the son of a French armament manufacturer, who saw the seaplane as the great hope for the future, with the vast areas of water over the Earth's surface potentially providing cheap airports. In Europe, the name of the trophy varied with different languages. In Britain and America it was sometimes called the Schneider Cup, though it bore no resemblance to a cup.

The rules for the race, drawn up in Paris, stated that the contests must take place over water and that the machines must be seaworthy. The entries had to be sponsored by a governing body – in Britain the Royal Aero Club – and the number of entries for each nation was limited to three. The winning country had to stage the next race, and any nation with three consecutive victories would retain the trophy. The length of the race was to be approximately 350 km, and this distance had to be flown in a number of laps round a closed circuit.

The Schneider Contests proved to be spectacular events, with aircraft roaring round at a very low height, giving the crowds of spectators a clear view of what was happening. Each turning point on the course was keenly watched because it was here that a race could be lost or won.

In the years between 1919 and 1931, there was keen competition for the coveted trophy, and aircraft firms and latterly governments spent a great deal of money designing racing flying boats and seaplanes.

The first Schneider Contest, held at Monaco in April 1913, was won by a Frenchman, Maurice Prevost, in a monoplane flying at a speed of 45.75 mph. His machine was powered by a French Gnome rotary engine.

The following year, 1914, there were two British competitors at Monaco, Lord Carberry in a French flying boat and Howard Pixton in a Sopwith Schneider biplane fitted with floats. Pixton won the race at an average speed of 86.78 mph – a seaplane record – and his victory brought the Schneider Trophy to Britain for the first time. Unlike many of the early pilots, Pixton was a quiet, reserved character. At the celebration party, when invited to drink vintage champagne, he replied: 'Thanks very much, but mine's a small Bass.'

Stella Pixton, Howard's daughter, wrote in the *Aeroplane Monthly* in October 1984: 'My father was the first British Schneider winner and the man who put Britain in the lead for the first time in aviation history. For what he did, his name should be honoured.' Indeed it should be.

The outbreak of war in August 1914 put an end to the Schneider races until 1919, by which time Mitchell, as has been described, was well established at Supermarine. Both he and Scott-Paine were eager to compete, but there was not enough time to produce a new aircraft. It was decided that their best chance lay in making some alterations to the Supermarine Baby, the biplane flying boat built during the war. This aircraft was powered by a 450 hp Napier Lion engine mounted below the top wing. A forward seat in the hull gave the pilot a good view. At that time there were no fuel pumps, and petrol from the tank above the wing reached the engine by a gravity feed system.

In the early days at Supermarine, Mr Pickett was the only man capable of stripping a Napier Lion engine. He had a young assistant, Trotter, nicknamed 'Sparrow' because of his size – he weighed seven stone. It was 'Sparrow's' job to fill up the flying boat's tanks. Petrol in two-gallon cans was rowed out to the aircraft, and then 'Sparrow', clinging on to the wing struts, poured the petrol into the tank from the cans hauled up by ropes. Quite often his clothes were soaked with petrol and he had to be left outside the factory to 'dry out' to avoid the risk of fire!

The modified version of the Supermarine Baby, renamed the Sea Lion, was entered for the 1919 Schneider race, together with two other British aircraft, a Sopwith Schneider and a Fairey IIIA, plus an Avro 539A as reserve. France and Italy were also competing.

The race, arranged for 10 September, was to be flown over Bournemouth Bay, where the surrounding cliffs would provide excellent viewing points for spectators, The circuit, roughly triangular in shape, had to be flown ten times, starting and finishing off the pier. Because there were no sheds or slipways at Bournemouth, the competitors had to come up from Cowes on the morning of the race and then drag their aircraft up on to the beach amidst swarming crowds of holidaymakers. The race was supposed to start at 2.30 p.m. but, owing to a dense sea mist, it was postponed until 6 p.m., by which time the judges hoped the fog would have lifted. The local boatmen were pessimistic, but by 4 p.m. visibility had improved and competitors were told to prepare for take off. Cdr James Bird, the Supermarine director with experience of local conditions, begged the committee to call off the race but his request was ignored. The French, having run into trouble during the navigability tests, had withdrawn, leaving the British and Italians in competition. As pilots ran up their engines in preparation for take-off, Bournemouth beach was suddenly blasted by a whirlwind of flying sand and scattering sun hats.

The three British pilots took off first, but within a very short time two of them returned, saying it was impossible to see the Swanage marker boat because of the fog. Since there was no sign of the third British pilot – Basil Hobbs in Sea Lion – the Italian Janello took off, determined to see what he could do.

The delay of the Sea Lion was caused by Basil Hobbs' search for the Swanage marker. In an effort to locate it he landed on the water, then, since it was still impossible to see it, he took off again. As he did so he felt a bump and knew that he had hit an obstacle. When he alighted near the pier, the hull, which had been ripped open in the collision, immediately filled with water and Sea Lion sank. Hobbs took to the water and the Supermarine launch, with a very worried Mitchell on board, roared off to pick him up.

Meanwhile, Janello was lapping the circuit until he too was lost to sight in the thickening fog. Eventually he was found drifting on the water and his aircraft was towed to the pier. On investigation it was discovered that he had mistaken the Studland warning light for the Swanage marker and he was therefore disqualified for flying shorter circuits. There were loud protests from the Italians who demanded a decision in their favour. An international committee finally decided that it would be unfair to give Italy the trophy, since the British pilots had tried to fly the correct course.

Mitchell's genius as an aircraft designer was made up of many qualities which combined to make him the right man at the time. He was a born leader, and one who could inspire in others his own dedication to hard work. One of the most amazing things about him was his versatility. In the twenty years of his working life at Supermarine, he designed no less than twenty-four different aircraft comprising flying boats, amphibians, light aircraft, racing seaplanes, the Spitfire, and finally a bomber that he was working on at the time of his death. He had a tremendous power of concentration and when working on a design he could keep every detail of construction in his mind. Above all, Mitchell had one very important asset – he never let himself be discouraged by failure. If a design failed he went straight back to the drawing board and started again.

In 1920 Mitchell was given a chance to prove himself as a designer when the British government issued a specification for a new amphibian. Trials were to be held at Martlesham Heath near Ipswich, and the winners would be awarded cash prizes.

Mitchell worked very hard on the Supermarine entry because it was his first original design. He did all the calculations himself and carefully inspected every drawing submitted by his draughtsmen. He was always extremely painstaking in his work and he expected the same high standards from his design team. Normally a quiet, friendly man, he would contemptuously flick aside any drawing which displeased him. Sometimes he tore one to shreds before stamping off in a temper. When the work had been amended to his satisfaction, he calmed down.

Mitchell's amphibian for the Martlesham trials was a biplane powered by a Rolls-Royce Eagle VIII engine. It gained second place, but was considered to be so good that the second price of £4,000 was increased to £8,000, a considerable sum of money in those days. Hardly comparable to the Spitfire to come sixteen years later, nevertheless this amphibian represented an important landmark in Mitchell's career since it was his first success with an aircraft for which he had been primarily responsible, and the prize money was a fitting reward for all the work that had gone into its design. In 1921, Mitchell produced an improved version of the Martlesham amphibian, known as the Seal, later renamed the Seagull. It was powered by a 450 hp Napier Lion engine and was produced in quantity for the RAF and Australian Air Force and in the end had an operational life of twenty years. In 1920 he had another cause for celebration when his son, Gordon, was born. By this time the family had moved into their own house in Radstock Road, Woolston, which gave them more space to bring up a baby and was also nearer to the Supermarine works.

The 1920 and 1921 Schneider Contests were held at Venice. There were no British entries, and on both occasions the race was won by Italy. Only one more victory was needed and the trophy would remain in Italy for all time.

With the approach of the 1922 Schneider Contest, Scott-Paine began to consider the possibility of a private entry from Supermarine, as there was no government backing forthcoming. With this idea in mind, Mitchell made some alterations to the old 1919 Schneider Contest Sea Lion, with the hope of beating the Italians, now recognised as the world's leading designers of flying boats. Using experience gained with the Martlesham amphibian, he designed a flying boat again fitted with a 450 hp Napier Lion engine. He gave very special care to the design of the hull, fin and rudder, to achieve the best possible streamlining. The new flying boat, the Sea Lion II, was a small biplane and the wings, made of wood covered with fabric, had a span of 28 ft. In tests over Southampton Water it reached a maximum speed of 163 mph. The design, construction and testing of Sea Lion II was carried out under strict security. Only three people – Scott-Paine, James Bird and Mitchell – knew that it was intended as a challenge to the Italians.

Supermarine's test pilot at that time was Capt. Henri Biard, an enthusiastic aviator born in Guernsey who had gained his pilot's licence in 1912. Before the First World War he had been a flying instructor, and following that he served for a time with the RFC. Though Sea Lion II had an open cockpit, Biard refused to wear a flying suit. When asked if he wasn't cold up there, he merely shrugged his shoulders and replied: 'No. Not a lot.'

He was a likeable, jolly character, and a very good pilot, but once on the ground he was always up to some devilment. He told an amusing story of the early 1920s when things were not too good in the aircraft industry. He was put on to any odd job that was going when not flying and one day he was unloading coal from a lorry! Suddenly, Scott-Paine and Mitchell appeared with some foreign visitors who were potential customers. Scott-Paine introduced Henri Biard as his chief test pilot. Later Mitchell smilingly remarked that the visitors, seeing the chief test pilot shovelling coal, must have wondered what the firm's other pilots had been doing – probably cleaning out the lavatories!

The 1922 Schneider Contest was to be held in Naples, and when the date had been fixed, the Italians suddenly brought it forward fourteen days to 12 August. This meant that the men at Supermarine had to work night and day to get the Sea Lion II ready in time, though none of the men realised why there was so much fuss. The weather also took a hand in delaying matters, when days of high winds and gales restricted flight testing. Because of a faulty airspeed indicator, Mitchell had to calculate the estimated speeds, and he knew that if his sums were wrong the new aircraft would not beat the latest Italian Macchi flying boat. Mitchell hoped for a speed of 160 mph, and in tests Biard knew he was flying the fastest aircraft in Britain. Sea Lion II was so easy to handle that he even looped the loop in it, a very daring feat in a flying boat.

When tests had been completed, Sea Lion II was dismantled and stowed in packing cases ready for transport to Naples. Everything was still done under the utmost secrecy, and the ship *Philomel* was specially diverted into Southampton by the Steam Navigation Company to take the flying boat on board. Only four men travelled with the machine, Scott-Paine, Capt. Biard, the engineer 'Digger' Pickett, and a rigger, A. Nelson. There was no send-off and no good wishes; the men simply crept silently out of Southampton hoping to keep their destination a secret. All expert aviation opinion considered that Britain had not a hope of beating the Italians.

The triangular course over the Bay of Naples was set against beautiful scenery, with Vesuvius towering in the background. Britain, Italy and France were the three nations competing for the trophy, the British aircraft being the only one not backed by government funds.

At Naples, Biard's first task was to test Sea Lion II's performance in the hot Mediterranean climate. During one flight he flew too near Vesuvius, and faced near disaster when he was caught up in a thermal and suddenly found himself tossed 2,000 ft into the air.

During preparations for the race, the Supermarine team tried to discover the strength of the opposition, and particularly of their chief rivals, the Italian Macchis. At every Schneider meeting a certain amount of spying went on, while every pilot took care to give nothing away. Biard's cunning was equal to that of the French and Italian pilots. When flying Sea Lion II within sight of Naples, he flew slowly and cornered clumsily, cleverly disguising the true speed and manoeuvrability of the Supermarine entry.

Little was seen of the French aircraft, and the Italians were firm favourites to win the race and keep the trophy with a third consecutive victory. Since the Schneider Trophy had now been won in turn by France, Britain and Italy, the pilots jokingly called it the 'Flying Flirt'. In August 1922, Supermarine thought it was time she returned to Britain.

Unlike many men of genius, Mitchell had a highly sensitive, compassionate nature and was always deeply concerned about the pilots who tested and raced his aircraft. He could not bear to think that a man might be killed because of a fault in one of his designs. During every Schneider race he endured severe nervous strain which never changed with time. Normally, he had a great sense of humour and enjoyed a joke, but all his smiles disappeared on race days. Unable to bear the sound of frivolous chatter, he would stand alone, well away from the noisy crowds, and pray for the time that the race would be over and the pilot safely back on the ground. Throughout all his years of designing aircraft he suffered the same torments of suspense. He never got used to the idea that he was asking a man to risk his life in a machine that he had created.

The day before the Naples race, all the French flying boats retired with engine trouble, leaving just Britain and Italy in contention. The circuit was mapped out by three marker balloons, and the pilots had to fly round the course thirteen times.

On the afternoon of 12 August, Biard, the only British pilot, was the first to take off. With no other aircraft to get in his way, he hurtled round the first lap at a speed of 150 mph. Then the Italians took off to join him. Though at times he was impeded by some of the slower machines, Biard battled on, keeping the throttle wide open as he tried to build up a commanding lead. Having done so, he slowed down somewhat to save his engine and finished well ahead of his rivals. By achieving an average speed of 145.7 mph, he beat the Italians and regained the Schneider Trophy for Britain, although the Italian pilot Passaleva, who came second, was only 2.5 mph slower than Biard. A close thing!

The cost of beating the crack Italian team was somewhere in the region of £6,000. Sea Lion II was the only Schneider entry without government backing, but since the Napier firm lent the engine and Shell provided the fuel, the cost to Supermarine had been kept as low as possible.

There were great celebrations in Southampton when the Supermarine team returned with the trophy. The town turned out in force to welcome the heroes home, with scenes reminiscent of football Cup Final days. The mayor and corporation were at the station to receive Scott-Paine and Capt. Biard, and they led the procession to the Floating Bridge, colourfully decked with flags, to ferry the Schneider Trophy across the river to the Supermarine factory. The jubilation in Woolston, as crowds lined the river banks, has been described by an eye-witness:

> Capt. Biard was a colourful man, and at the peak of his flying career, as he then was, he was the hero of every boy in Woolston. His most famous exploit was winning the Schneider Trophy in 1922. When Biard brought the trophy back, I went down to the Floating Bridge and joined the crowd of workers who rushed out of Supermarine to cheer their hero home.

The *Southern Daily Echo* report of the contest made no mention of Mitchell, who remained quietly in the background, quite content in the knowledge that his machine had won the race.

Winning the Schneider Trophy was a remarkable achievement for a small company like Supermarine. Mitchell was now keen to create more ambitious designs, and with this in mind he set out to build up a team of skilled men to work with him. He knew exactly the kind of men he was looking for, and one of the first he appointed was Joe Smith. Smith was a draughtsman who had served an apprenticeship at the Austin factory in Birmingham and was destined to have a long and illustrious career at Supermarine.

After the 1922 victory, Mitchell felt that he had made an important advance as an aircraft designer, and he looked forward to the next Schneider Contest with an air of quiet confidence.

The most extraordinary thing about Mitchell's success as an aircraft designer was that he was, to a large extent, self-taught. As has been seen, all his early training had been done on locomotives, and with his creative ability he might well have ended up designing the now commonplace high-speed trains. Instead, by some fortuitous circumstances, he found himself in an aircraft factory and when he became chief designer, at the age of only twenty-four, a whole new world of exciting challenges opened up for him. He was always interested in speed, and his work on flying boats had given him the chance to design an entry for the Schneider Contest.

The foundation of Mitchell's success was undoubtedly laid in the early years spent as an apprentice at Kerr, Stuart & Co. There, thanks to his father's foresight, he had learnt how to use his hands as well as his brains. In all the years at Supermarine he never asked a workman to do a job that he could not do himself. But when all this has been said, it is a tribute to his imaginative genius that he could adapt himself so quickly to the skills required in designing aircraft. As we have seen, in 1920, only a few years after joining Supermarine, his amphibian won second prize in a government-sponsored competition, and two years later his Sea Lion II enabled the company to win the Schneider Trophy for England.

Mitchell always described his apprenticeship at Kerr, Stuart & Co. as turning him out as an engineer with his feet on the ground. He was not, it should be noted, at that time an aeronautical engineer.

4

The Americans
at Cowes

In 1923, Mitchell designed the Sea Eagle, a commercial amphibian that could carry six passengers and was powered by a 360 hp Rolls-Royce Eagle IX. It was the usual biplane and had a range of 230 miles and a cruising speed of 84 mph. Three were built and operated for a number of years without incident by the newly formed Imperial Airways.

It was the first civil aircraft to use RT – telephone communication with the ground – and for this purpose it needed a long trailing aerial ending in a lead weight. This sometimes caused outraged protests from the people at Calshot when the pilot forgot to wind it in on the approach to Southampton. A flight to Guernsey cost £3 2s 0d single, £5 return, and those daring enough to use this new method of transport thoroughly enjoyed the experience.

Under Cdr Bird, Supermarine began to expand. They badly needed more staff, and one important newcomer at that time was Alan Clifton, who came from London with a degree in engineering. Clifton had heard through a friend that Mitchell was looking for a new man, and after an interview he was appointed as first technical assistant. In a letter he wrote to Gordon Mitchell in 1967, Alan Clifton said:

It was one Sunday in the spring of 1923 that I rode down from London on a motor bike to interview your father at your home in Woolston and I remember seeing you. I realise now how extremely fortunate I was, indeed we all were, who worked with R.J. during those inter-war years.

Alan Clifton recounts his experiences over the years at Supermarine in Appendix 3.

Another who was to become an important member of Mitchell's team was Arthur Shirvall. He had joined the firm as an apprentice in 1918 and was later put in charge of hydrodynamic hull design, tank testing and future project design. He had a special gift for designing flying boat hulls, and his ability to visualise beautiful three-dimensional shapes made him of great value to Mitchell.

To cope with the expansion of business resulting from their Schneider victory, Supermarine bought another boatyard higher up the river. The owner assured his lads that they would not lose their jobs in the take-over. One of the boys, Don Farwell, proved to be an expert carpenter, and he was chosen to make the most difficult part of the hull – the 'step'. When a flying boat begins its take-off run, the entire hull rests on the water, but as the speed increases, first the tail and then the bow lifts off. When 'hump' speed is reached, the flying boat hydroplanes on the 'step' just before taking off. Situated about halfway along the hull, the step had to be very well constructed to withstand the pressures and strains.

After Scott-Paine left in September 1923, Mitchell was virtually in control of all the work at Supermarine. By this time he was firmly established in the top position, and was affectionately known by all the staff and all the factory workers as 'R.J.' He knew all the men on the shop floor, and he was always ready to listen to their problems and offer help. This good relationship was shown when his brother, Eric, paid a visit to Southampton. The two men went out for an evening drink, not to one of the high-class hotels as Eric had expected, but to the place where Supermarine workers gathered for their evening pint. There was no embarrassment over the unexpected arrival of the boss; the men liked to have R.J. with them and felt completely at ease with him.

Mitchell was less patient in his office, where he was usually to be found puffing at his pipe while he studied a drawing. Because of his high power of concentration he hated to be disturbed at work, and his team soon learnt to recognise the danger signal. When a man entered the office he stood just inside the door, waiting in a nervous silence. If Mitchell turned his head with a welcoming smile, then all was well. If, on the other hand, a red flush began to creep up the back of his neck, the man hastily fled before the storm broke. Mitchell could be brusque and quick tempered, and it was necessary to choose the right moment before interrupting him at work.

But R.J. could also be very charming. He had a great sense of fun, and the smile which lit up his face when he was amused utterly transformed his usual grave expression. Away from work he enjoyed many sports, and at such times he was a jolly, friendly companion. The one social event that he really enjoyed was the annual drawing office party, a 'men only' celebration usually held in one of the Southampton hotels. There were two opposing sides to Mitchell's character. He worked harder than any man at Supermarine, but when work was over he could throw himself wholeheartedly into a noisy party as though that was the only thing that mattered.

Basically Mitchell was a shy man. He suffered from a slight stammer which worried him terribly and made him nervous when talking to strangers. But in the company of men he knew and liked he relaxed and the hesitation in his speech was forgotten. At the drawing office parties, which often went on into the early hours of the morning, he was always the leader of every piece of tomfoolery. The Southampton hotels were slightly apprehensive when they were invited to play host to a Supermarine party.

To a large extent, Mitchell left the handling of the family budget in his wife's capable hands. He stuffed a wad of notes into his pocket for his personal needs, and when they were gone he asked for a fresh supply. His mind was so taken up with his work that he had no time to spare for the trivial details of everyday life. His latest design was never far from his thoughts, and if he was left alone for a few minutes at a social gathering he was quite likely to start drawing some component on a scrap of paper.

As soon as the Sea Eagle was ready for testing, Mitchell began to prepare for the 1923 Schneider race which was to be flown over Spithead on 28 September. Because of his previous success, he still favoured a flying boat as a contender. He changed the shape of the 1922 Sea Lion II by fitting new wings and redesigning the hull so that it offered less drag. He kept a Napier Lion engine, but used one with the power increased to 550 hp. With all these improvements, Mitchell confidently expected Sea Lion III to exceed 160 mph.

The course of the 1923 Schneider race was a long, narrow triangle mapped over Spithead, with the start and finish off Cowes. The two sharpest turns were off Selsey Bill and Cowes, with a wide curve over Southsea pier in between. Italy and France had provisionally entered aircraft, but the greatest interest was shown in the new challenge from America.

Tremendous curiosity was aroused when the three aircraft sponsored by the American Navy arrived at Cowes. This was not surprising, because the American entries were not flying boats but seaplanes; two of them Curtiss CR-3s, and the third a Wright NW-2. With them came the glamorous American Navy pilots, Lts Rittenhouse, Irvine, Gorton and Wead. Cowes was agog. The people were used to foreign yachts, but the sight of the powerful seaplanes roaring up from the water was something quite new. There was a lot of talk about the high speeds of the Curtiss seaplanes, but most of it was dismissed as 'Yankee Swank'. The American seaplanes had very long floats, and it was thought that they might be unable to cope with the rough water in the Solent. All England hoped for an extra strong tide on race day.

The Italian team failed to turn up, but the French flying boats duly arrived at Cowes. Britain entered two aircraft, the Blackburn Pellet and Supermarine Sea Lion III which would be piloted by Capt. Biard.

All Schneider Contests were preceded by tests held on the day before the race. The tests consisted of two parts. First came the navigability trials, in which the pilot had to taxi over the water, take off and alight several times. These were followed by mooring tests, during which each aircraft had to remain tied to a buoy for six hours. After that, no major repair work could be carried out. The tests were quite severe, and over the years many aircraft were disqualified before the actual race day.

In 1923 there were several casualties. The Blackburn Pellet overturned, two of the French retired with engine trouble and the Wright NW-2 crashed before tests. So the only competitors left in the race were Sea Lion III, the two Curtiss CR-3 seaplanes from America to be flown by Lts Rittenhouse and Irvine, and one French aircraft flown by Lt Hurel.

On the day of the race the sea was calm, and the sun shone down on the huge crowds lining the shores on both sides of Spithead. In Portsmouth betting was evens on the Sea Lion to win. The Americans had drawn the right to go first and second, and they would be followed at fifteen minute intervals by Biard in Sea Lion III and then the remaining French aircraft.

Immediately the starting cone was dropped, Lt Irvine roared off in the Curtiss CR-3, quickly followed by Lt Rittenhouse in the second Curtiss. Then it was Biard's turn. Unfortunately, just as he was beginning his take-off run, the two Americans thundered over the starting line, having completed the first lap at a phenomenally fast speed. As soon as he was airborne, Biard chased after the Americans, using every trick he knew to overtake them on the turns.

During the second lap, the French aircraft was forced down with engine trouble, leaving Biard and the two Americans to carry on. But the final result had never been in doubt after the tremendous speed established by the Americans on the first lap. When the race ended, Lt Rittenhouse's average speed of 177.38 mph made him the winner, with Irvine a close second. Biard's speed of 157.17 mph made him a poor third. It was a disastrous result for Britain, Supermarine and Mitchell.

The Americans had beaten Sea Lion III by 20 mph and established a new world speed record in an aircraft powered by an engine of only 465 hp, compared with the British engine of 550 hp.

There was a lot of discussion and argument after the race. The British press stressed the point that the American planes were backed by the US Navy, while Sea Lion III was only a company entry. Everything about the American team had been highly organised, even down to the pilots' waders. In Britain all this was considered rather too 'professional' in a race originally intended for private individuals or aircraft companies.

But the great performance by the Curtiss seaplanes won international acclaim, while the Italians were secretly relieved that Britain had not won the trophy for a second consecutive time. Sadly, the British people saw the Schneider Trophy triumphantly carried across the Atlantic. After that tremendous show of speed at Cowes, few believed it would ever return.

Although Biard was only placed third in the 1923 Schneider Contest, he had flown a good race. By flying low and cornering beautifully he had got the maximum speed out of his aircraft, but it simply was not fast enough to beat the government-sponsored American seaplanes.

In an interview after the race, Scott-Paine, Supermarine's managing director, said:

> Our drawing office people got all the speed they possibly could out of the machine. We did the best we could and have no regrets. Sea Lion III was 11 mph faster than Sea Lion II, and the credit for this fine perform-ance was due to several people, one of whom is Mr R.J. Mitchell, who designed both machines.

Failure in the 1923 Schneider race was a setback for Mitchell, who saw his design outclassed by a superior aircraft. He realised that the defeat of Sea Lion III marked the end of the racing flying boats. He knew that his next racing design would have to be something very special if Britain was ever to recapture the Schneider Trophy. The defeat at Cowes marked a milestone in his life, for out of failure came a new British seaplane, and its influence on aviation was to be profound.

On 16 December 1924, Mitchell signed an agreement with The Supermarine Aviation Works, under which they agreed to employ him as chief engineer and designer for ten years from 6 December 1923, and to offer him a technical directorship in December 1927. In view of the historical interest of this agreement, its provisions are recorded here in full:

> An Agreement made the sixteenth day of December One Thousand Nine Hundred and Twenty-Four between The Supermarine Aviation

Works Limited whose Registered office is situated at and in the City and County of Southampton (hereinafter called 'the Company') of the one part and Reginald Joseph Mitchell of 'Cranbrook' Avenue Road Itchin Southampton aforesaid (hereinafter called 'the Designer') of the other part whereby it is agreed as follows:

1. The Company will employ the Designer and the Designer will act as the Chief Engineer and Designer of the Company for the term of ten years from the Sixth day of December One thousand nine hundred and Twenty three (Subject to determination as hereinafter mentioned) and thereafter until this agreement shall be determined by either party hereto giving to the other three months notice in writing of such intended determination.

2. During the continuance of this agreement the Designer shall devote the whole of his time during the business hours of the Company to the business of the Company and shall use his best endeavours to promote the interests and welfare of the Company and shall not be concerned or engaged in any other business than that of the Company or as a share-holder in a commercial Company carrying on any business other than a business similar to that of the Company. He shall not either before or after the termination of this agreement disclose to any person or Company whatsoever any information relating to the Company or its customers or any trade secrets or designs of which he shall become possessed or originate while acting as designer for the Company.

3. The Designer shall be entitled to take six weeks consecutive holidays in each year at a period to be approved of by the Board of Directors of the Company and such other holidays not exceeding a total of Twenty one days in any one year as the Board may from time to time approve.

4. If the Designer shall at any time be unfit or incapacitated by illness or otherwise from performing his duties as Chief Engineer and Designer for six consecutive calendar months or if he shall commit a breach of this agreement the Company may by three calendar months notice in writing put an end to this agreement notwithstanding anything hereinbefore contained provided always that in case the Designer shall desire to contest the decision of the Board of Directors as to his unfitness or incapacity or as to whether he has committed a breach of this agreement the matter shall be made the subject of a reference to arbitration under the provisions in that behalf hereinafter contained and should the decision be in his favour the said notice shall be invalid and inoperative.

5. If this agreement shall be determined at any time before the Sixth day of December One thousand nine hundred and Thirty-three by the Designer or by the Company in consequence of any breach of this agreement by the Designer the Designer shall not at any time within three years from such determination of this Agreement enter the service of or be connected with any Company or person in the United Kingdom and

which Company or person carries on or is interested in a business similar to that carried on during this period of his employment by the Company except with the consent in writing of the Directors of the Company for the time being.

6. In consideration of the covenants hereinbefore contained on the part of the Designer the Designer shall be entitled by way of remuneration for his services to the salary following, that is to say: For the year ending the fifth day of December One thousand nine hundred and Twenty four the sum of One thousand two hundred pounds, for the year ending the fifth day of December One thousand nine hundred and Twenty five the sum of One thousand three hundred pounds and from the Sixth day of December One thousand nine hundred and Twenty five to the fifth day of December One thousand nine hundred and Thirty three at such salary as may be mutually agreed between the parties hereto but not less in any event than the annual salary of One thousand four hundred pounds which shall be the salary in default of Agreement provided always that the said sums shall respectively be paid exclusive of any sum or sums payable to the Designer under any Profit Sharing Scheme subsequently introduced by the Company but this Clause shall not be construed as making any obligation upon the Company to have any Profit Sharing Scheme.

7. An Endowment Policy Number 250687 for the sum of Two thousand five hundred pounds payable in the event of (1) the death of the Designer before the Twenty ninth day of December One thousand nine hundred and Thirty three or (2) of his surviving until that date at an annual premium of Two hundred and sixty one pounds and five shillings has been effected with the Sun Life Assurance Society and by an Indenture bearing even date herewith has been assigned to the Company and in consideration for such assignment the Company hereby covenants with the Designer:

(a) To pay the said annual premium of Two hundred and Sixty one pounds and five shillings in respect of the said Endowment Policy if and so long as the Designer remains in the employ of the Company and this Agreement or any mutual agreement between the parties varying the terms of service which shall not specifically vary the terms herein contained as to any matters relating to such Policy is still existing and binding.

(b) In the event of the Designer (1) voluntarily severing his connection with or (2) leaving the employ of the Company for any cause whatsoever under this agreement except as provided in Sub-clause (c) on or before the said fifth day of December One thousand nine hundred and Thirty three the said Endowment Policy shall become the absolute property of the Company.

(c) Should, however, the Designer complete the full period of his service as provided by this agreement the Company will re-assign the said

Endowment Policy to the Designer and the same shall thereupon be the absolute property of the Designer and further should the Company go into liquidation either voluntarily or compulsorily or should the services of the Designer be terminated under Clause 4 or by mutual agreement then in either of the said events the Designer shall be entitled to the paid up value of the Policy at the date of the event so happening and for such purpose the said Policy shall if necessary be assigned to the Designer but the Company shall be under no further liability of any kind in respect thereof provided always that until any such assignment as aforesaid upon the happening of any such event as aforesaid the Company shall be deemed to hold the Policy Upon trust accordingly provided further that in the event of the Company being reconstructed and the Designer re-engaged the Policy shall be kept in force upon and subject to the terms of this agreement.

(d) In the event of the death of the Designer during the continuance of this agreement and prior to the said fifth day of December One thousand nine hundred and Thirty three the said Endowment Policy shall be assigned to and become the absolute property of the wife of the Designer if living or in the event of her death to the next of kin of the Designer and until such assignment the Company shall be deemed to hold the said Policy upon trust accordingly.

8. The Company further covenant that provided this agreement is still existing they will on or shortly after the fifth day of December One thousand nine hundred and Twenty seven offer a Technical Directorship in the said Company to the Designer.

9. In the event of the Company being wound up either voluntarily (save for the purpose of amalgamation or reconstruction) or compulsorily IT IS HEREBY AGREED AND DECLARED that the claim of the Designer in respect of future salary or damages under this agreement shall be limited to one year's salary only PROVIDED ALWAYS that in the event of the Company being wound up voluntarily either for the purpose of reconstruction or amalgamation then the Designer hereby agrees that should the new Company require his services and gives notice in writing to him of such requirement and of their election to undertake the duties responsibilities and agreements of the existing Company under these presents within seven days of the formation of the new Company he will act for them in the same capacity as herein provided and will agree that these presents shall in consideration of such undertaking as aforesaid be transferred to the reconstructed or amalgamated Company and everything herein contained and the rights of both parties hereunder shall be in full force and existence as if the present Company were identical with the new Company.

10. In case of any dispute or difference arising between the parties hereto as to the amount of the remuneration payable under any of the

foregoing stipulations as to the validity of any notice given hereunder or as to the construction of these presents or as to any other matter or thing arising hereunder or in the course of the Designer's employment every such dispute and matter in difference shall be referred to a single Arbitrator if the parties can agree upon one or otherwise to two arbitrators to be appointed by the Company and the Designer respectively and their Umpire in accordance with the provisions of the Arbitration Act 1889 or any statute for the time being replacing extending or modifying the same.

IN WITNESS whereof the Company has caused its Common Seal to be hereunto affixed and the Designer has hereunto set his hand and seal the day and year first before written.

SIGNED sealed and delivered by the
said Reginald Joseph Mitchell in the
presence of:

J. Smith
Draughtsman
3 Devonshire Road
Southampton

It is interesting to note Clause 5, under which if Mitchell should terminate his post before December 1933, he must not enter the service of any company or individual involved in work similar to that carried on at Supermarine without the directors' written consent. Clause 9 is of particular interest in the light of the company being subsequently taken over by Vickers Ltd, in 1928. Under this clause, Mitchell agreed that following the company being wound up voluntarily for the purpose of reconstruction or amalgamation, he would continue to serve the new company if they wished him to do so. Presumably Vickers would have been aware of the details of this agreement when they bought Supermarine (see Chapter 10).

One final comment which might be made is that this agreement with its legal language is not the easiest of documents to read and fully understand, with sentences in some of the clauses extending without a break to several lines. It was drawn up by a solicitor from Mitchell's home town (Stoke-on-Trent) and Mitchell would, no doubt, have been entirely happy before putting his signature to it, which, it is interesting to note, was witnessed by Joe Smith.

5

A Royal Visit to Supermarine

The fine performance of the American Curtiss seaplane was an eye-opener to all aircraft designers and Mitchell began to wonder what type of aircraft would be needed to beat the new record speed of 177.4 mph. As well as considering the next Schneider entry, he was busy on other projects. Following Sea Eagle's success, Mitchell developed it further to produce a larger version called the Scarab. This was an amphibian bomber, with twin fuel tanks placed above the upper wing. It carried a 1,000 lb bomb load, and twelve were sold to Spain for use in its war against Morocco.

At about this time another draughtsman joined Mitchell's team: Eric Lovell-Cooper, who had trained with Boulton & Paul Ltd, Norwich. He arrived at Woolston one dreary Sunday afternoon, and the sight of the shabby Supermarine buildings standing on the bank of the Itchen did nothing to cheer him up. However, having come so far, he decided to give the firm a try before moving on to better things. Two days later he had his first interview with Mitchell and from that moment there was never any doubt where his interest lay. Lovell-Cooper knew he had met the man with whom he wanted to work. Mitchell, who was often brusque and curt in dealing with his staff, had a strength of character and gift of leadership which was a true inspiration to those who worked with him. Joe Smith, Alan Clifton, Harold Smith and Eric Lovell-Cooper were among those who spent the whole of their working life with Supermarine, and they all had the same quiet manner and dedication to their work. Mitchell has rightly been described as a leader rather than a driver. He had an invaluable ability to assemble a team of young (like himself) experts round him and to inspire great loyalty and effort in them. He never failed to emphasise that without this specialist team he could have achieved little.

It is easy to picture Mitchell in his office, pipe alight and golden hair glinting in the sunlight as he studied the drawings for his latest design. As Joe Smith said in giving the 1st Mitchell Memorial Lecture –

> He was an inveterate drawer on drawings, particularly general arrange-
> ments. He would modify the lines of an aircraft with the softest pencil
> he could find, and then re-modify over the top with progressively thicker
> lines, until one would finally be faced with a new outline of lines about
> three-sixteenths of an inch thick. But the results were always worthwhile,
> and the centre of the line was usually accepted when the thing was
> redrawn. [1]

When starting work on a new design, Mitchell spent most of his time in the office discussing problems with his team. He was always ready to listen to anyone who had some useful, constructive comments to make. He was unquestionably a listener rather than a talker.

For Mitchell, 1924 was a busy year. When the Scarab went into pro-duction, he designed the Swan, a commercial amphibian powered by two Rolls-Royce Eagle IX engines. This aircraft was the first of its type and had a range of 300 miles, a cruising speed of 85 mph and an ingenious mechanism for retracting the undercarriage, actuated by an air-driven propeller. The wings folded forwards. Following excellent reports from its tests at Felixstowe, an immediate order from the Air Ministry was received, but the real importance of the Swan was that it laid the founda-tions for the world-famous Southampton flying boats.

The Swan attracted the attention of HRH The Prince of Wales (later King Edward VIII), who was fond of flying and always inter-ested in the progress of aviation. In June 1924, when he opened the new Floating Dock in Southampton, he visited the Supermarine works especially to see the latest product. The event was reported in *Flight* magazine of 3 July 1924, under the heading, 'A Gala Day for Southampton':

27 June 1924, was a red-letter day for Supermarine Aviation Ltd, Woolston. HRH The Prince of Wales arrived in Southampton to open the new Floating Dock, but before going to the docks the prince spent considerable time inspecting the Supermarine factory. After being received by Maj. Gen. J.E.B. Seely, Lord Lieutenant of Hampshire, the Prince was presented to the mayor and driven across Southampton to the Floating Bridge, which took the party to Woolston. Here they were met by the chairman of Supermarine, Mr Low, who presented Cdr J. Bird, managing director, R.J. Mitchell and Capt. Biard. The Prince also received the chief of the Royal Spanish Naval Air Services, who was interested in the purchase of flying boats for his country.

The Prince was then conducted on a tour of the works. In no 1 shop he inspected amphibian bombers under construction for the Spanish government, and he saw a completed aircraft of that type moored in the Itchen ready for delivery.

In no 2 shed he watched sheet metal work, wing assembly and engine erection. Proceeding through the works, offices and stores, the prince was shown a display of stainless steel fittings, a special feature of Supermarine.

In no 3 shop the building of the Seagull flying boat hulls was greatly admired by His Royal Highness.

He then spent some time in the hangar of Imperial Airways Ltd, which adjoined the Supermarine premises. Here he was presented to Hubert Scott-Paine, the man who had helped to found the company.

His last visit was to the Swan, Mitchell's latest design for a large passenger-carrying aircraft. Before leaving to open the Floating Dock, he congratulated Supermarine on their splendid achievements.

At the end of this article the reporter commented: 'Mr R.J. Mitchell is now regarded as one of our foremost flying boat designers.' This, at the age of twenty-nine, was only after some five years as a chief designer.

This report of the royal visit clearly shows the small size of the Supermarine works. Yet, at that time, the Swan was the largest commercial amphibian in Britain and one of the first aircraft to carry freight.

Many of Mitchell's early designs were built with Napier Lion engines. Maintenance work on these engines, even to the extent of major dismantling, was entrusted to the able fitter nicknamed 'Digger' Pickett. The diminutive 'Sparrow' served as his assistant until his transfer for training as an electrician.

While working late shifts in the electrical department, 'Sparrow' was sometimes called in to assist Mitchell in testing cable wires. On one such occasion Mitchell asked him if he would like to work in the drawing office. When 'Sparrow' said that he couldn't draw, Mitchell offered to teach him. It was this natural friendliness and interest in others which earned

Mitchell the affection and respect of the Supermarine workers. 'Sparrow' did not stay long a Woolston. His early departure may have been due to his mother, who once asked him: 'What do you want to work there for? They only wants them nasty things when there's a war on.'

It probably had no connection with the diminutive 'Sparrow', but a light plane designed by Mitchell in 1924 was called the Sparrow. This was built for the two-seater Light Aeroplane Trials at Lympne for which the Air Ministry had put up relatively large amounts of prize money. Supermarine had not built a landplane since the days of Pemberton-Billing, so this was a new departure for Mitchell and it is an interesting piece of history that Sidney Camm – who was, of course, later to design the Hawker Hurricane – also designed a two-seat biplane, the Cygnet, for the Lympne competition.

Mitchell's Sparrow was a sesquiplane, the two wings being of different section and was powered by a Blackburn Thrush three-cylinder radial engine of 35 hp. It achieved a maximum speed of 72 mph but throughout its life it suffered from trouble with the Thrush engine which proved to be both temperamental and unpredictable. In the Lympne trials, the Sparrow failed to pass the elimination test due to engine troubles, which was a bitter setback for Mitchell. In 1926, the Sparrow was converted into a high-wing monoplane called Sparrow II and the Thrush engine was replaced with a Bristol Cherub III flat twin engine. It took part in the 1926 Daily Mail Light Aeroplane Competition, piloted again by Henri Biard, but unsuccessfully. Finally, it was used in Air Ministry trials to investigate full-scale the merits of different wing sections.

It was not one of Mitchell's noteworthy successes, but undoubtedly it provided him with much useful experience when he turned once again to landplanes ten years later.

Further details of the Sparrow can be found in an article in *Aeroplane Monthly*, 13, 498 (1985) by Richard Riding.

> Following the 1923 Schneider Contest, the next race in 1924 had never been far from Mitchell's mind. In June 1924 the Air Ministry ordered two experimental racing aircraft; a flying boat from Supermarine and a seaplane from the Gloster firm. Although Mitchell had lost faith in the flying boat as a racing machine, he did design one powered by a Rolls-Royce Condor engine. Difficulties occurred during construction and the design, which was to have been called the Sea Urchin, was abandoned. Mitchell had a good eye for the right design and he knew that this one was wrong. He was convinced that a seaplane was needed to challenge the Americans.

With Sea Urchin on the scrap heap and the Gloster seaplane damaged in a crash, it became obvious that Britain would have no entry for the 1924

Schneider Contest. Neither Italy nor France had produced new racing aircraft, and without any foreign challengers it was generally accepted that America would score a walkover victory with the Curtiss racing seaplanes. To everyone's surprise, America sportingly announced that the race would be postponed until 1925 to allow time for competing nations to produce new aircraft, a fine gesture which Britain did not feel able to repeat seven years later in 1931.

This breathing space was just what Mitchell needed to work on his design for a new seaplane. The Curtiss seaplanes were biplanes but, in December 1924, he decided to make his a monoplane. Ever since the 1914 Schneider Contest, the biplane had been generally accepted as the best shape for racing aircraft. Now Mitchell was about to change all that. His revolutionary new design was one more proof of his creative ability but, as will be seen, he was to face many setbacks and disappointments before achieving success.

6

The S.4

Mitchell's new design for a Schneider seaplane, known as the S.4, was as revolutionary as the Curtiss, with one very important difference. It was a monoplane, with a wing of cantilever construction thus having no external bracing struts or wires. The production of such aircraft was expensive and the Air Ministry had agreed to give both the Supermarine and Gloster companies financial assistance for the design and construction of high-speed racing seaplanes which would subsequently be loaned to the respective firms to take part in the 1925 Schneider Contest.

In March 1925, having received approval for the design from the Air Ministry, Supermarine began work on the S.4. It was designed round a twelve-cylinder 700 hp Napier Lion engine. The streamlined fuselage had an open cockpit set back behind the wing, a position which put the pilot at some disadvantage, since it limited his visibility at the critical moments of take-off and landing.

The design of the S.4 is of special interest because it showed Mitchell's inventiveness and unquestionably represented an extremely important landmark in his career. It is, therefore, appropriate that some of its many completely new features and methods of construction should be described. The 30 ft 7½in. span single wing was made in one piece, and its two wooden spars were covered with plywood sheeting as the stressed skin. The monocoque construction fuselage was built in wood apart from the two tubular steel A-frames and metal fittings, and the fin and tailplane formed an integral part of this structure. Plywood skins covered the entire fuselage apart from the engine bay which was entirely cowled in with aluminium sheeting. Rigid tubular rods were used for control runs and the long ailerons extended from the wingtips to mid-span of the wing trailing edge. Radiators were mounted on the wing undersurfaces to provide cooling. The two-bladed metal propeller was of the Fairey-Reed type.

The wooden floats were single stepped and the undersurface was of vee form. They had watertight bulkheads and were strong enough to withstand rough water.

The S.4 had clean and elegant aerodynamic lines. The only parts which protruded and caused some drag were the underwing radiators. It was a wonderful and revolutionary design by any standards.

By August 1925, the S.4 was ready to fly. It had been built in only five months, a magnificent achievement for Supermarine, considering its complexity and unorthodox design. No doubt the sight of its strange shape aroused considerable curiosity as it was towed down Southampton Water to the RAF station at Calshot.

Henri Biard was to pilot the S.4 on its first flight, and as he climbed into the cockpit, Mitchell stood by, his face plainly showing signs of nervous tension and the deep concern for the pilot which, as has already been stressed, he always showed before a test flight in any of his aircraft throughout his career. So much hard work had gone into the new machine, and now he was about to find out if it would live up to expectations. While Biard prepared for take-off, Mitchell went out in a speedboat with Lord Louis Mountbatten, then a lieutenant commander in the Navy and very interested in Supermarine's new seaplane.

One story says that Mitchell wore bathing trunks under his suit. 'If anything happens,' he told Biard, 'I'll dive into the water and pull you out.' Both Biard and Mitchell were powerful swimmers.

That first flight revealed some possible defects in the design. There appeared to be a slight wing vibration occasionally, a fault likely to cause trouble because a Schneider course always included at least two sharp turns. The poor visibility for the pilot was evident when Biard only narrowly missed the White Star liner *Majestic* which happened to be cruising along at the entrance to Southampton Water as he came in to land. Nevertheless, in the light of the S.4's fine speed performance it was decided to make an attempt as soon as possible on the world seaplane speed record.

On 13 September, Biard, flying a straight 3-km course along Southampton Water, set up a new world record of 226.75 mph. The

S.4 was certainly very fast; the question was, how well would it handle under racing conditions?

In its issue for 24 September 1925, *Flight* reported:

> One may describe the Supermarine Napier S.4 as having been designed in an inspired moment. That the design is bold no one will deny, and the greatest credit is due to R.J. Mitchell for his courage in striking out on entirely new lines. It is little short of astonishing that he should have been able to break away from the types with which he has been connected, and not only abandon the flying boat type in favour of a twin float arrangement, but actually change from braced biplane to the pure cantilever wing of the S.4.

The technical press also commented on the new features of design and construction used in the S.4, drawing attention to the stressed skin, the operation of the ailerons, and the flaps on the trailing edges of the wing to reduce landing speed.

In mid-September the Supermarine team, including Mitchell and Biard, left London for America on board the liner SS *Minnewaska*. The S.4 was not the only British entry for the 1925 Schneider Contest. Also on board were two Gloster III racing biplanes with their pilots. One of them was a friend of Biard's, Bert Hinkler, who set up a fifteen-day record flight to his home country, Australia, in 1928. The other was Broad.

During the stormy Atlantic crossing, Biard slipped and sprained his wrist and then had an attack of influenza. Mitchell was worried stiff in case he would not be well enough to fly in the race.

Things were not much better when they reached Baltimore on Chesapeake Bay, over which the Schneider course would be flown. The British machines were housed in makeshift canvas hangars, and during a gale one of the tent poles broke and damaged the fin of the S.4. Repairs were hastily carried out in time for the Navigability Tests on 25 October, the day before the race.

In the test flights, a Curtiss R3C-2 racer took off first, followed by one of the Gloster IIIs and then the S.4. Biard made a perfect take-off but ran into trouble on the first turn. Mitchell, who was out on the water in a rescue boat, anxiously watched the seaplane's performance. After rounding the first marker he saw the S.4 crash into the sea with such force that it was temporarily hidden from sight by the huge mountain of water which shot into the air. The rescue boat roared towards the spot, with Mitchell in a fret of anxiety in case Biard had been killed.

That day, 25 October, was Mitchell's unlucky day. The speedboat carrying him towards the floating debris from the S.4 suddenly developed engine trouble and nearly an hour elapsed before Biard was picked out of the icy water. The first man to spot Biard was the pilot of the Gloster racer flying low overhead, who saw Biard's head pop up above the water. In their mutual relief at seeing each other, Biard and Mitchell exchanged grins.

It was a miracle that Biard had lived to tell his story. The force of impact as the S.4 hit the water broke the fuselage and knocked him unconscious, and he went down strapped in the cockpit. Luckily the ice-cold water revived him, and he managed to free himself from the harness. Holding his breath, he rose to the surface and, after inflating his lifejacket, he waited for the rescue boat.

After the pieces of the fuselage and part of the wing of the S.4 had been salvaged, an enquiry was held. Biard thought that wing flutter at the turn had caused the accident, but he admitted that the aeroplane had always frightened him. Aviation experts believed that Mitchell's ambitious use of a cantilever wing had exceeded the bounds of aerodynamic and structural knowledge available at that time. One expert later suggested after extensive research that the cause of Biard's accident was in fact a stall but that it was possibly aileron flutter that had led to the stalled condition. 'Jack' Davis's comments in Appendix 4 are of great relevance and interest to this view concerning possible aileron problems.

The 1925 Schneider race was won for America by Lt Jimmy Doolittle flying a Curtiss R3C-2 racer at an average speed of 232.57 mph. A Gloster III came second, piloted by Hubert Broad. After the race, Doolittle set up a new world speed record of 245.71 mph. More than ever it seemed certain that America would keep the Schneider Trophy.

Mitchell returned to Southampton with all his hopes of victory dashed but, despite the accident to the S.4, Mitchell still believed that the monoplane format was best for a racing seaplane. He considered that the biplane offered too much drag, and over the years he was proved right. Mitchell's ideas were often way ahead of their time and the construction of the S.4 cut across accepted ideas of aircraft design when the biplane reigned supreme.

In a newspaper article, written a few years later, the following comment was made:

> One of the greatest contributions to high-speed flying has come from what is known as the cantilever wing; that is, a wing fastened to the fuselage at its roots, without visible means of support. This idea was tried out by R.J. Mitchell in the S.4. It sometimes happens that the freak of today becomes the commonplace of tomorrow.

So the 1925 Schneider Contest was another bad setback for Mitchell, even worse than those which he had encountered in the 1923 Schneider race and with the Sparrow landplane the following year. This was where the true genius and ability of the man really came to light, since, as subsequent events were to show, Mitchell knew that he was basically on the right track with his S.4 design and refused to be put off by the, albeit severe, setback. A man with the courage of his convictions, which this country would later have every reason to be thankful that he possessed.

7

The Southampton
Flying Boat

Apart from the S.4, 1925 was a busy and successful year for Mitchell and the Supermarine company. The era of racing flying boats was over but they still had an important role to play in civil and military aviation. When the Air Ministry issued a specification for a replacement for the ageing Felixstowe flying boats, Mitchell set to work to design a new one.

Using knowledge gained from production of the Swan amphibian, he designed an armed military flying boat called the Southampton. The Southampton Mk I, with its shining mahogany hull, made its first test flight in March 1925, piloted by Biard. It was an immediate success. In due course, the Air Ministry, who wanted to use the type for reconnaissance and anti–submarine patrol, were amply satisfied with its performance, an order was given and it went into production.

The Southampton had a very distinctive shape. The triple fins and rudder were mounted on the monoplane tail which was carried on the upswept rear end of the hull. It was powered by two 490 hp Napier Lion V engines, with the two fuel tanks below the upper wing. It was of a wood and fabric construction with an unusual arrangement of steel interplane struts. It carried a crew of five: two pilots, a wireless operator, a gunner and a bomb-aimer. The cruising speed was 85 mph, the maximum speed was 107 mph and its range was 680 miles. The first Southampton was built and tested in 7½ months, a tribute to the efficiency of Mitchell and his team of engineers, draughtsmen and craftsmen.

Southampton flying boats entered service with the RAF and were also exported to Japan, Argentina and Australia. This meant increased business for the Supermarine factory, and carried the name of Southampton to the distant corners of the world.

Following the success of the Mk I, a Mk II version was built in 1926. This was the same in all significant details as the Mk I, except that it had a duralumin hull and a slightly more powerful Napier Lion Va engine of 500 hp. The metal hull was a great improvement, since a wooden hull tended to absorb water and, in hot climates, it was attacked by underwater parasites. The saving in weight thus achieved increased the range to 900 miles. The Southampton was the first new flying boat to enter service with the RAF after the end of the First World War, and six squadrons were equipped with them.

In 1927–28, four Mk II Southampton flying boats led by Grp Capt. H.M. Cave-Browne-Cave, DSO, DFC, made a historic Far East Flight, flying in formation. They covered a total distance of 23,000 miles, and places visited included Athens, Basra, Karachi, Columbo, Calcutta, Singapore and a complete circuit of Australia. They then returned to Singapore where they took up station and formed the basis of 205 Squadron RAF. Of the many press reports on the flight, that in the *Daily Mail* of 17 September 1928 was typical: 'As a demonstration of reliability the flight will rank as one of the greatest feats in the history of aviation.' With very little alteration, the Southampton remained operational for eleven years until 1936, double the lifespan of most military aircraft of that time.

While it would be considered fairly routine today, the 1927–28 Far East Flight by the RAF Southamptons was considered an impressive performance which aroused tremendous interest and established Britain's leading position in marine aviation. It also added to Mitchell's reputation. The king of Afghanistan came to England in 1928, and during his visit he went to Calshot to watch a flypast of Southamptons. One of the pilots on that occasion was AC E.H. Richardson, who said: 'The Southampton Mk I was a lovely boat to fly. In spite of all the advantages, we were sorry when metal superseded wood.'

In those early days of long-range flights, when aircraft were only just beginning to circle the world, a flying boat had a great advantage over a land plane. It did not require an aerodrome, and it could operate from the water in distant countries where airports had not been built. People felt safer in flying boats; if trouble developed they knew that the aircraft could always alight on the water. The establishment of permanent British flying bases in Basra, Singapore and Hong Kong owed much to Mitchell's Southampton flying boats.

While the Southampton became world-famous, very few people out-side of the aircraft world had heard of R.J. Mitchell. This was perhaps his own fault. He was a quiet, reserved man, who avoided publicity whenever possible. He could not be idle and was always thinking about the next step forward. Once the Southampton was flying, his thoughts began to centre on a design to replace the ill-fated S.4. Next time his ideas must be made to work successfully to enable Britain to win back the Schneider Trophy.

Before moving on to the events associated with the S.5, it is of interest to describe some events of a rather different nature that took place at Supermarine in the 1925–26 period, which show clearly that neither Mitchell nor his colleagues were all work and no play!

They concern three social events, details of which have come to light only recently and for which Ernest Mansbridge (see Appendix 5) must be thanked for their unearthing from his little box of mementos of his many years at Supermarine.

1.   The menu for the:
SUPERMARINE DRAWING OFFICE ANNUAL BINGE
Held on 22 December 1925 at Price's Cafe.

2.   The menu for the:
SUPERMARINE TECHNICAL STAFF'S ANNUAL DINNER
Held on 21 December 1926 at Price's Cafe.

The menu was of the conventional Christmas fare, including turkey and Christmas pudding and a very comprehensive wine list. The signatures of many of those who attended are on the back of this menu, and many well-known names can be readily deciphered, with Mitchell's firm signature clearly visible.

3.   Programme for the:
SUPERMARINE SPORTS and SOCIAL CLUB ROWING
SECTION
Inter-departmental four-oar galley race for the Easton Rowing
Challenge Cup. Monday, 19 July 1926 at 5.15 p.m.

Among the officers of the day were Cdr J. Bird, judge; Capt. H. Biard, assistant judge; Mr R.J. Mitchell, time-keeper; Mr R. Pickett, umpire.

Taking part in the four-oar galley race were the following teams: Boat Shop 'A', Metal Shop, Mill Joiners, Boat Shop 'B', Technical Dept,

Drawing Office 'B', Drawing Office 'A', Joiners (Assembly Shop) and Machine Shop.

Ernest Mansbridge rowed at bow in the Technical Dept team, with Arthur Black at 2, H.H. Holmes at 3, Alan Clifton at stroke and H.O. Sommer as cox. Unfortunately, Ernest cannot remember which team were the final winners of the galley race but he does recollect his boat having a close scrap with the Drawing Office 'B' team, both teams being, however, some ten lengths behind the Boat Shop 'B' boat!

In addition to this main event, there was a staff race in pair-oar pleasure boats with lady coxwains. There were nine teams entered, one of which was led by Cdr J. Bird. One team which raced in the third heat was Mr R.J. Mitchell and Capt. H.C. Biard, with Miss E. Allen as cox; how they got on was unfortunately not recorded by Ernest Mansbridge, but it would seem to have been a team with plenty of muscle, if perhaps lacking in rowing skills!

To complete the evening's enjoyment, there was also a four-oar gig race (prizes presented by Cdr J. Bird and R. Kemp, Esq.) and a rubber dinghy race (prize presented by the foreman of the works).

The start of all four races was from stake boats moored opposite the Supermarine works slipway at Woolston.

8

The S.5:
A Triumph for
Mitchell

The 1926 Schneider Trophy Contest took place in Virginia, USA, and, because the one-year interval had not given Mitchell enough time to design a new machine, there was no British entry. This meant that the three scarlet Italian Macchi M.39s, designed by Mario Castoldi, were the only seaplanes to challenge the fast American Curtiss R3Cs. Mussolini had now seized power in Italy and he ordered his pilots to bring back the trophy! The Italians were so confident that they smuggled in a supply of Chianti, hidden in the seaplane floats, ready to celebrate victory. Their hopes were realised when Maj. de Bernardi won the race at an average speed of 246.50 mph, 15 mph faster than the American Lt Schilt, who came second. Two days later, de Bernardi raised the world speed record to 258.87 mph. So the trophy, the 'Flying Flirt', went on her travels again, much to Mussolini's satisfaction. He sent de Bernardi a personal, although somewhat flowery, message of congratulation on Italy's behalf.

While the Italians snatched the trophy from America, at Supermarine Mitchell was beginning to think about the design for the 1927 Schneider Contest. Before this took shape, a comprehensive series of wind tunnel and tank tests were carried out at the Royal Aircraft Establishment and the National Physical Laboratory. As the results of these tests became available, Mitchell began to work towards the final form of the S.5. The main aims which Mitchell sought to achieve in his development of the S.4 were (a) reduction of weight, (b) reduction of drag, and (c) a satisfactory water performance. The latter was achieved by trying out no less than ten different forms of float in the RAE and NPL tests. His main innovations were:

1. Flat-surfaced copper wing radiators to reduce drag. These covered nearly all of the upper and lower surfaces of the wing.
2. Lowering the wing and moving the cockpit forward to improve visibility.
3. Streamline wire bracing between floats, wing and fuselage to reduce weight compared with the unbraced cantilever design of the S.4.
4. Reduction in cross section of the fuselage and of frontal area of the floats to reduce drag.
5. A higher-powered geared engine to improve propeller efficiency.

These differences between the S.4 and the S.5 were given in detail in one of the very few lectures that Mitchell gave during his career. This lecture was given to the Royal Aeronautical Society in 1928, following the 1927 contest.

An interesting comment made by Mitchell in his lecture, giving an insight into the way his mind worked, was that while his comments served to indicate what was done in the case of the S.5, and whilst these efforts resulted in a success which was gratifying, their real value lay in the experience gained.

As the design work on the S.5 advanced, two problems arose. Who would pay for the aircraft, and who would race it? The cost of production was now too high for a small firm like Supermarine and therefore the government would have to supply the money if it was to be built. It was generally recognised that much of the American success story was due to their well-trained naval pilots, and it seemed that Britain's only hope of regaining the trophy lay in using a team of RAF pilots. Many British officials at the time, including Sir Hugh Trenchard, Marshal of the RAF, thought that the Schneider Contests were of little value to aviation and that they merely produced 'freak' machines. There was also a lot of talk on both sides of the Atlantic about the impossibility of reaching higher speeds. According to some views, the record of some 260 mph marked the maximum speed at which man could fly. However, it did not escape the notice of certain Air Ministry officials that the nation with the winning Schneider machine also appeared often to possess the best military aircraft.

In March 1926, with this in mind, the government issued a specification for a Napier-powered aircraft able to fly at a speed in excess of 265 mph with a landing speed of 90 mph. It was interesting that for this specification, Supermarine submitted Mitchell's monoplane, the S.5, while their closest rivals, the Gloster firm, submitted a biplane. Eventually, when the government financial backing had been agreed, contracts were given for three Supermarine and three Gloster aircraft, plus one Short-Bristow Crusader monoplane.

It was a testing time for Mitchell. After the failure of the S.4 it was vitally important that his next design should succeed. Apart from altering the basic shape, he made other improvements in the S.5, the most important being the use of duralumin in place of wood for the fuselage and the incorporation of a fully braced wing and float structure. The wing was of all-wood construction. The Napier Lion VII engine of 900 hp was closely cowled and fitted into a streamlined nose which made the S.5 somewhat smaller than the S.4. It was generally believed that the Napier engine had been developed as far as possible, and that a Rolls-Royce engine might produce higher speeds, but after discussions with his engineers, Mitchell decided to keep the Napier Lion for at least this year.

In 1926, while he was working on the S.5, Mitchell added another man to his team, Arthur Black. Black was a metallurgist, and his expert knowledge proved extremely valuable at a time when metal alloy was rapidly replacing wood in aircraft construction. Supermarine was one of the first firms to employ a metallurgist full-time.

The following extracts from an article Arthur Black wrote in a commemorative brochure produced in 1959 by the Reginald Mitchell County Primary School (see Item 2, page 251) are of interest, written as they were by someone who worked with Mitchell for many years:

Mitchell built up around him the team of men, mostly a few years younger than himself, who were to carry on his ideas and enthusiasms after his death. I am proud that I was one of those men and grateful to R.J. Mitchell for the technical standards he so ably established in our minds.

I remember how R.J.'s well-built figure, medium height with fair colouring, could be seen in the workshop each morning, studying with complete concentration the developing shape of the aircraft being built. He would walk round it and study it from all angles, now and then examining a detail minutely. I sometimes wondered if he was aware how closely he was watched for some clue as to what his reactions were going to be. If he was satisfied, he would pass on to the next job; but if he was not satisfied, then much of the design work and manufacture might well have to be done again. But his outlook was strictly practical and having discussed the matter with those concerned, a satisfactory compromise was usually arrived at.

His technical genius was only part of the story; he was also a born leader of men. Although he was universally and familiarly known by his initials R.J., there was never any question as to who was the boss and at the same time he inspired devotion and affection in all his staff. His decisions were firmly given and faithfully carried out; he took a great interest in new developments and was always ready to listen to a technical argument and remained always open to conviction...

There were, however, things which one didn't do. His best work arose from a power of concentration and in the picture of him which most springs to mind, he is seated with his elbows on the drawing board, face cupped in hands, thinking out the latest problem. Woe betide the unwary but enthusiastic technician who broke in on that concentration! When early test flights of a new aircraft were in progress, his concern was so great that it paid not to attempt polite conversation. He could never escape the feeling of personal responsibility for the safety of the pilot.

R.J. was happy in his generation of aircraft designers, and his particular talent for brilliant new ideas, combined with a practical compromise, found full scope. His engineering training enabled him to grasp fully every detail of the construction of his aircraft, and he used these powers to the full, resulting in extremely successful aircraft which were indelibly stamped with his thinking. Thus, the Schneider Trophy racers and the original Spitfire were much more the designer's brain children than would now be possible with the greatly increased complexity.

Despite his quick temper, Mitchell built up an enviable working relationship with his design team. He was absolutely loyal to them and never allowed anyone to criticise them in public. If they made a mistake he would take them aside and point out their error and, because they knew he would always stand up for them, they worked hard to please him. They soon learnt to forgive his fiery outbursts. It was just R.J.'s way and the stormy scene was soon forgotten. In some strange way Mitchell had the power to get the best out of people. Speaking of her husband, his wife once remarked to a friend: 'He can make people do things they would have thought impossible.'

Mitchell worked very hard on the designs for the new seaplane. As already described, the fuselage was all metal while the wing was of all-wood construction with two spars and plywood skins. Tailplane, rudder and elevators were of similar construction. Before the cockpit was finalised the pilots were measured, so that they would fit in, rather like the way that today's racing driver fits into his car. The fuselage was smaller in cross-section than any previous design. It was less than that of the S.4 and the narrow opening made it impossible for a large man to wriggle into the cockpit.

When the S.5 was in Venice for the 1927 Schneider Trophy Contest, an Italian gentleman of rather generous proportions did manage to get inside, but trouble arose when he tried to get out! After several painful and unsuccessful attempts, he had to be winched out by a crane.

The space in the fuselage was so limited that part of the fuel was carried in the starboard float, where it helped to counteract the effect of torque – a twisting action caused by the propeller – on take-off. In addition, for the same reason, the starboard float was offset about 8 in. further from the fuselage centre line than the port float. Everything in the S.5 was designed to reduce drag. The frontal area was as small as possible and rivet heads were finished flush with the surface. During a Woolston cricket match, a player was accused of dropping an easy catch. He excused himself by holding up his sore hands, caused by hours spent polishing the skin of the S.5.

Sir Hugh Trenchard was fully aware that the British defeat in the 1925 Schneider Trophy Contest was mainly due to the technical superiority of the other competitors, but that the lack of team organisation also played a part. He also knew that the latter defect could be remedied by the RAF. Consequently, in May 1927, when the Air Ministry had finally agreed to finance and organise the 1927 British entry, an RAF High Speed Flight was formed to operate and fly the aircraft in the race.

The RAF High Speed Flight consisted of Sqn Ldr L.H. Slatter in command, Flt Lt S.N. Webster, Flt Lt O.E. Worsley, and Flg Off. H.M. Scholfield, who were later joined by the South African Flt Lt S.M. Kinkead. By the beginning of July the team moved to Calshot to try out the S.5s and the Gloster biplanes. The S.5s were allocated the serial numbers N219, N220, N221, and the Glosters followed in sequence, N222, N223 and N224.

Early in July, Webster flew the S.5 for the first time and after flying at over 275 mph, he recorded in his diary: 'Very nice. No snags.' Once it was airborne the aircraft performed well, but it was not easy to get it off the water. Owing to torque, the port float had a tendency to dip below the water, which swung the aeroplane round to the left. The bow waves from the floats sent up so much spray that the pilot in the open cockpit was unable to see for the first few minutes. Bringing the S.5 down on to the water also demanded skilled handling, since its approach angle was very flat and its landing speed was relatively high. A clear stretch of water up to two miles was desirable, because forward view from the cockpit was severely limited.

Mitchell got on very well with the RAF pilots, for whom he had the greatest respect, and when they were flying one of the S.5s he was always down at Calshot, anxiously watching each performance. He soon became known as 'Mitch', a familiarity never permitted at Supermarine.

The pilots spent most of their time practising take-offs and cornering. If the race in Italy was hotly contested, correct cornering technique might be the deciding factor; correct cornering meant achieving a turn of optimum radius, pulling neither too much nor too little 'G'. Flying time was limited, and sometimes had to be stopped altogether, depending upon weather conditions. If the sea was rough and the wind blowing up a high sea, the pilots were not allowed to take the seaplanes out for fear of their sinking. Even in calm conditions, they had to keep a close watch on all shipping movements. Thus, for example, the wash from an Isle of Wight ferry caused sufficient disturbance to make take-off or landing impossible. Floating debris was another hazard; a punctured float could be dangerous, with the possibility of sinking if a tow was long delayed.

The 1927 Schneider Trophy Contest course in Venice was marked out over the Lido, where the long beach would provide excellent viewing for the thousands of spectators. Since America and France had now withdrawn, Britain and Italy were the only competing nations. The American government refused to back any entry, arguing that further participation would be unlikely to be cost-effective in terms of new knowledge gained. It is interesting to speculate whether subsequent events led them to regret this decision. The race was to take place on Sunday 25 September, and early in August the S.5s were dismantled and packed in crates ready for the sea voyage to Venice. It was impossible to send them by the quicker land route because the crates were too large to go through the Simplon Tunnel.

The S.5 N219 and the Gloster N222 left Southampton on the SS *Eworth* on 11 August. Mitchell, with the other seaplanes, sailed ten days later on the SS *Egyptian Prince*, which took them to Malta. Here they transferred to the carrier HMS *Eagle* for the last part of the voyage to Venice.

The Italians had built hangars for the British seaplanes at the northern end of the Lido, which meant that the new S.5s and the Gloster were clearly visible across a narrow strip of water. But they kept their latest Macchi well out of sight, and were careful to give nothing away concerning their performance.

After all the RAF pilots had reached Venice, it had in due course to be decided which of them should take part in the race. After some discussion it was decided that Flt Lts Webster and Worsley would each fly an S.5 while Flt Lt Kinkead would pilot the Gloster IVB. Because they had no idea how fast the Italian Macchis could fly, the pilots decided to lap the course at full throttle and just hope that the Napier Lion engines would stand up to the strain.

Sunday 25 September came, with the Italians noisily excited about the race and fully confident of victory. Venice had been specially decorated for the occasion, with brightly coloured flags, banners and tapestries waving from every building. The coveted trophy, 'The Schneider Cuppa', was on view in St Mark's Square. The gondoliers did a roaring trade as tourists scrambled for transport to take them out to the Lido. The Excelsior Palace Hotel, on the start and finish line, was jammed with visitors. Then came the anti-climax. When everybody was worked up to a peak of excitement, it was announced that the contest had been postponed until the next day because strong winds and a swell made racing impossible.

On Monday the weather improved, and the British team were told to get ready for take off at 2.30 p.m. The 50-km triangular course, which had to be lapped seven times, covered the length of the Lido, with a sharp turn at each end. From the spectators' point of view it was an ideal position, and crowds of around 200,000 had gathered in eager anticipation of a glorious Italian victory. Just before the race, the crown prince arrived, ready to share in the jubilation.

At 1.40 p.m. the British and Italian seaplanes were towed from their hangars and an excited roar surged up from the crowd at the sight of the scarlet Macchi M.52s. Two of their pilots, Maj. de Bernardi and Capt. Ferrarin, were well known from previous races and they received a tumultuous welcome. Ferrarin was a local man and the crowds, who adored him, gave him a very special ovation.

As the cheers grew louder, Mitchell stood alone, trying to control his nervous fears. Two men were about to risk their lives hurtling through the air in his machines. Suppose something went wrong and there was another disaster? Mitchell knew they were well trained and knew what they were doing but however hard he tried he could not shrug off his concern for them.

Kinkead in the Gloster IVB N223 had drawn the right to go first, and as the starting gun went off he roared across the line. His first lap reached 266.5 mph but Bernardi, who followed him, reached an opening lap speed of 275 mph. The British officials, watching from the roof of the Excelsior, quickly realised that only one of the S.5s had a chance of beating the Italian's high first-lap speed.

Webster in N220 was next away, going nicely and cornering well. Worsley in N219 took off after Guayetti, who had followed Webster. All Italian eyes were now fixed on the scarlet Macchis. Then it began to rain. Almost at once disaster struck the Italians. Ferrarin's seaplane came down in a cloud of smoke as he dived towards the shore. Soon afterwards, Bernardi was forced to retire with engine trouble, leaving the three British pilots and the one remaining Italian, Guayetti, to fight it out.

After the fifth lap, Kinkead was forced to retire with engine trouble. It was found that a loose strip of metal had wrapped round the propeller blade and he was very lucky to have escaped alive. The two British pilots, Webster and Worsley, were still flying against one Italian. The latter came to grief when one of his fuel tanks was punctured and he came down on the lagoon, narrowly missing the Excelsior Hotel.

The British pilots carried a simple but effective device for recording each lap as they completed it. It consisted of a small board with holes in it which where covered by paper, one of which was punched out after each lap. Webster thought he might have made a mistake with his hole punching and ended up doing an eighth lap. His little board with its holes is still in existence fifty-eight years later.

The race was won by Flt Lt Webster in the S.5 and his average speed of 281.66 mph set up a new world speed record for seaplanes and land-planes. Flt Lt Worsley was second.

Flt Lt Webster's terse comment when he heard the news of his victory was: 'Now let's celebrate.'

These words must have echoed in Mitchell's heart. He had done what he set out to do and regained the Schneider Trophy for Britain, and he had every reason to feel pleased and proud. His first attempt to design a racing monoplane had ended in disaster but his second aircraft, the S.5, was a world beater.

In an interview a few years before his death, AVM S.N. Webster was rather reluctant to talk about his victory. He explained that he was stationed at Martlesham Heath when the Air Ministry invited him to take part in the 1927 Schneider Trophy Contest and he had jumped at the chance. He loved flying and, though he would not admit it, he was an exceptionally good pilot and the race gave him an opportunity to show what he could really do.

As a test pilot at Martlesham, Webster had flown a large variety of aeroplanes, but before leaving for Venice he flew the S.5 only twice, once in July and once in August. He liked the seaplane and, in spite of being a well-built man, he managed to get into the cockpit fairly easily by twisting his broad shoulders. Speaking of the race, he commented: 'You just went up and flew as fast as you damn well could.' He shrugged off any idea of danger. 'If you were afraid you were no use.'

He said that the British pilots planned to fly round the course as low as possible, adding: 'If you lost too much speed rounding the pylons it took a long time to make it up. The Italians used a different method of cornering which involved a climb to 600 ft followed by a steep dive into the next leg to regain speed.'

From his brief acquaintance with Mitchell, Webster knew him as, 'An ideal man to know; kind, steady, duty-minded, with no conceit. He was a good mixer and got on well with his workpeople and the RAF pilots.'

Watching his smiling face as he talked of those far-off days, it was easy imagine the parties and celebrations that went on in the Excelsior Hotel on the day when Britain regained the Schneider Trophy.

AVM Webster sadly died on 5 April 1984. In a letter Mrs Webster wrote to Gordon Mitchell at the time, she told him that, a day or so before he died, 'Webby' had said to her that the most marvellous thing that ever happened to him was winning the Schneider. A very interesting and illuminating comment by a man who had had such a long and distinguished career in the RAF. On a later occasion when Gordon visited Mrs Webster in her home, she proudly told him about a ring consisting of a ruby stone in a heavy gold setting, which 'Webby' had been given after his victory by an influential Italian businessman and well-known poet by the name of d'Annuncio. 'Webby' greatly treasured this ring.

9

Welcome Home

When the Supermarine team arrived back in the city of Southampton they were accorded a great welcome. The RAF pilots had returned to their bases, but Mitchell, Cdr Bird and E.L. Ransome of the Air Ministry were met at the station by the mayor who, in a brief speech of welcome, said:

> The city of Southampton may well be proud of the fact that the machine which gained the coveted Schneider Trophy for Britain, as well as the machine in second place, were built in Southampton by Southampton people.

The crowd which packed the station platform broke into a loud cheer as they recognised Cdr Bird and Mitchell. The latter, looking bronzed, was accompanied by his wife, who had been with him in Italy. They were rather embarrassed by the presence of so many people, but they were pleased to shake hands with Capt. Biard, who was at the station to congratulate them on their success.

As the party squeezed their way through the exit, they were faced with another tremendous crowd gathered on the forecourt to welcome the heroes home.

Ransome managed to escape, but Bird and Mitchell were driven to the mayor's parlour for the official reception. The route to the city centre was lined by cheering crowds, many of them relations of the workers employed at Supermarine.

After toasting the victors in champagne, the mayor said: 'These are two fellows we are all proud and honoured to know.' Turning to Bird and Mitchell he added, 'You have done something for England that will live through generations to come. You have regained our proud position as first and foremost in the world of aviation.'

Cdr Bird replied briefly, giving credit to Mr Mitchell who had designed the machine, and Mr Wilkinson of Napiers who had designed the engine. He was sorry that their duties prevented the winning pilots from being present. He also paid tribute to the men of Supermarine who had worked night and day to get the S.5s ready in time.

Mitchell replied, in one of his rare speeches:

> I feel proud of being a member of the team which has brought back the trophy. We gained considerable pleasure in the fact that we had won something for old England, because lately she has been losing sports laurels. I think our victory will raise the Union Jack a little higher. We have all worked very hard to win, and I am sorry that the mechanics are not present to share in this reception because they worked harder than anybody. Four hours before the Schneider race, a leak was discovered in a wing radiator but everybody got down to work and it was repaired just in time.

Because of his stammer, Mitchell was very reluctant to speak in public, but on the few occasions when he did he always praised the Supermarine workers.

Amidst the celebrations, Mitchell and his wife received an urgent telephone message informing them that their son had been involved in a car accident in Stoke-on-Trent, where he had been staying with relatives during his parents' absence. A heavy lorry had skidded on the wet road and crashed into the front near-side of the car in which Gordon was sitting next to his uncle. He was severely concussed, but fortunately suffered no serious physical injury, although the car was a complete write-off. Mitchell and his wife dropped everything and rushed off to Stoke. After Gordon had had three weeks' rest in a darkened room they were able to take him back home to Southampton. It was a lucky escape from what might have been a family tragedy, and Eric took a long time to get over his accident.

Subsequently, the Air Council gave a dinner at the Savoy to celebrate the victory in Venice. In his after-dinner speech, Sir Samuel Hoare, minister for air, said that, as the mouthpiece of the nation, he was proud to congratulate the Schneider Trophy team. He also announced that Flt Lt S.N. Webster had been awarded a Bar to his AFC.

Webster, a modest man, said in his reply: 'I just happened to get the fastest machine. I did no more than anybody would have done.'

After the Schneider Trophy victory, the RAF pilots became public heroes, but outside of Southampton there was little mention of Mitchell. His total lack of vanity and self-importance led some people to believe that the S.5 was the result of a lucky chance. Only the members of his team knew of the months of concentrated effort and dedicated work which had been needed to design the fastest aeroplane in the world.

On 7 October, Cdr Bird, Mitchell and Flt Lt Worsley were honoured at a Rotary meeting in the city of Southampton. Before the speeches were made, there was a preliminary discussion concerning the venue for the next Schneider Trophy Contest which was to be held in Britain. It was generally agreed that the Solent provided an excellent setting, and that the lack of suitable accommodation for important visitors and officials could be overcome by anchoring one or two liners offshore.

After apologising for Flt Lt Webster's unavoidable absence, Bird paid tribute to the designer of the S.5. 'Mr Mitchell secured a great triumph. You would all agree with me when I say he completely out-designed the Italians.'

In reply, Mitchell said:

> I would hate anyone to think it was an individual triumph, as I have been considerably helped by a large number of people, my personal assistants and draughtsmen, as well as those engaged on the construction side. The machine itself has been a source of anxiety to me right from the start, and I am pleased to know that at this moment it is safely shut up in a box. The designing of such a machine involved considerable anxiety because everything had been sacrificed to speed. The floats were only just large enough to support the machine, and the wings had been cut down to a size considered just sufficient to ensure a safe landing. The engine had only five hours' duration; after that time it had to be removed and changed. In fact everything had been so cut down it was dangerous to fly. Racing machines of this sort are not safe to fly, and many times I have been thankful that it was only a single seater. The pilots were the real heroes and they deserved all the credit [loud applause]. The Italians showed a fine sporting spirit and immediately the race was over they offered their congratulations.

Although the Italians had been beaten at Venice, they were determined not be left behind, and six weeks later de Bernardi in a Macchi M.52 recaptured the world air speed record at 297.76 mph.

The success of the S.5 was a personal triumph for Mitchell. His creative brilliance as an aircraft designer was now recognised in aviation circles, not only in England but in Europe and America. This brought increased orders for Supermarine and, as he had been promised in the agreement he signed in 1924 with Supermarine, Mitchell became one of the firm's directors. As has already been emphasised, he had always got on well with the workers. He knew them all by name and they liked and respected him. When he became a director, he acted as a liaison officer between management and the shop floor. At the first sign of trouble Mitchell was asked to deal with it, and the men always took notice of what he had to say.

An interesting letter which has recently come to light was that written by Mitchell to an old friend, dated 26 October 1927.

My dear Mrs Frost,

I was very delighted to receive your letter of the 29th inst. Please excuse me for not replying before but since returning from Italy I have been away from Southampton and have not been able to attend to my correspondence. Your letter brought back many happy memories and of course I remember all you mention in your letter perfectly well together with lots of other things. I was very pleased to hear you were now settled down and had a boy of fourteen years. This seems incredible and only shows how the years slip merrily on. Do send me a snap of yourself and boy. I am enclosing one of myself to show you how badly I have developed, and also one of our winning seaplanes.

If you are in Southampton any time be sure to call in at the works to see me.

I have a boy seven years' old. That seems incredible too, doesn't it? I have been looking for a photo but cannot find one at the moment. I will send you one at a later date.

With kindest regards
Sincerely yours, R.J. Mitchell

From what is said in the letter, it would seem that Mrs Frost knew Mitchell in his teens in Stoke-on-Trent. Mrs Frost's daughter, Mrs Myra Cecil, originally had the letter in her possession and passed it on to Keith Fordyce, curator of the Torbay Aircraft Museum, where it was in due course seen by Gordon Mitchell on a visit to the museum. Mrs Cecil told him that her mother (née Annie Griffiths) was a qualified nurse and had possibly nursed Reg Mitchell at some time. The letter is of interest in being a rare example of a personal letter written by Mitchell during that period of his career, which has survived.

Another change which followed the 1927 victory was the purchase of a new home. Up to this time, Mitchell had continued to live in

Radstock Road, Woolston, but when he was made a director he bought a plot of land in Russell Place, Portswood, a pleasant residential area on the west side of Southampton. A colleague at Supermarine drew up the plans for the new house to meet the requirements of Mitchell and his wife. This was H.H. Holmes, generally known in the office as 'H cubed', who worked on stressing but was previously an architectural student. The house was to stand in a fair-sized garden with plenty of room for Gordon, now aged seven, to play in. The house was called 'Hazeldene', perhaps a reminder of Hazel Road, Woolston, the site of the Supermarine works. Happily, the house survived the bombing raids over Southampton during the Second World War although one bomb did drop at the bottom of the garden.

When the Mitchell family moved into their new home they employed three servants: a gardener; a home help to do the rough work; and a maid who lived in. The maid, the late Miss Eva Ledger, went to them in 1927 when she was only fifteen, and she stayed until 1936 when she left to get married. Now, as Mrs Elliss, she clearly remembers her early life at 'Hazeldene': 'I was very happy there. I was fond of Mr Mitchell, he was so kind-hearted – they all were. Mrs Mitchell liked housework, and when we had visitors she and I did the cooking together.'

'Hazeldene' was a pleasant, two-storey detached house, and at that time Russell Place was a quiet road, well away from the bustle of Portswood Broadway, yet near enough for Mrs Mitchell to walk to the local shops, such as Addis', which stood on the corner opposite Alec Bennett's garage. Russell Place now has a few more houses in it but 'Hazeldene' remains much the same as it was in Mitchell's day and is currently owned by a professor at the University of Southampton. The main feature of the house was the large lounge, extending from front to back, with a French window opening on to a lawn edged with flower beds. The garden was a peaceful place, with tall trees shutting off the noise of the outside world and giving an air of quiet seclusion. Mitchell was very fond of his garden, but preferred other people to do the necessary work in it!

A great attraction was the large adjacent grounds, to which the surrounding houses had private access, reached through a gate at the bottom of the garden; these grounds contained several first-class grass tennis courts and were much used by all of the Mitchell family.

Mitchell developed a great interest in dogs later in life but they were never allowed to run wild either in the house or in the garden. One favourite red setter had a habit of escaping, and was often returned home by a patrolling policeman. Later on, he obtained an Alsatian but when this went for him one day, he decided this breed was not for him!

The rooms at 'Hazeldene' held many of Mrs Mitchell's treasures. She had a good collection of Staffordshire china, but the prize possession in later years was a silver tea set and tray presented to her husband in 1931.

The solid silver tray is engraved: 'Presented to R.J. Mitchell, Esq., CBE, by his fellow directors of The Supermarine Aviation Works (Vickers) Ltd to mark their admiration of his skill in designing three consecutive winning seaplanes in the International Schneider Trophy Contest thus retaining the trophy for Great Britain.' The tray is currently on exhibition in the RAF Museum, having been loaned to them by Gordon.

Another presentation which Mitchell was equally proud to receive following the 1931 contest was a circular, solid silver salver which is engraved: 'Schneider Trophy Contest 1931'. This heading is followed by an engraving of the S.6B with its number, S.1595, clearly shown. 'Presented to R.J. Mitchell, Designer of Supermarine Rolls-Royce S.6B by the Members of the Royal Aero Club.' On the reverse, the names of all eight members of the 1931 RAF High Speed Flight are engraved. Gordon is glad to be able to say that this beautiful and unique item has survived to the present day and is still in excellent condition.

The house was run with clockwork efficiency, and visitors were always welcome. Family relations often came to stay and, during the Schneider Contests, RAF pilots would come to Mitchell's home to discuss usually anything except aeroplanes. A time and place for everything, Mitchell used to say.

Both Mitchell and his wife enjoyed sport, and often played tennis on the nearby courts already mentioned. They also liked golf, and if Mrs Mitchell was alone she went out to the Bramshaw Golf Club in the New Forest, taking Eva – who was always treated as one of the family – to walk round the course with her. At holiday times the family usually went to the seaside, often to nearby Bournemouth.

There was great excitement at 'Hazeldene' when Mitchell came home with his Rolls-Royce car. He was as proud as a schoolboy, and he insisted on taking his wife out for a drive immediately. Later, after she had a ride in the car, Eva said: 'It was smashing, I had never ridden in such a beautiful car. It was black with a snakeskin roof.'

Shortly after becoming a director, Mitchell decided that his design team needed an extra typist. The post was advertised in the Southampton paper and his secretary, Mr Spencer, was told to interview the applicants. Mitchell never interviewed the girls employed by the firm; that job was always left to someone else. In this particular case Mr Spencer appointed a young girl of nineteen, Miss Vera Cross (later Mrs Vera Cherry), who was destined to play an important part in Mitchell's career.

When Miss Cross had left school, she had intended to take a university degree, but the sudden death of her father caused her to change her plans. In the reduced family circumstances she considered it her duty to earn some money, and after taking a secretarial course at a Southampton college she worked for a short period with a shipping firm. Passing the Supermarine factory on her way to work, she became fascinated by the sight of seaplanes and flying boats standing on the slipway. When she saw the post of typist to the design team advertised in the local paper, she immediately sent in an application.

Miss Cross soon became Mitchell's personal secretary, with her own office next to his, and in the ten years she worked in that capacity she gave him invaluable service. She was hard-working, competent and highly efficient, and she relieved Mitchell of much of the routine paperwork which he detested. At first, Miss Cross found Mitchell a difficult man to work with, since he was sometimes moody and she never quite knew what he was going to do or say next. He had no idea of a proper filing system, which made it difficult for her to find a particular letter he wanted. However, she soon had things organised, and when Mitchell realised how efficient she was, he decided to rid himself of the hated task of writing letters.

One morning, as Miss Cross entered his office for dictation, Mitchell took one look at the in-tray which was full of letters, seized it in both hands, and tossed it up in the air and let it fall to the floor. 'There you are,' he said with his charming smile. 'I don't want anything more to do with letters. From now on you can answer almost all of them.'

After that Miss Cross always dealt with most of Mitchell's correspondence herself. If a letter required technical information, she soon discovered which member of the design team could provide the answer and, having consulted him, she would compose a suitable reply. All Mitchell had to do was sign the letters at the end of the day, although sometimes there would be, of course, the occasional letter which only he could deal with.

Miss Cross performed another useful service for Mitchell by keeping a vigilant eye on all his visitors. Very few people were allowed to enter his office without first consulting her, and in this way she saved him from many unnecessary interruptions. When she knew R.J. was concentrating on a particular problem she would not let anyone near him.

'His mood is not right,' she would tell the caller, 'Better leave it until later.'

It was not only Mitchell who learnt to depend on Miss Cross. Mrs Mitchell soon found that she had a valuable ally who would help to look after her unpunctual husband. When Mitchell was absorbed in his work, he lost all sense of time, with the consequence that Mrs Mitchell would often be waiting at home with the dinner cooked and no husband to eat it. In desperation she would phone Miss Cross.

It might require two or three more phone calls before the culprit was finally tracked down and persuaded to go home. Mitchell would have only one idea in his mind, and that was his latest design problem. The fact that his wife was kept waiting was, unfortunately, liable to be forgotten. Work was what mattered, and everything else had to wait.

Often, Miss Cross also had the task of giving Gordon something to do in her office on the many occasions his father brought him in to the works with him on a Saturday morning. Playing with the typewriter was one of his delights; Vera Cross undoubtedly made him do more than just play with the machine as Gordon is now an accomplished two-finger typist! Recalling the years when she worked for Mitchell, Miss Cross said:

He was a very handsome man, with a lovely smile, but he was rather nervous with female members of the staff. He always dictated slowly, with only a slight hesitation in his speech. He was an inspiration to all the men who worked with him. If he took to a man and gave him a special job to do, then he would trust him to get on with it and in that way he got the best out of his design team and workmen. If he didn't care for a man he would have nothing to do with him. He went through the drawing office regularly, and when one of his designs was under construction he would haunt the workshops, his eagle eye ready to spot any faulty detail. If you were keen on your job he was a good man to work for. You soon got used to his moods and learnt to keep out of his way when he was concentrating on a problem if you wanted to survive!

R.J., as he was known to his staff, was a man of high principles. He was very attractive and had a charming personality but was very reserved and retiring, and was invariably to be found in the background on important occasions. He was a born leader of men and was capable of drawing out the best from his staff, in whom he placed complete confidence. His design work meant a very great deal to him, and he would spend much time alone in his office meditating on various problems before he held consultations with others on his staff.

He was a great driving force and once his mind was made up he went all out to achieve his end. Normal working hours did not interest him, and if he was engaged on some important project he would work until quite late in the evenings and expect his staff to do the same.

He was very temperamental, particularly in the latter years of his life, and also when his planes were to make their first flights.

He had a great opinion of his staff and would stand up for them at all times. This was borne out at the end of his life when he requested that the design staff should be given first place at his funeral; his wishes were carried out. He was very loyal to them and much loved by them.

Although so much of his life was devoted to designing, he still enjoyed to the full a game of golf or tennis and was always ready for a practical joke.

He enjoyed a happy home life with his wife and son, and bore his final illness with great fortitude, and was an example to us all.

As a postscript, it is appropriate that mention be made of a letter dated 10 June 1985 which Mrs Vera Cherry wrote to Gordon Mitchell and which she ended with these words: 'It is strange that I should be writing to you on the eve of the anniversary of R.J.'s death. It is a day I always reserve for him. God bless him!' No man could wish for a more loyal and understanding secretary. Vera Cherry sadly died on 16 December 1999.

After the victory at Venice, Mitchell received many messages congratulating him on the success of the S.5. The year 1927 was a milestone in his career. As we have seen, he had become a director at Supermarine and now owned a beautiful home. But to him the most important thing was the success of the S.5. Unlike certain others in high places, Mitchell firmly believed in the long-term value of the Schneider Trophy Contests and subsequent events were to prove only too clearly the validity of his views.

10

The S.6: Victory at Cowes

The outstanding success of their flying boats and of the S.5 in 1927 brought Supermarine to the attention of Vickers, who wanted to expand their aviation interests, and in autumn 1928 they began negotiations with Sqn Cdr Bird with the idea of acquiring the whole of the issued capital of the firm. Vickers really wanted Mitchell and it was a condition of the purchase – a highly important and significant condition – that he was bound to the company without option of terminating his service agreement before the end of 1933.

By November 1928, agreement had been reached by all parties on the basis of £390,000 for the issued capital plus eleven-twelfths of the profits of the company for the year. James Bird was to remain in charge. Under the terms of the service agreement that Mitchell had signed in 1924 (see Chapter 4), it would appear that if Vickers wanted his services then he had no option other than to remain with the newly formed company, at least until his service agreement ended in 1933. As already suggested in Chapter 4, presumably Vickers were well aware of this when they began negotiations with Cdr Bird. Eventually, in June 1931, the name was changed to 'The Supermarine Aviation Works (Vickers) Ltd'.

In the same year that Vickers acquired Supermarine, the main Vickers board appointed a new chairman of both their aviation companies, namely Vickers Aviation at Weybridge and Supermarine. This was Sir Robert McLean, a Scottish engineer of immense integrity and independence, and he had direct responsibility to the Vickers board. Those in his organisation that he considered to be effective and efficient, he supported and protected to the limit of his immense authority, and the rest just fell apart! Into the former category, Mitchell was quickly placed, and from then until his death nine years later, Sir Robert played a dominant role in Mitchell's life, giving him all the support he could muster. As is discussed later, in 1934 Sir Robert in effect 'set the scene' which made it possible for Mitchell to create his masterpiece, the Spitfire. Sir Robert's appointment as chairman was, therefore, unquestionably one of the major landmarks in Mitchell's career. The high regard and esteem that Sir Robert had for Mitchell is clearly shown in the Appreciation of Mitchell which he wrote for *Vickers News*, shortly after Mitchell's death, and which is reproduced on pages 21–23.

Under Sir Robert McLean, certain alterations were made in administration as Vickers replaced some Supermarine staff with their own men. However, Mitchell retained his position as chief designer and chief engineer and kept his design team together. One significant new arrival was that of T.C.L. Westbrook in 1929. His appointment as general manager, and later as works superintendent, was a milestone in Supermarine's history, and his contribution to the production side of the firm, from then until he moved to Weybridge in 1937, was enormous. He was a man of untiring energy and drive and it was not unexpected when Lord Beaverbrook insisted on him joining the Ministry of Aircraft Production in 1940.

The future now looked bright for Mitchell, with an increasing number of orders and the possibility of being able to design new and advanced aircraft now that he had Vickers behind him. A few months before Vickers acquired Supermarine, a sad event occurred which caused Mitchell much distress and sorrow.

It happened in March 1928. Earlier in the year, a new RAF High Speed Flight had been formed, and from that team Flt Lt S.M. Kinkead had been chosen to make an attempt on the world speed record, currently held by Italy. On the afternoon of 12 March, Kinkead took off from Calshot in a tuned-up S.5 N221, the reserve machine at Venice. The weather had been bad for several days, but on this particular afternoon there was a break in the clouds and a calm sea. The regulation 3-km straight course lay between Hillhead and Lee-on-the-Solent, and Kinkead climbed up high over the Isle of Wight in preparation for his record attempt. By the time he had turned and was ready to begin, the light was fading, and the mirror-like surface of the sea made judgement of height very difficult. But Kinkead was determined to have a go, and he set off, roaring down in a shallow dive before straightening out over the course. He never pulled out of the dive and hit the water at maximum speed. He was killed instantly.

Mitchell was deeply upset by Kinkead's death. He could not easily accept the fact that a man he had known and liked had been killed in one of his creations, even though all the evidence indicated that the accident had not been caused by a fault in the plane. He brooded for many days over the tragedy but gradually he came to accept what his colleagues at work kept telling him, that it was a most unfortunate accident but that there was no reason for him to believe that he was in any way to blame. A plaque at Calshot honours Kinkead.

In the same month as Kinkead's death, the Italian de Bernardi, in a modified Macchi M.52R, pushed the world speed record up to 318.57 mph. The 300 mph mark had now at last been passed, and the next target was 400 mph. Flt Lt D'Arcy Greig was posted to replace Kinkead in May 1928 and in November that year made an attempt on a new record in S.5 N220. Flying over the Solent he reached a speed of 319.57 mph, the fastest time in the world, but not high enough above the Italian speed to qualify as a new official record.

Another person who played an important part, albeit at a distance, in Mitchell's life, died that same year in May, and that was Jacques Schneider who was, of course, initially responsible for creating the Schneider Trophy Contests. Even though Schneider's original aims for the contest, namely to further the development of reliable long-range passenger and freight aircraft using the sea as their airports, had not come to pass, the long-term benefits of the Schneider Contest to aviation development were in the end to prove invaluable. One can certainly question whether either the Spitfire or its Merlin engine would have been created so successfully had it not been for the vast experience and know-how that Mitchell and his team derived from their deep involvement in the contests over a period of nine years, and likewise Rolls-Royce from the 1929 and 1931 contests.

Soon after Sir Robert McLean became chairman of Supermarine, he made it a routine to visit the firm every Tuesday and on these occasions Miss Cross acted as his secretary. Before setting out on his journey from Weybridge, McLean dictated his letters over the telephone, expecting them to be ready to sign when he reached Southampton. It was an exacting task, but Miss Cross usually coped, being, as we have seen, a highly capable and understanding secretary.

Mitchell worked irregular hours, often staying late in his office when he was engrossed in a particular problem, and at such times his staff were expected to remain on hand. He was quite unpredictable. He was fond of sailing, which in those days could be done on the River Itchen. If it happened to be a warm, sunny afternoon he might suddenly decide to go out for an hour's sailing and, having no idea when he would return, Miss Cross had to sit and wait for the day's mail to be signed. As the minutes ticked away and the usual time for going home receded, she became angry and resentful. Why couldn't he be like other men and work normal hours? Eventually she heard footsteps racing up the stairs, and the clicking of thumb and fingers which always heralded R.J.'s approach. She firmly intended to voice a complaint, but one sight of that magical smile and all her anger was forgotten. The letters were quickly signed and she was driven home.

The Vickers takeover caused some awkward repercussions. At that time, Barnes Wallis, one of the two designers at Weybridge, the chief designer being Rex Pierson, was working on the airship R.100, and he very much wanted to be on board when it made its trial flight to Canada. Sir Robert McLean had other ideas, however, and decided instead to send him to Supermarine to act as a sort of back-stop to Mitchell with the idea that he assist him with the Guinness flying yacht that Mitchell was working on and generally help with organisational matters. The thought of working with Barnes Wallis angered Mitchell so much that he could scarcely bring himself to speak to him. If Barnes Wallis came into the office at one door, he marched out through the other. Unable to stand the situation, Mitchell absented himself from Supermarine, and no one had any idea where he was. He must have made his objections known to Sir Robert in no uncertain terms for, on his return, Barnes Wallis was recalled to Weybridge, much to the relief of the two men. Both were brilliant designers and leaders, but they approached aeronautical design from entirely different angles, and it was unwise and undiscerning of Sir Robert to expect two men of such stature and individual personalities to work together within a small organisation such as the Supermarine design office.

The two men had very different views on aircraft construction; Wallis felt that geodetic construction was the answer (such as he later successfully applied to the Wellington bomber). While seeing its merits, Mitchell was convinced that there were better methods (such as he later applied very successfully to the Spitfire). Mitchell was not alone in having reservations about geodetic construction as some members of the Air Staff held similar views at the time.

Peace was restored when Barnes Wallis was replaced by a pilot, Maj. H.J. Payn, who became Mitchell's personal assistant; he became generally known at Supermarine as 'Agony'!

Mitchell was a totally democratic man and he was not impressed by wealth or rank. He was just as likely to speak kindly to the man sweeping up the workshop floor as to a visiting VIP. What really mattered to him was the way in which a man did his particular job. His language in men's company was sometimes colourful, but he never swore if a lady was present.

One day he was chairing a meeting which included high-ranking officials from the Air Ministry, and Miss Cross was sitting beside him taking notes. The discussion became rather heated and at one point the argument was backed up by some forceful language. Mitchell immediately sprang to his feet in protest and, glaring at the offender, he said: 'I will not allow such language to be used in the presence of my secretary!'

Away from work, Mitchell had a lively sense of fun, and even after he became a director at Supermarine he often indulged in boyish pranks. His son remembers being taken by his father to the RAF pageant at Hendon when he was about nine. As they approached the entrance gate, Mitchell suddenly remembered that he had no tickets for his son.

'Lie down on the floor in the back, Gordon,' he said. 'I'll cover you up with the rug until we get through the gate and hopefully they'll never know you are there!' It worked and Gordon was in, but it could have been a little embarrassing for Mitchell, having to explain who he was, if the chap on the gate had peered under the rug.

Another example was when he played a trick on one of his neighbours, Mr Mackie, who lived close by in Russell Place. Although Mitchell was very fond of his garden, he had no expert knowledge or practical experience of growing flowers or vegetables. But Mr Mackie justifiably fancied himself as a gardener and he often exhibited his produce and prize blooms at local flower shows. One day Mr Mackie called at 'Hazeldene' and began boasting about his fine tomatoes.

Mitchell said: 'I'd like to see your tomatoes. Why don't you bring some round just to see if they are as good as mine?' The following morning, after breakfast, Mr Mackie arrived with a bowl full of very fine tomatoes. After examining them critically, Mitchell said: 'Yes, they are quite good, but I'm sure mine are better. I tell you what, we'll both enter our tomatoes in the show and see who wins the best prize.'

Mr Mackie agreed. Before Mackie left, Mitchell added: 'You had better leave those tomatoes here. We shall enjoy eating them.' When the visitor had gone, Gordon looked up enquiringly: 'What were you talking about, Dad? You know we haven't even grown any tomatoes.'

Mitchell grinned. 'Get me a cloth, and we'll soon have these polished up and looking really first class.' The shining tomatoes were duly entered in the show, and, yes, Mitchell was awarded first prize! But it was all in fun, and he quickly confessed and Mr Mackie got the prize he had really earned.

Mitchell might have played such pranks in his spare time, but at Supermarine he was completely dedicated to work. J.R. Rice, who joined the firm as an apprentice in 1922 and later became head of electrical design, spoke of him as: 'A good leader with the ability to get the best out of his men. They respected him and would not have a word said against him, but they also knew he was a strict taskmaster who would not allow any timewasting.'

At one time, Mr Kimber, son of the one-time mayor of the city of Southampton, worked at Supermarine. He was an extrovert character, and one day he decided to liven up the office with a demonstration of centrifugal force. Picking up a fire bucket full of water, he began to whirl it round, raising it higher with each revolution until it reached shoulder height without spilling the contents. Delighted with his success, Kimber gave an exultant yell, but just at that moment the door opened and there stood Mitchell, his scowling face a picture of outraged fury. 'What the bloody hell do you think you are doing in the firm's time?' he demanded.

Unfortunately, Kimber could not let the bucket drop. He had to swing it slowly down to the ground and silently endure the indignity of Mitchell's scowling face.

The year 1928 saw another new Mitchell design which had nothing to do with racing. This was a flying boat developed from the Southampton and powered by three Armstrong Siddeley Jaguar engines. Named the Nanook, it was ordered by the Danish Navy for use as a torpedo carrier. When it proved unsuccessful in trials, it was converted and renamed the Solent and sold to the Hon. A.E. Guinness, a member of the wealthy Guinness family, who used it for many years as a luxury flying yacht.

It is of historical interest that the Nanook was one of only two aircraft produced at Supermarine in Mitchell's career which did not follow the famous 'Supermarine alliteration' by beginning with 'S'. The other was the little Walrus amphibian which in fact started life as the Seagull V and then commonly became affectionately known in service as the Shagbat. As seen, even the Nanook was later renamed the Solent. So the letter 'S' was to prove of special significance in Mitchell's career and, who knows, if his son had been born a little later, Mitchell and his wife might even have chosen a name such as Stephen or Stuart for him, instead of Gordon!

Also in 1928, a Mk III Southampton was designed and built essentially as a refined version of the Mk II but with metal wings.

Shortly after moving into Russell Place, Mitchell met Alec Bennett, who lived close by. Bennett was a one-time Canadian pilot who had come over to England to join the RFC in the First World War and later became world-famous in motorbike racing. Mitchell and Bennett became great friends and remained so until Mitchell's death in 1937. Outside his work, Mitchell did not have many really close friends but Alec Bennett figured prominently amongst these. It was an interesting and, to Mitchell, an important friendship and it is related in greater detail in Chapter 18.

In early 1928, the Schneider Contest rules were changed. It was agreed that it should be held every two years instead of annually, to give competing nations more time to build and test their new machines. This was a great help to Mitchell, since it gave him more time to produce a new design ready for the 1929 Schneider Contest, which was to be held in England. An early decision was taken that government backing would be available for the next contest and Supermarine and Gloster were approached to develop new aircraft.

When starting work on the S.6, the successor to the S.5, Mitchell made one very important decision which was to affect all his future designs. As we have seen, up to this time all of his Schneider aircraft had been fitted with Napier Lion engines, which had always proved very reliable over the years. After 1927, there was a belief that the Napier engine had been developed to its limit, but Mitchell found it very hard to change to another engine. Unable to make up his mind, he sought the advice of Maj. G.P. Bulman, an Air Ministry official responsible for the development of aero-engines. The only possible alternative to a Napier was an engine from Rolls-Royce, and Mitchell knew very little about the firm then. 'What do you think of these chaps at Derby?' he asked Bulman.

Bulman, who knew Rolls-Royce well, said he had a hunch they could do it if given a chance. 'Right,' replied Mitchell eventually after much thought, 'That's settled it!'

To make quite certain that he was doing the right thing, Mitchell discussed the question of an aero-engine with Sir Henry Royce, and so began a partnership between Supermarine and Rolls-Royce that was later to prove so invaluable with the Spitfire, in particular its wartime development, when the ability of Rolls-Royce to continuously increase the power of their Merlin engine ensured that the Spitfire continued as the RAF's primary fighter weapon throughout the 1939–45 war. Sir Henry Royce, who was very impressed by Mitchell's ability, once said of him: 'He is slow to decide but quick to act.'

At that time Sir Henry Royce was a semi-invalid, as described in Chapter 18, living in retirement at West Wittering. A.J. Rowledge, the firm's chief designer, together with two engineers, A.C. Lovesey and E.W. Hives, visited West Wittering to discuss the new engine for Supermarine. It was finally decided that they could develop the 925 hp Buzzard engine, the most important feature being the incorporation of a larger centrifugal supercharger supplied with ram air from a special forward-facing air intake. With this and other changes, Rolls-Royce gave Supermarine an assurance that they would supply an engine of at least 1,500 hp initially, with development to upwards of 1,900 hp, and, most importantly, with little or no increase in frontal area. On Rowledge's recommendation, the firm employed a new engineer who was an expert on supercharging, Jimmy Ellor from the Royal Aircraft Establishment.

All Rolls-Royce engines had to undergo stringent tests, which lasted anything up to one hundred hours. The engines were usually started up in the early hours of the morning, and since the loud roaring could be heard over a radius of five miles, it was hardly surprising that the people of Derby began to complain. But because Supermarine had given Rolls-Royce only six months to produce the engine, the roaring had to go on until the tests proved satisfactory. The engine finally produced was called the 'R' engine, which was destined to achieve great fame in the years to come.

Mitchell designed the S.6 round the slim-line 'R' engine. Its basic lines were very similar to those of the S.5, but it was larger to accommodate the new engine. Because of increased fuel consumption both floats were designed to serve as fuel tanks, with interior baffles to prevent sloshing.

Apart from the new engine, Mitchell made other innovations in the new machine. He moved the forward float struts' position in order to provide extra support for the heavier engine. Unlike the S.5, the wings and fuselage were both made of duralumin, and the double skin radiators were made of light alloy instead of copper, and were applied to the top of the floats as well as to the wings. The fin was used as an oil tank and its surfaces for oil cooling; additional oil cooling was provided by double skin internally baffled radiators attached to the fuselage sides. These were a very prominent externally visible feature.

Early in January 1929, Mitchell was made a fellow of the Royal Aeronautical Society (FRAeS), a great honour which he was naturally delighted to receive.

In February 1929, a new RAF High Speed Flight was formed, led by Sqn Ldr A.H. Orlebar. In the team were: Flg Off. H.R.D. 'Dick' Waghorn; Flg Off. R.L.R. 'Batchy' Atcherley; Flt Lt G.H. Stainforth; Flt Lt D'Arcy Greig; and Flg Off. T.H. Moon, the engineer officer. In April the team moved to Calshot, where they had practice flights on the old S.5s, since Supermarine was still awaiting delivery of the 'R' engine. As in 1927, Mitchell quickly established friendly relations with the RAF pilots. He confided in Orlebar, or 'Orlie' as he not surprisingly became known, that he expected the S.6 to reach at least 340 mph.

During the weeks preceding the 1929 Schneider Contest, the RAF pilots often gathered at 'Hazeldene' where Mrs Mitchell enjoyed entertaining them. She was essentially a home lover, and liked nothing better than looking after her home and family. She did not care for parties or social occasions, and much preferred receiving people in her own home. She usually left her husband's guests to talk amongst themselves, and the pilots often sat up into the early hours of the morning, lost to time in their lively discussions. Mitchell had the highest regard for Sqn Ldr Orlebar, and the two men became great friends and developed an excellent understanding which was to continue right through the 1931 contest. Orlebar, then aged thirty-three, was not the usual light-hearted RAF officer. He was the son of a vicar, and had joined the RFC in 1916. After the First World War, he became a test pilot at Martlesham Heath. Like Mitchell, he was self-effacing – one of the reasons why the two men got on so well – and being a good organiser and a superb pilot there could not have been a better man to lead the High Speed Flight team.

The days of test flying the new Schneider aircraft were always difficult times for Mitchell's staff. He became so worked up with anxiety that he tended to be very tense and irritable and very difficult to live with at times. Miss Cross very soon learnt to accept his moodiness; one look at his face and she recognised the danger signals. Mitchell's former secretary, Mr Spencer, also found it a difficult situation, and if the boss treated him badly he blamed himself for making a mistake. 'What is the matter with R.J. this morning?' he once asked Miss Cross. 'I can't do a thing right for him.' 'Don't worry,' she replied. 'It's nothing you have done. You must know he's always like this on flight testing days.'

It wasn't only Supermarine staff who were upset by Mitchell's awkward moods. The night before they were testing a new Schneider aircraft he would go home to 'Hazeldene', but not for an early night. Flo patiently endured her husband's moody silences, and over the years she learnt to come to terms with them. He was, in her view, a genius and therefore she had to accept that he was different from most other men, but she often wished he could take things a little more calmly. She had watched his unhappiness after Kinkead's death, but she knew that he would never change; that he would go on trying to design better and better aircraft whatever the consequences.

As soon as the first 'R' engine was delivered to Southampton, it was fitted into S.6 N247, and Orlebar was quick to notice that the numbers added up to thirteen, but Mitchell shrugged off any suggestion of superstition and merely remarked that the numbering had nothing to do with him. The S.6 was launched at Woolston on 5 August, bank holiday Monday, and towed down to Calshot on the pontoon for the first test flight by Orlebar.

Because of the streamlined design, the cockpit of the S.6 was narrow – about 14 in. across – and Orlebar, who was a fairly large man, had some difficulty in getting in. He only managed it by twisting his hips sideways, and then giving his shoulders a quick wriggle. Once seated he felt remarkably comfortable, and saw that, while only small, the windshield provided a reasonable field of vision.

When Orlebar first started the engine, he enjoyed its full-throated roar, but he was not so pleased when he found that he could not get the S.6 off the water. At each attempt the S.6 swung round violently to port, with the port float digging into the water, due to torque from the engine's propeller. Mitchell, who was watching Orlebar's struggles from a speedboat, was worried, but he thought that this torque effect could be at least reduced by carrying most of the fuel in the starboard float. Eventually this proved to be the answer and Orlebar managed to get the S.6 'on the step' and then into the air. A number of fairly readily overcome minor problems were encountered. One minor fault which occurred in later flights was leaking wing radiators, probably due to wing-flexing in high-speed turns. D'Arcy Greig had experienced the same sort of trouble in the radiator of his Austin 7, and had solved it by sealing the holes by the use of 'Neverleak' bought from a local garage. Mitchell, always ready to try anything if it seemed sensible and par-ticularly if it was simple, decided to try this remedy in the S.6 cooling water. It did the trick!

As maximum speed was gradually approached as the trials progressed, engine cooling began to be a problem. Mitchell had, therefore, to incor-porate more surface cooling and even designed a way of allowing some flow of air through the wing itself.

By this time, there was less than a month to go before the race, and the RAF pilots needed all the practice they could get on the two S.6s, N247 and N248. Their flying was limited by weather conditions. A wind of more than 15 mph produced an unacceptable sea-state, and great care had to be taken to avoid all debris floating on the water which might damage the floats and sink the machine. The S.6 was not an easy aircraft to fly. It needed quite a lot of force to move the ailerons, while the eleva-tor control required a very light touch. Good cornering was essential for the Schneider circuits, and as has previously been mentioned, this demanded special skills for, owing to the pull of centrifugal force, pilots temporarily 'blacked-out' on every sharp turn.

The 'R' engines installed in the S.6s had only a limited life, and flying time had to be carefully recorded. Engines had to be dismantled at frequent intervals and taken back to Derby for overhaul. So it was impor-tant to have a rapid transport system between Calshot Flying Station and Rolls-Royce in Derby.

For this purpose, the experimental department at Derby built a spe-cially designed 'lorry' fitted with a cradle to carry the engine. Because the lorry usually travelled at night, it earned the nickname of 'The Night Phantom'. When news leaked out about its performance, it was rumoured that police were stationed along the route to check the speed of this strange vehicle.

Britain was not the only country with problems. Following the death of their best pilot, the French withdrew, and the single American entry failed to turn up. But the Italians had entered two of their new Macchi

M.67s and one older Macchi M.52R, and they were determined to take part in the contest even though they had also lost one of their best pilots. Interestingly, the horsepower of the engine in the M.67 was only 1,400, compared with the 1,900 hp 'R' engine in the S.6s.

The Italian team, now the only threat to the British entry, arrived at Cowes at the end of August. During their first trial flights they found the crowded waters of the Solent a strange contrast to the peace and quiet of Lake Garda where they had done their early training.

Wg Cdr Smith was in overall charge of the contest scheduled to take place on 7 September, and acting as his secretary was aircraftman T.E. Shaw, better known to the world as Lawrence of Arabia. Orlebar's choice of pilots for the race was: Flg Off. 'Dick' Waghorn in the S.6 N247; Flg Off. 'Batchy' Atcherley in the S.6 N248; and Flt Lt D'Arcy Greig in the S.5 N219.

The inclusion of the S.5 became necessary when the Gloster VI aircraft had to be withdrawn due to persistent engine problems.

The four-sided 50-km course, which had to be lapped seven times, and which differed considerably from that used in 1923, was plotted over Spithead, with the start and finish off Ryde pier. The turning points, off Seaview, Hayling Island and Cowes, were marked by pylons, painted in yellow and black and mounted on destroyers. A simple lap recorder similar to those successfully used in the 1927 race was provided for each pilot – a piece of board having eight holes covered with thin paper. Each time the pilot passed Ryde Pier he jabbed a hole in the paper to mark a lap completed.

The navigability tests were carried out on the day before the race and when they were over, each aircraft was towed back to Calshot for the watertightness tests. As they rested on the water, tied to a buoy, Atcherley's aeroplane – the S.6 N248 – began to list. The mechanic who rowed out in a dinghy located a puncture in one of the floats, but he dared not mend it because this would mean disqualification. Unfortunately, three hours of the mooring period still remained, and from the way things were going it looked as though the aircraft would sink.

Poor Orlebar! He could not just stand by and watch it happen. Mitchell, who had been at work all through the previous night, was now asleep in the officers' mess, but as the water slowly crept up the float, Orlebar decided to wake him. Mitchell saw what was happening, and after watching for a time he said he thought the plane would just about last out the test. He was proved right. At the end of six hours, though listing badly, the S.6 was still afloat and had passed the test. It was hauled out of the water and the leak was sealed.

At 8 p.m. that night, Mitchell returned to the officers' mess, needing a good night's rest before facing the anxieties of race day. An armed guard kept watch over the aircraft, and he felt confident that everything was

in order. A mechanic, who was fitting new spark plugs to the engine of
N247, noticed a piece of white metal on the electrode of one of the plugs
he had removed. He showed it to Flg Off. Moon who knew at once it
spelt trouble. Lovesey, the Rolls-Royce engineer, was called. He decided
that a piston must have scored one of the cylinders. It was a major disaster
calling for either an engine change or a block change. The former was
not allowed under the rules so it had to be the latter. The cylinders were
arranged in two blocks of six and the damage meant that an entire block
would have to be changed. What made the task almost impossible was
the fact that the repair would have to be done without removing the
engine from the aircraft, since the rules forbade it once the preliminary
tests had been completed. Lovesey was in a fix. He roused Mitchell, and
together they tried to think of a way to solve the problem. None of the
mechanics at Calshot could change a cylinder block, but the engine was
useless as it was. While they tried to decide what to do, someone said
that a party of fitters had come down from Derby to Southampton to
watch the contest. If only they could be found, they would be capable
of changing the cylinder block in situ. But by now it was past midnight,
and the chances were that they would all be in bed.

In a great hurry, Lovesey drove to the Crown Hotel in Southampton,
where he found some of the Derby men and got them out of bed. They
had spent a merry evening and were hardly in a fit state to find their
shoes, let alone repair an engine! With the help of the police, he rounded
up the rest of the party and drove them to Calshot.

By a great stroke of luck one of the fitters was left-handed, and he
could knock out a gudgeon pin which was beyond the reach of a right-
handed man. The Rolls-Royce fitters worked through the night, and
early next morning N247 was moved out on to the slipway. Lovesey
climbed inside, started the engine and listened. The familiar roar told him
that all was well. He clambered out, and when Waghorn later strapped
himself into the cockpit, ready for the race to begin at 2.30 p.m., he was
quite unaware of the previous night's panic. Lovesey and his colleagues
decided that it was a prolonged period of slow running of the engine
that had been the primary cause of the damage which, if correct, demonstrated the enormous care that had to be given to these 'R' engines.
Hardly ready yet to install in a Spitfire!

The 1929 Schneider Contest aroused tremendous interest throughout
the country, and hopes were high that Britain would beat Italy for the
second time in succession. The Prince of Wales, always interested in aviation, flew from Broadlands to the Isle of Wight to stay with his friend,
Sir Philip Sassoon. On the Tuesday before the race, the prince went
to Calshot to see the British and Italian aircraft and talk to the pilots.
Afterwards he donned a flying suit and was flown round the course in a
Southampton flying boat. On his return he watched an S.6 being taken

down the slipway for launching. He was amazed to see the mechanics throw themselves across the floats to hold the machine down, and was forced to retreat a few steps as the tremendous slip-stream from the propeller tossed their caps into the air.

The weather played a vital part in every Schneider Contest, as poor visibility, a rough sea or a high wind made it impossible for the seaplanes to fly. In 1929, Calshot set up its own meteorological office to collect information from weather stations at Portland, St Catherine's Point and Southsea. There was also one at Plymouth which would give advance warning of any sudden change in weather conditions.

As the day of the race approached, thousands of visitors flocked to Southampton and the surrounding area, and all hotels and boarding houses were quickly filled to capacity and many had to camp out. Everybody wanted to watch the epic duel for supremacy in the air, to be fought between Britain and Italy across the Solent sky. Supermarine arranged for one of the Floating Bridges, that operated by their Woolston works, to be re-floated after it had sunk, its superstructure removed and then towed to Calshot and used as an ideal viewing platform of the race for their workers.

Race day, 7 September, turned out to be a perfect day, and by first light the roads leading to the best vantage points on the coast were blocked with cars. The Solent resembled one vast floating arena, alive with craft of every shape and size. The aircraft carrier HMS *Argus* was there with the Prince of Wales and the Prime Minister, Ramsay Macdonald, on board. There were two liners, the *Orford* and the *Orontes*, on one of which were the wives of the pilots, no doubt their excitement being mixed with a natural anxiety. As well as ensuring that his wife and son had good viewing positions on one of the ships, Mitchell made arrangements for his mother and father and his brothers and sisters to have VIP treatment and a first-class view of the race. A proud day for them on which they saw at first hand how far their son/brother had by now advanced up the ladder of success in his chosen career. Gen. Balbo, the Italian under secretary for air, was on board an Italian battleship. Even though there was no French entry, excursion trains brought people from Paris to Dieppe, where they embarked on a ship bound for the Solent. Besides the big ships, there were hundreds of yachts and motor boats, the latter doing a roaring trade as they took people out to see the sights. It was estimated that 1.5 million people came to see 'The World's Greatest Aerial Spectacle' in which six courageous pilots were prepared to risk their lives flying at speeds never before achieved by man.

In the starting order for the race, Britain had drawn first, third and fifth positions, with the Italians alternating at second, fourth and sixth. Waghorn was to go first, followed by D'Arcy Greig and finally Atcherley.

The seaplanes took off at fifteen-minute intervals, and the RAF pilots knew that they would have to fight hard to beat the Italians.

Mitchell, in his usual state of nervous anxiety, watched the race from a launch. As Waghorn roared across the starting line in a fountain of spray, a few moments elapsed before he realised that the S.6 had made a perfect take off. The collection of ships of all shapes and sizes made the sighting of the Seaview and Hayling Island pylons difficult for the pilots, and on his first circuit Waghorn lost valuable time making wide turns to be sure of not missing them. After he had completed the first lap and notched up one hole in his counter, the location of the pylons became easier with experience.

Down below, lap speeds were recorded and loudspeakers announced the figures to the excited spectators thronging the shores on both sides of the Solent. A feeling of optimism surged through the crowds as Waghorn's first lap speed of 324 mph was given out, but the greatest thrill came when Waghorn overtook Dal Molin, in his older Macchi M.52R. He chased the Italian hard down the straight stretch beyond Southsea pier, and as Molin cornered at the Cowes turn, Waghorn climbed up and then dived down past him on his way to the Ryde pier. Both Macchi M.67s had to retire on their second laps, due to engine problems, leaving only Dal Molin in his scarlet M.52R to fight it out with the two silver-blue S.6s and the S.5. One of the former was, however, quickly disqualified; Atcherley in N248 was judged to have cut inside one of the pylons on his first lap. This was most unfortunate, because not knowing that he had been disqualified, he flew his full seven laps and in doing so set the best lap time of the whole race at 332 mph.

Six times Waghorn had holed his lap counter. The S.6 had flown so well that he felt certain of victory. Then, as he began the last lap, the engine suddenly cut out. It picked up again slightly, but Waghorn knew that something had gone wrong. He climbed up to 800 ft, hoping that if the engine packed up altogether he might be able to glide over the finishing line. As he rounded the Cowes pylon the engine began spluttering and then stopped altogether, and he was forced down on to the water. It was a cruel disappointment to lose the race with victory in sight, and he knew that Rolls-Royce would blame him for pushing the engine too hard.

He sat in the cockpit feeling utterly miserable and dejected. When the rescue launch pulled in beside him he could not understand why the men were cheering and waving. Then they told him that he had won. During the excitement of the race, he had miscounted on his lap counter, exactly as Webster had done in 1927, and he had already in fact completed the course when the engine ran out of fuel.

Waghorn's average speed of 328.63 mph made him the winner, with Dal Molin in the older Macchi M.52R coming second at 284.2 mph and

D'Arcy Greig third in the S.5 just behind him with a speed of 282.11 mph. When Waghorn reached Calshot he was given a hero's welcome. Later he was to be awarded the AFC. Lovesey, who was exhausted by the anxiety of the previous night, had to be woken up to hear the result. Once again, Mitchell had produced a winner, but while Waghorn was rightly being feted at the celebration dinner, the designer again remained quietly in the background.

Vickers Supermarine, Rolls-Royce and the fuel and oil companies all used the Schneider victory in extensive advertisements with no mention of the designer's name. Shortly after the race, Orlebar set up a new world absolute speed record of 357.7 mph in S.6 N247.

'Dick' Waghorn's Schneider victory made him a public idol. If there had been television at that time his face would have become well known; many older people still remember his name.

At the Schneider banquet held at the Savoy, the Socialist Prime Minister, Ramsay Macdonald, spoke a few words of praise for the British achievement and warmly congratulated the Italians on their competitive spirit. When asked if his country would compete again, the Italian Minister replied: 'I don't know. The cost of taking part in this race is simply staggering.'

Britain had now scored two consecutive victories and only needed a third to win the trophy outright. In his design of the S.6, Mitchell had completely outclassed Italy, but no one at that time could have foreseen the tremendous influence that the advanced technology embodied in his racing seaplanes would one day have on the future history of Britain.

Apart from the recognition Mitchell got in the aviation world, the winning of the Schneider Trophy brought him other perks. From this time he always drove a Rolls-Royce car provided by the firm in appreciation of his designing skills. The first Rolls-Royce that Mitchell had was in 1928 and was a sombre, black soft-topped limousine nicknamed 'The Hearse'. In 1932 came the easily recognised Rolls with its distinctive yellow colouring to which Jeffrey Quill refers in his book *Spitfire – A Test Pilot's Story* – he relates how he could easily recognise it when he came in to land at Eastleigh after a test flight in the prototype Spitfire, showing him that R.J. was there to greet him!

The last car he had was a magnificent Rolls-Bentley DLA 372. Mitchell enjoyed driving these splendid cars, and he became a familiar figure as he drove from his house in Russell Place to the Supermarine factory (see also Item 19, page 269).

News of his successful Schneider racers created quite a stir abroad. Foreign aircraft manufacturers, impressed by his brilliance, began to offer him work, tempting him with salaries much above those paid him by Supermarine. If he had accepted any of them he could have become a very wealthy man, but even if he had wanted to, which he didn't, he was committed by his agreement of 1924, and that with Vickers in 1928, to remain at Supermarine at least until 1933.

A story is told of Mitchell's reaction when he first heard that Waghorn had won the Schneider Trophy. As he stepped off the launch and walked up the Calshot slipway, a Supermarine man moved forward to shake his hand: 'Congratulations, sir. I am pleased we have won for your sake.' To which Mitchell replied: 'Thank you, but it is not really for my sake, you know, it is for our country's.'

Although 1929 was dominated by the Schneider Trophy Contest, work on Supermarine's bread-and-butter aircraft, flying boats, did not stop. One which Mitchell produced in that year was the amphibian the Sea Mew. It was a three-seat reconnaissance plane fitted with two Armstrong Siddeley Lynx engines with a maximum speed of 100 mph. It had the appearance of a miniature Southampton. The Hon. A.E. Guinness had been very satisfied with his 1928 Solent air yacht, and in 1929 he placed an order for another to his own specification which was designed and built that year. This was an unusual design for Mitchell in that it was a parasol monoplane incorporating sponsons in place of wing-tip floats. It had three Armstrong Siddeley geared Jaguar engines mounted in the wing leading edge. The interior was luxuriously equipped and had sleeping accommodation. It was an interesting 'one-off' design which again demonstrated Mitchell's extraordinary versatility, but it failed to reach its specified performance, as Alan Clifton recounts in Appendix 3.

The following year, Mitchell designed the Southampton Mk X flying boat. In contrast to the original Southampton, it had three engines, Armstrong Siddeley Jaguars, and a sesquiplane superstructure, the two wings being of different section. Another novel feature was that the underwater part of the hull was plated with stainless steel with the obvious aim of preventing sea-water corrosion. The performance of the Southampton Mk X was very disappointing and it certainly cannot be included among Mitchell's successes. Lessons were learnt from it, however, and in particular he decided to return to the well-proved twin-engined concept of the flying boat which later resulted in the more successful Scapa and Stranraer. The Southampton Mk X did not receive any production order.

Finally, in 1930, the government gave Supermarine a contract for a large six-engined flying boat powered by Rolls-Royce 'H' engines and able to take up to forty passengers. The design work on it was well advanced when the government decided they had to cancel the contract as a result of the depressed state of the country's economy. The following year (1931) was to see the scheduled Schneider Trophy Contest very nearly abandoned for the same reason.

11

1931: Britain Wins the Schneider Trophy Outright

The early 1930s were times of worldwide economic depression during which the British people suffered many hardships. Over 2 million were out of work, and the unemployed had to exist as best they could on the 'dole'. Supermarine, like so many other firms, was faced with problems. In order to keep the men in work they had to reduce salaries and wages.

'We were so thankful to have a job, we didn't really mind,' Alan Clifton recalls, and probably everyone felt much the same way. The Vickers board promised that pay would be restored to its former level when conditions improved and, in due course, that promise was kept.

The date of the 1931 Schneider Contest was approaching but it seemed highly unlikely that the government would provide money for any new aircraft. It was very sad, for if Britain could gain a third consecutive victory she would win the trophy outright. Mitchell felt frustrated and disappointed. The S.6 had been an outstanding success and now he was to be robbed of the chance to design an even faster aircraft. He knew that the RAF was ready and eager to form a new High Speed Flight team, but it seemed that it was not going to be possible to squeeze any money out of the treasury in spite of the continuous efforts of many influential people and organisations, including the Royal Aero Club and the Society of British Aircraft Constructors.

The argument over whether there should or should not be a British entry dragged on and on. By the end of 1930, Italy and France had announced their intention of competing, but the outlook for Britain continued to look black. The cost of building two new aircraft was estimated to be a minimum of £100,000; in the depressed economic state of the country it was unrealistic to think of raising such a large sum by public subscription.

In January 1931, the Labour government, under Prime Minister Ramsay Macdonald, announced their final decision which was that in the present financial situation, expenditure of public money to support the contest was not justified.

Their attitude was largely due to the chancellor of the exchequer, Philip Snowdon, a bitter opponent of the Schneider races, who wanted to put an end to what he called 'The pernicious rivalry between nations.'

The government's decision not to back a British Schneider entry was attacked in newspaper articles, in which they were accused of being 'pacifist', 'defeatist' and 'anti-British'. There were many attempts to persuade them to change their minds.

Mitchell, in an interview with a newspaper reporter in January, and quoted by the *Stoke-on-Trent Evening Sentinel* in August 1931, said:

> It takes several years to develop a position in regard to aviation such as Britain holds today.
>
> It means really prolonged effort and concentration over four or five years, but it takes only about two years of relaxed effort to lose that ascendancy.
>
> British aircraft today are unquestionably superior to any other aircraft in the world, but if we drop our research work now and allow things to drift, in a year or two's time we may have lost that position.

Sir Samuel Hoare, in a letter to *The Times*, said:

> Now, when every other industry is passing through a period of unprecedented depression, the export of aircraft, valued in millions, is steadily rising. This is due to the reputation earned in winning the Schneider Trophy.

The Society of British Aircraft Constructors, in a petition to parliament, begged them to reconsider their decision:

> The British victories in the last two Schneider Contests have given the British techniques, both in aircraft and engines, a prestige in the eyes of foreign buyers. A loss of the trophy will mean a loss in export trade.

The government refused to budge, and Mitchell gave up all hope of there being a contest in 1931. Then, quite out of the blue, the situation was saved by Lady Houston, who made an unsolicited gift of £100,000. Lady Lucy Houston, the widow of a millionaire shipowner, was a very determined patriotic and wealthy woman, who spent most of her time living on board her private yacht. She intended to embarrass the Labour government by her offer of money and her message to the Prime Minister ended on a mocking note: 'I know I can confidently rely on the kindly help and co-operation of all who will rejoice if England wins.'

Ramsay Macdonald accepted her offer and informed the Royal Aero Club that the preparation of a British entry could now go ahead. But he had not heard the last from Lady Houston. She had a lot to say in the papers about the spirit of her forefathers, who considered one Englishman equal to three foreigners, and about the attitude of the Labour government who, according to her, were trying to reduce Britain to a third-rate power.

'We are not worms to be trampled under the heel of Socialism, but true Britons,' she declaimed in an outburst of patriotic fervour.

Lady Houston's gift delighted Mitchell. By a stroke of good fortune he was going to get the chance he wanted, namely to improve his S.6 design and thereby, he hoped, win the trophy outright for Britain – an ultimate goal he had long cherished. It has been suggested that without Lady Houston's generous gift which enabled the 1931 race to be held, there might not have been a Spitfire produced in 1936. However, as the S.6B was essentially only a modified version of the S.6, the major part of the vital experience R.J. gained from the Schneider Races, later to be of such value in designing the Spitfire, was in fact obtained in 1927 and 1929 with the S.5 and the S.6.

The 1931 Schneider Contest was now only seven months away, and in that time he could not hope to produce an entirely new S.7. Instead, he decided, rightly in the event, to concentrate on making some changes in the S.6 design, with the primary aim of accommodating the more powerful version of the 'R' engine promised by Rolls-Royce. This, in due course, they miraculously managed to do, raising the power output of the 1,900 hp 1929 'R' engine to about 2,350 hp, primarily by making both the crankshaft and centrifugal blower run faster, and increasing the air intake. Another important innovation was the use of sodium-cooled valves.

The major problem was to allow for the dissipation of the extra heat produced by the more powerful engine; a total of some 40,000 BTUs of heat per minute had to be got rid of. All major changes were directed to this requirement. Thus, the length of the floats was increased, firstly to provide more cooling surfaces and secondly to hold more fuel, while other modifications to the intricate oil-cooling system also had to be made. Even then it was found necessary to fly the S.6Bs according to water temperature rather than simply at full throttle. Mitchell often referred to his S.6B as essentially a flying radiator!

Two new S.6B seaplanes were built and given the military serial numbers S.1595 and S.1596. The two 1929 S.6s, N247 and N248, were modified to take the new S.6B floats and the new engines when they became available. As such, they were designated S.6As and would be available as reserves for the race.

The final responsibility for getting the S.6Bs built in time for the 1931 race fell firmly on to the shoulders of Supermarine's young general manager, Trevor Westbrook. By his immense drive and unceasing energy he succeeded, and his contribution to the successful outcome of the last Schneider race was vital.

While Supermarine raced against time to build the airframes, Rolls-Royce in Derby similarly raced against time to upgrade the 1929 'R' engine, and during the extensive trials of the engine, the people of Derby had to endure once again the ear-shattering roar from the testing sheds. By mid-July the first engines had passed the tests and were on their way to Southampton. The vital part played by Rolls-Royce, led by their experimental manager, Ernest Hives (later Lord Hives), in the successful outcome of the 1931 race cannot be over-emphasised and Mitchell was only too ready to acknowledge their outstanding contribution.

A new RAF High Speed Flight was formed under the command, once again, of Sqn Ldr A.H. Orlebar. The pilots eventually selected for the team were Flt Lt J.N. Boothman, Flt Lt G.H. Stainforth, Flt Lt F.W. Long, Flt Lt E.J.L. Hope and Flg Off. L.S. Snaith, later to be joined by Lt R.L. 'Jerry' Brinton from the Fleet Air Arm. Flt Lt W.F. Dry was appointed engineer officer. They arrived at Calshot in May.

The first aircraft to arrive was one of the modified S.6s (N247), now designated S.6A, and Orlebar took it up for the first time in June. This developed an alarming rudder flutter at speed and everyone, not least Mitchell, breathed a sigh of relief when Orlebar brought it down safely. As a result of this experience, mass balances were fitted both to the rudder, elevator and the ailerons, not only to N247 but also to the second S.6A (N248) and to the two S.6Bs under construction.

Later in June, N248 became available with its uprated engine and Orlebar took it up. After only a short period of time the engine began to splutter and lose power, and he had to come down. Choked fuel filters were the problem. They were cleaned but the trouble soon happened again and it was discovered that it was due to certain components of the new fuel being used taking away the surplus compound which sealed the tanks and the new 'Superflexit' pipes. As Sir John Boothman recalled later on the occasion of the 1st Mitchell Memorial Lecture, Mitchell's answer was short and to the point: 'You will just bloody well have to fly them until all that stuff comes off!' And, in the end, just this was done and it worked. Yet another example of Mitchell's urge to try the simple answer to a problem first.

All members of the team were able to have flights in the two S.6As while awaiting the arrival of the first S.6B. Flt Lt Hope in N248 had unfortunately to make a forced landing in a swell from a liner and the plane turned over and later sank. Hope damaged an ear-drum in the landing and he was grounded and replaced by Lt 'Jerry' Brinton of the Fleet Air Arm, a change which was later to result in much distress for Mitchell.

At last, on 21 July, the first S.6B (S.1595) arrived at Calshot. Its first flight, piloted by Orlebar, caused some anxious moments for Mitchell since, try as he might, Orlebar could not get the aircraft off the water. It would swing through 120 degrees and Orlebar once found himself heading straight for Calshot 'Fort'. After that nerve-racking experience he abandoned the flight and recorded in his notebook:

'When I first took her out she gave a good imitation of a kitten chasing its tail. I had many attempts to take off, but each time she swung round so violently I had to stop.'

Two days later, in another attempt, Orlebar collided with a barge and the S.6B (S.1595) was towed up to Southampton for repairs. This gave Mitchell a chance to make some alterations.

Mitchell was always at his best when things went wrong. While others fussed and grumbled, he quietly went on with his work, quite certain in his own mind that he could probably sort out the problem. He knew the main cause of the trouble was the extra torque due to the increased power of the engine. He could do nothing about this, but one thing he might possibly do was to modify the propeller. After careful calculations and tests, including fitting the smaller diameter propeller of the S.6B on to N247, when exactly the same problems occurred, he determined that a larger propeller of 9 ft 1½ in. diameter was required. It was the complete solution, and in subsequent test flights both S.6B (S.1595) and then, later in August, S.6B (S.1596) took off without any serious trouble.

Another problem did, however, show up in the S.6Bs, and that was a tendency to instability, particularly in turns. The pilots had complained that the aircraft felt nose-heavy but Mitchell diagnosed that the real cause of the instability problem was due to the centre of gravity being too far aft and caused by the extra oil in the tank near the fin. Accordingly, he reduced the amount of oil held in this tank to just that required to complete the race course and put about 25 lb of lead in the nose of each float. The result was a great improvement in the handling properties of the S.6Bs and is a particularly good illustration of Mitchell's sometimes uncanny ability of getting to the root of a problem even though, as in this case, his cure was the exact opposite of what, on the basis of the pilots' reports, was at first sight going to be needed.

It was also yet another good example of Mitchell's firmly held tenet that you should always first look for a simple solution to a problem before looking for a complicated answer. If a few pounds of lead and emptying a few gallons of oil out of a tank will do the trick, why get involved in making complicated design changes?

Then, just as things seemed to be going smoothly, a disaster occurred which seriously upset Mitchell. Lt 'Jerry' Brinton of the Fleet Air Arm who, as we have seen, had been posted to the team to replace Flt Lt Hope, was delayed in making his first flight in an S.6A owing to bad weather, but conditions at last improved on the afternoon of 16 August. Orlebar decided that the sea was calm enough for Brinton to have his first flight and N247 was towed out on a pontoon. Orlebar, with so much experience of these far from easy-to-fly aircraft, knew that the greatest danger was at the moment of take-off. He gave Brinton strict instructions about not pushing the stick forward when the nose went up, and as Brinton strapped himself into the cockpit he repeated the warning: 'You must hold the aircraft in a near-stalled condition immediately after you leave the water. If you get into trouble, close the throttle and keep the stick back.'

Brinton did one perfect practice run, then went away for take-off. Things went wrong the moment he left the water. He had reached a height of only 10 ft when the tail went up and the aircraft fell back on to the water. Then it jumped off at a steep angle and fell again, this time hitting the water with such force that it bounced 30 ft into the air. Finally, it nose-dived into the water and the floats were ripped off. It was an extreme case of a phenomenon known as 'porpoising'.

It was all over in a few seconds. A speedboat raced to the spot where the tail was still visible above the water, and men jumped into the water and struggled to reach the cockpit to rescue Brinton. But the tide was running so fast that they were swept away, and in the end they were forced to give up. The only thing they could do was to tow N247 back to Calshot. When a crane lifted it out of the water, Brinton was found dead in the cockpit with his neck broken. He had been killed instantly by the terrific rush of water.

It was a terrible blow for Mitchell. Once again he had to face the vexed question of whether it was right for men to risk their lives in this way in high-speed flying. But again, as with Kinkead's death a few years before, there was no reason to believe that Brinton's crash was in any way the result of a failure in the aircraft and Mitchell knew he had to put this latest tragedy behind him and carry on.

The 1931 Schneider Contest had been planned to take place on 12 September. All hopes of it being an exciting race began to fade when France withdrew her entry. Then in August, Monti, one of the top Italian pilots, was killed in a crash over Lake Garda testing the new and revolutionary MC.72, which was later, in 1934, to set up a new world speed record of 440.7 mph.

On 3 September, both France and Italy requested a postponement of the race, but the British Royal Aero Club refused to even consider it – in marked contrast to the Americans' agreement for a postponement in 1924. Thus, Britain was left as the only competitor, and it was feared that there would be little interest in the race without any foreign challengers. However, plans went ahead, and it was announced that Boothman in the S.6B (S.1595) would try to win the trophy with, if unsuccessful, Snaith and Long as first and second reserves, in S.6A (N248) and S.6B (S.1596), respectively. Later, Stainforth would attempt to establish a new world air speed record. Leonard Snaith comments further on the strategies for the race in Appendix 8.

In spite of the depressed state of the country and the very unfortunate absence of the new MC.72s, which could have provided stiff opposition to Mitchell's S.6B, the race aroused tremendous interest. People who were sick and tired of the hopeless struggle to find work and of the humiliation of the 'dole' queues longed for some excitement to relieve the monotony of everyday life. The sight of Mitchell's seaplanes thundering across the sky at breathtaking speeds raised a cheer from lips which had forgotten how to smile. England might be in a depression, but in the world of aviation she still had something of which to be proud.

With the approach of the 1931 Schneider Contest, Mitchell's family in Stoke-on-Trent eagerly discussed the possibility that Britain might win the trophy outright. Again, as in 1929, his father and his brothers were keen to see the new S.6Bs in action, but they could not all leave the Wood, Mitchell & Co. printing works. It was finally settled that Mr Mitchell senior should travel down to Southampton, leaving Eric in charge of the works. One can well imagine the joy in Herbert Mitchell's heart as he craned his neck to watch the seaplanes designed by his eldest son roaring across the sky. Sadly, he died in 1933 at the age of sixty-eight, without knowing of the greater triumph of what was to be Mitchell's masterpiece, the Spitfire, which was destined to take the air only three years later.

The day before the race, Miss Cross was anxious to see the S.6Bs in action, so she rang up Mitchell, who was down at Calshot, and said: 'If I bring the letters down to you by the afternoon launch, will it be all right for me to stay and watch the planes fly?'

'Yes,' he told her. 'You come down.'

With all his correspondence ready for signing, she was just stepping on to the launch when she was suddenly confronted by Sir Robert McLean.

'Where are you going, Miss Cross?' he demanded.

'I am taking the letters to Mr Mitchell at Calshot.'

'You can forget about that,' he said tersely. 'I want you with me on the SS *Homeric*.'

So Miss Cross was given a cabin on the promenade deck of the White Star liner, and in between taking dictation from McLean she was able to watch the flying in comfort and to enjoy to the full the weekend cruise.

Saturday 12 September began fine, and by early morning the Solent coasts were crowded with spectators, all jostling for good positions as they waited for the flying to begin. Suddenly it started to rain, and with strong winds whipping up the sea, the race had to be postponed. However, thankfully next day the wind dropped and once again the crowds gathered, Southsea being one of the most popular vantage points.

For the 1931 contest, the Royal Aero Club had earlier proposed some changes in the rules. The most important of these, all of which were subsequently agreed, was that the navigability and watertightness tests be dropped and be replaced by a single take off and landing immediately prior to the take-off for the start of the race proper. The idea behind this proposal was to enable the whole contest to be completed on a single day which had been impossible under the old rules. That was an undoubted improvement but the new rules introduced a new factor for Mitchell and that was that the floats now had to be strong enough to stand up to a landing at maximum take-off weight.

The 50-km course followed much the same plan as in 1929, but was triangular instead of four-sided, with sharp turning points off Cowes and West Wittering. Mitchell, feeling, as always on race day, extremely nervous and anxious, and no doubt also this time remembering Brinton's recent tragic death, went out in a speedboat with Lovesey of Rolls-Royce. As the starting gun went off, Boothman in S.1595 carried out his preliminary take-off and landing and then roared into the air towards Seaview, before heading for the West Wittering land pylon. After banking round the sharp turn, he flattened out and raced along the straight course over the Hampshire coastline. Southsea beach was packed with spectators, who craned their necks to cheer and wave as his seaplane thundered past over their heads. Seven times Boothman flashed past in an ear-splitting roar as he headed for the Cowes turn. When he alighted at the end of the final lap, the howling of the ships' sirens greeted his tremendous performance. He had flown at an average speed of 340.08 mph, nearly six miles a minute, and this with the throttle not fully open to avoid over-heating, and had won the Schneider Trophy outright. The last contest was over and the trophy would remain in Britain for all time, much to the great joy and relief of everyone at Supermarine and Rolls-Royce, and, of course, of Lady Houston.

At 4 p.m. on that same afternoon, Stainforth went up in S.6B (S.1596) in an attempt to set up a new world air speed record. He flew four times along the straight 3-km course off Lee-on-Solent, twice with the wind and twice against it. He achieved an average speed of 379.05 mph, a new record which delighted the cheering crowds.

Lady Houston came over from Jersey on her steam yacht, *Liberty*, to watch the flying, and two days later she gave a celebration lunch on board which was attended by Mitchell and the RAF High Speed Flight (see illustration 34, page 180).

Following the fine performance of the two S.6Bs, the city of Southampton local paper, *The Echo*, published an interview with Mitchell. The introductory paragraph stated that:

> Supermarine has been prominent in every Schneider Contest, and Mr Mitchell is the man whose genius has created all these remarkable aircraft. Conceived in his remarkable brain, they placed this country in the forefront of aircraft design, and established the supremacy of their creator in aeronautical technique.

Mitchell was not fond of making public speeches or giving interviews, but, as has already been emphasised, on the rare occasions that he did, he never failed to give full praise to his design team and the Supermarine workers. In his interview with the *Southern Daily Echo* reporter, he began by saying that hundreds of skilled workmen shared in the credit for the great performance of the S.6B, together with his draughtsmen and technical design staff. Supermarine had not been able to start work on the new S.6Bs until February, yet five months later the first one was delivered to Calshot, followed very closely by the second. He went on:

> I am by no means disappointed over the results produced yesterday. So far as the attempt on the world speed record was concerned, it was only an initial effort and we may yet achieve a greater speed. With a specially tuned up engine, I am very hopeful we may get very near to an average speed of 400 mph, which is our ambition. Flt Lt Stainforth has been trying out different methods of flying the course and varying the steepness of the dive before entering the straight. The conditions were fairly good but not ideal. It would be presumptuous of me to assume that speed has reached its finality; continuous development will lead to further progress. Speeds which amaze us today will be the commonplace of tomorrow.

> I have the greatest admiration for the city of Southampton as one of the
> most progressive seaports of the world. It has always shown an interest in
> aviation, and one day it could have one of the finest airports in the world.
> The Schneider Trophy Contests have established British supremacy in the
> air, and any work I have done was as a member of a big team.

At this point he referred to and praised all those who had been responsible
for the production of the Rolls-Royce engine, the finest in the world,
and without which little, if anything, could have been achieved. He
praised the work of the Air Ministry, and paid tribute to the RAF pilots
of the High Speed Flight, with special reference to Sqn Ldr Orlebar, who
had carried out the first flights of all new machines. 'His experience and
expert advice have been invaluable in bringing the machines to their
ultimate efficiency.' He ended his interview by saying: 'I feel that the one
predominating feature in our success has been the close co-operation of
all concerned. Without this co-operation we would all have failed.'

As Mitchell had said in his interview, Flt Lt Stainforth's attempt for
a new speed record had only been the first, and certainly Rolls-Royce
were not satisfied with the result. They had spent a lot of time and money
producing the 'R' engine, and they wanted it to be the first to establish a
speed of over 400 mph. In spite of the fact that the Air Ministry wanted
Calshot prepared for the return of the flying boat squadrons, Rolls-
Royce insisted that there must be a second record-breaking attempt.
After a special request from Sir Henry Royce, the Air Ministry relented
and rather grudgingly allowed the High Speed Flight team to remain
at Calshot to give Stainforth a second chance.

On 29 September 1931, with a tuned-up sprint 'R' engine, producing
2,530 hp, in S.1595, and using a special fuel 'cocktail', George Stainforth
achieved an average speed of 407.5 mph. This broke the previous world
speed record by over 20 mph and satisfied Rolls-Royce. It was a truly
remarkable performance, and it made Mitchell's seaplane the fastest aircraft in the world. Flt Lt Stainforth later was promoted to wing
commander but was killed in action in 1942, piloting a Beaufighter in
the Middle East.

The man responsible for mixing the fuel 'cocktail' – 30% benzole, 60%
methanol and 10% acetone, and including one part per 1,000 of tetra-
ethyl lead – was F. Rodwell Banks (later air commodore) of the Ethyl
Export Corporation. Great credit is due to Rod Banks for devising these
special fuel mixtures without which such tremendous power outputs of
the 'R' and special sprint engines developed by Rolls-Royce, and of the
Napier Lion in 1927, could not have been achieved.

Following the 1931 contest, Rod helped the Italians with their
potentially excellent Macchi–Castoldi MC.72, which had two engines
in tandem, and with which they had encountered serious fuel problems.

He duly solved them and the 'engine' achieved a power output of 3,100 hp. In April 1933, in a MC.72, Agello set up a new world speed record of 423.8 mph, increasing it to 440.7 mph in 1934. F. Rod Banks, CB, OBE, CEng, sadly died in June 1985 – he made unquestionably an outstanding contribution to the world of aviation.

The attainment of the record speed of over 400 mph by Stainforth did not pass unnoticed, and for the next few months Mitchell was kept busy going to meetings and attending dinners given in his honour. As a modest man he did not really enjoy being feted and he always hated making speeches. Nevertheless, it at least gave him further opportunity to stress that he had only been one of a team.

Early in October, the mayor of the city of Southampton, Councillor E.W. Cross, gave a dinner at the South Western Hotel in Mitchell's honour. It was attended by a large gathering which included: Sir Robert McLean; Hubert Scott-Paine; Sqn Ldr A.H. Orlebar, the captain of the RAF High Speed Flight; Grp Capt. H.M. Cave-Browne-Cave, leader of the famous Far East Flight of four Southampton flying boats in 1927–28; and Mrs Mitchell (see illustration 35, page 180).

In toasting the guest of honour, the mayor said that Mr Mitchell, at the age of thirty-six, was one of the most brilliant aircraft designers in the world. He named the list of Schneider Contest successes which had ended with the outright winning of the trophy, and said that he believed Mr Mitchell was now working on a six-engined flying boat, Britain's answer to the German Dornier. As Mitchell rose to reply he was given a tremendous ovation, lasting several minutes.

'I feel I shall never be able to thank you sufficiently for this great honour and this wonderful reception. I shall always look back on this evening as one of the greatest events in my life.' After paying tribute as usual to the Supermarine workforce, he went on to speak of the pilots.

> These men are the real heroes of this high-speed flying. The work they have done will help in the design of normal machines and will continue to do so. I believe, however, that we have now reached the stage when we can safely leave further development in high-speed flying for some considerable time, in order that we may digest and utilise the mass of knowledge and experience that we have now gained.
>
> Two questions most often asked about high-speed flying are:
>
> 'What is the use of it? Where is it leading?'
>
> I think that the answer is quite simple. In the first place, it was always important to strive after knowledge. Secondly, in a time of economic depression, an increased benefit to British aviation trade which could be directly attributed to the winning of the Schneider Trophy, could be of enormous value to Britain.

Afterwards, Sqn Ldr Orlebar made a brief speech in which he described the flight of the S.6B as 'an imitation of lightning'. He continued:

> I would like to thank the mayor of the city of Southampton for this dinner, especially as it is in honour of 'Mitch'. It is good to know that people realise what he has done. He is the brain behind it all. It was his brain that produced the S.6B which won the race and set up a new world air speed record.

In a letter dated 15 July 1978, Mrs V. Orlebar recalled the days when her husband captained the RAF High Speed Flight in 1929 and 1931:

> I remember 'Mitch' so well, working with my husband and the Schneider Trophy Teams, such a brilliant and very unassuming man, full of enthusiasm that his design of the S.6 should be made to work superlatively. How very easy my husband and the other members of the team found him to work with, and all knew that he would overcome difficulties and technical problems which were bound to occur during the testing of that wonderful machine – the forerunner of the Spitfire. My husband's account of the testing of the S.6s contains many examples of Mitchell's brilliance, as shown in the following quotations:
>
> 'It was extraordinary how very accurate Mitch's forecast of the machine's behaviour had been. He had foreseen exactly how the machine would behave in the air.'
>
> On another occasion, when there was some difficulty with the balance of the S.6, my husband wrote:
>
> 'The main point is, however, that Mitch produced a very effective cure.'
>
> I know my husband felt that the team's successes in winning the Schneider Trophy in 1929 and 1931, and then the world air speed record, were largely due to Mitchell's brilliant design concept and unflagging enthusiasm in helping them to make the very best of the machine. My husband always spoke very warmly of the quiet but enthusiastic help 'Mitch' gave to them all, always.

The celebrations to commemorate the Schneider Contest victory went on. The experimental department of Rolls-Royce held a dinner to mark the success of their 'R' engine. It took place at the assembly rooms in the Market Place at Derby, with A.F. Sidgreaves, OBE, in the chair. Speeches were made by the chairman and Sqn Ldr Orlebar, and the toast to the S.6B was proposed by E.W. Hives, MBE, later Lord Hives. Mitchell and A.J. Rowledge responded, and a total of 219 guests spent a very enjoyable evening.

Amidst so much jubilation, Stoke-on-Trent also wished to honour the man who was born in, and had spent his early years in, their city. A lavish banquet was arranged in a North Staffordshire hotel and when all the company, including Mitchell's two brothers, Eric and Billy, were assembled, the guest of honour was missing. After some searching he was eventually tracked down in a remote corner. By way of apology he explained: 'It is harder for me to make a speech than to design an aircraft.'

However, he did agree early in 1932 to make a record, which was broadcast on BBC Radio. After it was broadcast, his brother Eric said: 'He did it so well; in spite of his slight stammer, there was only one very slight pause in the whole of the long recording.'

The full text of this historic recording is as follows:

Mr R.J. Mitchell, CBE, of Southampton, England, will talk to you on the design of the Schneider Trophy Seaplanes:

The Vickers Supermarine Rolls-Royce S.6B was designed and constructed by the Supermarine works of Vickers Aviation Ltd. It is the latest of a long series of high-speed seaplanes, four of which have won Schneider Trophy Contests and three established world speed records.

By winning the third successive victory in 1931, the S.6B won the Schneider Trophy outright for Great Britain. This machine later established the world speed record of over 407 mph. In a very few words I will endeavour to describe one or two of the interesting features of the S.6B and also some of the problems of the designer.

In the design of a seaplane of this type, the one outstanding and all-important requirement is speed. Every feature has to be sacrificed to this demand. The result of this is that every part of the aircraft just and only just fulfils its requirements. A very exact knowledge is, therefore, essential of the functioning of every detail, requiring an enormous amount of research and investigation. It is not good enough to follow conventional methods of design. It is essential to break new ground and to invent and involve new methods and new ideas.

The important aim of the designer is to reduce air resistance. Of the total air resistance of the S.6B, as much as 70% is brought about by the friction between the air and the surface of the aircraft. The shapes of the fuselage and floats are such that their air resistance is very little higher than that of the purest streamline form. The floats are made so small for the load they have to carry that their reserve buoyancy is less than 40%. The usual reserve buoyancy for seaplane floats is about 100%. The problems of float design are further increased by the enormous torque developed by the engine. The effect of this torque is to raise one float and depress the other resulting in the aircraft swinging off its course if the balance is not maintained in some way. This is overcome by carrying a larger load of fuel in one float than in the other, calling for a very sensitive device to ensure that the balance of fuel is maintained during flight.

The underwater lines of the floats are of extreme importance. Before taking the air, the aircraft must accelerate to a speed of over 100 mph – almost equivalent to the world speed record on the water. The floats must run perfectly smoothly. Any instability at high speed would be fatal. The cooling of the engine presents many interesting features. The usual method employed either by aircooling or by means of honeycomb radiators have very high air resistance. On the S.6B the engine is cooled without adding any air resistance. The cooling water is circulated over both surfaces of the wings and most of the surface of the floats, the covering being of a special double skin construction. Similarly, the oil is circulated along the sides of the body and over the surface of the fin. During flight, heat equivalent to 1,000 horse power is being given to the air from these surfaces. The S6.B has been aptly described as a flying radiator.

The air controls and stability in flight must be exactly right. The pilot must be very efficiently protected from the enormous air pressure and from exhaust fumes. He must get a very adequate supply of fresh air and he must have a very good view. I must express the very greatest admiration for the pilots of the High Speed Flight of the RAF who carried out trials and operated these machines. Their job required great courage and great skill and they played a very important part in developing the machines to their final state.

The question is often asked: will higher speeds be obtained in the future? I feel quite sure they will. The problem of still higher speeds are no more intense at this stage than they have been at any period in the past. For the present, however, it is generally considered that high-speed development has served its purpose. It has accumulated an enormous amount of information which is now being used to improve the breed of everyday aircraft and is helping to develop our great airliners and ocean-going flying boats and it is thus bringing closer together the outlying parts of the British Empire. This indeed is an objective worthy of all our greatest efforts.

J.N. Boothman, the winning pilot in the 1931 race, and A.J. Rowledge, chief designer at Rolls-Royce, also made recordings at the same time and the full text of these equally historic recordings follows:

Flt Lt J.N. Boothman, AFC, RAF, the pilot of the Vickers Supermarine Rolls-Royce S.6B will give his impressions of the Schneider Contest of 1931 when winning the trophy outright for Great Britain at a speed of 340.08 mph:

It is rather difficult to record impressions after an event such as the Schneider Trophy Contest because at the time one is concentrating so utterly on the job in hand that the prospect of having to make a record later does not enter one's head.

For the contest last year, the former navigability test had been abolished and replaced by a take off, a climb to fifty metres and an alighting, following which the machine had to taxi for about two minutes before taking off to cross the starting line of the speed test proper.

These new conditions meant take off at full load – always an extreme test of a racing seaplane – followed by an alighting and a take off at practically full load.

On 13 September 1931, the day when the contest was flown, the weather conditions were fairly good, the sea being rather rough but improving rapidly. After a preliminary flight to test the conditions, I took my seat in the Vickers Supermarine Rolls-Royce S.6B and was slipped from the pontoon; the starting gun was fired at two minutes past one. The first take off was effected in forty seconds, the machine making no difficulty about lifting her 6,000 lb weight, despite the enormous loading of nearly 42 lb to the square foot of wing surface. As soon as we were off the water, the engine was throttled down to half speed in order to conserve fuel, and a left-hand circuit made. Over Cowes the throttle was shut and an alighting made close to the take-off position. In spite of the heavy load and the high landing speed of about 110 mph or more, the floats took the roughish water beautifully. After taxiing throttled right down for the specified time, the second take off was started. This one was not so pleasant with the floats running into the wash left from my first effort. The machine was receiving rather a hammering from the rough water. Forty seconds saw us in the air again and after a right-hand turn, the nose was pointing at Ryde Pier – the starting line of the speed course. This course consisted of seven triangular laps of just over thirty-one miles each. With the throttle wide open we passed over the pier towards the destroyer marking the southern turn near Bembridge in the Isle of Wight. Then a gentle left-hand turn round the pylon and across the eight miles of open sea to Wittering.

The sea here was bad; a heavy swell rolling in from the Channel making any hopes of a successful forced alighting rather small. However, the consistent running of the engine and the perfect way the machine was flying banished any unpleasant thoughts of trouble. The eastern turn at Wittering was an enormous tower built on the foreshore and coloured like the other two with rather a violent yellow paint. This turn was a sharp one of about 150 degrees followed by the long straight of over fourteen miles past Hayling Island and Portsmouth and a sharp western turn – a destroyer anchored in the Solent. The next leg was flown at full throttle and the turn was taken rather wide in order that there should be no risk of disqualification. After about 1.5 laps, the water temperature started to rise above the maximum allowed for the race and so the throttle had to be eased back slightly for the remainder of the contest. Weather conditions were good; the visibility was excellent and over the sea the air was smooth, but near Southsea where the course was slightly inland, bumpy air was experienced. Bumps on a high-speed aircraft are rather disconcerting because instead of the aircraft moving gently up or down, one experiences a sudden jar that can be felt right throughout the aircraft structure. In view of this, after the fourth lap I flew out to seaward at Southsea in order to miss the disturbances.

After about twenty minutes, the cockpit became very hot and stuffy and I was glad of the breathing tube that led a draught of cold air on to my face. During the fifth lap my legs began to get slightly cramped owing to the small cockpit and I rested my knees on the side of the fuselage. However, I quickly moved them when I found the cockpit walls were blisteringly hot. I considered that the cramp was the lesser of the two evils.

During the last lap the engine was still giving the same healthy noise and the aircraft was still flying perfectly. The combination, in spite of the higher speed, being much smoother than a normal aeroplane. As we rounded the last turn, I opened the throttle full out once more for the final four or five miles to the finish and then a climbing turn and an amble back to Calshot on about a quarter throttle of 200 mph; a final closing of the throttle, left-hand gliding turn and an alighting and the last Schneider Trophy Contest was over. A few days later, in the same aircraft, Flt Lt G.H. Stainforth established a world speed record of 407.5 mph.

Mr A.J. Rowledge of the Rolls-Royce company will describe the design and construction of the Schneider Trophy racing engine:

It was not until Lady Houston so generously came forward with her offer to defray the cost of the machines that a decision was made that Great Britain should take part in the 1931 Schneider Trophy Contest. This indecision might easily have been fatal to our chances as very little time – only seven months – was left for the development of the design to the new standard and the construction of the actual racing engines. Fortunately, the problem had already been considered and informal discussions had taken place between representatives of the Vickers Supermarine and Rolls-Royce companies, and later the matter was further considered at a conference presided over by the late AVM Holt. At this conference the Rolls-Royce company as engine builders undertook to increase the horsepower output by 400, thus bringing it up to 2,300 at 3,200 rpm. On the one-hour full throttle acceptance test the power given was over 2,300. This increase in horsepower brought several problems forward affecting the seaplane and also the propeller maker. More fuel had to be carried and more cooling surface provided. As regards the fuel, we were able to help by reducing the fuel consumption per brake horsepower per hour.

In preparing the engines for the 1929 contest, we were in many ways at the beginning of the development of this particular engine. In 1931 we had more knowledge and data to enable us to tackle the job but at the same time we had a smaller field for development. The 1931 engine, besides giving more power, was a more efficient engine than its predecessor. As the development of a given engine proceeds, the balance of the design improves, thus making it more difficult to obtain further improvement and almost every piece of material in the engine is working at its limit of stress or heat capacity, even for the short life required of such an engine.

However, the limit of development has not yet been reached as regards engine construction.

We think it will be agreed by most people who saw the engines perform that they did their work in quite a gentlemanly fashion and that besides giving good power they were docile and ran smoothly. Looking at the aircraft it is perhaps difficult to believe that the engine fitted to it can possibly give more power than a railway engine which has such an imposing size and weighs so many tons. Again, a three-litre car engine if it gave the same power in relation to its cylinder capacity would have to develop 190 brake horsepower or a car engine of 20 horsepower British Tax Rating develop 266 brake horsepower.

For the speed record the conditions were different and the engine was allowed to run at a higher maximum speed. This involved a further series of tests after the race standard had been settled. A very considerable further increase in power was obtained but, as the runs at full throttle were comparatively short, the difficulty of providing adequate cooling for the engines was no greater than in the race for the trophy.

When taken down and examined after the race, the engine was in particularly good condition. No parts were damaged and the bearings looked almost as new. The engine used for the speed record was equally good.

In conclusion the satisfactory result was due to team work and, in addition to the people already mentioned, a word of praise is due to the suppliers of the material and to all the work people.

Perhaps the celebration Mitchell enjoyed most was the dinner held in the South Western Hotel, in the city of Southampton, on New Year's Eve 1931. He was happy to be in the company of his old friends from Supermarine, and the pilots of the High Speed Flight. With a midnight cabaret to bring in the New Year, it was an exceptionally enjoyable party. A menu of the dinner survives in the RAF Museum at Hendon, and among the signatures on the front cover are the names of Boothman, Stainforth, Hope and Lovesey. Alongside it is an interesting relic of the 1931 Schneider Contest, a pound note signed by J.N. Boothman with the added inscription: 'The only one to go round the course'.

New Year's Day 1932 brought Mitchell a surprise when he was awarded the CBE in the New Year's Honours List. His family in Stoke-on-Trent were delighted that his great work in designing high-speed aircraft had been officially recognised, and so were all his colleagues at Supermarine. Mitchell himself was pleased up to the time when, early in February, he received an official letter from Buckingham Palace informing him of the correct dress to be worn at the investiture, to be held on 23 February.

The order for Levee Dress read:

> Black evening dress coat. Black or white evening dress waistcoat. Breeches of plain black of evening dress material or stockinet, with three small black cloth or silk buttons, and black buckles at the knee. Black silk hose, plain court shoes with bows and no buckles. White evening dress tie and white gloves.

Mitchell rebelled and his first reaction was to positively refuse to dress himself up like this, and it needed all his wife's persuasive pleadings to make him change his mind (see illustration 1, page 169).

Eva, Mrs Mitchell's maid, described the occasion.

> He was very thrilled about the award of the CBE; we all were, because he really deserved it. Mrs Mitchell went with him to Buckingham Palace to receive the honour. He made great objections to wearing court dress, and he particularly hated the bows on his court shoes. But Mrs Mitchell talked him round, and he knew deep down that it was right. He had a great respect for the Royal family.

The official Buckingham Palace portrait of him wearing the insignia of the order shows a very handsome but very stern, solemn-faced Mitchell, looking so different from the informally dressed man to be seen walking round the Supermarine workshops.

In spite of all the praise and congratulatory speeches, Mitchell never became pompous or conceited, and beneath the customary quiet, reserved manner he presented in public, there always lurked a boyish sense of fun. Over the years the Supermarine drawing office team continued to hold their annual parties, and on several occasions they were held in Paris. At one of these celebrations Mitchell enjoyed a jovial evening at the Folies Bergere, in the company of Maj. G.P. Bulman of the Air Ministry (later president of the Royal Aeronautical Society). When the party was over, the two men went to the cloakroom to collect their coats, and Mitchell discovered that he had lost his ticket. He could see his coat quite plainly hanging on a peg; it happened to be a new one, which he didn't want to lose. But the French attendant was firm, and to all of Mitchell's pleas he repeated: 'No ticket! No coat.'

Bulman came to the rescue by creating a noisy disturbance at the far end of the counter. The attendant rushed forward to quell the fracas and while his attention was distracted, Mitchell leapt over the counter and retrieved his coat!

In 1931, the S.6Bs were believed to be the last of the high-speed seaplanes. They had been specially built to fly at high speeds for very short periods of time and were useless for commercial purposes. In 1968, Sir George Edwards, then chairman of the British Aircraft Corporation, paid an important tribute to Mitchell and his racing seaplanes, which Sir George includes in his contribution in Appendix 1.

Sqn Ldr Orlebar, who had shared with his friend 'Mitch' both triumphs and disasters, wrote in his book, *Schneider Trophy*: 'The credit belongs to the brains which conceive, not to the hands which hold. But the hands had very good fun.'

'Batchy' Atcherley, member of the 1929 Schneider Contest team, made the following pertinent comment which David Mondey quotes in his book, *The Schneider Trophy*:

> He [Mitchell] was a man with an alert and inquisitive mind, and in spite of his very considerable attainments in the world of aircraft design, he was always ready to crack a joke or take on (in conversation) anyone on his own wavelength. He was always keen to listen to pilots' opinions and never pressed his views against theirs. He set his sights deliberately high, for he had little use for 'second-bests'. Yet he was the most unpompous man I ever met.

For a particularly germane comment on the Schneider success, the words of J.D. Scott[2] cannot be bettered:

> The aeronautical world at large had been profoundly impressed by the boldness of Mitchell's 'S' (Schneider seaplane) designs; but it was his passion for engineering detail, which always got these aircraft to the scene of the contest and always got them into the air, which made a special impression on his colleagues. They knew that he was a great designer, and suspected that he was a great man.

As the penultimate comment before leaving the Schneider story, one might perhaps contemplate the thinness of the thread on which history sometimes rests. If the Royal Aero Club had not turned down the request of the Italians and the French in early September to postpone the 1931 race, with the result that the former were able to solve the problems with their MC.72s in time for the new race date, the Italians might well have won that contest. Indeed, a MC.72 did, as we have seen, eventually break Stainforth's record by a substantial margin. Pure speculation, of course, but the history of the Schneider Trophy races might have been very different if these changes had come to pass and, who knows, might even still be taking place!

Be that as it may, Britain did win the trophy and won it to keep for all time. Following the race, the trophy was put into the care of the Royal

Aero Club and was on display in their premises in Pall Mall, London, until 1977 when they decided to close these premises.

After some discussion, it was decided that the obvious place for the trophy to be located for the future would be in the Science Museum in London, since in 1932, the S.6B (S.1595) in which Boothman had won the 1931 race, and in which Stainforth had broken the world speed record, had been transferred to the Science Museum by the Air Ministry and had been on display there ever since. It was accordingly agreed that the trophy should be handed over to the Science Museum for safe keeping and for display alongside the S.6B. On 15 March 1977, Vice-Admiral Sir Richard Smeeton, representing the Royal Aero Club, formally handed over the Schneider Trophy to Dame Margaret Weston, director of the Science Museum. The ceremony took place alongside the S.6B and was attended by a large gathering of notable guests including several former members of the Schneider RAF High Speed Flights. Gordon Mitchell was delighted to receive an invitation to attend this ceremony to represent his father.

Finally, it is appropriate to record that a weather vane, consisting of an S.6B in bronze, was erected on the roof of George Stainforth's old school, Weymouth College, and unveiled on 23 July 1932, to commemorate his great achievement in breaking the world air speed record on 29 September 1931. When the college closed in 1940, the weather vane was presented to the town of Weymouth and in 1952 it was erected in the town's Greenhill Gardens where it stands today.

12

The Last of Mitchell's Flying Boats and Amphibians

'A boat that will fly, not an aeroplane that will float.' That was how Noel Pemberton-Billing, the founder of Supermarine, had described the flying boats which he set out to build. As we have seen, throughout the years of the Schneider Contests, Supermarine continued to build flying boats. This was the bread-and-butter work which kept the firm going through the years of the Depression. The outright winning of the Schneider Trophy ended the production of racing seaplanes, and Mitchell returned to the less exciting, but no less important, work of designing flying boats with the hope of securing government contracts. One of the men closely associated with Mitchell for many years was Arthur Shirvall, who had joined the firm as an apprentice in Mitchell's early days. He recalled those days:

> At that time R.J. had a motorbike and a sidecar, and I remember him driving into the yard on two wheels. He was very good looking and wore

riding breeches and brown gaiters. He was a down-to-earth engineer who
did things in the simplest possible way and was pretty successful. He was
a nice man with plenty of drive and I count myself fortunate in coming
under his influence when I did.

Shirvall always had an eye for a good line, and as a junior apprentice he
worked on the hull of the Sea Lion II, the flying boat that won the 1922
Schneider Contest in Naples. He spent the last years of his apprenticeship in the works, and then became an 'improver' with a wage of £2
15s 0d per week.

To increase his knowledge of hulls and floats, Shirvall was attached to
the drawing office of a qualified naval designer seconded to Supermarine.
One day, Mitchell, who happened to be showing a visitor round, paused
by his drawing board. Turning to his companion he said: 'Shirvall always
makes things look very nice.'

When the naval designer left Supermarine, Shirvall became Mitchell's
hydrodynamic specialist designing hulls and floats and conducting the
required tank tests; in this capacity he was involved in the design of the
floats for all the Schneider racing seaplanes from the S.4 to the S.6B. In
the latter, the skin on the top of the float used for cooling was a specialist
job which kept two or three people busy for some time.

One of Arthur Shirvall's most notable designs was the hull of the very
successful Southampton flying boat. He was reluctant to talk about it,
and merely said that it was based on something he had read, and added,
'It worked like a charm.' Shirvall was later made responsible for all
future project design at Supermarine, a very important position. This
work brought him into even closer contact with Mitchell, and gave
him a better understanding of the boss. Shirvall recalled stories of R.J.'s
impish sense of humour.

On one occasion he was at Teddington, tank testing hulls, when R.J.
rang up to ask him how he was getting on.

'I would like you to come up and see for yourself, if you could manage
it,' Shirvall replied.

'Right,' said R.J. 'I'll come up tonight.'

Shirvall's immediate task was to find accommodation for Mitchell.
The small hotel where he himself was staying was full up, and he could
not find another in the immediate vicinity. 'It would be possible to
set up another bed in your room, if that would be all right?' the hotel
manager suggested. So this was agreed, and when R.J. arrived the two
men enjoyed themselves over dinner and an evening out. When it was
time to retire for the night, R.J. sat down on his bed to remove his shoes
and socks, when it suddenly collapsed under his weight, leaving him
sprawled on the floor. Unable to control his laughter, Shirvall made a
hurried dive for the bathroom. When he returned he sat down on his

own bed, which immediately collapsed in the same manner; in Arthur's absence in the bathroom, R.J. had, of course, removed the supports of his bed. This episode ended in much laughter, as both men set about reconstructing their beds.

Although he often enjoyed this sort of prank, Mitchell was a very practical man and as a director his main aim was to get orders for the firm and to obtain the best conditions for his design staff and everyone at Supermarine. His team worked hard to please him, but not entirely from a sense of duty.

'We all regarded him with affection,' Shirvall said, a wonderful tribute from a man who had endured his exacting standards of workmanship and fiery outbursts of temper.

Arthur Shirvall recalled another occasion when Mitchell found a joke irresistible:

> The design staff had for several years held a Christmas dinner to which no 'bosses' were invited, until one year it was suggested that we were being a little unkind in not asking R.J. to join us, and he was accordingly invited. He accepted with evident pleasure, on being assured that he would be coming along as one of the lads and not as a guest.
>
> It happened that I was in the chair at this particular dinner, and I thought it desirable to extend a few words of welcome in opening the proceedings. Unaccustomed to public speaking, and the world's worst speaker, I wrote my speech on a sheet of foolscap which I reckoned I could read from a standing position if I left it lying on the table.
>
> When the time came, I had R.J. sitting on my right hand, and after a nervous start he suggested that I should let him have the notes, and he would prompt me as necessary. The arrangement didn't work out too well because he interjected a good deal with remarks I hadn't written, so I hastily recovered my notes and carried on as before with the sheet in my right hand. I had not got very far when I found my notes were on fire! Blowing out the flames I sat down, considerably confused, amid roars of applause. It got the show off to a very good start!

In 1932 Mitchell designed a replacement for the Southampton Mk II flying boat to meet the RAF requirements for a new coastal reconnaissance aircraft. This was originally named the Southampton Mk IV but later was re-christened the Scapa. It was a twin-engined biplane powered by Rolls-Royce Kestrel IIIA engines of 525 hp. These were placed close under the top wing to increase the water clearance of the large propellers. Its hull was larger than that of the earlier Southamptons, while the fabric-covered wings and tail unit were, for the first time, constructed in light alloy. The Scapa had a wing span of 75 ft, a top speed of 142 mph, a range of 1,100 miles and an enclosed cockpit, and like its famous

predecessor could be flown on one engine at full load. It could carry
a torpedo. Its performance was better than that of any other British
military aeroplane at that time and fifteen were built for the RAF for
use in general reconnaissance work.

During the initial work on the Scapa, a new man, Jack Rasmussen,
joined the design team. He came from Hull where he had served
an apprenticeship with a shipbuilding firm, and had worked with
the Blackburn Aircraft Company as a draughtsman before moving
on to Southampton. At that time Supermarine employed about fifty
draughtsmen and Rasmussen's first task was working on a design for
a gun installation.

Rasmussen has a vivid memory of his first meeting with Mitchell
soon after he joined the firm. One morning R.J. walked into the
drawing office on his customary tour of inspection. There was always
a certain stir in the air when he appeared, because everyone wondered
what the visit would produce. On this particular day, Mitchell paused
by Rasmussen and then sat down. Leaning his elbows on the drawing
board, he cupped his face in his hands and for many long minutes
he stared at the design of the gun installation without saying a single
word.

'Mitchell's name had always meant a great deal to me,' Rasmussen
admitted. 'And it was one of the proudest moments of my life when
he first noticed my work.'

When Mitchell broke his lengthy concentration, he turned to
Rasmussen and said:

'Perhaps we had better go across to Hythe this afternoon to take a
look at the flying boat in the hangar there.'

Rasmussen was delighted at the prospect of being taken out by the
boss, and that afternoon the two men went across to Hythe in the
Supermarine speedboat with Skipper Grimes at the helm. While they
looked at the flying boat, Mitchell explained his own ideas for the
design of a gun installation.

Their meetings were not limited to working hours. Rasmussen was
a keen sportsman, and in 1931/32 he played tennis in the Supermarine
team. Much to his delight he was paired with Mitchell, and the two men
occasionally played matches against rival clubs. Rasmussen remembers
going to a tennis match at Brockenhurst in Mitchell's Rolls-Royce
– 'It was the first time I had ridden in such a smart car.'

Rasmussen subsequently took charge of design liaison at
Supermarine.

It was in 1932 that Mitchell first began to turn his attention to the
design of a landplane fighter based on a very restrictive specification,
F.7/30, which had been issued by the Air Ministry in 1930. This is
described in the next chapter.

Another important year for Mitchell was 1933 – for two reasons, one good and one extremely bad, since it was in August of that year that it was realised that he had cancer. This traumatic event in Mitchell's life is described later. The good event in 1933 was that it marked the birth of another of Mitchell's outstanding designs. This was the Seagull Mk V, which was later to become widely known with affection as the Walrus and will be referred to as such hereafter.

The Walrus was originally designed by Mitchell as a private venture. It was a biplane amphibian finally powered by a single 750 hp Bristol Pegasus VI radial engine driving a pusher airscrew, and carried machine guns fore and aft. The hull was of normal duralumin construction but the wings had spars of stainless steel and ribs of wood and were fabric covered. It had a totally enclosed cockpit for which many pilots were destined to say a prayer of thanks during its years of active service in the Second World War. Total wing span was 46 ft but the wings could be folded to a span of only 17.5 ft. Maximum speed was 135 mph.

The Walrus made its first flight (as the Seagull V) over Southampton Water in June 1933; shortly afterwards it was shown at the Hendon Air Display, flown by Capt. 'Mutt' Summers, the Vickers chief test pilot, who to the surprise of everyone, including Mitchell, entertained the crowd by looping the loop in it. Mitchell was highly delighted as he watched this demonstration of the high capabilities of his latest aircraft.

'He looped the bloody thing!' he kept repeating to everyone he saw.

In service, a crew of three was initially carried – pilot, navigator, and a third man who doubled up as gunner and wireless operator – but the crew was later normally increased to four. In addition to the two machine guns, it could also carry four 100lb anti-submarine bombs which were dropped by the pilot or gunner using a portable bomb sight. The Walrus could be catapulted from a ship and then, after alighting on the water, be winched back on board by a crane. This was often a tricky and dangerous operation because one member of the crew had to climb on to the top wing to fasten the crane hook on to the slinging point. There was a safety strap which he attached to his harness, but in rough seas it could be a very hair-raising experience because of the proximity of the propeller.

The Walrus was a design that was in marked contrast to Mitchell's 400 mph Schneider S.6Bs and demonstrated only too clearly the extent of his versatility as an aircraft designer. One of its features which was to prove invaluable was its outstanding ability to cope with rough seas.

Initially the Air Ministry were very lukewarm about it and it is reported that a certain high official who saw the prototype said that it was very interesting but felt they had no requirement for anything like that! How wrong can you be. Alan Clifton makes further reference to this interesting little episode in Appendix 3. The first orders for the Walrus came in 1934 from the Australian government who initially required twenty-four of them. The Australians had bought, and made good use of, some of the earlier versions of the Seagull which had not too good a performance on rough water but which suited the Australian conditions. They used some in 1926 in a survey of the Great Barrier Reef. It would appear, therefore, that they were more ready, as a result of this experience, to buy the Walrus than the government of the country which produced it.

However, Air Ministry orders started to be received the following year, and in April 1935, Supermarine were given an order for twelve. It was at this point that the name was officially changed to Walrus. Further substantial orders for the RAF followed and, in 1939, when Supermarine were more than fully occupied building Spitfires, Walrus production was transferred to Saunders-Roe in the Isle of Wight, who eventually built 461. Some of these were a Mk II version with a wooden, instead of a metal, hull, which helped reduce the demand for priority supplies of the latter during the war.

The original prototype Walrus had many interesting experiences before it finally collided with an anti-submarine boom in Gibraltar early in 1936 and sank, never to be recovered. One somewhat amusing episode occurred in October 1935 when the Walrus prototype was on the battleship *Nelson* serving as the admiral's 'barge'. On the day in question the new commander-in-chief was to be flown in the Walrus from Hendon to join the *Nelson*. In landing alongside, the unfortunate pilot forgot to retract the undercarriage and the aircraft turned over and the occupants had to be rescued, unharmed but very wet! The views of the commander-in-chief on this performance have not been recorded but it is noteworthy that when the prototype was salvaged and returned to Supermarine for repair, an undercarriage position indicator was fitted. Probably the first time such a device had been fitted to an aircraft as fully retractable undercarriages were not exactly common at that time. Accordingly, development of this new, fully retractable undercarriage for the Walrus involved much research and design work, all of which was to prove invaluable when it came to designing the retractable undercarriage for the Spitfire one year later.

In the Second World War, the Walrus played an invaluable role in the Royal Navy, the Royal Australian Navy and the Royal New Zealand Navy as the foremost fleet gunnery-spotting and observation platform. Later in the war it did sterling service in air-sea rescue operated from land bases by the RAF. Hundreds of airmen were rescued from the sea after their aircraft had been shot down. A total of 746 of Mitchell's Walruses were eventually built; one of these is today in the Fleet Air Arm Museum in Yeovilton and a second, an Australian Walrus, in the RAF Museum in Hendon.

The Walrus was the last amphibian that Mitchell designed and lived to see built and fly. He did design an improved version of the Walrus in 1936, which was eventually named the Sea Otter, but it did not have its first flight until September 1938, over a year after Mitchell's death. The Sea Otter took a long time to develop and overcome the problems encountered with it, so that, although 292 were built, it did not enter operational service until late 1944 and so had no chance of matching the war record of the Walrus. The service pilots did not take to the Sea Otter as they had to the Walrus and it took some time before they learnt to accept it.

While the Sea Otter was the last amphibian Mitchell designed, his last flying boat and, incidentally, the last twin-engined flying boat to be produced by Supermarine was the Stranraer, which he designed in 1934. This was essentially an enlarged version of the Scapa designed for a specific requirement of the Air Ministry for a coastal patrol aircraft capable of carrying up to 1,000 lb load for 1,100 miles, and able to fly on one engine. It was finally powered by two Bristol Pegasus X engines of 920 hp and had a top speed of 165 mph. It had a rate of climb of 1,000 feet per minute up to 10,000 ft, which far outclassed any contemporary flying boats and was double that of the Scapa. It carried three machine guns and a 1,160 lb bomb load. Special attention was paid to prevention of corrosion, which was always a problem with marine aircraft. Subsequent long-term use of the Stranraer, particularly in Canada, demonstrated the effectiveness of this preventative treatment. The prototype Stranraer first flew in July 1934 piloted by 'Mutt' Summers. It was another of Mitchell's very successful designs.

The first order from the Air Ministry for seventeen was received in 1935. These were extensively used on patrol flights for the first two years or so of the war. In addition, forty Stranraers were built by Canadian Vickers in Montreal for the Royal Canadian Air Force who used them continually during the war, the last one not being 'laid off' until 1946. Some were converted for civil passenger use in Canada and used as such right up until 1962.

One of the Canadian-built Stranraers is today in the RAF Museum in Hendon.

Thus, the Walrus and the Stranraer represented the end, as far as Mitchell was concerned, of his long association with the flying boat and amphibian. These were what Supermarine had been founded to produce and when Mitchell was first employed by Supermarine in 1917, it was this type of aircraft that he was to work on. With his departure into designing high-speed seaplanes, starting with the S.4 in 1925 and ending with the S.6B in 1931, it is hardly surprising, when the opportunity arose in the early 1930s for him to start thinking about a new area of design, namely a high-speed, land-based, single-seater fighter, that he grasped the opportunity with both hands. Undoubtedly, he missed the excitement of designing high-speed seaplanes, but this new departure promised to be every bit as stimulating.

It is worth recording at this point a very excellent record in relation to Mitchell's aircraft. It has frequently been stressed that Mitchell always felt great concern for the pilots who had to take his creations into the air for flight testing. It must, therefore, have given him the greatest satisfaction that in the whole of his career not one pilot lost his life due directly to some design or structural fault in any of his aircraft. Some were indeed sadly killed, such as Kinkead and Brinton, but there was no evidence that the aircraft itself was in any way to blame. This enviable record was retained through to Mitchell's death since in addition to all the aircraft that have been discussed so far, the same record with both the initial (unsuccessful) and ultimate prototype Spitfire was maintained.

It is now time to turn to what was unquestionably the most important and successful of Mitchell's designs, the legendary Spitfire, which is considered in detail in the next chapter.

13

The Spitfire

The outright winning of the Schneider Trophy in 1931 heralded the end of seaplane racing, but the 1925 to 1931 races had provided Mitchell and his unique young team with more experience of the design of high-speed aircraft than probably existed anywhere else. One of the great fears of any designer is structural failure, but Mitchell's aircraft had stood the test of high-speed flight with flying colours, and proved the basic excellence of his designs. Although he had limited formal training in aerodynamics, Mitchell seemed to have an intuitive understanding of aerodynamic problems and was able to envisage shapes that would move most effectively through the air.

In the same way, Arthur Shirvall could envisage and create graceful and effective boat hulls, and, as we have seen, there was always a good understanding between him and Mitchell.

So, following the success of the Schneider seaplanes and the steady output of successful flying boats, Supermarine became one of the world's foremost marine aircraft manufacturers and led the world in the technologies of high-speed flight. At a time when most firms were having to sack men, the Supermarine factory at Woolston increased its staff and, from this time, Mitchell's drawing office had fifty draughtsmen and ten technicians.

Towards the end of 1931, Beverley Shenstone arrived at Supermarine, looking for a job as an aerodynamicist. Shenstone, a Canadian with a degree in aeronautical engineering, had been working at the Junkers factory in Germany, where he had written a paper on wing design. He was interviewed by Mitchell, who followed up his questions by sending for the drawings of the wing of a six-engined monoplane flying boat which the firm was hoping to sell to the government. He invited Shenstone to comment on the design and, after studying it carefully, the Canadian suggested some minor alterations to improve the wing shape. Rather taken aback by criticism from a man ten years his junior, Mitchell ended the interview by saying he would contact Shenstone if his services were required.

Mitchell must have given some thought to the Canadian's ideas on wing design, for a few weeks later he sent for Shenstone and offered him a temporary job working on the wing of the monoplane flying boat. That particular aircraft was never built but Mitchell was sufficiently impressed by Shenstone's work to offer him a permanent post. This was to prove to be an important appointment since, later, Beverley Shenstone was destined to play a significant role in the design of the Spitfire wing, and for Shenstone the years he spent at Supermarine working for Mitchell were to prove to be both very happy and very stimulating. Although Mitchell was a director with an enviable track record to his credit, he was always ready to listen and take advice from anyone who had anything useful to say. Shenstone was also very interested in the German aircraft industry and, from his time at Junkers, he had some ideas of what was going on in that country. By the Treaty of Versailles, drawn up at the end of the First World War, Germany had been forbidden to have an Air Force, but they ran the civil airline, Lufthansa. At the same time, quite unknown to the Western powers, they set up a secret air base in Russia, some thirty miles north of Moscow, where they built military aeroplanes and trained pilots. To maintain secrecy, the German airmen did not wear a uniform but strolled about in shirts and shorts as though they were on holiday.

'Mutt' Summers, the Vickers chief test pilot, was a source of much useful, and disturbing, information about what the German aircraft industry was doing in the 1930s since he had many personal contacts, holding high positions, in that country. Although some were inclined to dismiss what he said, saying in effect that his job was to be a test pilot, not a sort of unpaid spy, others nevertheless took serious note of what he was saying and there can be no doubt that many people such as Sir Robert McLean and Mitchell, to name only two, had a pretty good idea of what was going on in Germany. They recognised the need for Britain to re-arm, and realised that one of the weapons sorely needed was an improved and modern fighter aircraft.

Nevertheless, some people in high government positions believed that it would be impossible to prevent bombers getting through, and therefore they considered it a waste of time and money building fighters. Luckily for this country, AM Sir Hugh Dowding (later Lord Dowding), then air member for supply and research, took the opposite view. He wanted to build up a powerful fighter force to serve as a defence against any future attack. From 1930–36 Dowding was responsible for specifications issued by the Air Ministry, and in that role he had a major influence on the designs of aircraft later to be used in the Battle of Britain.

In 1930 the Air Ministry, inspired by Dowding, issued Specification F.7/30, in which they asked for a day and night fighter to replace existing outdated fighters then in service with the RAF.

The essential requirements were:

1. Low landing speed and short landing run.
2. Maximum speed of 250 mph.
3. Steep initial climb rate for interception.
4. High manoeuvrability.
5. Good all-round view.

No specific shape of air frame was called for but the fighter was to be armed with four Vickers machine guns.

Because Britain was in the middle of a slump, orders were very difficult to obtain, and there was keen competition between aircraft companies to win the F.7/30 competition. Sir Robert McLean wanted Supermarine to compete, and Mitchell was thus given the chance to start creating the fighter he had had in his mind for some time; the operative word here is 'start'.

It has been suggested that Mitchell felt the requirement of a speed of 250 mph would be 'dead easy' when his S.6B had achieved over 400 mph. Certainly, certain aspects of the resulting Type 224, as it was known in Supermarine, suggested a degree of general over-confidence by Mitchell and his team. At the same time, the F.7/30 Specification was constricting and tied Mitchell down severely. The first proposals submitted by Supermarine early in 1932 underwent considerable changes in design before Type 224 eventually emerged ready for its first flight in February 1934. It was a monoplane with a narrow, streamlined fuselage with open cockpit and powered by a 600 hp Rolls-Royce Goshawk II engine, a derivative of the successful Kestrel engine but with water evaporative cooling. It had the military serial number K2890, a two-bladed wooden propeller, and a fixed undercarriage with 'trousered' wheels. The aircraft was unofficially christened Spitfire, a name chosen by Sir Robert McLean as is discussed further later.

Type 224 might well be described as a near disaster – with a maximum speed of only 230 mph, its performance in general fell short of what had been considered to be an 'easy to achieve' specification. Moreover, the evaporative cooling of the Goshawk engine had many serious shortcomings.

Mitchell was never really happy with Type 224, and even before it was ready for testing he was back at the drawing board working on something which he felt would be better. Then disaster struck. He had not been feeling well for some time and, when he was taken ill in late summer 1933, his doctors diagnosed cancer of the rectum and advised an immediate operation. Mitchell entered St Mark's Hospital in London in August 1933, where he had a major operation which left him with a serious physical disability in the form of a permanent colostomy. Fuller details of Mitchell's operation and, in particular, the potential consequences of it, both physical and mental, are given in Chapter 18.

Mitchell was told by his doctors that there was a grave risk that the cancer would return, in which case it was unlikely that anything could be done for him. He went to Bournemouth for a short convalescence, accompanied by his wife and a nurse. By early 1934 he was back at work. He could not and would not accept the life of a semi-invalid or think of retiring for the rest of what years he might have left.

Testing of the F.7/30 entries took place at Martlesham Heath in the early months of 1934, and in the event neither the Supermarine Type 224 nor any of the other submissions were accepted and a contract was in fact given for the Gloster Gladiator biplane under a different specification, thus delaying further the entry of the RAF into the monoplane age.

Both Mitchell and Sir Robert McLean were now convinced that Type 224 was a mistake and an irreparable one. As J.D. Scott[3] describes, when the Air Ministry tried to persuade Supermarine to replace the Goshawk engine with a Napier Dagger, the Vickers (Aviation) Board, with Sir Robert as chairman, turned down the proposal, saying that it would take up the company's time to little purpose. This took place on 6 November 1934.

Sir Robert, who had resigned from Vickers in October 1938, wrote in *The Sunday Times* of 18 August 1957:

> I felt that they [his design team] would do much better by devoting their qualities not to the official experimental fighter [i.e., F.7/30] but to a real killer fighter. After unfruitful discussions with the Air Ministry, my opposite number in Rolls-Royce, the late A.F. Sidgreaves, and I, decided that the two companies together should themselves finance the building of such an aircraft.
>
> The Air Ministry was informed of this decision, and were told that in no circumstances would any technical member of the Air Ministry be consulted or allowed to interfere with the designer.

Strong words indeed, and of great historical importance. They demonstrate a number of things very clearly. First, how strong, determined and forceful Sir Robert McLean was and what a vital role he played in the creation of the Spitfire; second, the total confidence he by then had in Mitchell and in his ability to produce this so-called 'killer' fighter; and thirdly, that, as will be seen, the Spitfire did start as a private venture, as indeed did the equally famous Rolls-Royce Merlin engine, although the Spitfire soon became an official Air Ministry project. It is worth mentioning here, in order further to establish the close relationship and understanding that existed between Sir Robert and Mitchell, that this had now extended beyond a purely work relationship. Thus, for example, Mitchell and his family were invited to go on a private skiing holiday in Austria with Sir Robert and Lady McLean, a fabulous holiday as Gordon Mitchell remembers it (see illustration 38, page 181).

This strong action by Sir Robert clearly stirred things up in the Air Ministry, since, less than a month later, on 1 December 1934, they issued a contract for £10,000 for the new 'killer' fighter, and the covering Specification F.37/34 was received by Supermarine at the end of December, which basically agreed with and approved the Supermarine Type 300 proposals.

The suggestion sometimes made that the Spitfire was entirely a private venture designed and built by Supermarine in a complete vacuum outside of government participation, is, therefore, entirely wrong. Nevertheless, Sir Robert McLean and Mitchell had to play a vital initiating role to get the project officially under way.

Many years later in 1967, in *The Barnes Wallis Story* television programme, Wallis paid a great tribute to Sir Robert, who had died in 1964 'virtually unknown'. He said he did not receive the recognition that was his due. The reason, he thought, was because he was a fighter not a diplomatist and made enemies in high places. It was all very wrong.

Mitchell was also a fighter; and although Type 224 was not a success, he had gained a lot of useful experience from it and he refused to be beaten. He knew that he could design a better aircraft, and his failure on the first attempt stimulated him to make sure he succeeded at the second attempt. Now he concentrated all his energies on the new fighter.

An intensive period of design studies was initiated and Mitchell and his team all worked long and hard on them. It goes without saying that a complicated piece of machinery, like the Spitfire was to be, did not just happen.

None of the people working closely with him realised the seriousness of his illness. Mitchell never wanted to talk about himself, only about getting the new fighter design right this time. His attempts to gloss over his illness are revealed in a letter written to Alan Clifton in April 1934, from a London nursing home where he had gone for a check-up after the operation.

50 Weymouth Street, London Wl.
26 April 1934.

Dear Clifton,

Many thanks for your letter with specifications and drawings of the four-engined boat design. I have been through them generally, but not in complete detail and consider they are very good, and have no criticism to offer. You must have worked very hard to get them finished in time and must still have a lot to do. Sorry I have had to leave it to you like this. I did not think I would be away so long. Afraid I shall be at least another week. You seem to have managed extremely well.

Sincerely yours,
R.J. Mitchell.

It is interesting that in spite of his close association with Mitchell, Clifton had no idea that he had a colostomy until Gordon Mitchell told him only a few years ago.

On returning to Southampton, Mitchell resumed his normal working routine and his leisure activities were also resumed. During all the years that he had been designing aircraft, he had often flown as a passenger in his own planes, but he decided it was time to learn to fly himself. Accordingly, he started taking flying lessons in a Gipsy Moth at Eastleigh Airport, and in July 1934 – less than a year after his operation – he gained his pilot's licence (see illustration 39, page 181).

His pilot's logbook, now kept at the RAF Museum, Hendon, makes interesting reading. Here was a man whose doctors had told him he might not have long to live, occupying his spare time in learning to fly. The first entry in the logbook is on 22 December 1933, when he had his first flight with W.H. Dudley, his instructor at Eastleigh. In the following six months he recorded regular flights concerned with straight flying, turning, climbing, taking off and landing. Then, on 1 July, comes the brief but all-important entry: 'First Solo.'

But flying was only a pleasant distraction from his major task of developing his Type 300 fighter. Throughout 1935, Mitchell worked on the fighter, primarily because he was inspired and motivated to do so but, at the same time, the knowledge that his cancer might return at any time and kill him could never be completely dismissed from his mind. Would he have time to complete his task? was the question he must have asked himself many times.

To create the new fighter, Mitchell made several important revolutionary changes to the F.7/30 design. After several straight-winged designs and after detailed discussions with Beverley Shenstone, his aerodynamicist, the wing shape was changed to the now famous, and almost unique, elliptical configuration. The wing, which had a single main spar, was also made as thin as possible consistent with strength, but towards the root it had to be thick enough to accommodate the retractable undercarriage and the machine guns. This concept was completely opposite to the aerodynamic thinking at the time, which was for high-lift, thick wings. It also had a unique induced twist built into it. The wing, like the fuselage, was of stressed skin construction, while the fin was integral with the tail end of the fuselage, which was detachable. A good wing, it is said, makes a good aeroplane, and there is no doubt that Mitchell's final decision for the wing design of the Spitfire was a feature of major importance in relation to its success. That it was so complicated and advanced was to be shown later when it proved initially to be so difficult to mass produce. It is interesting that for the hand-built prototype, the skin on the wing surfaces aft of the D nose leading-edge configuration was fixed in long, narrow overlapping strips, after the fashion of a clinker-built boat. This method was never used again on any of the production Spitfires.

Mitchell replaced the 'trousered' wheels with a retractable undercarriage, and the cockpit was given a sliding canopy which improved streamlining while allowing the pilot a good all-round view in the air. All these changes reduced the drag which had impaired the performance of the Type 224. Joe Smith, as chief draughtsman, was responsible for the whole of the detail design of the new aeroplane.

A very important change was the replacement of the unsuccessful 600 hp steam-cooled Goshawk engine. In 1933, Rolls-Royce had developed a new engine, the PV.12 (PV meaning private venture). This was the engine which was destined to play such a prominent role in the Second World War. It powered Spitfires, Hurricanes, Lancasters and many other aircraft, and its deep-throated roar became a familiar sound. The decision to fit this Merlin engine into Mitchell's Type 300 fighter was a vital turning point in the development of the Spitfire.

It was developed from the Kestrel, used so successfully in the Hawker Fury but, unlike the Kestrel, originally it had steam cooling as used on the earlier Goshawk engine. However, when the shortcomings of this cooling system became obvious, the PV.12 engine was changed to a pure ethylene glycol cooling system in which form it eventually emerged as the Merlin of approximately 1,050 hp.

It is sometimes wrongly suggested that the Merlin was a direct descendant of the Schneider Trophy 'R' engines. The confusion is understandable, since an engine that was descended from the 'R' family was later to be very successfully fitted to the Spitfire, and that was the Griffon, an engine of some 1,735 hp which became available in early 1943.

Thus, Rolls-Royce played a crucial role in providing the power source for the Spitfire. It is also of interest, in relation to the discussion between Sir Robert McLean of Vickers Aviation and Rolls-Royce described earlier, that Rolls-Royce in addition contributed £7,500 towards the development of the prototype Spitfire, a considerable sum in those days (see Supermarine expenditure statement at 29 February 1936, on fighter K5054, reproduced as illustration 41, page 182).

Mitchell was a true patriot and he was deeply concerned about the slow development of British aviation and, on 23 October 1934, an article appeared in the *Daily Mirror*, headed: 'What is Happening Now in Air Transport?' by R.J. Mitchell, CBE, designer of the successful Schneider Trophy machines and many types of service flying boats.

Some of the points he raised have such a familiar ring that they might almost apply to the present-day situation:

> The MacRobertson Air Race to Australia has captured public imagina-
> tion as a great sporting event. It had done much more than this. It has
> given a very good indication of our position as a nation in the race for
> supremacy in high-speed aerial transport over long-distance flying routes.
> It is regrettable that this indication is rather unfavourable to ourselves.
> The list of competitors included a number of foreign machines which
> are practically standard airliners, well established on the American and
> European aerial transport routes. Their performance was such that they
> stood high in the list of favourites for the race. We had no such British
> competitors. We could do better.
>
> The fact that a British machine gained, and for long held, such a clear
> lead in the Melbourne Air Race, is proof of that. But it was a machine
> specially built and designed, and by no means a standard airliner. As far as
> technique is concerned, British aviation is well to the front. Our Empire
> is so widely spread that fast aerial transport is perhaps the most vital neces-
> sity of our existence. Why are we so slow in the development of our big
> airliners? Why are we being left behind by other countries?
>
> It is largely a matter of the policy which has been pursued. We have
> concentrated too much on safety and economy to the detriment of speed.
> We have been too slow in putting to practical use new developments
> which have been proved to possess great advantages.
>
> It is difficult to predict the extent of development of the airliner during
> the next decade or two. The improvement in flying instruments may
> play an important part, in particular the perfection of one which would
> indicate the close proximity of land or water when flying blind.
>
> Weather is always the greatest enemy. Much can be done to elimi-
> nate this danger, such as better ground organisation, improved W/T

communication with pilots, more reliable weather reports, lighting arrangements, closely spaced emergency landing grounds on the main routes, and even higher cruising speeds. Progress will probably be on the lines of improved methods of combustion, better materials, and aerodynamic developments which will enable aircraft to be built more nearly to the form of the flying aerofoil, which is the ideal to be obtained, and higher efficiency engines and improved fuels.

There is no doubt whatever that in the comparatively near future flying will become the safest form of transport.

Before the construction of the new fighter began, a wooden mock-up was made, and Air Ministry representatives visited Supermarine to approve the final layout of the whole aircraft. Sir Ralph Sorley (later AM Sir Ralph Sorley), of the operational requirements department of the Air Staff, had studied the question of fire power and calculated that for the brief time an enemy aircraft would be in sight, it would be necessary to be able to destroy it in a single burst of two seconds' duration. He concluded that eight Browning .303 guns, firing 1,000 rounds per minute, would be essential for there to be any chance of a kill. Early in 1935, both Mitchell and Camm (with the Hurricane) had been thinking in terms of only four guns, but Sir Ralph easily convinced them of the need for eight guns located in the wing and they readily agreed to incorporate these in their designs.

In spite of being kept busy with his new brainchild, Mitchell managed to find time for some flying. On 7 May 1935, he logged fifty-five minutes' flying time with George Pickering, followed by three more flights with the same pilot.

Mitchell first met Flt Lt George Pickering, AFC, at the Marine Aircraft Experimental Establishment at Felixstowe, where the young RAF officer was a test pilot on flying boats. Pickering was a brilliant marine aircraft pilot and had been one of the first men to loop the loop in a flying boat. He was awarded the AFC for his part in a daring seaplane rescue. At Felixstowe he took part in the trials of the Supermarine flying boats, the Scapa and the Stranraer, and he often took flying boats abroad to test their performance under tropical and semi-tropical conditions. Besides being a first-rate pilot, Pickering was a very likeable, light-hearted character, always cheerful and ready for a joke.

Mitchell was regarded with some awe at Felixstowe, and whenever he went over to see his flying boats in action a whisper went round the station: 'R.J. is coming'. He greatly admired Pickering's ability as a pilot, and the two men became great friends.

In 1934, George Pickering left the RAF and became a test pilot with Supermarine at Mitchell's suggestion; he and his family took up residence in a house in Cobbett Road, Bitterne, Southampton. Their friendship with the Mitchell family continued, and they became frequent visitors at 'Hazeldene'. Speaking of R.J., Mrs Pickering said: 'I grew very fond of him,' and then she added with a smile: 'It was impossible not to like him, he was so kind-hearted and such good company.'

On 25 July 1935, Mitchell's logbook records: 'Stranraer flying boat, test flight over Southampton Water, 25 mins with Flt Lt Pickering'.

Mitchell's solo flights did not always end with a successful landing. One day he was returning home after a flight to Bristol when his aeroplane developed a mechanical fault and he was forced to come down at Middle Wallop in Hampshire. Knowing that his wife would be worried if he was late home, he telephoned Supermarine, explaining the reason for his delay and asking them to notify his wife. The telephonist had obviously never heard of the strangely named Hampshire village, for when Mrs Mitchell answered the phone she was told: 'Your husband has had an accident. He has come down wallop!'

During the summer of 1935, the prototype fighter began to take shape in the works, and hardly a day passed without Mitchell giving it a close inspection. By autumn, the airframe was approaching completion ready for the installation of the engine and so the new fighter was gradually moving towards being ready for its first flight. Since it had been built under government contract, it had RAF markings and was subject to strict security control.

During the long months of work on the F.37/34 prototype, George Pickering was a good friend to Mitchell and often helped him to forget his worries for a while. George liked his pint of beer, and if he found R.J. in a tense mood, anxious in case something should go wrong at the last moment, he would say: 'Come on, Mitch. Let's go out for a drink.' Since it was impossible to be gloomy in George's company, Mitchell temporarily forgot his worries. But there was an ominous ring about the entry in his personal diary for 31 December 1935: 'Fairly severe BA. Rather concerned re. future.'

It is not certain what 'BA' refers to; Gordon Mitchell thinks it meant either backache or bowel activity but, bearing in mind his colostomy, feels that the latter is the more likely.

By the beginning of 1936, the prototype Spitfire, bearing the serial number K5054, was nearly ready for its first test flight. Once again, Sir Robert McLean insisted that it should be called the Spitfire, a name which did not meet with general approval at Supermarine. The first plane with that name had been a failure, and no one wanted that to happen again. Mitchell is said to have said that it was, 'Bloody silly to call it by the same name as a previous failure.'

Various stories are told about the name's origin. One says that at the first firing of the eight machine guns, a mechanic standing close by was blackened by the spitting flames. But in fact it was Sir Robert McLean who first suggested it and it is believed that it first originated from Sir Robert calling his young daughter, Ann, 'a little Spitfire'!

We have seen how Mitchell never failed to stress that he was 'only one of a team', and it is fitting, therefore, as Mitchell would have wished, that due credit is given to the men who, at this period of Mitchell's career, were closely involved in the production of the Spitfire. In Appendix 12 (page 366), the names of the senior members of Mitchell's team, in or around 1936, are listed and this list includes the test pilots and senior members of the inspection department, who came directly under Mitchell. It is hoped that this table is complete but as the author has indicated, if there should be any omissions, he offers his sincere apologies.

Many other individuals, having a particular expertise, and such organisations as the Air Ministry, the RAF Martlesham Heath and the Royal Aircraft Establishment at Farnborough were all involved in various ways. Mitchell was always ready to listen and was never too proud to ask for other opinions. A good example of this was the work done at Farnborough on low-drag, ducted radiators by Dr K. Meredith. Mitchell was quick to appreciate the significance of this work and promptly adopted Meredith's designs for the Spitfire.

At that time, cooling drag was one of the major obstacles to increased speeds for fighter aircraft. The demands for engine cooling in a fighter were far more stringent than for a racing seaplane, because rapid climb to high altitudes had to be catered for, involving high power outputs at low speeds and in rarefied air. In other words, the fighters had to cope with a far wider and more stringent range of operating conditions than the Schneider seaplanes and surface cooling was obviously not practicable. Dr Meredith's experimental work at the RAE on a ducted cooling system, which had the great merit of providing some thrust and thereby significantly reducing the cooling drag, led to a major breakthrough which contributed to the ultimate performance achieved by the Spitfire and Hurricane. The radiator on the prototype Spitfire was placed under the starboard wing where it became an easily recognisable feature.

In February 1936, K5054 had its first engine runs at the Woolston factory and was then ready for its first test flight, in which the efficient management of T.C.L. Westbrook and W.T. Elliott, who were in charge of the works, played a vital role. The prototype was dismantled and transported the short distance to Eastleigh, where it was reassembled. Then, on the afternoon of 5 March 1936, two days before Hitler's troops marched into the Rhineland, it flew for the first time. Parts of the aircraft, such as the engine cowling, were, at that time, unpainted while the rest had a sort of dirty yellowish-green factory finish. The fine painting by Jim Mitchell of the first flight of the prototype Spitfire, reproduced on page 184, illustration 48, shows well the authentic finish of the aircraft at the time of its first flight.

Capt. J. 'Mutt' Summers as the Vickers chief test pilot, had the task of carrying out the first flight. Mitchell had the greatest confidence in 'Mutt' since he had very expertly carried out the first flights of a number of Mitchell's earlier aircraft. On landing, 'Mutt' said: 'I don't want anything touched,' meaning that there were no major snags which needed fixing before the next flight. Many months of testing and alterations lay ahead but a successful first flight was one large obstacle overcome.

An eyewitness account of that first flight is given by Jeffrey Quill, then assistant test pilot at Vickers Supermarine and later chief test pilot:

> As I recall it, 'Mutt' did not retract the undercarriage for the first flight on, I believe, Mitchell's instructions. The take-off run was short because the aircraft was fitted with a special fine pitch propeller specifically for the first flight. 'Mutt' took the aeroplane up to about 3,000 ft, checked the low-speed handling and then came straight back to land.

Incredibly, no records of this historic first flight of K5054 existed prior to January 2000, sixty-four years after the flight. Arthur Falcon, a former engineer at Supermarine, had taken home, when he retired in 1957, a pile of papers from his office. These were about to be burnt so Arthur decided to rescue them as souvenirs, but it was not until January 2000 that he decided to go through the papers and found amongst them a copy of 'Mutt' Summers' actual test flight report of his first four flights on K5054. This was stamped 'Supermarine Chief Designer' and dated 19 March 1936, and is reproduced as Appendix 14.

No doubt R.J. would have been very pleased with this report on the first four flights recorded of his Spitfire by the first man ever to fly one, particularly that recorded under the heading of 'Flying', but maybe not totally surprised! Of course, these four flights totalled only 112 minutes in the air and so much further work and flight testing was required following the fourth flight, firstly to deal with the suggestions made by 'Mutt' Summers and secondly to try and improve the performance and achieve the target maximum speed of 350 mph (which was successfully obtained in due course) before R.J. could be satisfied that K5054 was ready for its RAF acceptance trials.

It has already been mentioned that Rolls-Royce contributed to the cost of K5054 and it is of interest to see this figure of £7,500 duly recorded on all the expenditure statements referred to, including the one reproduced on page 182, illustration 41.

Mitchell must have been very relieved as he watched the fighter return safely to earth. As already mentioned, the section from 9 February to 7 March 1936 is missing from Mitchell's personal diary and so what he entered in it on 5 March is regrettably unknown. However, there is an entry on 10 March which reads: 'third flight of F.37/35.' Interestingly, not F.37/34, the specification under which K5054 was built. According to Andrews and Morgan,[4] F.37/35 was in fact a specification for a cannon-equipped fighter, and only a few weeks after the first flight on 5 March, Mitchell produced a Supermarine specification for a Spitfire equipped with four 20-mm cannons. It would seem that he was already in little doubt what the armament of Spitfire would have to be in the future.

The semi-unpainted condition of K5054 at the time of its first flight has already been described. About one month later, in April 1936, it was given an immaculate coating of cerulean blue paint which it retained to the end of its life on 4 September 1939, the day after war broke out, when it crash landed due to a misjudgement on the part of the pilot, Flt Lt 'Spinner' White. Sadly, he was killed and K5054 never flew again.

Throughout the summer months of 1936, Mitchell's diary constantly refers to the flying dates of the prototype, accompanied by the name of the pilot. Often in the late evenings, his 'yellow' Rolls-Royce was seen parked on the edge of Eastleigh Airport, as he sat there alone, watching the aeroplane on which he had worked so long, being put through its extensive test programme.

Shortly after the initial flight, Summers was recalled to Weybridge to work with the Wellington, designed by Rex Pierson and Barnes Wallis, and all the subsequent test flights of the Spitfire were left in the very capable hands of Jeffrey Quill and George Pickering.

Just twenty days after the first flight of the prototype, the following report appeared in the Southampton local paper, the *Southern Daily Echo*:

NEW SUPERMARINE FIGHTER
FIVE MILES A MINUTE MONOPLANE
HUSH-HUSH TRIALS AT SOTON

Keen observers in and around Southampton have recently been interested in the high-speed performances of a remarkable plane which has made occasional flights from Eastleigh Airport.

This machine is the very latest type of single-seater fighter, designed and built for the RAF by The Supermarine Aviation Works (Vickers) Ltd at their factory in Woolston.

Produced amid great secrecy, the plane is one of the fastest of its category in the world. Like all Supermarine aircraft, the new fighter was designed by Mr R.J. Mitchell, CBE, director and chief designer of the firm, who designed every British winner of the Schneider Trophy since the war [the First World War].

Even the uninitiated have realised when watching the streamlined monoplane flash across the sky at five miles a minute (300 mph) and more, that here is a plane out of the ordinary.

Mitchell allowed himself one very special celebration to mark the successful flight of the Spitfire. Although he had lived in Southampton since 1917, he had always kept in close touch with his family in Stoke-on-Trent. After his father died in 1933, and when he himself was seriously ill, he drove up to Staffordshire to satisfy himself that everything possible had been done for his mother's comfort. Now, in 1936, he felt he would like to share his success with his two brothers, so he went to Stoke-on-Trent and took Eric and Billy out to dinner in the town's best hotel. As the evening wore on, they re-lived boyhood memories, and talked of the days when they had flown model aeroplanes in the garden of Victoria Cottage.

It was amazing what a busy life Mitchell led, right up to the end of 1936. One glance at his diary shows how hard he drove himself: 'April 5 – Flew F.37/35 Pickering. Breakfast for eight at Eastleigh Hotel; April 6 – F.37/35 to RAE; April 7 – RAE with Gordon. Lunch (2).' Gordon remembers his visit to the Royal Aircraft Establishment at Farnborough. He was fifteen at the time and found it very exciting to see all that was going on there. 'May 15 – Dinner (5). Summers stayed night. £2 1s 0d; August 5 – Oyster season opens' (see Chapter 18, page 229). The following entry in Mitchell's logbook is of special interest: 'April 21 – Heinkel HE70 (R.R. Kestrel) Hucknall Sheppard.'

There was a curious interplay between Mitchell and Heinkel in Germany. The German designer had shown considerable interest in the S.5, the 1927 Schneider winner, and subsequently he created a very elegant cantilever monoplane. Rolls-Royce, keeping an eye on foreign developments, purchased one of these and powered it with their own Kestrel engine, and this was the one Mitchell was interested in looking at for possible new ideas to mull over. Another entry in his logbook on 9 May reports: '40 mins photographing F.37/35 in flight.'

Mitchell also maintained his interest in sport; he was fond of rugby football, and early in the year he took Gordon to an international match at Twickenham. Other entries in his diary refer to further outstanding events in the sporting calendar: the Grand National, golf matches, and partridge and pheasant shooting.

The prototype Spitfire eventually proved successful at Eastleigh but, before it could achieve RAF acceptance, it had to undergo RAF tests at the Aeroplane and Armament Experimental Establishment at Martlesham Heath.

An entry in Mitchell's diary for Tuesday 26 May 1936 reads: 'F.37/35 delivered to Martlesham.' A very significant day for him, giving him cause for concern whether any problems would arise at Martlesham which would jeopardise the official order, which he now had high hopes of getting from the Air Ministry. The initial testing at Martlesham is described at first hand in Appendix 2 by AM Sir Humphrey Edwardes

Jones who, as a flight lieutenant, had the responsible task of making a quick, initial assessment of the Spitfire. As will be seen, his report was fortunately very favourable and as a result Supermarine received their first order for 310 Spitfires on 3 June 1936 to the value of £1.25 million. This only three months after it had first flown – unprecedented speed of action on the part of the Air Ministry and showing unequivocally the confidence they now had in Mitchell's fighter. Nevertheless, as Sir Humphrey relates in Appendix 2, that initial test flight he made in the prototype on 26 May 1936 very nearly ended in disaster when he almost forgot to lower the undercarriage before landing! The likely dire effects both to himself and to the whole Spitfire programme if Sir Humphrey had crash landed K5054 do not bear thinking about, bearing in mind that it happened a mere eighty-two days after the prototype had first flown and a very large amount of test-flying still remained to be carried out on it. Events having potential consequences of vital importance can sometimes have their outcome hanging on a very fine thread!

This historic order was signed by Capt. Harold Balfour, the under secretary of state for air, the late Rt Hon. The Lord Balfour of Inchrye, who very generously wrote the Foreword to this book.

It is of interest that on 8 July 1936, King Edward VIII visited Martlesham on his tour of RAF stations and, as photograph 42, page 182, shows, Mitchell was present for the visit. The King spent a long time inspecting the aircraft lined up on the tarmac and, as the photograph shows, climbed up to inspect K5054's cockpit. It was one of the rare royal visits undertaken during his brief reign.

The interim performance report on the Spitfire, issued from Martlesham in July 1936, included the following data:

> True air speed at 10,000 ft, 330 mph.
> True air speed at 16,800 ft, 349 mph.
> True air speed at 30,000 ft, 324 mph.
> Climb to 15,000 ft in 5 mins 52 secs – rate of climb 2,300 ft/min.
> Climb to 20,000 ft in 8 mins 12 secs – rate of climb 1,770 ft/min.
> Climb to 30,000 ft in 17 mins 0 secs – rate of climb 680 ft/min.

Supermarine had never received such a large order. The firm were delighted but at the same time rather concerned. The design team could cope, but the works were far too small to build so many aircraft, and the only way they could fulfil the order was by subcontracting a good deal of the work. T.C.L. Westbrook had to grapple with the enormous task of getting the Spitfire into production.

At first, Supermarine built only fuselages, the remainder of the work being sub-contracted to a number of outside firms. The various components were collected and assembled in the Supermarine factory at

Eastleigh, and the finished aircraft were tested on the adjoining airfield. It was the first time that a British aircraft firm had so extensively sub-contracted and, inevitably, it led to many very serious complications when the various 'pieces' did not match up, the wings proving to be the major problem. The production of the Spitfire is described in more detail in Chapter 17.

Before the final tests were completed, the prototype Spitfire made its first public appearance at Hendon Air Display on 27 June 1936. It made a fly-past at about 4.30 p.m., but it roared across the sky so quickly that people had only a vague idea of its spectacular performance.

Later in 1936, the Spitfire returned to Martlesham Heath for final handling trials, and the detailed report summed up its performance by saying: 'The aeroplane is simple and easy to fly and has no vices.'

Sometime during the latter half of 1936, Mitchell and Camm – later Sir Sidney Camm – were summoned to attend a meeting of important Air Ministry officials to present the merits of their respective fighters, the Spitfire and the Hurricane. When Mitchell returned to Supermarine his design team gathered round, anxious to know how he had got on.

'Well, I think I've made it,' he told them. 'But while the argument was going on I couldn't help feeling that I should have done much better if I had been on the opposite side.'

What were the features in the design of the Spitfire that resulted in it being one of the greatest single-seater fighters of all time? J.D. Scott suggests that the answer lay in aerodynamic refinement and cleanness down to the slightest detail, its very advanced and efficient structure, and its low weight to power ratio. C.F. Andrews and E.B. Morgan[5] in their publication, *Supermarine Aircraft since 1914*, sum it up by saying:

> There was in fact no mystique about Mitchell's design. It was a straight-forward merger of all the technical knowledge of the time into one composite piece of machinery, including its power plant which, with the airframe, had embodied all the experience of high-speed flight gathered from the Schneider Trophy races. In the case of the Merlin and the Spitfire everything came right at the psychological moment – a rare event in aircraft and engine design.

Throughout 1936, Mitchell continued to fly, sometimes solo, at other times in one of the Supermarine flying boats or the Walrus with George Pickering. On 2 November his logbook records: 'Pickering, Supermarine Walrus Amphibian. Take off and landing tests over Southampton Water.'

However, Mitchell's health was not improving and 28 November marks the last entry in his logbook:

'Gipsy I, Southampton Airport, 30 min. solo.'

Nevertheless, as the following report in the local *Southern Daily Echo* of 12 December 1936 shows, Mitchell was still feeling sufficiently well to attend what could have been a somewhat exhausting social occasion for even the fittest of men:

> The fifth annual dinner and dance of The Supermarine Aviation Works (Vickers) Ltd was held last night. Heads of the firm with their ladies, and a large number of guests were entertained to dinner at the South Western Hotel by Sir Robert McLean, chairman of the company and his co-directors, Sqn Cdr James Bird, OBE, RN (Ret'd), and Mr R.J. Mitchell, CBE, who was accompanied by Mrs Mitchell. Lt Col. J.B. Neilson, CMG, DSO, deputy chairman of Vickers Ltd and Mrs Neilson, were also present.
>
> After the dinner, the entire company went to the Royal Pier Pavilion, where the works dance was in progress, and joined in the revels there.
>
> Mr T.C.L. Westbrook, general manager of the Supermarine works, was responsible for the general organisation of the dinner and dance.

In the description that followed of the aircraft under production at Supermarine, it is interesting that their latest product, the Spitfire, is described as the fastest single-seater fighter in the world. This shows that the press had decided that this was the case, in the same year that the Spitfire first flew, in spite of the 'atmosphere of secrecy' surrounding Supermarine mentioned earlier in the report!

Mitchell was not an easy man to understand. His colleagues at Supermarine saw him as a down-to-earth, practical engineer with an intuitive eye for a good aerodynamic shape. He was also a great thinker, with a sensitivity disguised by outbursts of rage and impish pranks. He cared deeply for the welfare of his country. Perhaps his greatest asset was his ability to inspire affection, which made him a great leader in every sense of the word.

He had a great kindness of heart, and often helped people in trouble. Some time after Mitchell's death his youngest brother, Billy, spoke to the press:

> Reg was always generous. If he got something, he liked to share it with others. He once gave me a car which had cost him £100. It was the first I had ever had, and I was very proud of it.

By the end of 1936, preliminary work on the production of the Spitfire had started but, meanwhile, the only person who really knew and understood the difficulties under which Mitchell had had to work was his wife, Florence. During the Battle of Britain, when the Spitfire first attracted widespread public attention, a reporter tracked her down to Dorset, where she was staying. He described her as a 'quiet, brown-eyed, smiling lady', and she agreed to talk about her husband's work on the Schneider seaplanes and the Spitfire:

> In those days we lived aeroplanes. There were always people from Supermarine or pilots in our Southampton house, talking about their aircraft and the speeds at which they could fly, and they often sat up into the early hours of the morning. Sometimes my husband would ring me up at nine o'clock at night from work and apologise for being late for dinner!

'Was your husband excited when his designs took to the air?' she was asked. 'He was more worried than excited,' she explained.

> You see, George Pickering, Jeffrey Quill, 'Mutt' Summers and all the Schneider pilots were his friends. He was just relieved when they landed safely because he could not bear to think that they might be killed or injured flying his planes.

Mrs Mitchell described her husband as a square-jawed, quiet, strongly built man:

> He'd be talking to you one moment, and then the next minute he'd be miles away, and you knew he'd thought up something new. He loved snooker, but even in the middle of a game he'd suddenly put down his cue and out would come an old envelope or a scrap of paper and, as he began to draw, he would give me a rapid explanation of the diagrams he was making.

Many people outside the world of aviation think that the Spitfire was the last aircraft that Mitchell designed but this was not so. The Spitfire was indeed the last plane he designed that was built and flown, but, when the major design work on the Spitfire was completed, he gave his attention more and more to a very different project. The Air Staff had issued, in early 1936, Specification B.12/36 for a four-engined bomber. Tenders for this were in due course submitted by Weybridge, Supermarine and Shorts. As Weybridge were more experienced in building large aircraft of this type, it came as a great surprise to many people when the Weybridge submission was rejected and contracts awarded to Supermarine and Shorts, the latter to produce eventually the Short Stirling bomber of Second World War fame.

There were no doubt a number of good reasons for the decision to reject the Weybridge tender and accept Supermarine's but one could well have been the high standing Mitchell now had as an aircraft designer par excellence.

Be that as it may, Mitchell and his team got down to the job of producing a design which would satisfy the B.12/36 Specifications and ideally improve upon them. The result was a very advanced design incorporating a number of novel features, many of which have since become commonplace. It was a single-spar, mid-wing monoplane, with a swept back leading edge and a straight trailing edge. There was a choice of engines, Rolls-Royce Merlin, Bristol Hercules or Napier Dagger. The main fuel supply was carried in wing leading-edge tanks which were part of the structure. It carried three gun turrets, the one situated amidships being retractable.

It had an estimated all-up weight of 55,000 lb, a maximum speed of 360 mph – well in advance of the 275 mph of the Lancaster which did not come into service until 1942 – a maximum bomb-carrying capacity of over 21,000 lb, and a range of 3,000 miles, carrying 8,000 lb of bombs, all in the wings. If it had matched the estimates and had gone into production, it could have given Britain a bomber far in advance of anything else then available and it could, moreover, have come into service before the Lancaster was ready. It is interesting to reflect that this bomber would have been faster than the prototype Spitfire and hence, of course, faster than the contemporary German fighters.

The first entry in Mitchell's diary for 1937 is: 'January 7 – Heard the news re. B.12/36.'

His design was accepted by the Air Ministry which authorised the building of two prototypes but, in the event, this did not commence until some time after Mitchell's death. Some delay was inevitable because of Supermarine's vast (for them) programmes of Spitfire and Walrus production but eventually work did begin on building two fuselages.

They were nearing completion when, in September 1940, they were both completely destroyed by a German bombing raid over the Woolston factory.

So Mitchell's final design was destined never to fly and his last memorial must be his elegant and highly effective aerodynamic masterpiece, the Spitfire, but an impression by the artist, Cliff Machin, of how the B.12/36 bomber would have looked if it had been built is reproduced as illustration 46, page 184. It bears every indication of being just as elegant, and beautiful to the eye, as the Spitfire.

Before moving to the final chapter in Mitchell's life, it is appropriate to be reminded of what Joe Smith, a long-standing and senior colleague of Mitchell at Supermarine, said when he presented the Royal Aeronautical Society's 1st Mitchell Memorial Lecture on 21 January 1954 to a large invited audience.[6] This included many of Mitchell's former colleagues and pilots, representatives from the RAF and Navy, and from many aircraft companies, chief designers, representatives from Southampton City Council, and many of Mitchell's close friends and relatives, including his son, Gordon. The president of the Royal Aeronautical Society, Sir William Farren, took the chair:

He was known as 'R.J.' to everyone from the lowest to the highest, and the fact that he accepted this nickname is one illustration of his friendliness and absence of false dignity. I shall call him R.J. from now on, because that is how I think of him. He was a well-built man, pleasant faced, of medium height and fair colouring, with a very determined chin. He possessed great charm, an engaging smile which was often in evidence and which transformed his habitual expression of concentration, He was rather shy with strangers, although preserving an outwardly easy manner, and only when one came to know him well did his chief characteristics become evident. Foremost among these characteristics was a clear thinking ability to create, which made him a designer in the truest sense of the word. This creative ability was the driving force of his life and, as we shall see, resulted in a tremendous output of new types of aircraft in an incredibly short span of years. Thinking back, I have realised that no other man in my experience has produced anything like the number of new and practical fundamental ideas that he did during his relatively short span of working life. The wholehearted and continuous application of this genius was an inspiration to all who worked with him.

The next most important characteristic of the man was his notable capacity for leadership. He never shirked full responsibility, and his technical integrity was unquestioned. He won the complete respect and the confidence of his staff, in whom he created a continuous sense of achievement. He placed himself firmly at the helm, and having made decisions, expected and obtained the full co-operation of all concerned. But, in spite of being the unquestioned leader, he was always ready to listen to and consider another point of view, or to modify his ideas to meet any technical criticism which he thought justified. He was always open-minded and took a great interest in aeronautical developments. The effect of this attitude on the team of young and keen engineers which he collected around him can well be imagined, especially as he was kindly and approachable and took a lively and sympathetic interest in the personal problems of those with whom he worked. He was, well, just R.J.

As a person, R.J. was a modest man who hated publicity and shunned public occasions. He was a shrewd assessor of other men and often showed great restraint in dealing with strangers, with whose point of view he disagreed. He had a good sense of humour, or perhaps I should say, of fun, and a capacity to relax completely. If you were away on a business visit with him and the day's work was over, there was always the possibility of some prank developing. He was literally the life and soul of the party on such occasions as the annual drawing office dinner, when with no thought of dignity he became the ringleader in any sort of fun and games, usually aided and abetted by the firm's test pilots. He smoked a pipe, with the aid of a plentiful supply of matches, and was keen on sport. He played tennis, and later, golf, not in order to excel, but as a relaxation, and he was a good loser. He was also fond of a game of snooker and took up sailing as a hobby in later years.

It has been said that he would break off from his social activities to make sketches of aeroplanes on the backs of old envelopes, and that one minute he would be talking, and the next would be 'miles away' in the throes of a problem. Be that as it may, it is certain that his work was never far from his mind and I can remember many occasions when he arrived at the office with the complete solution of a particularly knotty problem which had baffled us all the night before.

Sir Henry Royce summed up R.J. as 'a man slow to decide and quick to act', and I feel that this is the keynote of the way he worked. A mental picture which always springs to my mind when remembering him is R.J. leaning over a drawing, chin in hand, thinking hard. A great deal of his working life was spent in this attitude, and the results of this thinking made his reputation. His genius undoubtedly lay in his ability not only to appreciate clearly the ideal solution to a given problem, but also the difficulties and, by careful consideration, to arrive at an efficient compromise.

One result of his habit of deep concentration was that he naturally objected to having his train of thought interrupted. His staff soon learned that life became easier if they avoided such interruption. I have often wondered how I could manage to apply a similar ban to my present staff! If you went into his office and found that you could only see R.J.'s back bending over a drawing, you took a hasty look at the back of his neck. If this was normal, you waited for him to speak, but if it rapidly became red, you beat a hasty retreat! In more serious vein, R.J. was an essentially friendly person, and normally even-tempered, and although he occasionally let rip with us when he was dissatisfied with our work, the storms were of short duration and forgotten by him almost immediately – provided you put the job right!

Another very human aspect of the man, which soon became known to his staff, concerned his state of mind during flight trials of a prototype. One did not indulge in silly chatter in light-hearted manner on such occasions. He was always worried for the safety of his pilots and although he witnessed the first flights of so many aircraft, he never grew accustomed to it. During such periods as the testing of Schneider trophy machines, he was in a continual state of tension lest a pilot be injured or killed, and felt that he carried a personal responsibility in the matter...

When in the throes of a new design, the arrangement of which had been decided, he would spend almost all his time in the drawing office on the various boards. Here he would argue out the details with the draughtsmen concerned, and show a complete grasp of the whole aircraft. It is appreciated that such a method could only be used with the type of aircraft then being built but it illustrates the practical outlook of the man.

Construction of the machine having begun, he would spend some time each day examining and assessing the result. If he was not satisfied with the way something had turned out, he would go back to the drawing office and, having discussed the matter with the people concerned, either modify it or leave it, as the case might be. And always the practical aspects of the proposed alterations would be borne in mind in relation to the state of the aircraft, and the ability of the works to make the change.

Finally, in this attempt to show you Mitchell the man, I turn to his magnificent courage. In the whole range of human emotions there can be nothing as terrible as the realisation that an incurable disease makes one's death inevitable within a short space of time. To have the courage to face such a tragic fate unflinchingly must be the hope of everyone, adding a fervent prayer that it may never happen to them. It did happen to Mitchell, and I can personally vouch for the fact that he behaved in a way which was beyond praise. To talk to him during this period was to see the highest form of courage, and the memory must always remain an inspiration...

The most outstanding feature of R.J.'s technical achievements is the number of aircraft which he designed in the sixteen years between 1920, when he became chief designer, and 1936, when his last illness began. There were twenty-four different types, rangeing through bombers, flying boats, amphibians, racing seaplanes, fighters and even light aeroplanes. The amazing diversity of this work is no less remarkable than its amount.

Sadly, Joe Smith died only two years after giving this excellent lecture, at the age of fifty-eight, also from cancer.

These aircraft that Mitchell designed have been described and discussed in the present, and in the previous twelve chapters, reflecting as far as possible how they were seen through the eyes of Mitchell himself. It is now time to turn to the sad, but inspiring, story of his death.

14

Mitchell's Death

Each year, as August came round – the month of his operation in 1933 – he made a note in his diary. Thus, on 15 August 1936, there is the entry: 'three years on.' He knew that if he lived about four years without the cancer recurring, his chances of living to a good age would be increased many times.

All through the second half of 1936, while Supermarine and the sub-contractors were busy preparing for the building of the first Spitfires, Mitchell grudged every moment that took him away from his bomber design. It was this overpowering urge that drove him to work, in spite of the severe bouts of pain which began to occur more frequently through autumn 1936. Day after day Mitchell continued to go in to work, only remaining at home when the discomfort became too severe, and in spite of everything he continued to hope.

But at last, in February 1937, he was forced to give in. The fact that his cancer had returned could no longer be hidden. Mitchell faced the last challenge with the same courage that he had shown throughout his career. His main concern was that his affairs should be left in order, to help his wife and son. Gordon was now at the age when he wanted to leave school, and his father was anxious to help him choose the right career. In a letter written early in February he suggested an engineering apprenticeship with Rolls-Royce:

Hazeldene,
Russell Place,
Southampton.
10 February 1937

My dear Gordon,

   I am enclosing correspondence with Rolls-Royce. It seems that this
part of the story is fixed up satisfactorily – do you think? They seem very
keen on keeping you longer than two years. I asked Hives if this could be
left in abeyance, then you can make up your mind in the dim and distant
future. He seems to agree.

   Your housemaster has written quite a nice letter suggesting you are leaving too early, and that you would be better going to Cambridge straight
from school. The more I think about it the surer I feel that you are doing
the right thing. It is probably OK for boys who wish to be high-brows
on the academic side – schoolmasters and such like. I really think you
are more suited to the practical side – you notice they give complete
instruction for BSc at Derby Technical.

   Well, big boy, I don't feel too good. I have been in bed for about a week,
and feel rather sorry for myself. I hope I shall be better soon. Pick [Dr
Picken] comes to see me twice a day, so you see he is quite matey.

   Cheerio Gordon,

All the best,
Yours affectionately,
Dad.

Towards the end of February, Mitchell went into a London hospital. He
still hoped that a second operation might be effective, but when all the
tests had been carried out he was told that there was no hope, and that
at best he had only four or five months to live. He wrote to Gordon
from the hospital in a letter dated 21 February 1937:

My dear Gordon,

   Thank you so much for your nice long interesting letter. You seem to
have done very well with your shooting. Mr Gabriel (the surgeon I had
before) came back from holiday and saw me this morning, and is coming
again on Monday night. He seems to think I may have appendicitis (that
is easy, they soon get through with that).

   Mum has been in London, and today we went to the Trocadero for
lunch and then to the pictures on Saturday.

   Cheerio, big boy and don't you get the 'flu!

Yours affectionately,
Dad.

Mitchell returned home to 'Hazeldene' knowing that his days were numbered. He had accepted the highest medical opinion in England that there was nothing more they could do for him.

'They think the end will probably be about June,' he told a visitor. 'Until June,' he mused, ignoring the murmurs of sympathy. 'I – who have so much to do – have only until June.'

Mitchell wanted to live, but since the doctor's verdict, he was quite prepared to die, and seldom has any man accepted his cruel fate with such coolness and courage. He could no longer go to work, but he received visits from members of his design team who wanted to discuss technical problems. Miss Cross was a regular visitor, and she dealt with his official correspondence, but all the letters to Gordon, and others on personal matters, were written in Mitchell's own hand, which remained firm and clear to the very end. Another letter to Gordon in early March showed how cheerfully he tried to hide his suffering.

Hazeldene,
Russell Place,
Southampton.
10 March 1937

My dear Gordon,

I am sending this letter with your chicken and orange squash. I hope you find the chicken up to standard.

Very many thanks for your letter. We were very pleased to hear from you to know that you had arrived safely.

To answer your questions, Gordon. Yes, I think it would be a good plan to stay another term, especially as you say you would like to, and as our arrangements have been rather messed about by my inconsiderate behaviour.

I hope the evacuant worked OK, big boy!

About your visit next weekend, Gordon, I really don't know what to say. You know how delighted I should be to see you, and yet I suppose there is a limit to these things. So far we have been perfectly justified in what we have done, as at one time I was very, very ill. I tell you what, we will ring you up on Friday evening and then decide whether to ask you to come or not.

I am feeling better since you left, Gordon. I get up for half an hour each day, and may go downstairs this weekend.

It is snowing heavily this morning and the lawn is covered already – be able to make your snowman if you come down.

Mum joins me in love to you, Gordon.

Yours affectionately,
Dad.

By this time Gordon had been told of the serious nature of his father's illness, and he was allowed time off from school to go home at weekends. Mitchell was now so weak that he had difficulty in getting out of bed, and yet he could write cheerfully about making a snowman. It was typical of his character, always thinking of others rather than himself.

As the days passed, Mitchell continued to give a great deal of thought to arranging his affairs, in order to make things as easy as possible for his wife. He made his will, and then wrote to his solicitor in Stoke-on-Trent just to make sure that everything was legally correct.

Hazeldene,
Russell Place,
Southampton.
20 March 1937

Dear Mr Breaton,

I am writing to you with regard to my will, a copy of which was sent to you a few days ago.

I have read with considerable interest your letter, and have given the points you raised very careful consideration. I have decided not to alter this will with its terms and provision and also not to have a third trustee. I thoroughly realise the soundness of your advice and your reasons for putting this forward, but I think in this particular instance I have very great confidence in my wife and son so I feel quite safe in leaving matters as they stand. I have already discussed this very fully with my wife, and to a certain extent with Gordon, as I have now told him that there is a very good chance that I shall not get better. I have explained to him, to the best of my ability, the various points.

I feel quite confident that he will respect these all his life, and will act accordingly.

It must be remembered that I am leaving my wife and boy at a time when heavy expenses will be incurred, and there will be no income whatever except from the capital that I leave them. I have made a verbal understanding – I might perhaps put it in writing – that both my wife and son will always, to the very best of their ability, see that my mother is never short of anything she requires throughout the rest of her life.

Is the will, a copy of which has been sent to you, properly and efficiently drawn up? Or, what I mean is, is the wording of the will such that it definitely indicates my intentions, and leaves no ground for any further indecisions or actions of any sorts? I am afraid I have expressed myself very badly in this, but no doubt you will understand what I am driving at.

Do you think there is anything at all which I have overlooked, and which should be given attention? Your advice upon these matters will be very greatly appreciated. With many thanks and kind regards.

Yours sincerely, R.J. Mitchell

By March, news of the serious nature of Mitchell's illness had reached the Air Ministry, and the Chief of the Air Staff sent a letter paying tribute to his great work. There were very many other letters, and to all of them Mitchell sent a personal reply, but what really pleased him was the recognition of his work and the hopes expressed that – even after his death – the production of the B.12/36 bomber would go ahead. A very small sample of these letters and Mitchell's replies follows.

Letter from ACM Sir Edward Ellington, GCB, CMG, CBE:

Chief of the Air Staff,
Air Ministry,
Adastral House,
Kngsway, WCR.
16 March 1937

Dear Mitchell,

This is to say how extremely sorry I am to hear of your serious illness. I think I have never told you before how much your great services to the RAF and aviation as a whole are valued. I am fully aware, as are all the other members of the Air Council, of the unsparing manner in which you have devoted your great abilities to the task of design, and I wish you to realise that however incomplete you may feel your work to be at the present time, we know that you have always given us of your best. More especially I should like to recall how your success with the Schneider machines placed British aeroplane design at the top of the world.

Yours sincerely, Ellington.

Mitchell's reply:

Hazeldene,
Russell Place,
Southampton
20 March 1937

Dear Sir Edward Ellington,

I wish to acknowledge with many thanks your letter of the 16th instant. I cannot tell you how grateful I am to receive a letter of this nature from you and how happy it has made me feel that my efforts in the past in connection with the RAF machines have been so appreciated. I always got very great pleasure from working with the personnel of the Air Ministry and the RAF, and any success which I have achieved is due to a very large extent to the friendly, healthy co-operation which I feel has always existed. Your letter has made me feel very happy. Very many thanks.

Sincerely yours, R.J. Mitchell

A letter from AM Sir Wilfred Freeman, the air member for research and development, was written in his own hand:

Air Ministry,
Savoy Hill,
WC2
16 March 1937

Dear Mitchell,

I have had it in mind for some time to write to you but felt that you did not wish to be worried with letters.

You must not worry yourself with thinking that you have let us down – you have never done that, and I hope that your B.12/36 will be a great success, and as good as ever you could wish.

I can assure you that your illness has been a blow to the whole department – but the blow is not because you cannot get on with this aeroplane, it is only our grief at the illness of a personal and greatly respected friend.

Yours sincerely,
Wilfred Freeman.

Mitchell's reply:

Hazeldene,
Russell Place,
Southampton
20 March 1937

Dear Air Marshal Freeman,

I was delighted to receive your letter of the 16th instant. It is extremely
kind of you to write to me in this way. I must admit that I have been rather
worried that circumstances have arisen which will prevent me from taking
very much further interest in the B.12/36. I have always been very enthusiastic
about the design. I have felt that my enthusiasm had quite a lot to do with
your decision to place an order. I am very pleased to be able to say that I have
always trained my staff to be thoroughly up to date with all new ideas and
proposals being carried out at Supermarine. I feel very confident that they
will be able to carry on without me, with complete success, particularly as
the close co-operation of the Weybridge staff has always been available. I shall
always feel extremely grateful to you for the friendly sentiments expressed in
your letter. I now feel very much happier about everything.

Yours sincerely, R.J. Mitchell

Some of the letters came from close friends in the RAF, and one was
from H.M. Garner, stationed at Felixstowe:

Felixstowe,
19 March 1937

Dear Mitch,

I was terribly sorry to hear you were ill with the old trouble and
hope you will make the same great recovery as you did before. The best
of luck.

Now that you have deserted flying boats, we do not see so much of your
products, but I see and hear of the Spitfire occasionally, and it seems to be
getting on very well, although you seem to have had the usual production
difficulties. I went to the last Paris Air Show, and found the French have
nothing in the same street as the Spitfire.

What do you think of the international situation? I am one of the
optimists who thinks that the present building up of armaments may lead
us all into seeing how silly it all is. Then we shall stop making military
aeroplanes and turn to civil aeroplanes. How is Gordon getting on? He
must be almost grown up now. Is he going to become a great aeroplane
designer, or are his interests in another direction? Our son Clifford is at

Westminster and doing well and enjoying life. He is very fortunate in being able next term to attend the Coronation ceremony [of George VI] in the Abbey — all the Kings scholars attend.

I suppose you are having the same sort of weather we have had. This has been the worst winter on record. Well, once more the best of luck.

With kindest regards to Mrs Mitchell,

Yours sincerely,

H.M. Garner.

Mitchell's reply:

Hazeldene,
Russell Place,
Southampton
20 March 1937

Dear Garner,

Many thanks for your letter of the 19th instant. I am sorry to say that the medical profession have me in their clutches again, and I propose to leave the aeronautical part of your letter for attention at a later date. I am very pleased to hear that your son is getting on so well at school, and hope he will enjoy his visit to the Coronation.

I have seen quite a lot of my boy this last week or two, as he has been allowed to come over at the weekends to see me.

With kind regards to Mrs Garner and yourself,

Yours sincerely,
Mitch.

After twenty years of happy married life, Mitchell and his wife, Flo, faced the separation which now seemed inevitable. The British doctors had said there was no hope, and Mitchell had arranged his affairs, leaving no loose ends for those left behind to clear up. During his long illness his wife had always been close beside him, visiting him in hospital and sharing the weeks of convalescence at the seaside after his operation in 1933. She faced the ordeal bravely, and endeavoured to hide her own sorrow as she tried to match her courage with his. But it was hard just to sit and wait, without being able to help.

March was moving into April, and already the spring flowers were blooming in the 'Hazeldene' garden, when Mrs Mitchell turned to her husband one day and said: 'There must be something more we can do.'

Sitting beside her, Mitchell suggested an idea that he had been turning over in his mind for some time.

1 R.J. Mitchell in formal attire on the occasion of the presentation to him of the CBE in the 1932 New Year Honours

Above: 2 41 Squadron Mk XII Spitfires with 1735 hp Rolls-Royce Griffon engines

Right: 3 The Old Genius – bust of R.J. Mitchell by James Butler R.A., commissioned by the Royal Air Force Club, London. February 2002 (see Item 47)

Above left: 4 Gordon at one year of age

Above right: 5 Gordon today

6. R.J. Mitchell the amateur artist – a hunting scene painted in 1916

Clockwise from top: 7 R.J. with his two sisters and a brother, at their parents' house in Hanley, Stoke-on-Trent. Left to right: Eric, Doris, R.J., Hilda and Hilda's husband, Bert

8 R.J. Mitchell on his wedding day in 1918

9 Mrs R.J. Mitchell (*née* Florence Dayson), in 1942

Left: 10 Picture taken shortly after R.J. Mitchell joined Supermarine. Left to right: Henri Biard, R.J. Mitchell, *et al.*

Below: 11 Sea Lion II, the victorious 1922 entry. From the left: Hubert Scott-Paine, Henri Biard, R.J. Mitchell, H. Victor Scott-Paine (Hubert's half-brother)

12 The Schneider Trophy

Right: 13 HRH The Prince of Wales with members of the Supermarine management (R.J. Mitchell to the right of the prince), with the Swan flying boat

Below: 14 The Sparrow light aircraft at Eastleigh. R.J. Mitchell and A. Shirvall on extreme right

15 The S.4 shortly before the accident in which Biard was lucky to escape with his life. The naval officer second from the left is believed to be Lord Mountbatten

16 R.J. Mitchell (fifth from left) and Biard (third from right), *et al.* with the S.4

Above: 17 Henri Biard, R.J. Mitchell, Henry Follard and Hubert Broad on SS *Minnewaska* on their way to the USA for the 1925 Schneider Trophy Race

Left: 18 Southampton flying boat on the Far East Flight flying over India between Akyab and Rangoon on 6 February 1928

SUPERMARINE NAPIER S. 5.

SUPERMARINE STAFF
Schneider Cup Victory Dinner
at the
BAROVA RESTAURANT, DECEMBER 20TH, 1927

MENU

GRAPE FRUIT

CLEAR SOUP
PEA SOUP

FILLET OF SOLE, WHITE WINE SAUCE

ROAST TURKEY
BRUSSELS SPROUTS, RISSOLEE POTATOES

PEACH MELBA
WAFERS

COFFEE

Burgundy
Sauterne
Spirits
Ale
Minerals

Above: 19 The S.5 Schneider Trophy seaplane at Calshot

Left: 20 Menu of the Supermarine staff's Schneider Cup Victory Dinner, 1927

21 The S.5 with R.J. Mitchell and members of the 1927 High Speed Flight

Clockwise from top left: 22 Eva (Mrs Elliss), Mrs Mitchell's maid

23 The second Rolls-Royce car owned by Mitchell

24 R.J. Mitchell enjoying a contemplative pipe in the garden of 'Hazeldene'

Above: 25 Spitfire being re-armed under monsoon conditions in Burma

Left: 26 R.J. Mitchell and Sir Henry Royce at Calshot in 1929

Below: 27 R.J. Mitchell with Sqn Ldr Orlebar at Calshot in 1929

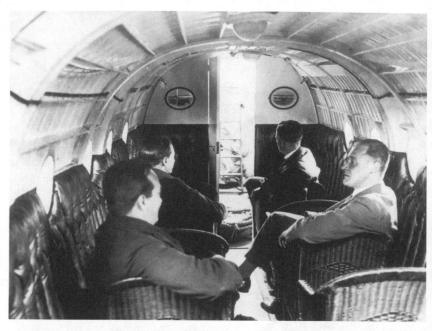

Clockwise from top: 28 R.J. Mitchell and colleagues in the cabin of a flying boat

29 R.J. relaxing on a picnic with Mrs Mitchell and his beloved 1932 Rolls-Royce car

30 Newly built S.6 N247 at the Supermarine factory. It was in N247 that Waghorn won the 1929 Schneider Trophy Race. The eight-year-old boy in the back of the rowing boat is the author, and the man in the trilby hat near the front of the group is his father, R.J. Mitchell

Clockwise from top left: 31 The S.6B

32 R.J. Mitchell with Lady Houston at Calshot

33 R.J. Mitchell with the 1931 Schneider Trophy pilots at Calshot. On extreme right is Lt Brinton who was sadly killed shortly afterwards. Stainforth is on R.J.'s right

Above: 34 The 1931 Schneider Trophy RAF High Speed Flight with Lady Houston, on her yacht, *Liberty*, 1931. R.J. Mitchell on the right standing

Above: 35 Schneider Trophy Dinner given by the mayor of Southampton, Councillor Cross, in honour of R.J. Mitchell at the South Western Hotel on 7 October 1931. From the left: R.J. Mitchell, Councillor Cross, Mrs R.J. Mitchell

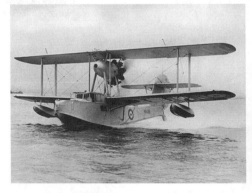

Right: 36 Supermarine Walrus during take-off. This aircraft gave sterling service in the Navy and the RAF during the 1939–45 war

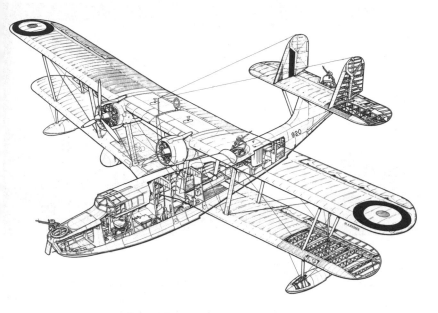

Above: 37 Fine cutaway drawing of a Stranraer flying boat by M.A. Barnes

Left: 38 Lady McLean (wife of the chairman of Vickers Aviation and Supermarine) with Mrs R.J. Mitchell on holiday in Austria, *c.*1934

39 R.J. Mitchell's pilot's licence

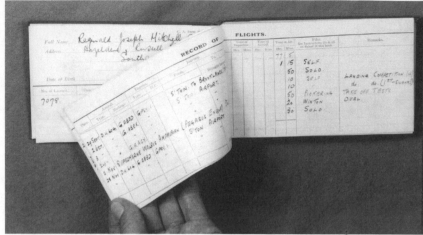

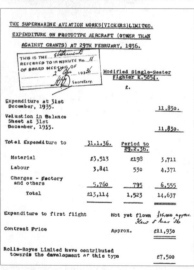

Above: 40 R.J. Mitchell's logbook

Left: 41 Statement of expenditure on K5054 at 29 February 1936. See note 'Flew 5 Mar '36' at lower right. Entry following 'Not yet flown' is '£15,000 approx.' The original document is now lodged in the Vickers Archives at the Cambridge University Library

Below: 42 HM King Edward VIII inspects the prototype Spitfire at Martlesham. R.J. Mitchell is standing next to the propeller

Left: 43 The prototype Spitfire K5054 at Eastleigh, 11 May 1936

Below: 44 The prototype Spitfire

Below: 45 After the first flight of K5054. From the left: 'Mutt' Summers, 'Agony' Payn, R.J.Mitchell, S. Scott-Hall, Jeffrey Quill

Above: 46 Artist's impression of Mitchell's last design – the B.12/36 four-engined bomber

Right: 47 Pass for R.J. Mitchell to enter the Royal Aircraft Establishment, the Aeroplane and Armament Experimental Establishment, and the Marine Aircraft Experimental Establishment

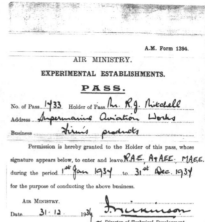

48 First flight of the prototype Spitfire K5054, painted by Jim Mitchell, R.J.'s nephew

Top: 49 Mitchell embarking for Vienna, 29 April 1937, assisted by Mr Gingell from Supermarine

Above left: 50 A few of the floral tributes

Above right: 51 R.J. with his wife in their garden, shortly before his death

Clockwise from top left: 52 Three Battle of Britain Mk I Spitfires from 19 Squadron, Duxford

53 Two 610 Squadron Mk Ia Spitfires. This photograph is one of the few available of Spitfires in action during the Battle of Britain

54 A Spitfire Mk IXc of the 306 (Polish) Squadron

Right: 55 Clipped wing Mk XII Spitfire with Griffon VI engine. Primarily used in low-altitude operations

Below left: 56 Spitfire Mk IXc. On 26 April 1944, Spitfires flew into Germany for the first time

Below right: 57 241 Squadron Mk IXc Spitfires with Rolls-Royce 1710 hp Merlin 63A engines passing Mount Vesuvius following a sortie south of Rome

Right: 58 The Supermarine works at Woolston after the German bombing raids, 26 September 1940

Right: 59 One of the three Mk I Spitfires (serial number R7058) donated by the city of Southampton

Above: 60 Gordon's prep. school Fathers' Cricket Team. R.J. Mitchell is sixth from left and the headmaster is on the extreme right

Left: 61 R.J. Mitchell convalesces in Bournemouth after his operation in 1933, accompanied by his wife and a nurse

Left: 62 The prototype Spitfire at Eastleigh. R.J. Mitchell poses for a photograph by his son, Gordon, taken on 8 March 1936, three days after the first flight of the prototype

Middle: 63 The matching shot of Gordon taken on the same occasion by his father

Above left: 64 Mitchell with Instructor Dudley in a Gipsy Moth, c.1934

Above right: 65 19 Squadron Spitfire Mk Ia being re-armed at Duxford in early October 1940

Left: 66 *Pride of the West Country* – one of several excellent Spitfire paintings by Mark Postlethwaite. This one depicts Spitfire Mk Vc AR 501 flying over the Westland Aircraft factory in Yeovil. It is currently owned by the Shuttleworth Trust and is regularly flown by them

Below: 67 Gordon with his his family standing by the statue of his father in the Science Museum in London. From the left: Penny, Adrian, Nicky, David, Gordon and Emma

Left: 68 Gordon unveiling the English Heritage plaque on his father's house in Southampton

Above: 69 Gordon's wife, Alison, who did so much to help him in the earlier editions of this book but who sadly died on 30 April 2005 after a long illness. (Photograph taken August 2002)

'I have been told that there is a man in Vienna, Professor Freund, who is one of the greatest cancer specialists in the world. If you will come with me, I will go and see him.'

'Of course I will come with you. When can we go?'

The invaluable Miss Cross handled all the necessary arrangements. She contacted Mr F. Pearson, director of the Cancer Clinic in Vienna, and when a date had been fixed she hired a private aeroplane to fly Mitchell, his wife and the nurse, Miss Jones, from Eastleigh Airport to Vienna. They departed for Vienna on 29 April 1937.

Before he left, Mitchell had paid his last visit to the Supermarine works, where he stood for a few moments in his office at the top of the new administrative block. He gazed out of the wide windows overlooking the River Itchen and thought over what might have been. Then he spoke to each member of his design team, and in saying goodbye he thanked them for all the work they had done for him over the years. His last words were to Miss Cross: 'I shall never come back to this office.'

In the clinic, Mitchell was given the most advanced treatment for cancer, and he and his wife desperately hoped for a last-minute cure. A letter written to Gordon at this time shows that his concern that his son should find a suitable career was still very much in his mind in spite of his other overwhelming problems.

Wien.
17 May 1937

My dear Gordon,

At last I am writing to you. I have read all your letters with great interest. You seem to have been very busy in Southampton during the Coronation. Do you remember

(a) Is that special iris (pink) in bloom and was it very good?

(b) How are the tom-tits progressing? Have they laid yet?

I shall leave Mum to answer your letters, except to say that I shall be very non-committal at this stage about my treatment. It is early days yet. I think I feel a little benefit. Now Gordon, your housemaster has written about you and your time at school. I have just answered him and so that you will know everything, I enclose an extract from my letter. Try to find out if you are on the right subjects for accountancy. Do you still favour it? I am trying to get more information about it through Gen. Caddell.[7] I will say cheerio as mum wishes to add a few lines.

Yours affectionately,
Dad.

Extract from Mitchell's letter to Gordon's housemaster:

You may take it as quite definite that we should like Gordon to stay at school for at least one more term after the present term, and I trust you will make the necessary arrangements. The question of Gordon studying to become a chartered accountant has recently arisen, but nothing definite has yet been decided. At present I am trying to find out if the big London firms of accountants prefer to take their articled pupils direct from school, at what age and at what stage of education, or if they take them from Cambridge. Any information you can give me at this stage will be very gratefully accepted. Gordon is trying to see the careers master on this subject.

These letters of 17 May that Mitchell sent to Gordon and to his house-master were written a mere twenty-five days before he died, knowing in his heart that he had not much longer to live. While Mitchell was in Vienna, he wrote to Vickers concerning his financial situation, and in reply he received a letter from Cdr Sir Charles Craven, chairman of The Supermarine Aviation Works (Vickers) Ltd, and chairman and managing director of Vickers-Armstrongs Ltd:

Vickers House, Broadway,
Westminster, London.
25 May 1937

Dear Mr Mitchell,

Mr Jamieson[8] showed me your letter of 2 May, and I am so pleased to know that the financial arrangements we had made for you have given you satisfaction. I do hope that this at any rate will let you know that we have very sincere sympathy with you in your serious illness, and that we do wish to put your mind at ease for the future.

Your letter sounds most hopeful, and all I can say is that I do sincerely hope that the Viennese doctors will be right, and that I shall soon hear good news of you.

With every good wish,

Yours sincerely,
Charles Craven.

He added a postscript in his own handwriting: 'I want you to feel that if I can help in any human way I should like to.'

The days in the Vienna Clinic passed slowly, and hope began to fade. The disease had gone too far and the doctors could not save him. At the end of nearly five weeks' intensive treatment, the cancer specialist told Mitchell that nothing more could be done for him.

He accepted the verdict calmly, merely saying: 'Then I will go back to England.'

All his work had been done for Britain, and he did not want to die in a foreign country. Once again a private aeroplane was hired, and on 25 May 1937, Mitchell, his wife and Miss Jones made the homeward journey back to Eastleigh Airport, where they were met by Miss Cross with a car.

Mitchell was very weak and had some difficulty in walking, so when the aircraft landed a problem arose about transferring him from the aircraft to the waiting car. Miss Cross took command of the situation and, sending Mrs Mitchell away and the nurse on an errand, she said: 'Leave it to me. He will never let me see that he cannot walk.'

She was right. Summoning up all his strength, Mitchell stepped out of the aeroplane and drove home to 'Hazeldene'. He knew now for certain that he would never live to see his bomber fly and it was fortunate for his peace of mind that he did not know that in the event nobody would ever see it fly. His courage did not falter. Mitchell had always liked his garden, and in the quiet summer days of late May and early June he spent a lot of time sitting outside with his wife.

He had many visitors, and one of the most frequent was Mrs Gladys Pickering. In recalling those sad days, she said: 'Sometimes it was difficult to know what to talk about. He did not want sympathy, he just wanted to forget.'

Mitchell had a soft heart for anyone in trouble, and one day Mrs Pickering told him that her little daughter, Ann, had whooping cough. Anxious to help the child, he said: 'I tell you what, you borrow my sun lamp. It might do her good.'

'I couldn't do that,' she protested. 'You might need it.'

'No, I won't. What I've got, no sun lamp will cure.'

Mitchell felt at ease in Mrs Pickering's company. He had known her and her husband, George, the test pilot, for a long time, and they had always been great friends. He looked forward to her visits, and the last time she went to see him he said:

'I thought you were never coming.'

'Don't let's talk about flying today,' she suggested.

'Why should we?' he replied. 'There are more important things in the world than flying.' He gazed at his favourite flowers, all in full summer bloom. 'There is so much beauty all around us. I wish I had spent more time appreciating beauty. It is too late now but tell George that there are more important things in life than speed. Tell him to look at beautiful things while he has time.'

Eric, Mitchell's brother, who had been so close to him in boyhood days, visited 'Hazeldene'. One morning he asked Reg what had meant most to him in his life and was told quite simply: 'My work was important but there are other things as well that are important in life.'

In his last days, Mitchell remembered all the people who had been part of his life for so many years; one person he particularly asked about was Mrs Pitman – the Mitchells' maid for many years – and hoped she might visit him. Miss Cross often went to the house, but Mitchell could not bear her to see him as a helpless invalid. Lying on a sofa, he would apologise at least half a dozen times for being unable to stand up.

When Arthur Shirvall called to see him, Mitchell looked up from his bed and said: 'I had great plans for you, Arthur. Sorry about that.'

Shirvall made no reply, but it did cross his mind that it would have been better for Britain if he could have exchanged places with the dying man.

Another regular visitor from March 1937 was the vicar of the nearby Highfield Church, the Reverend Stretton Reeve, who subsequently left Highfield to become the 95th Bishop of Lichfield from 1953 to 1974. From his home in a quiet Shropshire village to which he retired, he recalled his talks with Mitchell.

> It was only towards the end of his life when I came to know Reginald Mitchell; it was a few months after I had become vicar of Highfield, the parish in which he lived, that his wife told me after a service that he was ill and would I visit him. So, of course, I did and he at once showed me that I was welcome and put me at my ease. After that, I visited him almost daily during the last three months or so of his life.
>
> He was battling against the illness from which he eventually died, and, looking back on this over the years, what stands out in my memory is the indomitable courage he showed. He was only young and did not want to die but he faced the situation in which he found himself with bravery and steadfastness. He was obviously suffering much, but he refused to give in and he fought on in a way which was truly remarkable.
>
> What I also remember very clearly was his growing and deepening religious faith as the end drew nearer. After I had got to know him fairly well he asked me to pray with him, and not only did he ask me to bring the Holy Communion to him at home, but also on his last Easter Day on earth he summoned up his strength and came to church.
>
> I regarded it as a very great privilege to have known Reginald Mitchell and I am proud that he gave me his friendship in the closing months of his life; I only wish I could have done more to help him in his time of need. It was also a privilege to be able to pay a tribute to him at his funeral in my church. From our human standpoint, it was sad indeed that he should have been taken from us at such an early age, but there was a sense in which his great work had been done, because he left us the Spitfire which played so vital a part in saving our country in the Battle of Britain. Chiefly, however, I remember him as a man whom it did one good to know. I shall never forget him.

The Right Reverend Reeve died in January 1981 at the age of seventy-three, seven years after his retirement.

The Reverend Frank Cocks, the curate at Highfield Church, also visited Mitchell at this time. He assisted the Reverend Reeve at Mitchell's funeral and subsequently he gave much comfort to his wife in the weeks following his death. The Reverend Cocks later became Chaplain-in-Chief to the RAF and then after the war, the Bishop of Shrewsbury. Frank died in August 1998 (see Item 45 on page 285).

Mitchell's last letter to Gordon, on 27 May – a mere fifteen days before his death – was written in his usual cheerful style:

Hazeldene,
Russell Place,
Southampton
27 May 1937

My dear Gordon,

Very many thanks for your letter. I am hastening to enclose the £1 note which you fairly and squarely won from me over the FA Cup Final – good luck to you.

I have got nicely settled here now – spent all day in the garden today – examined the tom-tits [blue tits?]. How you counted eleven, I don't know. The iris blooms are beautiful, don't you think? I feel quite proud of them. I am going to be very careful what I say about myself at present, but I think I feel better and decidedly more optimistic. Dr Picken is carrying on with the treatment, injections, etc. Mr Pearson of the Vienna Foundation is in England and is calling to see me tomorrow. Your housemaster has written to say he is making enquiries about chartered accountants, and I will let you know.

Well, cheerio for the present,

Mum joins me in fondest love,

Yours affectionately,
Dad.

Mitchell sat in the garden for the last time on 6 June. Two days later he became unconscious, and he died at noon on 11 June 1937.

In paying tribute to Mitchell, an article in the local *Southern Daily Echo* for 11 June was headed: 'The World of Aviation has lost one of its most Brilliant Designers.'

It recalled his four-year fight against illness, during which time he went on working with remarkable courage, and how all of his friends marvelled at his indomitable spirit. 'He will be remembered as a very brave man.'

As was to be expected, Mitchell's death was widely reported in the national press; the following may be quoted as being representative, including being accompanied by a photograph of Mitchell:

PLANE GENIUS DIES AT forty-two – Mr R.J. Mitchell – Designer of Schneider Trophy Machines.

One of the world's youngest and most brilliant aircraft designers, Mr Reginald Joseph Mitchell, CBE, designer of the seaplane which won the Schneider Trophy for Great Britain, died yesterday at the age of forty-two.

For four months he knew that after the last series of operations, he was soon to die.

He accepted the verdict with amazing fortitude; and set about arranging his affairs and the future of his wife and sixteen-year-old son.

Regarding it as a gleam of hope, Mr Mitchell flew to Vienna for treatment by Professor Freund, the famous specialist. He was in a Vienna sanatorium for a month, but his illness had advanced too far for the treatment to succeed – so he flew home again and resigned himself to the end, which he knew was very near.

Last Sunday he sat in the garden of his home in Russell Place, Southampton, for the last time. On Monday he became unconscious, and remained so till his death.

Gordon felt that this was a reasonably accurate report – in Chapter 18, he refers to the writing of these obituaries relating to Mitchell's death.

The funeral Service at Highfield Church on 15 June was attended by Mitchell's family and a vast congregation, including representatives from every branch of aviation. Among the many RAF officers was his great friend Sqn Ldr A.H. Orlebar. The city of Southampton was represented by the mayor and other civic dignitaries. Four cars carrying the wreaths preceded the hearse, and on the coffin lay two crosses; pink roses from his wife and carnations from his son. One hundred men from Supermarine, comprising staff and workers, followed the cortege up the gently sloping hill to Highfield Church.

The service was conducted by the vicar of Highfield, the Reverend Stretton Reeve, assisted by the Reverend Frank Cocks. Reverend Reeve concluded his address with the words:

'It seems a tragedy that his genius should have been removed just when he was most needed, and when he was at the height of his powers.'

The service ended with the singing of the Nunc Dimittis.

After a private cremation service his ashes were laid to rest in South Stoneham Cemetery near Eastleigh Airport, and at the moment of interment three RAF aircraft flew over in formation, dipping their wings in a final salute to the man who had given Britain the Spitfire.

The floral tributes were too numerous to list, but out of the vast number, three are representative of the esteem and affection with which Mitchell was regarded.

From the Air Council: 'In homage to the memory of a distinguished designer and a great-hearted gentleman.'

The Supermarine design team's wreath – an S.6B outlined in blue cornflowers on a background of white carnations – bore the words: 'In memory of our deeply mourned leader.'

A floral design in the firm's colours of blue and white said: 'In memory from the Schneider boys, Orlie.'

R.J. Mitchell died with courage and in peace, knowing he had left three outstanding gifts to his country – the Spitfire fighter, the Walrus amphibian and, as he hoped, his B.12/36 bomber. The first and second of these were destined to become respectively, the fastest and the slowest aircraft in the British services.

Following Mitchell's death, his wife received a very large number of letters and telegrams of sympathy from his friends and from those associated with his work.

A few of the latter are reproduced below. The very high regard felt by the aviation world for Mitchell and what he had achieved in his seventeen short years as a chief designer cannot be better illustrated:

The Royal Aeronautical Society:

> The president, council and all members of the Royal Aeronautical Society tender you their deepest sympathy in your personal irreparable and overwhelming loss. Aviation has lost its most brilliant member in this country and all who knew him have lost a great and loyal friend.
>
> Pritchard, secretary.

A.F. Sidgreaves, Rolls-Royce Ltd:

> On behalf of the chairman and directors of Rolls-Royce, I send you deepest sympathy.
>
> Sidgreaves.

The Society of British Aircraft Constructors Ltd:

Permit me on behalf of the council and members of the Society of British Aircraft Constructors to offer you the profoundest sympathy of the society on the death of your husband.

His death is a great loss to the British aircraft industry, and everyone in aviation who knew him will feel a deep sense of personal loss. He was indeed well admired and liked by everyone who met him. Gillman, secretary.

The Institution of Civil Engineers:

I have learned with deep regret of the death of your husband, an associate member of this institution, whose association with the institution was much appreciated and valued here, and I ask you to accept my sincere sympathy in your bereavement.

Clark, secretary.

Aeronautical Research Committee, National Physical Laboratory:

May I express my deepest sympathy with you in your loss. With Mr Relf, I knew Mr Mitchell well in a business capacity and have always appreciated his cheery ways and the pleasant manner in which all our business connections were carried through. Others more competent than I will no doubt mention to you his great skill as a designer and we at NPL were only too pleased to have been able to help him a little from time to time when he has been designing the many fast aircraft with which his name is associated.

Nayler, secretary.

The Bristol Aeroplane Company Ltd:

I felt I must write to say how much you are in our thoughts at Bristol, during the troublesome time through which you are now passing.

Mr Mitchell was very well known to all of us in every direction with regard to aeroplanes and flying boats, and we all feel that we have lost a great friend, as he was associated with us for so many years.

My staff join me in offering you the deepest sympathy in your bereavement.

A.M.R. Fedden [chief designer (aero-engines)].

The Staffordshire Society:

I was extremely sorry to see in the press an announcement of the death of your husband.

Some two or three years ago we elected him as one of our very few honorary members in recognition of his distinguished services to aviation in this country.

On behalf of the council and myself, I wish to say how grieved we are at the premature termination of such a brilliant career.

Brindley, vice-chairman.

Cdr Sir Charles Craven, chairman of The Supermarine Aviation Works (Vickers) Ltd:

My wife and I send you our most sincere sympathy in your great sorrow.

Charles Craven.

Col. Sir Donald Banks on behalf of The Air Council:

The Air Council have learned with profound regret of the death of your husband whose name will long be remembered for his brilliant work in helping to secure the highest distinction for this country in high-speed flying. On the council's behalf I beg to offer an expression of our deepest sympathy in your bereavement.

Donald Banks [secretary of the Air Ministry and a member of the Air Council].

Marine Aircraft Experimental Establishment, Felixstowe:

I am writing to offer you my deepest sympathy in the loss of your husband... I always regarded him as one of the most brilliant men in aeronautics today; there are few with his ability and soundness of judgement. You will have plenty of testimonies from all the distinguished men in aeronautics as to his qualities, and I am sure you will be very proud of them. But I should like also to say how very much I admired his personal qualities. I feel I have lost a real friend...

H.M. Garner.

A.V. Roe & Co. Ltd:

Please accept my sincere sympathy in your very sad bereavement.

I was a great admirer of your late husband's work. It is a big loss to British aviation.

A. Verdon-Roe.

Joe Smith, Supermarine Aviation Works (Vickers) Ltd:

On behalf of the drawing office staff, I have been asked to convey to you and your son our very sincere sympathy in your great bereavement. It was with deep regret that we learned yesterday of this irreparable loss. Mr Mitchell was much admired and beloved by us all here, and as our leader for a number of years has set us a very high example of courage under trial and of great devotion to duty. In deepest sympathy.

J. Smith.

Col. J.B. Neilson, deputy chairman of Vickers Ltd:

I was terribly sorry to learn the sad news. Please accept my deepest sympathy in your great loss. Mr Jamieson, our chairman, asks me to convey to you also his deep sympathy.

J.B. Neilson.

Lord Swinton, Secretary of State for air and president of the Air Council:

May I write a few lines to say how truly we all at the Air Ministry sympathise with you.

You know, without any letter, the high regard everyone in the service and the ministry had for your husband. His was real genius, a flair all his own and an infinite thoroughness! His work is his memorial.

Swinton.

In Mrs Mitchell's replies, with which she had great help from Miss Cross, Mitchell's secretary, there was, when appropriate, reference to her husband's great regret that he was not able to see his four-engined bomber design finished in detail. However, he had, she said, been able to guide the earlier stages until quite a short time ago and so he felt it would be carried successfully to completion by his team at Supermarine.

It is clear from this that Mitchell felt deeply about not being able to see his bomber in the air and that his concern, on his death-bed, lay with that aircraft rather than with the future of the Spitfire.

As seen in Chapter 11, Mitchell was awarded the CBE in 1932 following the winning of the Schneider Trophy outright by Britain. However, in relation to his much more important contribution to his country, his Spitfire, Mitchell, like several great men and women before and after him, died before the importance of his last, and most significant, years of work could be appreciated. Consequently, he could not be awarded any official honour due to the fact that posthumous awards for anything other than gallantry cannot be given under the present system in this country. Had Mitchell lived, few can doubt that he would in due course have been awarded an appropriate honour, such as a knighthood.

Posthumous honours have only ever been awarded in this country for gallantry. In February 1997, Gordon wrote to the Rt Hon. Tony Blair, leader of the opposition, about posthumous honours awards and whether consideration might possibly be given to the introduction of a new posthumous award for outstanding lifetime achievement.

A very positive reply was received from Mr Jonathan Powell, Mr Blair's chief of staff, in which he described R.J. as a remarkable man who would have been a prime candidate for such a posthumous award if such had existed. Following the general election, Gordon wrote a further letter to Mr Powell, now chief of staff to the Prime Minister, who in his reply stated that he would certainly see that the question of posthumous awards (for other than gallantry) would be looked at if the Prime Minister had a review of the honours system (see the letter to Gordon received from 10 Downing Street in December 1999, reproduced on page 9). At December 2005, position remains the same.

Be that as it may, there exist now in this country a large number of memorials and tributes to Mitchell and these are all described in detail in Chapter 19. Some were initiated during the war but most were established in the post-war years. Their existence is a true reflection of the genuine esteem felt for Mitchell and of a widespread determination that he should never be forgotten.

A further fine example of this wish to remember R.J. occurred on 15 September 2000 when the Air Force Board held a dinner to commemorate the sixtieth anniversary of the Battle of Britain in the officers' mess at RAF Bentley Priory. It was held in the gracious presence of HRH The Duke of York, HRH The Princess Margaret, Countess of Snowdon, and HRH Princess Alexandra The Hon. Lady Ogilvy. Following the dinner, ACM Sir Peter Squire, KCB, DFC, AFC, ADC, FRAeS, RAF, chief of the Air Staff, gave a fine address embracing the outstanding achievements of the RAF since its foundation.

Gordon was delighted to receive an invitation to this memorable occasion, showing as it did that his father had most certainly not been forgotten by the RAF.

It is appropriate to conclude this chapter with a tribute by the late Grp Capt. David Green, the chairman and founder of the Spitfire Society, since one of the aims of the society is to preserve the memory and life of R.J. Mitchell.

> Throughout my flying years my curiosity has grown consistently about the man whose brain spawned what has always been to me an artistic masterpiece even before its engineering excellence. The latter was always present in the work of R.J. The Southampton, the Stranraer, the Walrus

were all fine examples of his engineering skill. But the explosion of aesthetic genius, first with the S.4 and culminating with the Spitfire, was the ingredient which raised the man to a level unattainable by the most brilliant of his contemporaries.

It should be borne in mind that all of these very fine letters sent to Mrs Mitchell were, of course, written long before the vital role the Spitfire was to play in 1939–45 was known. The writers no doubt at that time considered the Spitfire to be a beautiful and quite good little aircraft. Only the designer and a handful of others knew that it was indeed an exceptionally good aeroplane!

15

The Spitfire
Goes to War

So R.J. Mitchell, with great achievements behind him and great plans and ambitions for the future, had died prematurely at the age of forty-two. He lived only long enough to see the prototype of his Spitfire in the air, to see that it performed up to his expectations, and to know that 310 of them had been ordered by the government. But he could not know that it was to become what many considered to be the most famous fighter of all time, that it would be a prime instrument in the salvation of his country, and that it would serve with the utmost distinction in every major theatre of what was to be the most extensive war in history.

Nor did he know, of course, that 22,789 Spitfires and Seafires would eventually be built, or that sixty-five years after his death, Spitfires would still regularly be on show to the public, both on the ground and in the air (see page 251).

After Mitchell's death, there were inevitable changes in the design organisation at Supermarine. Joseph Smith became chief designer, with Alan Clifton as his principal assistant and Eric Lovell-Cooper as chief draughtsman. Smith, a man of great energy, determination and courage, fully recognised that he had inherited an aircraft of exceptional quality, and his task would be to develop it to its maximum potential. In the years to come he was to direct the unprecedented development of the Spitfire which was to keep it in the front rank of fighter performance throughout the war years and extend its capabilities over a range of military roles which even Mitchell could not have foreseen.

J.D. Scott,[9] writing about Joe Smith, says:

> Although he had been a great admirer of Mitchell, Smith had never tried to imitate his visionary boldness, for his own talent lay in developing things which were already known to be good. If Mitchell was born to design the Spitfire, Joe Smith was born to defend and develop it.

At Mitchell's death, the immediate tasks facing Supermarine were to complete the development tests of the prototype and to press on with the production of the 310 Spitfires then on order by the government. On 15 May 1938, Jeffrey Quill took the first production Spitfire, K9787, into the air at Eastleigh. On 4 August he delivered the first RAF Spitfire, K9789, to 19 (Fighter) Squadron at Duxford, which was commanded by Sqn Ldr I. Cozens. Thereafter deliveries continued, and by September the squadron was fully equipped. Early production Spitfires were fitted with fixed-pitch wooden propellers, because the variable-pitch metal propellers were not yet in production. This gave the early Spitfires a rather sluggish performance at take-off and at low altitudes, and they tended to 'float' on landing. In spite of this, the pilots of 19 Squadron, all of whom were accustomed to much slower biplanes, adapted very quickly to their new aircraft, although some accidents inevitably occurred. Sqn Ldr Cozens later commented on the Spitfire's ease of handling.

It soon became clear that demands for Spitfire production would be greatly increased, and that Supermarine alone would not be able to meet the task. Two things happened at about this time. First, an internal reorganisation in Vickers put the aircraft interests directly under the control of Vickers-Armstrongs Ltd, wherein were concentrated all the armament activities of Vickers. Second, the government decided to set up a major 'Shadow Factory' for Spitfire production at Castle Bromwich near Birmingham, under the management of the Nuffield organisation. This shadow factory was later transferred to the management of Vickers-Armstrongs Ltd.

Ever since the prototype Spitfire had first flown in 1936, all information concerning it was strictly secret. However, it was decided to exhibit a Spitfire at the 1938 Salon Aeronautique in Paris, a static exhibition in the Grand Palais in the centre of Paris. Accordingly, Jeffrey Quill flew a standard production aeroplane, K9814, from Croydon to Le Bourget on 14 November 1938 without any attendant publicity, in spite of establishing a very fast point-to-point time. However, on the return journey, on 16 January 1939, Quill completed the trip from take-off to landing in forty-one minutes without assistance from wind conditions en route. This record attracted the attention of the aeronautical press, and the more discerning aeronautical correspondents at once drew the conclusion that the Spitfire was an aircraft of exceptional performance. Shortly after this, the Air Ministry decided to release performance figures to dampen down the wilder forms of press speculation. They gave a top speed of 362 mph, which put the Spitfire significantly ahead of its rival, the Hurricane.

In May 1939, the general public had an opportunity to see the Spitfire at several RAF open days, when Flt Lt George Stainforth, of Schneider Trophy fame, toured several RAF aerodromes in the north. A more limited and specialised public audience had also seen the Spitfire prototype fly at the RAF display at the SBAC Show at Hendon in 1936. Gradually the British public began to take notice of Mitchell's new fighter.

At the outbreak of war, in September 1939, there were some 400 Spitfires in RAF service. Spitfire production at that time was concentrated at the Supermarine works in Southampton, and the completed aircraft were assembled, test flown and delivered from the aerodrome at Eastleigh. Production was at last going at a brisk rate, and the 'phoney' war gave a welcome period for consolidating the build-up of the RAF's Spitfire force. At this time George Pickering and Jeffrey Quill were joined by a young pilot of exceptional talent and ability, Alex Henshaw, and the three of them were kept hard at it testing the steadily increasing output of production aircraft.

The story of the Spitfire at war is a huge subject and has been dealt with extensively in official and unofficial war histories and in numerous books specifically about the Spitfire. During the 'phoney' war, as the early months became known, the Spitfires were not sent to France, as the Hurricanes were, but were kept at home. Subsequent events showed this to be a wise and prudent decision, for which Sir Hugh Dowding, commander-in-chief of Fighter Command, had to fight a 'battle' within the War Cabinet.

Although Spitfires were engaged in the interception of random raiders against the UK during this period, they were not truly 'blooded' until the extensive operations from UK bases in support of the Dunkirk evacuation, fought at the extreme limit of the Spitfire's range and endurance. At Dunkirk, the Spitfire was pitted against the German Messerschmitt Bf109E, which became popularly known as the ME 109, which was able to operate from airfields in Belgium, Holland and France as the German army advanced. Many important lessons were learned, RAF confidence in the Spitfire was strengthened and, although Fighter Command suffered substantial casualties, they also gained invaluable experience both in the air and on the ground, which was to serve them well when the supreme test came.

The Battle of Britain was essentially a fighter battle. After the fall of France, Hitler paused in the hope of achieving a negotiated peace with Britain. This gave Fighter Command a short but much-needed respite, for during the French campaign, the RAF had lost nearly 1,000 aircraft, of which about 450 were fighters. Worse by far, nearly 400 pilots had been killed or taken prisoner.

Eventually, Hitler realised that Britain under Churchill's leadership was in no mood to negotiate and so he would have to invade. This required command of the Channel and, since Germany had no hope of achieving this through the use of its naval forces, it fell to the Luftwaffe to secure complete air superiority to enable the invasion to proceed. So Goering was instructed to destroy the RAF Fighter Command on the ground and in the air, and indeed he confidently proclaimed to Hitler that the Luftwaffe could do this.

The Battle of Britain can be said to have started on 10 July 1940. Throughout the operations, the German strategy was to bring Fighter Command to battle by all possible means and to destroy it, or so severely weaken it that Operation Sealion – the invasion of Britain – could be safely launched across the Channel.

The fall of France and the capture of French airfields near the Channel coast enabled the German fighters, principally ME 109s and ME 110s, to operate as escorts to the German bomber raids and thus destroy, so it was planned, the opposing British fighters.

It is now a matter of history that Germany failed in its prime objective of bringing Fighter Command to its knees. By the end of September, Germany had broken off this phase of the battle and had switched to night bombing attacks, by which time Operation Sealion had been called off. The main factors which contributed to Goering's failure to destroy Fighter Command, in spite of numerical superiority, were:

1. The quality of the British fighters – Hurricanes and Spitfires.
2. The existence of radar (known then as RDF), the tactical significance of which the German High Command were very slow to grasp.
3. The courage and determination of the British and Allied fighter pilots and ground crews.
4. The quality and determination of the RAF's command structure and leadership.

Another important factor, more on the negative side, was that the Luftwaffe suffered greatly from high-level leadership which was too politically oriented and which made continual changes to the main tactics of the battle. They would probably have done much better without

Goering. Moreover, both at the political and the command levels, the ease and speed of their victories on the continent had made them over-confident and arrogant. They learned a salutary lesson when it came to straight battle against the RAF fighting in defence of its own country.

It took both the Hurricane and the Spitfire, two aircraft which ide-ally complemented each other, to win the Battle of Britain, and honour should always be accorded to both, but see Chapter 20. At the start of the battle, Hurricanes in Fighter Command outnumbered Spitfires by about two to one, although in 11 Group, which largely bore the brunt of the fighting, the ratio was more even. As the battle proceeded, however, the rapidly increasing production at Supermarine brought the ratio of Spitfires to Hurricanes closer, especially within 11 Group.

It is perhaps not generally realised that during the Battle of Britain the combined output of Spitfires and Hurricanes was about 100 a week, and that in the four months from June to September, British fighter produc-tion exceeded that of Germany by quite a substantial margin.

Sir Maurice Dean, in his excellent history of the RAF, wrote:

> The British defence during the battle depended on our operational force of 600–700 Hurricanes and Spitfires, maintained from day to day through-out the battle fairly comfortably as to aircraft and far from comfortably as to pilots.

It was perhaps during the Battle of Britain that the British people first began to appreciate the qualities of the Spitfire, to recognise its elegant shape in the air, and to recognise the peculiar whistling note that was superimposed over the throaty sound of its Merlin engine. The newspa-pers gave publicity to the fact that German fighter pilots were frequently heard on their radios giving the warning cry, 'Achtung, Spitfeuer!', and the people of England began to take Mitchell's fighter to their hearts.

In both performance and manoeuvrability the Spitfire was superior to the Hurricane, and thus better able to fight the ME 109, especially at higher altitudes. The Hurricane, however, was a splendidly robust aeroplane and an excellent gun platform.

AC Alan Deere[10] made, from first-hand experience, the following two comments on the relative performance of the Spitfire and the ME 109:

(1)   There was a great deal of scepticism about my claim that the Spitfire was superior to the ME 109; there were those who frankly disbelieved me, saying that it was contrary to published performance figures. Later events, however, proved me to be right.

(2)   Before I could fire another burst, two ME 109s wheeled in behind me. I broke hard into the attack pulling my Spitfire into a climbing,

spiralling turn as I did so; a manoeuvre I had discovered in previous combats with ME 109s to be particularly effective. And it was no less effective now; the Messerschmitts literally 'fell out of the sky' as they stalled in an attempt to follow me.

The Luftwaffe mounted attacks by large formations of bombers flying at around 12,000 ft, escorted by large numbers of ME 110s and some ME 109s flying as close escorts, or as 'top cover' at much higher altitudes. When the situation permitted, the general pattern was that the Spitfires, with their superior performance, were 'scrambled' to engage the fighter escorts and shoot them down, or to draw them out of position while the Hurricanes tackled the bombers. It was not always possible, of course, to adhere to this tidy concept.

AC Alan Deere, who was one of those directly involved in this strategy, writes in his book, *Nine Lives* (1959):

> I am in a position to comment at first hand on the policy of using selected Spitfire squadrons to draw off the enemy escort fighters thus enabling the remaining squadrons, and this included the 12 Group Hurricanes, to concentrate more effectively on the bombers. Though this decision meant a much tougher and unrewarding job for the Hornchurch Spitfire squadrons, I do not recall a single pilot saying other than he thought it an excellent idea. I strongly support this view, and on numerous occasions witnessed the rewards reaped when enemy bombers, shorn of the majority of their escort, were set upon by the defending Hurricanes which, excellent as they were, could not have coped so effectively without the intervention of the Spitfires.

The Battle of Britain was a very closely fought and critical affair. It is entirely appropriate to remind ourselves of the Duke of Wellington's remark after Waterloo, quoted by Creevey: 'It has been a damned nice thing – the nearest run thing you ever saw in your life.'

If the vicious German attacks on the British fighter airfields had been pursued longer, it could have been an even 'nearer run thing'.

As far as the RAF was concerned, it was essentially a defensive battle, and the issue was as starkly clear as at Waterloo. Had the battle been lost, then the war would have been lost as a consequence.

Even if Mitchell's fighter had never flown again after September 1940, he could have had the satisfaction of knowing that his Spitfire had played a leading role in the salvation not only of Britain but also of Europe.

Over many years many words have been written by many people about the Spitfire. It is appropriate that this chapter should include a reproduction of just a small cross-section of these tributes:

Sir William Farren, president of the Royal Aeronautical Society in 1954, on the occasion of the 1st Mitchell Memorial Lecture.[11]

> I always felt, from my own experience of it [the Spitfire] that it was the nicest aeroplane to fly that anybody had ever produced; it was a beautiful piece of aerodynamics. Those of you who design aircraft should never forget that you can make aeroplanes which are really nice as well as good aerodynamically, which sometimes people think is almost a contradiction in terms.

Sqn Ldr Anthony Bartley in his book, *Smoke Trails in the Sky*, published by William Kimber:

> The Spitfire was the perfection of a flying machine designed to combat and destroy its enemy. It had no vices... an aerodynamic masterpiece and a joy to fly.

AC Alan Deere:

> The Spitfire, despite its classical lines, was the epitome of toughness and durability. Thus, it could be subjected to severe 'G' loadings without any danger to the airframe, enabling me to stay inside the ME 109 during the steepest of turns.

Mr H.V. Evatt, Australian minister of external affairs, in a broadcast from Sydney in March 1943:

> The Spitfire is more than the name of an aircraft, it is the epitome of some of the greatest qualities of the British race, their engineering genius, their refusal to be satisfied with anything less than the best, and, above all, their dauntless courage in the face of adversity.
>
> After Dunkirk the fate not only of Britain but of the Empire, the USA and the whole world hung in the balance, but the Spitfire smashed the German onslaught and destroyed for ever Hitler's chances of invading England.
>
> The presence here of Spitfires has cheered the hearts of Australians.
>
> Our land is gradually emerging from the shadow of death and disaster into the sunlight of victory, peace and rehabilitation.
>
> Spitfires will share in the process of transformation and salvation.

Jimmy Edwards, in his book, *Six of the Best* (Robson Books, 1984):

> I was airborne – in a Spitfire! My mate's cheers rattled in my ears, and I swung into a climbing turn to join him above the airfield. Already I was

glorying in the feel of this wondrous little aeroplane, with its fantastically quick response to the controls, and my spirits soared with every hundred feet I climbed.

This chapter would not be complete without mention of one vitally important organisation, the Air Transport Auxiliary (ATA) and in particular the largely unknown part played by the ATA women pilots. A major problem which arose as aircraft production rapidly increased was the transport of the aircraft from the factories to the operational squadrons and it was for this task that the ATA was formed.

The information that follows about the ATA was provided by Lettice Curtis, MA, MRAeS, a distinguished and long-standing lady member of the ATA, and to whom the writer is most grateful. The ATA included both male and female pilots who, having collected the aircraft from the various factories, had to fly them to RAF maintenance units, although it was not until mid-1941 that women members were allowed to fly operational types. Again until 1941, the aircraft had been usually flown from the MUs to the squadrons to which they had been allocated by pilots from the squadrons themselves, but as from around mid-1941, this task was also carried out by the ATA.

By 1943, ATA women pilots were flying four-engined as well as operational two-engined aircraft. In 1944 there were 110 women pilots in the ATA and from 1940–45 women pilots made no less than a total of 308,567 individual ferry trips, 57,286 being with Spitfires. In spite of the fact that flying conditions were often far from ideal, out of the 57,286 Spitfire ferry trips, there were only some 100 instances of mechanical failure, and from 150–200 accidents or incidents of one type or another. There were 103 fatal accidents recorded in total, of which only twelve were with Spitfires.

By the very nature of their not widely published job, the general public were largely unaware of the vital contribution the ATA made to the war effort. Those actively involved in the air war against Germany owe the ATA a great debt of gratitude for relieving them of a task which the squadron pilots would otherwise have had to undertake on top of their arduous operational flying.

16

Development of the Spitfire

The Spitfires which fought in the Battle of Britain were Mks I and II. The difference between these two marks was small, and their performance in the air was virtually the same. The principal difference in the Mk II (which was produced at Castle Bromwich) was the fitting of a Rotol three-bladed propeller, whereas the Mk I had a de Havilland three-bladed propeller. Shortly before the Battle of Britain, both were fitted with constant speed units – a very important factor for improving climb performance. One important characteristic of the Rotol propeller was that the blades could be set at a coarser pitch, enabling the aircraft to be dived to its maximum permissible diving speed without overspeeding the engine.

There were two problems with the Spitfire at this time which created some difficulties for the pilots. One was very heavy aileron control at high speeds, and the other was a limitation imposed by the float-type carburettor of the Merlin engine. If the stick was pushed forward to put the aircraft rapidly into a dive, the engine would 'cut' due to flooding of the float chamber.

The Daimler–Benz 601A engine of the ME 109E had no carburettor but used a direct injection fuel system and therefore did not suffer from this problem, and German pilots were quick to exploit this advantage. Luftwaffe pilots, finding a Hurricane or Spitfire on their tail, pushed sharply over into a steep dive, making it difficult (but not impossible) for the British pilot to follow them.

In the short term this problem was ameliorated by the ingenuity of a lady scientist at the RAE Farnborough, Miss Schilling, who thus earned the gratitude of the fighter pilots. It is interesting to recall that this device, a small disc with a hole in it, was generally referred to in the squadrons as 'Miss Schilling's orifice'. In the longer term, the problem was eliminated altogether by the introduction of the Bendix-Stromberg pressure diaphragm carburettor on all Merlin engines.

Immediately following the battle, Supermarine instituted a crash programme to improve the quality of the aileron control. This was achieved by the introduction of metal-skinned ailerons in place of the original fabric-covered type. This was just the beginning of the Spitfire's development under the overall technical guidance of Joe Smith.

By 1940, it was known that the Merlin engine had enormous potential for power growth. In 1938/39, Supermarine had built and flown a specially modified Spitfire to attack the world air speed record. This aeroplane, N17, was fitted with a very special Merlin engine, sometimes known as the 'Schneiderised' Merlin, producing some 2,000 bhp, or about twice the power of the standard Merlin fitted to the Spitfires Mks I and II. This 'Schneiderised' Merlin had a very limited life, and like the Schneider engines it burned a very specially prepared fuel; it had all the limitations usually associated with 'souped-up' sprint engines.

The war broke out before the attempt on the speed record could be made, but the power-growth potential of the engine was clearly demonstrated in flight trials, so Supermarine knew that it could look forward to Merlin engines of progressively increasing power up to at least 2,000 bhp and perhaps more. In addition, Rolls-Royce was planning to produce another engine which was a direct development of the old 'R' type racing engine that had been fitted to the S.6 and S.6B Schneider racing seaplanes. This engine, to be known as the Griffon, was of ten litres greater cylinder capacity than the Merlin, and Joe Smith realised that it had an even greater potential for power growth than the Merlin. He immediately put in hand the necessary design studies to find a way of installing this considerably larger engine within the fine lines of the Spitfire airframe.

So, with the glittering prospect of steadily increasing power, combined with the already demonstrated low drag characteristics of the

Spitfire and the advanced technology of its airframe structure, Joe Smith realised that the efforts of the Supermarine design department should be concentrated upon developing the maximum potential from what already existed and was already basically established in production, rather than on making any attempt to design and produce a completely new aircraft as a Spitfire replacement. In other words, Mitchell's original design had been fundamentally right and therefore development rather than replacement was the most advantageous policy.

This policy also had the great advantage that it saved time and man hours since it was shown after the war that the development of a new mark of Spitfire in no case required anything approaching the same design effort as the original Spitfire had necessitated. Thus, J.D. Scott, in *Vickers: A History*, quotes figures showing that the total design man hours devoted to the whole of the Spitfire development effort over a period of five years was 620,000, barely sufficient to design two new aircraft of the original Mk I type.

Thus, this partnership between Supermarine and Rolls-Royce played a vitally important role during the war: (1) The Spitfire because its advanced design and enormous structural strength, which enabled increasingly powerful engines to be incorporated without any major design changes, and (2) Rolls-Royce because of their ability to continually increase the power of the Merlin engine, as a result of the development of two-speed, two-stage supercharging by Sir Stanley Hooker, and subsequently by their development from the Schneider Trophy 'R' engine of the even more powerful Griffon engine.

The importance of this partnership is demonstrated by subsequent history. During the ensuing wartime years, no fewer than fifty-two separate marks, or variants, of the Spitfire were produced and put into operational service, and in this process many more were flown experimentally. The Spitfire variants included fighter versions of progressively increasing performance and armament; the Seafire naval carrier-borne fighters; specialised photographic reconnaissance (PR) versions; and some special high-altitude fighter versions (Mks VI and VII) for the interception of very high-altitude intruders.

Just one example of the way in which the development of the Spitfire kept it ahead of developments in the German fighter aircraft concerns the introduction of the Mk IX in the middle of 1942. Late in the previous year, a new German fighter, the FW 190, had made its appearance and this was soon shown to be superior to the current Mk V Spitfire in nearly every respect. This constituted a major setback in the Allied air offensive strategy and the urgent need for an improved Spitfire became critical. Fortunately, it proved possible for Supermarine to provide this in a relatively short time by basically making the necessary design changes to enable the Merlin 45 engine of the Mk V Spitfire to be replaced by the more powerful two-speed, two-stage supercharged Merlin 61 to produce the Mk IX. This was originally to be only an interim mark, but it proved to be such a superb fighting aircraft that in the event some 5,700 of them were built. Thankfully, it proved to be the answer to the FW 190, as AC Alan Deere[12] records:

> The Spitfire Mk IXB attained its best performance at 21,000 ft, or at roughly the same altitude as did the FW 190. At this height, it was approximately 30 mph faster, was better in the climb and vastly more manoeuvrable. As an all-round fighter, the Spitfire Mk IXB was supreme, undoubtedly the best mark of Spitfire produced, despite later and more powerful versions.

This comment is reinforced by one made by AVM 'Johnnie' Johnson in his book, *Wing Leader*, published in 1956 when he was a group captain. (Johnnie became the highest scoring pilot in the RAF.)

> We flew hard during those summer months of 1943 and scored some decisive successes against the Luftwaffe. Our Spitfire Mk IXs were superior to both the FW 190 and the latest Messerschmitt product, the ME 109G.

Another big tactical advantage that the Spitfire Mk IX had in battle was that at combat range it could not be distinguished from the Mk V. This gave the Luftwaffe many unpleasant shocks!

The Mks VI, VII and PR.XIX were the first aircraft in the world to enter operational service equipped with pressurised cockpits. The Spitfires Mks XII, XIV, PR.XIX, 21, 22 and 24, and the Seafires Mks XV, XVII, 46 and 47, all had Griffon engines. The Spitfires Mks XIV, PR.XIX and 21 to 24 were all versions with the latest development of the Griffon engine, and really represented the ultimate in Spitfire performance, achieving top speeds of around 450 mph at 28,000 ft.

In 1941, a Spitfire Mk V was flown experimentally fitted with floats. These floats were designed by Arthur Shirvall, who, as described earlier, had been responsible for the floats of the Schneider racing seaplanes. The handling characteristics on the water and the relatively small reduction of performance in the air were so promising that it was decided to convert the higher performance Mk IX to a float plane. Several were produced and served in the Mediterranean on special missions.

In parallel with the airframe and engine developments, there were progressive improvements in armament. The original eight Browning .303 machine guns gave place first to a combination of four Brownings plus two 20-mm Hispano-Suiza cannon, and then to four cannon. Installations for the carriage of bombs and rocket projectiles (RP) were introduced. Jettisonable external fuel tanks to extend the aircraft's fighting range were introduced in 30 gal., 45 gal. and 90 gal. sizes. Finally, a 'jumbo' version of 170 gal. capacity was produced to help ferry the aircraft to the Mediterranean (Maeta).

The last version to be produced was the Seafire Mk 47, and this aeroplane, compared with the Mk I and II of the Battle of Britain, had an increase of nearly 100 mph in top speed; around double the maximum rate of climb; 2.5 times the operational range; and it fired from its four 20-mm cannon more than twice the weight of projectiles per minute, as well as carrying a considerable load of secondary armament in the form of bombs and rocket projectiles. It is interesting to reflect that, at its maximum take-off weight, the Seafire Mk 47 was equivalent to the Mk I carrying thirty-two passengers at the standard post-war airline weight allowance per passenger. Such, in round figures, was the measure of Spitfire development during the war years, achieved by the combined efforts of Joe Smith and his team of dedicated designers and engineers at Supermarine, and the great engine firm of Rolls-Royce.

J.D. Scott in *Vickers: A History* makes the intriguing comment that almost all suggestions for development and improvement of the Spitfire during the whole period of the war came either from Supermarine, or from Supermarine and Rolls-Royce together, sometimes with Rotols. Rarely did the initiative come from the Ministry of Aircraft Production or from the Air Staff. When it did, it was usually in the form of an enquiry as to whether the company thought it would be possible to undertake some particular development. The Supermarine attitude was that although the integrity of the Spitfire design must be preserved, with the Spitfire anything that the RAF wanted was possible.

Spitfires in PR and fighter variants and Seafires of various marks served in every major theatre of war, and a grand total of 22,789 were built, made up of 20,334 Spitfires and 2,455 Seafires. These figures, about which there has been some disagreement in the past (see Chapter 19 describing the Spitfire plaque at Southampton Airport), were kindly provided for inclusion in this book by E.B. Morgan, co-author with C.F. Andrews of *Supermarine Aircraft since 1914*. It is appropriate to mention that Eric Morgan, with co-author Edward Shacklady, published in 1987 a 634-page book entitled *Spitfire – the History*, aptly described by Jeffrey Quill as being what must be as definitive a history of the Spitfire as is ever likely to be written.

The last operational sortie in which Spitfires fired their guns in anger was in 1951, flown by 60 Squadron RAF in operations from

Singapore against Malayan terrorists in the jungle. On that occasion the squadron was led by a very distinguished wartime Spitfire pilot, the late Sqn Ldr Duncan Smith (see Appendix 10). In celebration of the Spitfire's last flight, which ended its incredible career as a fighter aeroplane, Supermarine and Rolls-Royce presented 60 Squadron with a silver model, the plinth of which was engraved with the first line of the Nunc Dimittis: 'Lord, now lettest thou thy servant depart in peace.'

Undoubtedly R.J. would have derived great satisfaction from this.

17

Production of the Spitfire 1940-45

It has already been noted in the last chapter that the unprecedented development history of the Spitfire, which resulted in it being the only Allied fighter to remain in full production and front-line operational service throughout the whole of the Second World War, was made possible by Mitchell's fundamentally correct design, and by the highly successful and progressive development of the Merlin and Griffon engines by Rolls-Royce.

The man in charge of Merlin development at Rolls-Royce was the late Cyril Lovesey, and Griffon development was managed by the late Mr Cantrell.

One man very much concerned with the development of the Merlin engine at Rolls-Royce in Derby was Stanley Hooker, later Sir Stanley Hooker, who retired as group technical director of Rolls-Royce (1971) Ltd some years before his death in 1984.

Speaking in his office at Rolls-Royce Aero Division, Filton, where he was at that time acting as consultant, Sir Stanley Hooker briefly outlined his career. Born at Sheerness, Kent, he attended Borden Grammar

School. Moving on to the Imperial College of Science and Technology, he took a degree in mathematics, and afterwards did research work on high-speed aerodynamics at Brasenose College, Oxford. In 1935 he joined the Scientific and Research Department of the Admiralty, working on anti-aircraft rockets.

Like other men of that time, he recognised that war with Germany was coming and he was anxious to help in increasing the strength of British armaments. When told by a friend in 1938 that there was a vacancy at Rolls-Royce, he immediately applied for the post, and after a successful interview with E.W. Hives – later Lord Hives – he was installed in an office, not quite sure what sort of work he would be asked to do.

Sir Stanley Hooker admitted that he was attracted by 'the magic of the Rolls-Royce name', and said he still possessed the carved oak desk across which he faced E.W. Hives on that memorable day in January 1938. At that time he had very little practical experience, but during his first days at Derby he wrote a paper on superchargers. The expert on superchargers at Rolls-Royce was Jimmy Ellor, and after reading the paper he was so impressed by the new man's ability that Hooker was made assistant experimental chief engineer, with special responsibility for the development of superchargers.

In 1938, with war imminent, Rolls-Royce was working hard to improve the power of the Merlin engine. E.W. Hives was now general works manager, with A.G. Elliot as chief engineer, Col. Barrington as chief designer, Ellor as chief experimental engineer and Hooker as assistant experimental engineer. During the early years of the Second World War, Barrington and Ellor went to Packards in Detroit, who were manufacturing Merlin engines for US fighters, including the Mustang which, when fitted with a Merlin 61 engine, had a performance close to that of the Spitfire. Following this American move, Rubbra became chief designer and Lovesey became chief experimental engineer. At this time, Lovesey and Hooker shared the same office.

Throughout the war many different marks of the Merlin engine were manufactured, but basically there were three main groups:

1. The Merlin III, produced at the beginning of the war, which gave 890 hp for take off and 1,000 hp at 15,000 ft.

2. The Merlin 45, which gave 1,230 hp for take off and 1,200 hp at 17,500 ft. This improvement was achieved by development of the supercharger.

3. The final phase of high power was achieved on the Merlin 61 series engines by the introduction of two-stage superchargers with an after cooler, developed by Hooker. This type of engine gave 1,450 hp for takeoff, 1,550 hp at 11,000 ft, and 1,370 hp at 24,000 ft. Spitfires fitted

with Merlin 61 engines can be easily recognised by their longer noses, four-bladed propellers and radiators under each wing to cope with the increased cooling requirement of the more powerful engine.

During this development period, Rubbra worked on design, Lovesey on mechanical problems and Hooker on superchargers. They worked as a team, and all their efforts were directed at improving the reliability and performance of the engine. The Spitfire Mk IX was the first variant to go into production with the Merlin 61 engine, which increased the fighting altitude of the aircraft by 10,000 ft and added 70 mph to the top speed. It appeared in the nick of time to cope with the threat of the Focke-Wulf FW 190, which could outfight the RAF's Spitfire Mk Vs; this is also discussed in Chapter 16. During this development of the Merlin engine, Hooker was responsible for the improvements to superchargers. He was therefore one of the men most closely concerned with increasing the power of the engine and the speed of the Spitfires, which made them more than a match for the German fighters. While Hooker increased the power, Lovesey was responsible for preserving the mechanical integrity and reliability of the engine, and Rubbra incorporated their ideas into designs. Rubbra had trained under Sir Henry Royce, who had laid down very strict guidelines for design work at Rolls-Royce.

Speaking of Sir Henry Royce, Sir Stanley Hooker said that he was a meticulous mechanical engineer who had started his career on the shop floor. Everything done for him had to be perfect, and in his autocratic manner he would instantly sack a man for shoddy work. He was a creative genius with a natural gift for seeing what would work. During the latter years of his life he lived as a semi-invalid at West Wittering (see Chapter 18), but all design work at Derby had to pass his scrutiny and he countersigned with the 'R' which he used as his signature. 'Rolls-Royce treated him like jewellery', and gave him a villa in the south of France where he lived for certain months of the year. Sir Henry Royce died in 1933, and so never saw the final triumph of the Merlin engine.

The Merlin engine was designed and brought to a high standard of performance by a team of highly skilled and dedicated engineers and designers. Digging into his memory of those far-off days at Derby, Hooker commented: 'I think they were some of the most satisfactory years of my life.'

The development of the Griffon engine, larger and more powerful than the Merlin, was conducted along much the same lines. It was fitted in the later series of Spitfires and Seafires, and drove four-bladed, five-bladed and, ultimately, six-bladed contra-rotating propellers.

One of the most significant events leading up to the Spitfire was the record-breaking speed of 407.5 mph achieved by the Schneider seaplane, the S.6B, in 1931. In the words of Sir Stanley Hooker:

If Mitchell had not set his heart on gaining the speed record; if Lady Houston had not donated £100,000; if Sir Henry Royce had not had complete faith in Mitchell as an aircraft designer, then the history of this country might have taken a very different turn.

With the large number of aircraft in service in wartime there were the inevitable training accidents and a high incidence of combat damage in operations. It was essential that damaged aircraft should be repaired and returned to service with the minimum of delay. It was not practicable or desirable that this work should be undertaken by the main production factories, and therefore a number of special repair units were set up, notably at Cowley near Oxford, in an ex-Nuffield plant, and at Air Service Training at Hamble. Aircraft which had suffered only minor damage were flown in, repaired as quickly as possible and flown out. More seriously damaged aircraft were delivered by lorry, repaired as quickly as possible, test flown and delivered by air back to the RAF.

The nature of the damage caused by accidents and bullet and cannon shell strikes was infinitely variable and repair schemes had to be devised quickly and most carefully vetted to preserve the integrity of the structure and to ensure that the strength and safety of the aircraft in the air were not impaired. The devising or approving of repair schemes required an expert engineer with a detailed knowledge of the Spitfire's structure and stressing. Such a man was found in the person of Jack Rasmussen of the Supermarine design team. He constantly visited repair units to advise and approve the repair schemes, which had to be improvised on a case-by-case basis. The repair organisation did much to minimise the impact of accident and combat damage on Fighter Command's frontline strength.

Also in the course of large-scale and rapid production of new aircraft, there arose a continual stream of problems and minor modifications which required design approval. Rasmussen therefore visited all production units to give on-the-spot, rapid design advice as the need arose. It was a heavy responsibility.

At the beginning of 1944, Britain and her Allies were preparing for the invasion of Nazi-occupied Europe. In April, Sir James Bird, managing director of Supermarine, sent for Rasmussen and introduced him to a senior RAF officer, who said:

We are going into Europe soon and we need someone who can help us to keep the maximum number of Spitfires in the air. We expect to meet with great losses, and shall probably have to repair our Spitfires with anything at hand, Jerrycans or even captured German material. We are looking for a volunteer for this job, and you have been recommended as having the necessary qualifications. Will you take it on?

After a few moments' thought, Rasmussen accepted the challenge, even though it meant giving up a safe civilian job. 'How soon can you be ready?' was the next question.

He replied: 'By the end of the week'.

Rasmussen reported to Uxbridge, where he was kitted out with a uniform. Although not strictly an RAF officer, he was styled as a special duties officer to enable him to gain access to the highest ranks in time of emergency. Spitfire squadrons going to Normandy were stationed in the south of England, and in the pre-D-Day weeks Rasmussen visited them all to get to know the pilots, and more particularly the engineers, so that it would be easier to talk to them when he met them again in France.

Rasmussen went to France shortly after D-Day, and began visiting Spitfire squadrons and repair units. At each unit the engineer in charge would present his work plan. If it passed inspection, Rasmussen would sign it, and in due course the damaged Spitfire would fly again. By this time there were about 2,000 modifications on the Spitfire, and since it was impossible to memorise them they were listed for quick consultation. At regular intervals Rasmussen flew back to England for discussions with Joe Smith in the design office at Hursley Park. Smith and Rasmussen were old friends and played golf together whenever possible. Like Mitchell, Joe Smith drove himself hard, and even in peacetime he worked a 6½ day week.

Throughout the war, Rasmussen continued to work with Spitfire repair units. In the course of his duties he spent six months in Delhi, visiting Spitfire squadrons in India, and after VE Day he worked with Seafire squadrons based in Ceylon. The RAF recorded their appreciation of his services in a letter written by AC Disbrey in August 1945:

> The time has come for the Vickers-Armstrongs representative, Mr Rasmussen, to be returned to the UK, and I want to place on record our appreciation of the valuable services he has rendered.

Rasmussen was awarded the MBE in 1946 for his round-the-world work with the RAF. Jack died fifty-five years later in April 2001, aged ninety-six.

In June 1940 the Castle Bromwich shadow factory, now under the direct management of Vickers-Armstrongs, rolled out its first Spitfire. It was the Mk II, a derivative of the Mk I which was already in production at Southampton, and in service in Fighter Command. From this point onwards the rate of production of the Castle Bromwich factory was to build up rapidly. Ten aircraft were delivered in June, thereby winning a bet between the Castle Bromwich management and Lord Beaverbrook, and in due course the production of Spitfires at Castle Bromwich was to peak at the incredible rate of 320 per month, by which time the Mk IX was in production.

By the end of the war, Castle Bromwich was producing Spitfire Mk 22 aircraft. The chief executive of Castle Bromwich was Mr B.W.A. Dickson, and his chief assistant was Mr S.P. Woodley. Castle Bromwich constituted an autonomous production unit on its own, separate from the production organisation in the southern region. At a later stage in the war, Castle Bromwich was also producing Lancaster bombers concurrently with Spitfires.

Up to October 1940, all Spitfire production in the southern region (Southampton) had been concentrated at the Woolston and Itchen works, although many components were sub-contracted to outside firms. Final assembly and flight testing took place at Eastleigh Airport, and through-out the 'phoney war' and Battle of Britain, Southampton production was running at a brisk and increasing rate. Strangely, the Germans made no determined attempt to bomb the principal source of Spitfire production during this period. But in September 1940 a series of determined raids severely damaged the Woolston and Itchen works, causing considerable casualties amongst the workers and virtually bringing Spitfire produc-tion to a standstill (see illustration 58, page 188).

In these raids the Germans also achieved something of great potential importance that they knew nothing about at the time. The Woolston works contained two partially built prototypes of Mitchell's heavy bomber, designed to Air Ministry Specification B.12/36 and to be powered by four Merlin engines. They were totally destroyed and the project was abandoned.

It is interesting to speculate what might have happened if those prototypes had not been destroyed. If Mitchell had achieved the same degree of success with his bomber as he had with his fighter – bearing in mind that he was undoubtedly at his peak as a designer at that time – its impact upon Britain's bomber offensive against Germany might have been spectacular. Also, due to its superior speed, it would undoubt-edly have reduced the terrible 55,000 casualties suffered by Bomber Command 1939–45. The Luftwaffe raid on Woolston probably achieved far more than they ever realised. Further comments on this bomber are to be found in Chapters 14 and 18.

Supermarine were not totally unprepared for the damage to the works, for in 1939 the young works engineer Mr L.G. Gooch was given the task of planning a small-scale dispersion scheme for the Southampton area, which included the requisitioning of a bus station and two sizeable garages. Consequently, many of the vital production jigs and tools had already been moved before the bombing occurred.

However, when the extent of the damage to the factories was fully appreciated, Lord Beaverbrook, then Minister of Aircraft Production, immediately ordered 100% dispersal of Spitfire production (excepting Castle Bromwich), over southern England. On the day following the bombing, the company requisitioned the fourth floor of the Polygon Hotel in Southampton, and the works manager, W.T. Elliott, and Len Gooch moved in with their staffs and department heads to plan and implement the dispersion scheme and to get production moving again. They were joined by some senior MAP officials with substantial powers to ensure that no obstacles should be allowed to stand in the way of the dispersal scheme.

Len Gooch later wrote,

> My first action was to obtain large-scale ordnance maps of the counties of Wiltshire, Hampshire and Berkshire, and from calculations made of exist- ing areas of factories already in use, and scaled up to meet increased output, we prepared a plan whereby 25% of the output was selected to be made in each of four towns with nearby aerodromes; namely Southampton area (using Eastleigh Airport), Salisbury (using High Post and the racing gal- lops at Chattis Hill), Trowbridge (using Keevil Aerodrome) and Reading (using Henley initially, and later Aldermaston). In each of these towns we planned to put wing and fuselage jigs, and completely assemble these major components ready for marrying together at the aerodromes. So we planned four production lines, not one.

All this work was carried out in requisitioned premises – garages, laundries, etc. – dispersed throughout the four towns. Production of Spitfires was soon re-established, and the dispersion scheme continued through the war, resulting in a continually increasing rate of pro- duction. It turned out to be extremely flexible, as it was possible to introduce new Spitfire variants very quickly, and several variants were often in production at the same time. It is also notable that when the dispersion scheme was fully established, some 45% of the productive labour force were women.

Because of the bombing, it was also necessary to evacuate the design department, drawing office and associated departments. They moved to temporary quarters at Southampton University. Eventually the whole company, administration, works, design and commercial, moved into a large country house, Hursley Park near Winchester, where they remained for seventeen years.

When Mitchell died, he bequeathed to the nation two legacies of incalculable value. The first was the Spitfire itself, plus of course, the Walrus amphibian. The second was the design team which he had built up over the years, and which was destined, under the leadership of Joe Smith, to carry on and to build upon the work which R.J. had initi- ated with so much inspiration. Such a team takes years to grow into an experienced, effective and mature organisation, and its strength depends upon the quality of the leadership and the individuals who serve it.

Such men as Alan Clifton, Eric Lovell-Cooper, Arthur Shirvall, Ernest Mansbridge, Harold Smith, Wilfred Hennesey, Jack Rice and Arthur Black, to name but a few, made a contribution during the war years which cannot be over-emphasised. It was they who helped to develop the Spitfire and keep it in the front line from 1939 through to 1945.

As already described, the two Vickers test pilots most closely connected with the early test flights of the Spitfire were Jeffrey Quill and George Pickering, later joined by Alex Henshaw. George Pickering was a very experienced and skilled flying boat pilot, to which he owed his original employment by Supermarine. However he quickly adapted to fighter flying and became a first-rate Spitfire pilot; up to the end of 1941 he spent hundreds of hours test flying Spitfires.

In October 1941 he had a serious accident when the production Spitfire he was testing to its maximum diving speed broke up in the air. He was thrown from the cockpit, which virtually disintegrated around him, damaging his parachute in the process. George, who was unconscious at this stage, was saved by the fact that the parachute deployed on its own and, although the canopy was badly damaged, it arrested his fall, which was further broken by the branches of a tree.

When picked up he was desperately injured and spent many months in hospital. In spite of this he was determined to fly again and finally, after being 'grounded' for almost a year, he was passed fit for flying by a medical board at Oxford. On the return journey from Oxford, happy at the prospect of flying Spitfires again, he stayed the night with his sister at Leighton Buzzard, where he met some officers of an Army unit which was conducting a training exercise. They invited George to come and see the fun. While negotiating a steep slope at Ivinghoe Beacon, the Bren gun carrier in which George was riding overturned and he was killed. It was a most ironic twist of fate, and the sad loss of George Pickering was a very severe blow to Supermarine.

When the great factory at Castle Bromwich had begun to get into its stride in the latter half of 1940, it was clear that the production test-flying task would be a formidable one, and it was decided to transfer Alex Henshaw to Castle Bromwich to take full charge of the flying there, and to build up a team of pilots to assist him.

Henshaw was a pilot of quite exceptional ability and courage. Shortly before the war he had established, by a handsome margin, records for the London–Cape Town, Cape Town–London, and London–Cape Town–London flights in a tiny, specially modified Mew Gull racing aircraft. He had also won the King's Cup air race at record speed. He had an exceptional faculty for flying in extremely bad weather without external navigational or 'let-down' aids, and he was also a brilliant aerobatic and demonstration pilot. A vivid and enthralling account of his activities at Castle Bromwich is contained in his book, *Sigh for a Merlin*. In a Foreword to that book, Jeffrey Quill wrote:

> There is no doubt that the job of chief pilot at Castle Bromwich was one of exceptional difficulty and challenge. It was fortunate for us all that Alex was there to do it. I know of no other pilot who could have handled it as he did, nor who could have set such a high standard for his subordinate pilots to follow. It was a case of leadership by example if ever there was one.

The transfer of Alex Henshaw to his demanding task at Castle Bromwich, and the loss of George Pickering, left Jeffrey Quill with sole responsibility for the testing of the production output of the southern region – now dispersed over Hampshire, Wiltshire and Berkshire. Quill also had to cope with the rapidly expanding task of experimental test-flying, arising from the development of a whole new series of Spitfire variants (see Chapter 16), all of which had to be meticulously tested in prototype or experimental form. To handle the production testing task in the southern region, a team of RAF pilots, on secondment to Supermarine, was built up, and Quill also engaged an old colleague from RAF days, Flt Lt George Snarey. This left Quill free to concentrate his main efforts on the experimental and development testing.

A special experimental Flight Test Unit, operating independently of the production organisation and working directly with the design organisation under Joe Smith, was set up at the aerodrome of Worthy Down near Winchester. Later in the war this unit moved to High Post Aerodrome near Salisbury. The development flying task soon became well beyond the capacity of one pilot, and Quill was assisted at various times by Lt Cdr Don Robertson, RNVR; Frank Furlong, RNVR (in peacetime a noted amateur rider who won the Grand National in 1935), who was killed while test flying in 1944; G.B.S. Errington (on loan from Airspeed, of which company he was chief pilot); Lt P. Shea-Simmonds, RNVR; and Lt M.J. Lithgow, RN.

In the course of the 1939–45 war, Spitfires were flown in combat against the enemy by pilots representing almost every Allied country. It became the most famous and best-known fighter of all time and was much beloved by the pilots who flew it. It captured the imagination and the hearts of the British people when, in the desperate days of 1940, it became a symbol of defiance and brought the sweet taste of victory during the Battle of Britain, following an uninterrupted series of military disasters. The British public gave a particularly practical form to their feelings about the Spitfire and arrangements were made whereby individuals or organisations could present an aircraft to the nation. In the case of the Spitfire, an arbitrary figure of £5,000 was decided upon to represent the cost of a new machine, although, in fact, the real cost was more like £7,500, and in return for that sum of money a Spitfire was delivered to the RAF with the name of the donor painted on the side. Photographs were sent to the donor(s) with a letter of thanks from the government, and sometimes there was a naming ceremony.

Enormous sums of money were subscribed nationwide, and at one period almost every new Spitfire emerging from the southern unit factories had the name of a donor on it. The director of the Vienna clinic attended by Mitchell just before his death, Mr Fred Pearson, gave a Spitfire, serial no X4936, with the inscription 'In memory of R.J. Mitchell' painted on the side.

The city of Southampton, the home of the Spitfire, also contributed. In August 1940, at the height of the Battle of Britain, the following letter appeared in the local Southampton paper:

> The Mayor's Parlour
> Southampton.
> 12 August 1940.
> To the editor of the Southern Daily Echo
>
> Sir,
>
> In a response to a widely expressed desire on the part of the citizens of Southampton, I have much pleasure in initiating a fund for the purpose of presenting, on behalf of the town, a Spitfire to the nation.
>
> There is a special reason why Southampton should be identified with this movement, which is now being taken up throughout the country. It is that the designer of the Spitfire, the late Mr R.J. Mitchell, CBE, was himself for many years a citizen of this borough, until his untimely death three years ago.
>
> Besides being an outstanding aeronautical designer, he was a gentleman of most loveable personality who endeared himself not only to a wide circle of friends, but to all who came in contact with him during his many years at The Supermarine Aviation Works in Woolston.
>
> Nothing could be more appropriate, therefore, than that Southampton should present one or more Spitfires to the country in memory of this great man, whose genius may yet prove to be the means of enabling us to emerge triumphant from the greatest trial to which we have ever been subjected in our history.
>
> Robert N. Sinclair,
> Mayor.

That Southampton appeal realised a sum of £15,527, which therefore paid for three Spitfires; these were among the first to be presented under the scheme and each one bore the arms of the city of Southampton and the name 'R.J. Mitchell'. Their serial numbers were R7058, R7059 and R7060. (See illustration 59, page 188.)

R.J. would have been very gratified by this response by the citizens of the city in which he had lived all of his working life.

18

My Father as I Remember Him

I was only 16½ years old when my father died; I am now eighty-one (December 2002). It may well be asked whether I am really able to remember accurately any events that took place so many years ago. The human brain is, however, an incredible organ and it is my experience that I can today remember things that took place in my life fifty or more years ago, very often more vividly than I can recall something which happened to me a mere week ago!

I understand that this is by no means unusual and that the remarkable ability of the adult to remember quite vividly events that occurred during the period they were growing up between about six and seventeen years of age is very well recognised. I think my threshold of memories is somewhere around the age of six, namely from around 1926.

Starting from about this age of six, I remember well the annual trips we used to make at Christmas from Southampton to Stoke-on-Trent for my parents to visit their parents. Father had great respect for both his mother and father and felt that to visit them from time to time was both a pleasure and a duty he must fulfil no matter how inconvenient it was and however busy he might be. Hence the Christmas forays. Mother and I would pile into the car accompanied by our little dog. It was called 'Binkie' and was essentially mother's pet; somewhat surprising that I can remember the name of what was after all only a rather silly little dog!

Once father had started on a journey in his car, only reluctantly would he stop before he arrived at his destination. Accordingly, I have a vivid recollection, on more than one occasion, of father continuously putting off the requests of my mother to stop to let Binkie out. As a result certain acts of nature were performed over the back seat and sometimes over me. This did not make father in the best of tempers when he arrived, so that the whole visit started off very much on the wrong foot, not helped by mother repeating that it was all his fault.

This simple little episode does bring out one characteristic of my father, which I must add is one of several traits that I have inherited from him, and that is that he was a very impatient individual. He may take, and generally did, some time to reach a decision but having done so, the sooner the necessary action was implemented the better. Hence, if he had to drive from Southampton to Stoke-on-Trent, the sooner the journey was completed, the better as far as he was concerned.

My memories of these Christmas visits are mixed. I enjoyed them partly because I received a lot of attention from both of my grandmas and grandpas (Mitchell and Dayson) and partly because I was generally rather spoilt and given plenty of presents. But I got the feeling that sometimes things were rather hard going as far as my father was concerned. I think perhaps, in hindsight, that it was a case of not having much in common to talk about after the first few days of normal greetings. Father had, since he left home to work in Southampton, begun to live in a world completely foreign to that which his parents knew. He was, after all, by then on course to becoming recognised as one of the world's greatest aircraft designers and I have some doubts whether either his father or his mother would fully comprehend this in the light of their so completely different interests of a different generation.

I have an amazingly good recall of the Mitchell senior house in Hanley, namely Talbot House, 4 Mollart Street, to where my grandparents had moved from Victoria Cottage, Normacot. I remember the first room on the right, which was only used on special occasions, the large kitchen and especially the toilet which was situated halfway up the stairs! I also had good reason for remembering one of the bedrooms. It was in 1927 and it was arranged that I should stay with my grandparents while mother and father went to Venice for the Schneider Trophy Contest. Just before they were due back in England, I was involved in a car crash as described in Chapter 9. I received severe concussion and remember nothing of the crash. My parents were informed immediately they stepped off the boat and belted up to see me lying in bed in a darkened room, as I then was. Both were kindness personified and could not do enough for me. Father used to sit with me, I remember, for ages trying to cheer me up and telling me that his 'big boy' would soon be all right again.

In due course, I was, and returned home none the worse, I think, for this rather frightening experience.

Another clear memory I have of those early years was the annual event at my local preparatory school when the school cricket team played a team of fathers. I was not good enough to play for the school but father was always selected for the fathers' team. He was an exceptionally well-built man with broad shoulders and he used them to good effect to try and bash the ball all over the field. He usually succeeded in this for a time, much to the dismay of the entire school, but whether by accident or design (probably the latter) he normally did not last very long, being either caught, run out or stumped. I recollect one particular master who seemed to hang around father most of the day. I am not sure whether it was out of admiration or whether he hoped father would give him a job but I remember father telling my mother afterwards that he was a bit of a bloody nuisance!

I mention this cricket episode mainly to show that right from a quite young age, my father went to great pains to show a fatherly interest in me and, looking back, I realise how fortunate I was to have a father who was willing to spend so much time with me, taking me around with him all over the place on numerous occasions.

About this time, he began to take me into work with him to the Supermarine factory in Woolston, on a Saturday morning. I would spend quite a bit of time in the office of his secretary, Vera Cross, messing about with carbon paper or the typewriter and so on. I am sure she blessed me sometimes but I remember her kindness and understanding to this day. I enjoyed particularly one thing, and that was going out with Herbbie Grimes in the works' launch for a trip up the river. This was great fun and I used to pretend I was the skipper and Grimes was the crew. Although I did not appreciate it at the time, this was, of course, just one of the perks of being the boss's son.

However, it was not long before father indicated that these Saturday morning visits were not to be just fun and games for me. One day he said that he wanted me to go all round the factory and note all the various jobs that were being done both in the machine shops and in the assembly areas. After I had done this, I told my father I had enjoyed going round. He replied that he didn't want to know if I had enjoyed it but whether I had learnt anything from my tour. I was tempted to say 'very little', but approaching nine as I then was, I had learnt that that would not have been an exactly acceptable reply! So I then described some of the operations I had observed. By things my father said, I realised that he knew exactly the type of work that everyone in the factory was engaged on. He had not spent five years as an apprentice engineer in a locomotive works for nothing and this I firmly believe was one of the secrets of his success – he knew at first hand everything going on from top to bottom in the Supermarine works.

Father had a stammer which, although it was only slight, worried him a great deal. When he was preparing for the recording he made after winning the Schneider Trophy in 1931 (and which is reproduced in full in Chapter 11), I remember him going through his talk out loud to my mother time after time. This was not because he had to learn it but simply so that by saying the words often enough, he would not falter over any of them. That he succeeded is shown by the fact that he hesitated over one or two words only throughout the recording. His concern about this speech defect was, I would surmise, possibly that in his continual search for perfection in all things, he felt his speech fell short of this goal.

It was around this time that father went up to Buckingham Palace to receive his CBE. Oddly enough, I have very little recollection of this big event in his life, except being aware of his great dislike of having to be decked out in the court dress. One thing that is certain and that is that I did not accompany my mother and father to the palace; perhaps eleven-year-olds were not allowed to do so then?

At this point, it is important that I make it clear that although most of my memories about my father are happy ones, they are by no means exclusively so.

I was once asked, by the chairman at a Mitchell Memorial Lecture in 1981, what it was like to live with a genius. Even at the age of sixteen, when he died, I doubt whether I really knew what a genius was, but I did know that life with my father was at times extremely difficult although I did not feel it was an appropriate time to enlarge upon it at the lecture.

My father had an extremely short temper, and could become unreasonably angry, followed by a long period of moodiness when he would not say a word to anyone. He had no time at all for anyone he considered a fool and could be very rude if the individual concerned did not quickly get the message. I suffered from this aspect of his character myself only too often when I did or said something about which he felt I ought to show more sense. With such a person it was hardly surprising that just occasionally some heated rows took place at home. Fortunately, my mother, who was eleven years older than my father, having been born on 13 February 1884, was fairly placid and highly intelligent (she was, as is mentioned in Chapter 1, one time headmistress of Dresden Infants School in the Potteries). I think she knew in her heart that she had married an exceptional man, a genius, and that accordingly she had to make allowances for his occasionally erratic behaviour and do her best to calm things down. She undoubtedly did just this with great success and I believe my father was indeed very fortunate that he had married the one in a million who had the ability to understand exactly what was needed and to provide it. Interestingly, mother was always somewhat concerned that she was older than my father, although I could never understand why. One simple example of his temper stays clearly in my mind. Father was very partial to oysters and on one occasion at home when a new supply was opened, they were found to be bad and really stank. Immediately, father was on the phone to the fishmonger, who had supplied them, and subjected him to a verbal barrage bordering very close to pure rage. I had little doubt that father had concluded that the fishmonger was an incompetent fool and, in consequence, really let him have it with all guns firing.

I hope the reader will now have gathered that life at home with father was not always a bed of roses, but as I shall show, after 1933 there were overwhelming reasons why this should be so.

My father also had an intense sense of humour, which very often, thankfully, overrode his potential anger. Hence when, for example, I arrived home one evening accompanied by a police officer, having been caught riding my bicycle without any lights, or when I plunged our house into darkness by wiring up a torch bulb, fitted to the top of the Eiffel Tower I had built with Meccano, into the electricity mains, on both occasions, fortunately for me, he showed amusement rather than anger.

Another of his attributes, which I had good cause to remember, was the great importance he attached to the exercise of common sense, attention to detail, and hard work as recipes for success; but he always put special emphasis on the first of these attributes. This was drummed into me many times and I think I can say I learnt the lesson. Luck, he told me, rarely came into it. Joe Smith in giving the 1st Mitchell Memorial Lecture in January 1954[13] said, 'R.J. was, above everything else, a practical engineer, and possessed an abundance of plain, straightforward common sense.' In this connection, it is of interest to quote, by kind permission of Robert Hale Ltd, from the book *Air Crash – the Clues in the Wreckage* by Fred Jones, published in 1985:

> People have devoted a lifetime to studying and researching fatigue and associated matters and I have noticed over the years, having seen many accidents attributable directly to the fatigue failure of an item or component, that the failure was almost always due to the lack of good common sense engineering practice...

Reading this very interesting book on investigations into various aircraft crashes, drives home forcibly that the designing of structurally safe aeroplanes is not the piece of cake some people might imagine it to be.

Coupled with his great emphasis on the application of common sense at all times was a continual urge to simplify things. Jeffrey Quill, in his book *Spitfire – A Test Pilot's Story*, recalled what my father once said to him, while they were chatting together in his Rolls-Royce car between flights, and as it is such an excellent example of this particular attribute, it bears repeating: 'Jeffrey, if anyone tries to tell you something about an aeroplane which is so damn complicated that you can't understand it, you can take it from me it's all balls!' Father did not use quite the same words to me but he must have got the message over since I have precisely the same views as he had on this matter of simplification. Father had no time for people who tried to make out that something was so difficult to understand that only they could possibly do so.

On a more personal note, I feel, looking back, regret that my father and mother decided, for reasons best known to themselves, that I should be an only child. Brothers and sisters play a vital role in knocking off the rough edges, as manifest by my own fine family of three, and I realise now how much I missed by not having any. Both my father and mother came from large families but perhaps there were good reasons for me being an only child; it was a subject that was never discussed with me.

I come now to the traumatic events of the summer of 1933. These are described in short in Chapter 13 on page 142, but it is necessary and right, I feel, for me to enlarge upon them and their consequences in this chapter. Unquestionably, they had an indelible effect on father's character and were very much an integral part of the last four years of his life and of my memories of him. Furthermore, I am, of course, in a unique position to relate in true detail this all-important aspect of his life and so stop, I would hope, further incorrect statements being made about it, such as, for example, that he died of tuberculosis. This untrue statement has appeared several times, such as in an important 1985 publication about the RAF, *The Right of the Line* by John Terraine, published by Hodder and Stoughton.

I remember the time well, as we were due to go to Devon in a few days for our summer holiday. I believe that father had decided to have a routine check before going on holiday and that certain observed abnormalities would prove to be of no consequence. His doctor, Dr Picken, suspected cancer of the rectum and referred him to Mr William Gabriel, a leading colorectal surgeon at St Mark's Hospital in London, who advised an immediate operation. This was a success but involved extensive surgery in which his rectum was removed and the severed end of his colon brought out through an opening in the abdominal wall to form a colostomy, through which his bowel motions would have to be discharged for the rest of his life. It is of interest to recall here that typically my father had, within a few weeks, designed what he thought would be a more satisfactory appliance for covering his colostomy at night. A year or so after Mitchell's operation, Mr Gabriel published a textbook on colorectal surgery and in it appears the following: 'Fig. 157. Pad of wool and aluminium ring, which can be bent to fit the body, for night wear over a colostomy (R.J. Mitchell's design)'. I remember very well my father working on this design in our garage at home, showing that designing aircraft was not his only expertise!

Later, I contacted Mr Howard Jones, the director of the British Colostomy Association, about the adverse effects having a colostomy can have. In his letter of reply, he said:

> To be deprived of a perfectly natural body function can, in itself, cause great distress, and the thought of having to discharge faecal matter through the colostomy into a bag for the rest of your life, a cause of considerable repugnance. The inevitable odour, leakage and wind noises would, in your father's time, when all that was available was a pad of cotton wool held in place by a belt, have been much worse than today with the well-sealed appliances now available... Your father must have agonised over the fact that when he was in company, there would usually be unpleasant smells detectable which clung to his clothes. In the 1930s, it was considered a social stigma to have a colostomy which turned many of those with one into recluses, never venturing far from a toilet for fear of a sudden accident or onset of diarrhoea. How your father managed to overcome his disability to the extent that he was able to design such a complicated piece of engineering as a fighter plane, with all that it obviously entailed in meetings, travelling, long hours and mental strain, is quite beyond my belief. In your father's time, the best that most people so affected managed to achieve was just to more or less exist from day to day, the motivating power simply being gratitude for actually being alive.
>
> A major problem with a colostomy even today is that worry and anxiety can cause a nervous reaction which can easily result in diarrhoea. It says mountains for your father's constitution and will power that he achieved so much in a condition of such adversity.
>
> Another common problem, which is perhaps the greatest danger with a permanent colostomy, is acute depression, which is extremely difficult to treat, even today. All I can say in conclusion is that having personally helped several thousand colostomy patients, and being one myself, I do not know how your father did what he did for his country.

I have deliberately looked at this crucial part of my father's life at some length because it gives a greater insight than has ever appeared in print before, or been said before, into what a mammoth personal problem he had to cope with during the time he was designing the Spitfire, since he knew from what Mr Gabriel had told him that he was probably dying, there being the gravest risk his cancer would return.

This accurate description of my father's illness was, however, not accurately followed in the big film that was produced about him in 1942.

It was a great honour for R.J. that this film was made, starring Leslie Howard as my father, Rosamund John as my mother and David Niven as his test pilot, and was entitled *The First of the Few*, based on Churchill's famous words, 'Never in the field of human conflict was so much owed by so many to so few'. Churchill, in fact, gave his full backing to the film.

It was a sympathetic portrayal of my father but was inaccurate in several ways. Thus, for example, cancer was never mentioned, and R.J.'s illness and death were portrayed as being somehow due to overwork designing the Spitfire. The fact is, of course, that he would still have died on 11 June 1937 (see page 195) even if he had retired in 1933 after his operation for rectal cancer and never created the Spitfire. Nevertheless, the film was without doubt entertaining to the general public as witnessed by the fact that today, sixty-three years after it was produced, it is still being shown on TV from time to time.

It is sad to recall that Sir Henry Royce, whose engines played such a vital role in father's life, underwent in around 1912 an operation for cancer of the intestine which resulted in him also having a permanent colostomy. Following this operation, he was never without a personal nurse in attendance. Sir Henry visited his factory in Derby in 1914, but although he was the mainspring of his company until his death nineteen years later, he never visited Derby again. He had his design team with him at his home in West Wittering and communicated by memo and sketch with his factory in Derby. Sir Henry was seventy when he died in 1933.

Like my father, it is clear that Sir Henry showed a degree of courage and fortitude in the face of severe physical adversity that fortunately not many of us are called upon to endure.

Returning to the visits I used to make to the Supermarine works with father, I remember another occasion very vividly. It was a bit later on, when I was about fifteen. He went into his office where some three or four of his design staff were assembled and they began to discuss some problem that they had on the Spitfire that was connected with the radiator.

Father went round the group asking for the views of each individual; I listened but most of the discussion went in one ear and out of the other. Suddenly my father turned to me and said, 'And what do you think should be done, big boy?' I do not think I can claim to have influenced the Spitfire design in any way by my reply but it certainly taught me to keep on my toes when father was around and I have no doubt that all of his colleagues at Supermarine had learnt the same lesson. It was also a very typical action on my father's part in that he was a great listener and was always ready to listen to anyone, even, as on this occasion, to his teenage son.

Another visit I made to Supermarine that I have good cause to remember was when father asked me if I would like to go for a flight with George Pickering in the Seagull V (later named the Walrus) amphibian. Immediately, I said I would, little knowing that George would be throwing the aircraft around somewhat to demonstrate at first hand to my father its amazing flying capabilities. I enjoyed it at first but then things began to get a bit rough. It was not long before I disgraced myself by being violently sick all over the cabin floor. Both George and my father just laughed – I felt like anything but laughing at the time!

At a later visit in 1935, father proudly showed me the prototype Spitfire under construction in a screened-off part of the assembly building. It was in fact situated near to the stairs leading up to the offices, which I used to climb on my visits to the office of Vera Cross, which I mentioned earlier. Little did I realise at the time the significance of what I had been very privileged to see, but this was yet another example of how my father made a special point of keeping me informed about the designs on which he was working.

Three days after its first flight, on 5 March 1936, I was taken to Eastleigh to see the prototype Spitfire which by now, it was clear to me, had become father's pride and joy. My first reaction on seeing this historic aircraft was how beautiful and graceful it looked, but I thought (to myself) how much better it would look if given a good coat of paint (see illustration 63, page 189). This was, of course, before the prototype received its famous coat of cerulean blue. A photograph I took of my father, and the one he then took of me, alongside K5054, can be seen on page 189. Father was no photographer and this snap is one of the few he ever took; these are photographs that I treasure greatly.

A few years earlier, in 1929 and 1931, visits with father to Calshot to see the Schneider Trophy seaplanes being flown were quite frequent and, of course, he introduced me, as his 'big boy', to all the pilots and other important people! We would usually leave home at the crack of dawn without having had any breakfast; this was because often the best conditions for flying were very early in the morning. While I greatly enjoyed these visits, since again being the boss's son I could go more or less anywhere I wished, in no small measure the highspot for me was to go to the officers' mess for breakfast with father, the pilots and other notables.

Father was by no means all work and no play. Some of his leisure activities have already been described. Golf, tennis, rowing, dog breeding, snooker (I believe the need for a correct interpretation of angles appealed to him), private flying and shooting were his major sports. Particularly in the latter three activities, he developed a very close and long-lasting friendship with Alec Bennett. Alec was a Canadian by birth and a former RFC pilot and winner of the Isle of Man TT race on no less than five occasions between 1922 and 1928, plus four French and two Belgian Grand Prix victories. They got on like a house on fire, no doubt because they had so much in common, such as a passionate interest in flying. Most of father's really close friends were those connected with his work. Alec Bennett was a notable exception. Both found great relaxation in shooting; whether father was any good at it, I know not, since this was one activity to which I was never invited. He used to bring home a pheasant from time to time, but, knowing him, he could easily have bought it in a shop on the way home and said nothing until we were actually eating it a few days later!

On one occasion father bought home a rabbit which we presumed he had shot. He took it and me into the kitchen and proceeded to give me my first lesson in anatomy as he cut it open and began to remove the organs one by one. A rather gory and smelly business; mother kept well away.

Little did I realise at the time that this episode would represent the start, as it were, of the career which I was eventually to choose, namely to become a member of the academic staff of the University of Reading, working as a research scientist in the field of animal physiology and nutrition. No wonder I remember the occasion so clearly! I was not the only person to remember it; in the discussion following the 1st Mitchell Memorial Lecture in 1954,[14] AM Sir John Boothman, the winning pilot in the 1931 Schneider Trophy Contest, said:

> R.J. once said to me if he had his life again he would not have been an aeroplane designer but a surgeon – this was a long time before he was sick – and I remember around 1932 or 1933 an occasion when, having been out shooting with him in the early morning, there was a most gory procedure going on in the kitchen when he was explaining the inside of a rabbit to his son.
>
> R.J. was a very great man and I am very proud to have been allowed to say my little bit this evening.

One of father's leisure activities that he often shared with me in the 1930s was golf. We would all go off on a Sunday, quite often taking a picnic lunch, to nearby Bramshaw Golf Course. While mother and father played against each other, I was provided with a suitable iron with which I proceeded to hack my way round alongside them; I also used it for putting!

Father was very patient with me and would from time to time stop to give me a bit of advice and even occasionally a bit of praise. Then we would have our picnic lunch in one of the shelters on the course. It is of interest that, in 1999, Bramshaw Golf Club published 'The Millennium

Handbook' incorporating the history of the club and recording the names of famous people remembered as playing the course and these included, 'Mr & Mrs R.J. Mitchell (it was Mr Mitchell who was responsible for the Spitfire fighter plane)'.

I enjoyed these outings very much and developed a great liking and interest in golf thanks to father's encouragement. Mother also helped me a lot as she was in fact a very capable golfer and won several competitions in her golfing career. She was once hit sharply on the breast with a golf ball and she always blamed this for the breast cancer for which she later had to undergo an operation.

Father was a good average golfer and, although he played it essentially for enjoyment, in 1935 he won the prestigious Junior Scratch Championship of the Southampton Shipping Golfing Society, played over the Stoneham Golf Club Course in Southampton, a course which he knew well. Incidentally, 'Junior' here does not refer to age but to handicap, the Junior event being for the second league players as it were, with handicaps of between thirteen and twenty-four. For this achievement father received the King Cup, and the replica that was given for him to retain is still in my possession. Remembering his physical disability, this little episode is one more example of my father's determination not to allow it to interfere with his sporting and leisure activities during those stressful years between 1933 and early 1937.

While on the subject of golf, an interesting little story recently came to light. One day in 1936, father met at his golf club a Mr A.E. Payne, who turned out to be a technical representative of a watch-importing concern. Father told him that his watch always let him down when he played golf and so Mr Payne obtained a better one for him with a new type of shockproof movement. He was delighted with it and, having paid for it, gave Mr Payne his old watch, a services navigator.

During the war, Mr Payne spent four years as an inspector on Spitfire salvage and repairs and then many years later in 1964 he wrote a letter to Flight International saying he had this watch which had belonged to my father and would be glad to give it to the person who made the highest bid for it, the money to go to the RAF Benevolent Fund. A Mrs Falconer from Stroud in Gloucestershire duly acquired the watch and gave it to her son, Richard Falconer. Following a letter I wrote in August 1985, Richard Falconer contacted me and said he still had the watch, given by my father to Mr Payne forty-nine years earlier, and would be pleased to loan it to the RAF Museum should they be interested in having it!

In July 1934, father obtained his private pilot's licence (no 7078) and I remember watching him on 24 October 1936 win a 'spot-landing' competition at Eastleigh Airport against all the odds. This achievement was just eight months before my father died. I recall that he put some money on himself in the 'book' that was run for the event. He got good odds as nobody else gave him any chance of winning. Earlier, I have said that father did not put much store on luck, but he did admit after collecting his winnings that this was a case of being just a little bit lucky!

Father was a founder member of the Hampshire Aeroplane Club, of which Lord Mountbatten was one-time President. He really loved his flying and used to go around all over the country whenever he found any excuse to do so. A trip to Rolls-Royce in Derby – what better than to fly himself there? Of course, he never flew the Spitfire himself since his licence did not qualify him to do so, but perhaps his private flying experience made him feel he could understand some of the problems encountered by his test pilots, George Pickering and Jeffrey Quill, that little bit better. This could have been one reason for him learning to fly himself, but it was undoubtedly mainly because he enjoyed it.

Another sport, if it can be called that, which father took up around the 1934–36 period was so-called 'stagging' on the stock exchange. He would apply for shares in a new issue and sell them quickly once they were quoted on the exchange in the hope of making a small profit. His personal diary contains many references to this activity. By that time, his annual salary had reached £2,500; chickenfeed by today's standard, but equivalent in spending power to well over £100,000 at today's prices and tax rates (his overall tax rate was only 18.5%). So I guess father felt he could afford to indulge in this somewhat dicey pastime and he would often say to me that he had done very well stagging such and such a share. I must admit I really had no idea what he was talking about!

With reference, once again, to my father's personal diary, it is interesting that later in 1936, references to the Spitfire were replaced by references to his four-engined bomber, Specification B.12/36, a contract for which had been given to Supermarine by the Air Ministry early in 1936. As has been already emphasised, this bomber, and not the Spitfire, was the last aircraft my father designed.

I remember an occasion at home, sometime in 1936, when I overheard my father say to my mother that he was tickled pink by the thought that his relatively tiny Supermarine company might produce not only Britain's front-line fighter but also its number one bomber. As the latter had an estimated maximum speed of 360 mph (compared to the 275 mph of the Lancaster, which did not come into service until 1942), it has always seemed to me to have been one of the major mistakes of the war that the building of the B.12/36 (by another company if Supermarine could not cope), was not continued with after the setback when the first fuselages were destroyed in a bombing raid in 1940. I can only say that I know father had very great hopes for it and this is brought out very clearly in Chapter 14. Joe Smith, who succeeded him as chief designer, used to tell me, during my chats with him early in the war, of his great expectations for the bomber. In the 1st Mitchell Memorial Lecture in 1954, Joe said, '... there seems little doubt that it [the bomber] would have been highly successful'. It is, in my view, indeed a real tragedy it never flew, as it could have saved a great many lives in Bomber Command with its superior speed potential, which was in fact faster than that of the Mk I Spitfire!

Father was initiated into Freemasonry in the Jasper Lodge, Hanley, on 10 September 1923. His father, Herbert, was a very active and high-ranking Freemason and so no doubt told my father what Freemasonry was all about. I cannot recall any activities that father took part in as a Freemason but possibly it was something he just kept to himself. More recently, I was told by a close colleague of my father that he believed he attended the Royal Gloucester Lodge No 130 in Southampton. He added that R.J.'s personal qualities were consistent with the code of Freemasons.

He was quite a heavy smoker, both cigarettes and a pipe, this latter being something I have definitely inherited from him, which brings to mind the saying that a pipe stops a fool from displaying his ignorance by talking too much. May well apply to me but hardly to my father, I think! One of my delights was to go into my parents' bedroom before they got up (looking back, it seems rather surprising they allowed me to do this), open the cigarette packet on the dressing table and extract the card for my collection.

Another incident that occurred in this bedroom only a matter of days before my father died is one I shall never forget. I should explain that I had known for some time how ill father was and that he had not long to live – a shattering blow with which I did not know how to cope. In the light of this, my mother had gallantly tried to explain some of the facts of life to me a few weeks earlier. As I knew most of them already, I did not take a lot of notice of her, merely feeling rather embarrassed. So when one day my father said to me, 'I understand from mum that you know everything', I immediately thought he was referring to his grave condition. So I replied, 'Yes'. Then he said words to the effect that however tempted you may be it was best to wait until you got married. It took me a while to realise what he was on about but I think I can say that I managed more or less to stick to his advice in later years!

During this period of his life, my father wrote several personal letters to me either while I was away at school and later when he was in Vienna, and these are reproduced in Chapter 14. They are of considerable interest when it is remembered they were written by a man who knew he was dying, and I am so very glad that I kept them.

Even a matter of days before he died, he continued to show the greatest concern about my career and was still writing letters to various people on my behalf. In this connection, it is interesting to recall what Sir William Farren, then president of the Royal Aeronautical Society, said in the discussion following the 1st Mitchell Memorial Lecture in 1954:

> I think the only time he [Mitchell] and I ever really got down to some-
> thing was when he spent a considerable time one afternoon discussing
> with me the problem of the education of his son. I was busy, and had been
> for a number of years, in that field and only afterwards did I realise what
> a privilege it was to be asked about such a thing by such a man.

Father also went to great lengths to try and ensure that my mother and I would be well provided for after his death, and often used to talk to me about what he had done in this respect. Once, he said that whereas his solicitor had recommended that certain safeguards ought to be incorporated in his will dated 5 April 1937, he had complete confidence in both mother and myself and was sure such safeguards were quite unnecessary. I like to think that neither of us abused that trust.

Another important financial matter about which my father was involved in considerable discussion during the last weeks of his life and which again he made sure that I knew all about was a very personal and, at the time, private subject which very few people knew about then, or know about now. After consideration, I decided that my father would not object to me disclosing the broad outlines after the passage of so many years. It was a unique settlement agreement which Vickers, under the direction of Sir Robert McLean, made with my father; it would not be right, even now, for me to reproduce the details of the settlement or the amount of money involved, but I will just say that it was a very generous gesture on the part of Vickers which was greatly appreciated by my father and gave him, I know, peace of mind concerning the financial provisions for his wife after his death. It is of interest that all the arrangements leading up to the settlement were carried out by Henry Duvall, the Vickers company secretary, and I know that my father felt very happy with the excellent way in which Mr Duvall dealt with the settlement, as indeed was my mother subsequently.

I have seen it suggested that father had financial problems during his lifetime; he did indeed have problems but financial difficulties were not one of them as I think will now be clear, and any sensational statements suggesting otherwise should be ignored.

While on the subject of financial matters, another misconception, which I believe may be held by some people, is that my father had some form of patent rights on the aircraft he designed, which were subsequently sold by Supermarine, and which brought him very valuable royalty additions to his basic salary. Not so, unfortunately; he was an employee of the Vickers organisation and anything he produced belonged to them. He may well have received some special bonuses from time to time, but that was something he never talked to me about. It indeed makes an interesting subject for speculation if my father had in fact held patent rights on his Spitfire and had lived to see the 20,334 of them built, not to mention the 2,455 Seafires.

The last weeks of his life were very traumatic and distressing to both mother and I, but father remained outwardly cheerful until the end in spite of the pain he had to endure, which was never completely masked by the regular injections of morphia that he was then having.

One little incident illustrates that father retained his sense of humour right to the end. He was having some trouble, in that when he sneezed it caused him a lot of pain. His doctor suggested that he tried pinching his nose when he felt a sneeze coming on. He duly did this and it worked well at first but after a few aborted sneezes, a big one built up which completely overcame the nose pinch and produced more pain than ever. Father did not despair, he just smiled and said he would prefer several smaller pains than one really big one!

At the end of April, only a few weeks before he died, it was decided in desperation that he should fly to Vienna to consult Professor Freund, one of the leading cancer specialists in the world. I remember the sad occasion when I went to Eastleigh Airport to see my mother and father and his nurse take off in their chartered Dragon Rapide for Vienna (see page 185, illustration 49). His passport, which I still possess, shows that he departed on 29 April 1937 and returned on 25 May 1937. This passport, no 154587, was issued to my father on 23 November 1936 and in it is a 'disembarkment into Calais' stamp bearing the same date. In father's personal diary there is the following entry for 23 November 1936: 'Started for Paris from Victoria' with '£5.17.0' underneath, presumably his expenses for the trip entered later. On 29 November, there is an entry: 'Paris Show ends', and the implication must be that he travelled to Paris to attend this show. So far so good, but on the following day, 24 November, there is the entry in his diary: '12.30 Croydon'. Did he really intend to be in Paris for such a short time since this last entry must surely indicate that he flew back to Croydon on that day? If he had to curtail his visit for some reason, was this perhaps because he was feeling unwell when he got to Paris? It would certainly appear to have been a last-minute decision to go at all since he only got his passport on the day he departed; it was certainly his last ever business trip abroad.

However, this is not quite the end of the passport story since in it is another 'disembarkment into Calais' stamp, this time dated quite clearly 21 January 1938, some seven months after he had died! Who then could have apparently used his passport in January 1938? It had no endorsement on it to cover a child of his and so I could not have done so, nor are there any stamps of any description in my mother's passport, which expired in April 1942, other than those recording her entry into, and departure from, Vienna in April/May 1937, so it would seem very unlikely she went to Calais in January 1938 using her late husband's passport when she had her own. Passport control could have made an error in the date on the stamp, although I would doubt it, but could it have been 21 January 1937 perhaps? However, there is every indication from father's diary that he was in England at that time. An intriguing mystery which will probably never be solved now.

Finally, returning to father's personal diary, there is one further point of interest that I have not mentioned before and that is that the final entry in his 1937 diary is on 4 March and reads: 'Board Meeting'; this shows that it was around this time that he decided he could no longer continue his working life.

Naturally, I hoped and prayed there might be a miracle performed in Vienna, but it was not to be and father returned home a few weeks later to die.

I cannot emphasise too strongly what I know from first-hand experience, namely that my father displayed the greatest courage and fortitude in the face of severe physical adversity, resulting from his colostomy and his knowledge of the likely return of the cancer, during the whole of the last four years of his life and particularly so when all hope had gone and he knew he was going to die. As already discussed, a permanent colostomy frequently results in very severe psychological disturbances and one has only to think about it and what a most unpleasant disability it is to understand this. The suicide rate in those having this disability forced upon them is, for example, much higher than in the normal population.

He used to sit in the garden with my mother, well wrapped up in a big overcoat, until shortly before his death. I was told by my mother to try and behave as though nothing was wrong with father and chat naturally to him, about his dog, his pond that was full of his goldfish, and so on. Not always easy. Father also spent a lot of time with the Reverend Stretton Reeve, vicar of the local Highfield Church in which the funeral service was later to be held. These visits to father's home have been described in Chapter 14, but I would like to emphasise again that I know from personal experience that father, although not a religious man in his lifetime, derived much comfort from these talks with the Reverend Reeve. Both he and his curate, the Reverend Frank Cocks, gave invaluable support to both my mother and myself.

About a week before my father died, something happened which I remember vividly. This was that my mother was approached by a newspaper with a view to writing his obituary then so that, she was told, it would be all ready to include immediately he died. I remember my mother was initially somewhat shocked by this request but in the end understood the reason for it being made and co-operated with the person concerned. She acted in a more sensible manner, I now realise, than her young son would have done. I remember feeling that the whole episode was bizarre and would have been tempted to tell them that my father was still alive and so we wished to have nothing whatever to do with their request. Time enough if and when he was actually dead, was my reaction.

Then on 11 June 1937, my father passed away. Although we had both been expecting it for some weeks, it seemed impossible to accept that he had really gone. I just felt numb and very sad, but even at the tender age of 16½, I could comprehend that at least my father was no longer in pain.

The day of the funeral was, I remember, one of those really hot June days that we get occasionally. Very soon, the wreaths, which it had been requested should all be delivered to our house, began to arrive and were laid out on the lawn.

Eventually, there was hardly any lawn to be seen, so many were the wreaths. The names of those sending them would make an interesting chapter on its own; each wreath was accompanied by a wonderful tribute to the man they had all learnt to respect and had come to realise was one of the world's greatest aircraft designers. In the heat of the strong sun, the overpowering scent from all the flowers spread out on the lawn is something I shall never forget.

Highfield Church where the funeral service was held was full – it was a simple service but a very moving one, conducted in a most beautiful and sympathetic manner by the Reverend Stretton Reeve, assisted by the Reverend Frank Cocks. This was followed by a small family cremation service at South Stoneham Cemetery where my father's remains were later interred. When my mother died in 1946, her remains were placed in the same grave.

The outstanding memory of my father is that he was a good father, a caring father. Although, like us all, he had his faults, which made life with him extremely difficult at times, he helped me enormously, taught me a lot, and in particular taught me how to stand on my own two feet.

Nevertheless, it was a devastating blow to have your father taken away from you just when you began to need his help and advice most. I often reflect upon the many questions about his work that I would dearly like to ask him if he were alive today. How exactly did he evolve the final form of the multitude of components making up the ultimate configuration of his aircraft designs; to what extent, if any, was a touch of good fortune sometimes involved; to what extent were the beautiful curves and elegance of the Spitfire the result of his artistic family background? There can be no doubt that father was an artist in the true sense of the word, as well as a brilliant aerodynamist. It is relevant that both of his brothers, Eric and Billy, were accomplished artists; Billy spent his life producing the close and intricate designs for transfer on to high-quality china. Billy's son, Jim, is a member of the Guild of Aviation Artists and an example of his excellent work is shown on page 184, illustration 48, depicting the first flight of the Spitfire. The only known painting by my father was done in 1916 and is reproduced on page 170, illustration 6.

It is not then, I suggest, something to be surprised at, bearing in mind this background, that father's ultimate achievement, his Spitfire, should have been described over and over again as the most beautiful aeroplane that has ever been produced, before or since.

Finally, a question which perhaps only I would have had the nerve to ask, namely what was his reaction to being called a genius?

I could go on for a long time on this theme but it can, sadly, only be a dream.

In the Memorial Hall in the Garden of Rest, at South Stoneham Cemetery, is a book of remembrance; I would like to conclude this chapter on my memories of my father by quoting the tribute to both of my parents that is included in this book:

11 June
Mitchell, Reginald Joseph, CBE
Aircraft Designer and creator of the
legendary World War II Fighter, the SPITFIRE.
Born 1895, at rest 11 June 1937. Also his beloved
wife, FLORENCE, who died on 3 January 1946.
Both suffered long illnesses
and no son could have parents who are remembered
with greater love and pride.

19

Memorials, Tributes and Events Associated with R.J. Mitchell

Updated 2005

It may come as a surprise to some that there are so many individual items coming under this heading relating to my father. I had not realised myself how many there were until I started to collate them. For the reasons discussed in Chapter 14, there can be no question of my father being awarded a posthumous high civil honour in recognition of his work on the Spitfire but, as will become clear in this chapter, many people resolved that his name should never be forgotten.

The subjects to be described cover a very wide field and no attempt has been made to list them in any particular order of date or importance. In order to avoid the continual repetition of the words 'my father', I have used the initials by which he was popularly known, R.J., throughout.

1. *The Reginald Mitchell Memorial Fund, changed in 1944 to*
    The Spitfire Mitchell Memorial Fund.

The appeal was launched by the lord mayor of Stoke-on-Trent, Alderman C. Austin Brook, MA, at a special showing of the film *The First of the Few* in Hanley, Stoke-on-Trent, on 28 February 1943. The specific objective at that time was to raise enough money to build a centre for youth in Stoke-on-Trent as a memorial to R.J.

In July 1943, Austin Brook announced that he had been in touch with Councillor B.A. Corry, the mayor of Southampton, and with a number of prominent people in the aeronautical and engineering industries, and that it had been now decided that the city of Stoke-on-Trent should join with the city of Southampton in a national appeal. In consequence a joint national appeal was duly launched at an inaugural luncheon held at the Waldorf Hotel in London on 1 June 1944.

It is interesting to record that a very fine menu was provided for this luncheon, which was held at a top-class hotel in wartime Britain.

The chief officials of the memorial fund were:

Patrons:	AM Sir Leslie Gossage, KCB, CVO, DSO, MC.
	AM Sir Ralph Sorley, KCB, CB, OBE, DSO, DFC.
President:	Lady MacRobert, BSc, Jp.
Vice Presidents:	Alderman C. Austin Brook, MA.
	Councillor B.A. Corry, DCM.
Chairman:	Sir Francis Joseph, Bart, KBE.
Honorary Treasurer:	The Rt Hon. The Lord Swaythling.

The president, Lady MacRobert, was unfortunately unable to be present but sent the following tribute:

> We shall never forget that such immortal battles and victories were only possible because such a man as Reginald Mitchell had laboured to provide us with a fighter plane, his life's work... the Spitfire is a symbol of the British fighting spirit. Mitchell embodied that spirit.

It is interesting to record that I was reminded of this tribute in a letter I received dated 12 November 1985 from the Right Reverend Frank Cocks in reply to a letter I wrote to him about the book, and my proposed mention of him in it. Frank Cocks attended the luncheon on 1 June 1944 but more importantly was a source of great comfort to my mother and myself in 1937 as is mentioned in Chapter 18. Before this, I had lost contact with him for many years and it was very pleasing to renew this friendship of so long ago. Producing a book does have its perks!

In the brochure produced at the launching of the memorial fund, MRF Sir Charles Portal, GCB, DSO, MC, chief of Fighter Command during the Battle of Britain, wrote:

> Until the whole story of this war has been written by historians, we shall not know the full measure of the nation's debt to R.J. Mitchell. Indeed, in one sense we can never know it, for his Spitfire helped to deliver our country from a fate which had never before engulfed it, a fate whose horrors would certainly have far exceeded the worst that any of us could imagine. Be that as it may, no one can doubt Mitchell's title to one of the highest places among those who have done most for our deliverance.
>
> May the memorial to him, which is the object of this appeal, inspire future generations with some of the vision, perseverance and self-sacrifice for which we of his own time honour his name.

Speaking at the inaugural luncheon on 1 June 1944, AM Sir Ralph Sorley said:

> It was my fortune to be associated with Mitchell during the work on the Spitfire. He was an utter delight – his simplicity, his jollity – just an ordinary chap and he had the most delightful way of expressing himself and of seeking information.

It was Sir Ralph who, when he was in the operational requirements department of the Air Staff, determined that in order to get the required density of bullets to destroy an enemy aircraft, it would be necessary to have eight Browning guns in the wings of the new fighters being designed, rather than the four that had been considered sufficient up to then. Sir Ralph convinced R.J. and Sidney Camm of the need for the eight guns in the Spitfire and Hurricane, respectively, and it is this to which he referred in his speech at the luncheon.

The two main objectives of the appeal were now agreed to be:

> 1.   To build a youth centre in Stoke-on-Trent to provide facilities for the staging of spiritual, dramatic, musical, sporting, and other cultural projects, all for the benefit of young people. The declared intention was that youths should be given the opportunity of doing things for themselves rather than for them to feel that it was the duty of the state to provide them with everything.
>
> 2.   To establish a trust fund for the provision of scholarships in aeronautical engineering tenable at the University of Southampton and open to members of affiliated youth organisations throughout the world, and having the long-term objective that there may be in the aircraft industry

at all times potential successors to Mitchell, and who, through the fund awards, would be helped to succeed.

The Spitfire Mitchell Memorial Fund in due course achieved its objectives, a total of some £78,000 being raised, which enabled the following memorials to be established:

1a.   *Mitchell Memorial Youth Centre, now called The Mitchell Memorial Theatre.*

This is situated in Broad Street, Hanley, Stoke-on-Trent, and was completed at a cost of approximately £50,000. It contains a theatre and is designed to provide for almost every type of youth activity. It was officially opened on 28 October 1957 by Grp Capt. Douglas Bader, CBE, DSO, DFC (later Sir Douglas Bader). Among those attending the ceremony were The Right Worshipful The Lord Mayor of Stoke-on-Trent, Councillor Reverend A. Perry, JP, the chairman of the Spitfire Mitchell Memorial Committee, Alderman Mrs A.L. Barker, JP, and Alderman C. Austin Brook, MA, JP, who launched the original Mitchell Memorial Fund. It was also attended by members of Mitchell's family and they and myself were honoured to be present on this notable occasion in the history of the city of Stoke-on-Trent.

In November 1996 I was invited by Mr Stuart Clamp, manager of the Mitchell Memorial Theatre, to present the trophies at the 53rd Annual One-Act Play Festival in the theatre on 22 March 1997. I accepted the invitation with great pleasure and enjoyed the evening immensely. Having attended the opening of the theatre nearly ten years earlier, it was particularly appropriate to visit it once again. In addition to presenting the trophies, I had the honour of unveiling a plaque by the favourite seat in the theatre of Miss Mary Blakeman, chairman of the drama committee, who was associated with the theatre from the time the appeal for it was launched in 1943. Mary died in December 2000.

1b.   *Scholarships at the University of Southampton.*

As at December 2005, a total of thirty scholarships in aeronautical engineering have been awarded, twenty-four undergraduate and six postgraduate, for advanced research work in the School of Engineering Sciences, formerly the Department of Aeronautics and Astronautics. The awards are usually for either two or three years.

The postgraduate awards are currently for approximately £7,800 per annum and the total value of the scholarship fund remains at £120,000, all income from the fund having been used in the awards.

I had the pleasure of meeting several of the ex-Mitchell scholars when I attended the wind tunnel naming ceremony at the university on 17 May 1995 (Item 30) and, without exception, they said how grateful they were for the opportunity the scholarships gave them for advancing their careers. I am sure my father would have been delighted with this as he was always ready to help anybody willing to work hard!

2.   *The Reginald Mitchell County Primary School.*

This school is located in Congleton Road, Butt Lane, Stoke-on-Trent, and R.J.'s birthplace at 115 Congleton Road is in front of the school and can be seen from the school grounds.

The school on the present site was founded in 1909 as the Butt Lane Junior School; the name was changed to the Butt Lane Primary School in 1932. In 1956, the school managers met to choose a new name for the school and decided that the obvious choice, in view of the school's proximity to Mitchell's birthplace, was the Reginald Mitchell County Primary School. When I was approached by the then headmaster, Mr G.H. Shenton, for my approval of this proposed name change, I said I was delighted to give my agreement and that I was sure R.J. would have considered it an honour to have the school so named in his memory.

To mark the occasion of the name change which took effect in 1959, the school produced a special brochure which also commemorated the school's first fifty years of service. It contained tributes by a number of notable people, together with a detailed history of the school by the present and previous headmasters.

A new motto for the school was adopted, which being translated reads: 'An illustrious and honoured name'.

Today, the school has 250 pupils in the age range of five to eleven years. Mr H.J. Deakin, after fourteen distinguished years as headteacher, retired in March 1997, to be succeeded by Mr Stephen Mitchell.

A day in May 1968 will be one that will always be remembered by the Reginald Mitchell CPS pupils since a Spitfire flew low over the school and gave a special display for them.

3.   *The Mitchell Junior School.*

This school is situated at Hornchurch in Essex. On 1 April 1928 a new RAF aerodrome was opened and given the name RAF Hornchurch. This aerodrome was destined to play a vital role in the Second World War, both during the Battle of Britain and throughout the war. When the war broke out, all the squadrons based at Hornchurch were equipped with Spitfires; the aerodrome was used operationally until February 1944.

In 1967, the government decided to sell the aerodrome land for building houses on for a sum of £440,000 and the local education authority resolved to build a school on what was part of the airfield. It was, moreover, decided that the school should be named after R.J. Mitchell, designer of the Spitfire, for which RAF Hornchurch was so famous. Originally to be the Mitchell Primary School, it was subsequently given its present name of the Mitchell Junior School.

The school was officially opened on 2 December 1968 when AVM R.I. Jones presented a replica of the insignia of RAF Hornchurch, which now hangs in the main hall of the school. In 1970, a separate infant school was added to the main school.

The school has four houses with the following names: Broadhurst (ACM Sir Harry Broadhurst), Deere (AC Alan Deere), Stanford-Tuck (Wg Cdr Bob Stanford-Tuck) and Stephen (Wg Cdr H.M. Stephen). All of these famous fighter pilots flew Spitfires from RAF Hornchurch and have visited the school on several occasions and maintain contact with it. The squadron crests of 19, 54, 92 and 111 Squadrons, which were presented to the school shortly after it opened, are used as trophies for inter-house competitions.

Today the school has nearly 200 pupils and continues to have great pride in its name.

As a small token of my own personal interest in the school, I provide a number of 'Mitchell Endeavour Prizes' in the form of books for especially good progress which are awarded annually to pupils at the school.

On 5 July 1983, ACM Sir Harry Broadhurst unveiled the RAF Hornchurch Memorial in the grounds of Mitchell Junior School, to provide a permanent monument to the men and women who played such an important role in the Battle of Britain at RAF Hornchurch. Fifty-seven pilots lost their lives in action flying from this airfield. It took three years to raise the funds needed for the memorial under the patronship of Wg Cdr Bob Stanford-Tuck.

The inscription on the memorial stone reads:

SITE OF RAF HORNCHURCH
SECTOR AIRFIELD FOR No 11 GROUP
TO ALL AIRCREW AND GROUND PERSONNEL WHO
SERVED HERE
1928–1962

I am sure that all the staff and pupils of Mitchell Junior School must feel extremely proud that such a worthy memorial is situated for all time in the grounds of their school.

4a.   Hanley High School in Hanley, Stoke-on-Trent.

R.J. attended this school from 1909–11, leaving when he was sixteen to start his apprenticeship at the locomotive engineering firm of Kerr, Stuart & Co. in Fenton.

One of the houses at the school was named 'Mitchell House' and there was a commemorative plaque which stated that R.J. Mitchell attended the school 1909–11. Hung beneath the plaque was an old wooden Spitfire propeller.

It is of interest that twenty years after Mitchell left Hanley High School, he continued to keep in touch with the school and two weeks before the 1931 Schneider Trophy he sent the school a detailed article about the seaplanes he had designed for the race which was published in the December 1931 issue of *The Hanliensiaq*, the school's magazine. He concluded that, while he was satisfied with their new aircraft,

> ... it must remembered that everything with these aircraft, both mechanical and human, is working so near to the limit that an element of luck one way or the other may make the difference between complete success and failure. Let us hope it is on our side again.

Previously, in September 1929, Mitchell attended and took part in a meeting of the school's debating society.

4b.   The Mitchell High School in Bucknall, Stoke-on-Trent.

In 1985 Hanley High School and Carmountside High School were amalgamated to be renamed Brookhouse High School. Then in 1988, Brookhouse High School and Willfield High School were amalgamated to create a new school and given the name the Mitchell High School in memory of R.J. Mitchell. It was formally opened in a moving ceremony by HRH The Duke of Gloucester on 23 March 1990. In his address, HRH said that he would like to congratulate the person whose idea it was to name the school after a local hero. Mitchell managed through his intelligence and his skills as an engineer to create an aeroplane that was absolutely vital to this country.

The school's motto is: 'Pride, Care and Excellence'. Headteacher is Mr L.H. Wild.

5.   Commemorative plaque on R.J.'s birthplace.

A plaque on 115 Congleton Road, Butt Lane, Stoke-on-Trent, was unveiled on 25 June 1951 by AVM R.L.R. Atcherley, CB, CBE, AFC, a member of the 1929 Schneider Trophy Contest High Speed Flight.

It reads:

Reginald J. Mitchell, CBE,
AMICE, FRAeS
Designer of the 'Spitfire'
was born here
20 May 1895

The ceremony was attended by some 2,000 people and by many members of father's family and was held in conjunction with the local Festival of Britain celebrations. In his speech after the unveiling, AVM Atcherley said:

> Wartime pilots carried proof of Mitchell's bold, imaginative genius into the Battle of Britain. Looking back at the Second World War, we could perhaps understand a little more clearly the outstanding nature of the service which Mitchell performed for this country. The RAF owed a debt of gratitude to all those men who designed their aircraft, but to Mitchell they owed a special debt.

6.   *Spitfire Museum in Hanley, Stoke-on-Trent, housing Spitfire Mk XVIE.*

Hanley was where R.J. spent much of his youth and it was considered appropriate that an example of his most famous aircraft should be displayed there.

In 1969, Wg Cdr John Ashton, DFC, a famous wartime Spitfire pilot, was appointed chairman of a Spitfire appeal fund aimed at securing a Spitfire for the city. This was very successful and Spitfire no. 388 was duly obtained from the RAF and displayed in a jumbo-sized 'greenhouse' in Bethseda Street, Hanley, the official handing-over ceremony taking place on 28 June 1972 by ACM Sir Neil Wheeler, on behalf of the RAF. After the opening ceremony, John Ashton handed to Sir Neil two cheques as donations to the RAF Benevolent Fund and RAF Museum Fund, being the balance of money left over from the Spitfire appeal fund.

For many years it was hoped that the Spitfire could be moved to a more suitable location. This was finally achieved in May 1986 when it became possible to move it into the City Museum & Art Gallery in Hanley, where it is now on permanent display.

HRH Princess Margaret visited the Spitfire Museum a few years ago and was introduced to Sam and Charles Mitchell, the sons of R.J.'s brother Eric. She talked to them about their uncle's contribution in helping to save Britain in the Second World War.

7.   *Mitchell Memorial Lecture (Stoke-on-Trent).*

This is delivered annually under the auspices of the Stoke-on-Trent Association of Engineers, of which R.J. was a student founder member. On the occasion of the tenth annual meeting of the association on 24 February 1928, R.J. was the chief guest and gave the after-dinner speech. The first course of the dinner was native oysters which were a particular favourite of R.J.'s! The 1st Memorial Lecture was given by AC Frank Whittle in 1946. Subsequent speakers included: Sir R. Watson-Watt, Sir Geoffrey de Havilland, Sir Howard Florey, Sir John Cockcroft, Dr Barnes Wallis, Sir George Edwards, C.S. Cockerell, S.G. Hooker, Patrick Moore, Professor Sir Fred Hoyle, Brian Trubshaw, Sir Robert Lickley and Helen Sharmen. The 50th Memorial Lecture was given by Raymond Baxter in 1995, R.J.'s centenary year, the title of his lecture being, 'My love affair with Mitchell's brainchild'.

8.   *Mitchell Memorial Lecture (Southampton).*

This lecture is given annually in the University of Southampton and is organised by the Southampton branch of the Royal Aeronautical Society. It is funded by the society.

The first lecture, which was also given as a main lecture of the RAeS, was entitled 'R.J. Mitchell – Aircraft Designer', and was given in 1954 by Joe Smith, who succeeded R.J. as chief designer at Supermarine. As described in Chapter 13, it was a memorable occasion. Many distinguished guests attended to pay tribute to R.J. and the lecture was an outstanding delineation of the man, his life, his work and his contribution to the aircraft industry, in the short sixteen years of his working life as chief designer and chief engineer. The lecture, which was published in full in the *Journal of the Royal Aeronautical Society* (May 1954), serves as an excellent and accurate reference and was used as such in the preparation of this book.

To date, forty-five memorial lectures have been given and details are as follows:

Lecture No.	Year	Lecturer	Title of Lecture
1	1954	Mr J. Smith	R.J. Mitchell – Aircraft Designer
2	1954	Mr P.G. Masefield	Problems and Prospects in British Air Transport
3	1956	Mr A.C. Lovesey	The Aircraft Engine
4	1956	Prof. E.J. Richards	Noise and Aircraft Structures
5	1957	Dr S.G. Hooker	The Developments of Propulsion Systems for High Speed Flight

6	1958	Mr M.J. Brennan	Applied Rocket Power
7	1959	Mr D. Keith-Lucas	Vertical Take-off by Jet Lift
8	1960	Mr B.S. Shenstone	Man Powered Aircraft
9	1961	Dr Barnes Wallis	The Strength of England
10	1962	Mr A.N. Clifton	The Shape of Aeroplanes to Come
11	1963	Mr B.S. Shenstone	The Development of Civil Air Transport
12	1965	Mr L.F. Nicholson	The Work of the Royal Aircraft Establishment
13	1966	Mr S.L. Bragg	The Ideal Gas Turbine
14	1967	Mr R. Hafner	The Domain of the Convertible Rotor in Aircraft
15	1968	Mr J. Taylor	Kinetic Heating of Aerospace Structures
16	1969	Mr E.E. Marshall	The Role of Aircraft in Future Transport Systems
17	1970	Mr D.G. Brown	Short Haul in the Long Term – Projection in Aircraft Development
18	1971	Mr A.V. Cleaver	Astronautics after Apollo
19	1971	Mr P.G. Masefield	An Airports System for UK Air Services
20	1973	Sqn Ldr R.W. Richardson	MRCA – A Progress Report
21	1974	M.R. Chevalier	Technical and Operational Aspects of Concorde
22	1975	Mr G.S. Henson	Aero and Underwater Engineering
	1976		Special Spitfire Mitchell Memorial Symposium to mark the Fortieth Anniversary of First Flight of the Spitfire on 5 March 1936, held on 6 March 1976

The lecture which took place on 6 March 1976 in the form of a symposium must receive special mention. It took place in one of the main lecture theatres at Southampton University and was attended by a capacity audience of over 500. Following the presentation of papers, all the participants travelled to the College of Air Training, Hamble, where they were treated to a superb Spitfire flying display.

The symposium was organised by the Southampton branch of the RAeS, and the then president, Mr Alan Clifton, played a very important role in ensuring the success of the event, ably assisted by his hard-working organising committee.

The full proceedings of the symposium were published later in 1976, the editors being Dr East, honorary secretary, and Professor Cheeseman, chairman of the Southampton branch of the RAeS. The publication includes a complete account of the discussions that followed the presented papers, together with some additional material received after the symposium. An account of my reply to the toast proposed by Alan Clifton, 'The Memory of R.J. Mitchell and his Achievements', at the symposium dinner, was also included by the editors.

23	1976	Mr J.W. Fozard	Sea Harrier – The First of the New Wave
24	1977	Mr M.J. Brennan	History of British Flying Boats and the Final Stages
25	1978	Sir Stanley Hooker	The Merlin for the Spitfire and early Rolls-Royce Jet Engines
26	1980	Mr D.G. Brown	Airbus Industrie – Past, Present and Future
27	1981	Mr D.N. James	The Schneider Trophy – Fifty Years On
28	1983	Mr R.D. Boot	Fighter Aircraft Design
29	1985	Dr H. Pfeffer	Europe's Plans for Future Launchers
30	1986	Mr J. Davis	The Basic Design for the Prototype Spitfire

This was a special lecture to commemorate the fiftieth anniversary of the first fight of the Spitfire on 5 March 1936, and began with an introduction by Jeffrey Quill. Jack Davis then gave his first-hand knowledge of the design and construction of the prototype Spitfire with special reference to the elliptical wing and how it evolved. Following an extensive discussion, I had the privilege of making some concluding remarks about the memorable and nostalgic evening everyone had enjoyed so much, together with some personal anecdotes about my father. Finally, I gave the vote of thanks to Jeffrey and Jack for giving everyone such an instructive and historic evening.

31	1987	Mr J. Vincent	Europe's Future Fighter
32	1988	Mr A. Bond	Propulsion for Economic Space Transportation Systems
33	1989	Mr K.G. Hodson	Beyond 2000 with Hawk and Goshawk
34	1990	Mr S.G. Corps	Airbus Industrie – Today and Tomorrow

35	1991	Mr F. Turner	Rolls-Royce in Perspective, Past, Present and Future
36	1992	Sir Colin Marshall	G-Global – Britain's Role in World Air Transport
37	1993	Mr Oliver Boileau	B2 – the Stealth Bomber

This lecture was of particular interest in that it was the first R.J. Mitchell Lecture to be presented by an American citizen.

38	1994	M. Jean-Marie Luton	Space – Open to International Co-operation
39	1995	Brian H. Rowe	Five Decades of Progress in Aero Engines; Remembrance of the Past and Opportunities for the Future
40	1996	Mr Stewart Miller	Technology Transfer from Mitchell to the Millennium

This lecture commemorated the sixtieth anniversary of the first flight of the Spitfire and to mark the occasion was held for the first time at Hursley Park, to which Supermarine personnel were transferred during the 1939–45 war.

41	1997	Mr Stuart Lewis	The Importance of Technology Demonstrator Programmes to the Design of High Performance Military Aircraft
42	1998	Nancy J. Bethel	Changes in Commercial Aviation
43	1999	Mr Tony Edwards	Aspects of Technology in the Aircraft Equipment Industry
44	2000	Marsha S. Ivins	The Space Shuttle in the 21st Century
45	2001	Mr Brian A. Miller	The Ultimate System Aircrew Safety in the 21st Century
46	2002	Mr Lorne S. Clark	International Air transport after September 11th 2001
47	2003	ACM Sir Malcolm Pledges	The Next 100 Years of Military Aviation
48	2004	Prof. J.E. Ffowcs Williams	Aeroaccoustics
49	2005	Adam Brown	A380 and Beyond: An Airbus Perspective

9.   *Engraved stone memorial in Hazel Road on the site of The*
       Supermarine Aviation Works, Woolston, Southampton.

As has been described, the Supermarine factory was severely damaged
by German bombs in September 1940.

After the war, the remaining office block was eventually considered
to be unsafe and was demolished, and so nothing now remains of the
buildings where R.J. spent all his working life.

A new bridge, to replace the well-known Floating Bridges, was built
over the River Itchen and it is adjacent to the arch of this bridge that
the officers and members of the Supermarine Association decided to
erect a stone memorial in memory of R.J.

The memorial was unveiled on 10 September 1978 by Alan Clifton,
former chief designer at Supermarine. In his speech, Alan recalled R.J.'s
career and paid tribute to his many designs which had brought the small
Supermarine factory world-wide renown.

The ceremony was attended by many Supermarine Association members, and notable guests included Mr Bob Mitchell, MP for Southampton
Itchen, and Mr C.B.P. Pepper, vice-chairman of Rolls-Royce Ltd. The
424 (Southampton) Squadron of the Air Training Corps mounted a
guard of honour which greatly added to the impact of the ceremony.

The memorial, ornamented with outline drawings of the Spitfire, is
inscribed:

> To the memory of the designer of the legendary light aircraft, the
> Spitfire.
> Reginald Joseph Mitchell 1895–1937.
> On this site the first Spitfire was built by The Supermarine Aviation
> Works
> (Vickers) Ltd.
> Spitfires and their pilots played a decisive part in the Battle of Britain.

After the ceremony, a scale model Spitfire built by John Isaacs, president
of the Supermarine Association, flew overhead and gave an aerobatic
display.

10.   *'Spitfire', a documentary BBC-TV South production.*

This hour-long programme was produced by John Frost. It was aimed to
coincide with the fortieth anniversary of the first flight of the Spitfire and was
first shown on BBC South in two parts in February and March 1976; it was
subsequently repeated several times on the national BBC-TV channels.

I was one of many asked to take part in the programme and had
to report to the Supermarine site in Woolston on 10 January 1976 to

record my contribution. I duly arrived feeling a little apprehensive. I had, naturally, thought a lot about what I might say but there was no formal script and no question of reading your notes in front of the camera. Then when John Frost said he wished to film me first on the slipway, where the Schneider Trophy planes had once stood so that I could recall my memories of being there forty-seven years ago, this completely threw me as I had not expected such a scene!

Having been told where to stand, John said we would have a dummy run-through of my offering. If anything was ad. lib., this was it. However John seemed to think it would do and said we would now shoot it. I repeated, so I thought, what I had said before but when it was finished John said,

> Yes, that was OK, but unfortunately you omitted to bring in the word 'anguish' (to describe the general feelings of tension as the engine was run and the S.6 prepared for moving into the water) which you brought in in the dummy run-through and which I particularly liked.

So it had to be done again with 'anguish'; this time John was satisfied and we moved on to R.J.'s old office for the next shots. John and all of his colleagues were so patient, understanding and helpful that I was beginning to quite enjoy the experience. Duly installed on the balcony of R.J.'s office with the river in the background, I did my next piece. I had prepared myself for this and so I knew what I wanted to say. It went quite well, I think, as I only had to do it once, and that was my contribution completed.

The next interview to be shot was with Alan Clifton, former chief designer at Supermarine and ex-colleague of R.J. As a pre-liminary, John Frost asked Alan a few questions to get some ideas as to what might be included in the interview. The first question was, 'Were you not excited when it was realised how good the Spitfire was?' Alan replied, 'Not really, since most of what we produced at Supermarine was good!' The next question was, 'What did you think of the name Spitfire and were you not excited at such an apt name?' Alan replied, 'I did not think much of it. It sounded rather like an irate old woman!'

Subsequent history has shown that Alan Clifton was wrong in his initial reaction, since I think it would be generally agreed now that one would have to look a long way to find a more appropriate name than 'Spitfire'.

John Frost also speculated that the use of the name Spitfire for the aircraft had changed the meaning of the word in the English language. In this connection, it is interesting that in, for example, Chambers' *Twentieth Century Dictionary* 1985, the definition of 'Spitfire' is given as, 'that which emits fire, e.g., a volcano, cannon; a type of fighting aeroplane used in World War II; a hot-tempered person'.

The completed documentary was first-class, with every effort being made to ensure it was authentic in every detail, as well as being good entertainment.

Raymond Baxter, an ex-Spitfire pilot, did the commentary in his usual polished manner and this added greatly to the enjoyment of the production.

Following the showing of the documentary on BBC1 in May 1976, I was particularly pleased to receive a letter from R.J.'s brother, Eric:

> I thought it was an excellent and interesting programme – your part was very good indeed and you are to be congratulated on the efficient way you said your piece. It was particularly gratifying also to note the admiration and affection for your father expressed by all his associates. I consider that the family was well represented.

Sadly, Eric died six years later in 1982 at the age of eighty-six.

11.　*Mitchell Drive, Fair Oak, Eastleigh.*

In December 1965, Mr Walkden, director of Tom Jurd Ltd, a local company of builders, approached me to seek my approval of a suggestion to name a road after R.J. on a new estate of forty-three houses that they were building.

He pointed out that as Fair Oak was situated 2.5 miles east of Eastleigh, the Spitfire during its original test flights would have often flown over the fields of Fair Oak, and consequently he felt it would be very appropriate to honour R.J. in this way.

Eventually, the name Mitchell Drive was selected and accepted by Winchester Rural District Council. An appropriate road name sign was erected when the estate development was completed in 1967.

12.　*Mitchell House, Southampton Road, Eastleigh.*

In 1978/9, Miller Buckley Developments Ltd, based in Rugby, began work on the construction of a five-storey 40,000 sq. ft office block development in Eastleigh. The directors decided at an early stage that in view of the proximity of the development to Southampton Airport, it would be appropriate to name it Mitchell House in honour of R.J.'s association with the area.

Early in 1980, Miller Buckley invited me to perform the 'topping out' ceremony of the building. I agreed provided they told me exactly what I was supposed to do since the proposed ceremony was something that I had never previously been called on to perform!

The 'topping out' took place on 25 April 1980 on the top floor of the building; where, in the floor, a square had been left unconcreted. My job was to shovel some fresh concrete into this square and tamp it down in the recognised professional manner. I was handed a stainless steel spade for the job which, after duly using it, was presented to me as a memento of the occasion. An engraved plate was fixed to the handle which recorded the occasion.

Mr T.A. Roberts, chairman of Miller Buckley Developments, introduced the guests who included the mayor and mayoress of Eastleigh, Councillor and Mrs Patrick Hallifax; Mr David Price, the local MP; and Mr K. Hainsworth, managing director of Miller Buckley. After describing and expounding the virtues of the office property development, he invited me to say a few words. I thanked the directors for inviting me to perform the ceremony and said I was sure my father would have felt greatly honoured by having this fine building named after him.

It was, as I recall, extremely cold up on the completely open top floor of the building with the wind whistling across in all directions. This had the virtue of ensuring that all speeches, including mine, were short and very much to the point. My wife agreed!

13.   *Royal British Legion Reginald Mitchell Court in Eastleigh.*

This development by the Royal British Legion contains forty self-contained double luxury flats for elderly couples, many with ex-service connections.

Officers of the British Legion generously decided that it would be appropriate, in view of his association with the area, to honour R.J. by naming the court after him. Originally, it was to be named 'The Mitchell Court' but this was changed on the suggestion of Wg Cdr David Bennett to 'Reginald Mitchell Court'. I readily gave my approval to this proposal.

In a very impressive ceremony, the court was officially opened on 19 May 1977 by admiral of the fleet the Earl Mountbatten of Burma. In his speech, Lord Mountbatten made several references to R.J. In one, referring to the contribution to victory that the Spitfire made, he said, 'If it had not been for R.J., where would Britain be today? He was one of the world's most brilliant aircraft designers.'

I was glad to have the opportunity of formally thanking the organisers for honouring my father in such a splendid way. I mentioned that the date fixed for the opening of the court was particularly appropriate since if my father had lived it would have been the eve of his eighty-second birthday. I said that the Reginald Mitchell Court held a special interest for me, having been for many years on the management committee and a vice-president of the James Butcher Housing Association in Reading, an organisation devoted to establishing flats for the elderly in courts very similar to this court.

A long time after the opening of the Reginald Mitchell Court, I visited Broadlands and told one of the attendants I had a few photographs I had taken at the ceremony, which Lord Mountbatten might possibly be interested in seeing. Shortly afterwards I received the following letter which Lord Romsey kindly gave me permission to reproduce:

Broadlands, Romsey,
Hampshire S05 9ZD
19 June 1979

Dear Dr Mitchell,

Thank you so much for sending me photographs taken at the opening of Mitchell Court, named after your wonderful father, in May 1977.
I will put them both in my album.
With all good wishes.

Yours sincerely,
Mountbatten of Burma.

One of the great men of our time, whose life was to be dramatically and tragically cut short on 27 August, less than ten weeks later.

14.   *Three trees planted on the Whiteknights campus of the University of Reading in memory of the Spitfire designer.*

As a result of my association with the university (see page 25), I was able to put R.J.'s name forward as one who might be remembered and honoured by the planting of a tree on the university campus, a ceremony which the university arranged from time to time for certain selected people.

This was approved by the vice-chancellor, Dr Evan Page, but it was felt that it would on this occasion be appropriate that the ceremony should be a little more formal than I had originally envisaged. First, the two famous Spitfire test pilots Jeffrey Quill and Alex Henshaw were invited to plant trees in addition to the one to be planted by myself, an invitation which they generously accepted. Secondly, it was arranged that following the ceremony a number of guests should be invited to have lunch in the senior common room with the vice-chancellor. Finally, it was suggested that it would add greatly to the significance of the occasion if it could be arranged for a Spitfire to fly over the site following the tree planting. I was asked if I could organise this at short notice. With the help and generous co-operation of three people, it was eventually arranged; these were the Hon. Patrick Lindsay,[15] the owner of a Mk IA Spitfire who agreed that it could be used for the flight; Mrs Edna Bianchi,[16] a director of Personal Plane Services Ltd at Booker Airfield, who maintained the Spitfire; and Flt Lt Peter Thorn who agreed to fly the aircraft over the Whiteknights campus. It was indeed fortunate that Patrick Lindsay always enjoys displaying his Spitfire; he says he feels that people perceive this aircraft as the symbol of what won the war and consequently derive enormous pleasure from seeing it. The three trees, each bearing appropriate labels, were duly planted on the chosen site by Jeffrey, Alex and myself at noon on 8 March 1992 in the presence of Dr E. Page; Dr J. W. G. Porter, director of the NIRD; AVM P.R. Harding, air officer commanding No 11 Group RAF Strike Command; Mrs Edna Bianchi; the standard bearer and representative of the local RAF Association; and other officials and staff of the university and NIRD.

All eyes turned to the sky expecting to see the Spitfire approaching, but there was no sign of it. After many agonising minutes a message was received from Booker Airfield that Peter Thorn should be arriving shortly. The Spitfire appeared at last; it did a sharp 180 degree banking turn onto the line of the planting site and then made a spectacular low pass over the assembled gathering. A nostalgic moment.

The local *Evening Post* of 9 March 1982 reported the event:

> The sky was the limit for a Reading University lecturer's special tribute to his famous dad. High above the Whiteknights campus one of the few remaining Spitfire fighter planes flew past in memory of its designer, Reginald Mitchell.
>
> And on the ground yesterday his son stood proudly to watch the legendary warplane in action again.
>
> The nostalgic flight followed a tree-planting ceremony on the campus, and after the fly-past Dr Gordon Mitchell said, 'I am thrilled and delighted, not for myself but for my father and his memory'.

I felt, on reflection, that this ceremony, at the university where I had worked for so many years, in a way linked for the first time my father with my own humble career.

Following a letter I wrote to Peter Thorn thanking him for flying the Spitfire over so well in exactly the right place, I received the following reply:

> I consider it a great honour to have been able to participate on such an occasion and I am very grateful for the opportunity. I have been flying for thirty-six years now and I can honestly say that the greatest pleasure I get from doing a job that I really call my hobby, is the rare opportunity

to fly one of the greatest aircraft of all time. There is no aircraft that gives such satisfaction to a pilot as the Spitfire and I am conscious of the rare privilege I have to fly one. I know that whenever this aircraft appears it brings tears to many a mature eye...

Yours very sincerely
Pete Thorn

Flt Lt Peter Thorn was for three and a half years a member of the Battle of Britain Memorial Flight.

15.   *Cranfield University.*

The College of Aeronautics was established at this university in October 1946 and in the following year the two halls of residence were named 'Lanchester Hall' and 'Mitchell Hall'. The former had originally been the officers' mess, and the latter the Sergeants' mess. The principal at the time had decided that it would be appropriate to name one hall after a pioneer of aeronautical science and the other after a modern aircraft designer.

A portrait of R.J., presented to Cranfield by Vickers, hangs in the dining room of Mitchell Hall. Included in the portrait is a Spitfire, and framed prints of other Spitfires are also hung in the room.

16.   *(i) R.J. Mitchell Hall in the city of Southampton (1976–1983).*
       (ii) Southampton Hall of Aviation, incorporating the R.J. Mitchell Memorial Museum Ltd (opened 1984).

The idea of establishing a suitable memorial to R.J. in Southampton first began in the early 1970s and the local junior chamber of commerce made valiant but unsuccessful attempts to get a project under way. Then in 1975, the mayor of Southampton, Councillor Fred Goater, called a meeting at the civic centre to discuss the demise of the junior chamber of commerce efforts; he invited all persons in Southampton who had connections with aviation or the RAF, and among those who attended the meeting was Sqn Ldr Alan Jones, MBE, a local businessman and the officer commanding 424 (Southampton) Squadron of the Air Training Corps. All looked hopeless after this meeting, but shortly afterwards, Alan Jones came up with the idea of converting an old redundant building, Morlands Hall, into a suitable memorial to Mitchell. Alan was determined to succeed and raise the necessary funds and eventually, with the untiring help of his small band of dedicated committee members and of his ATC squadron, he did succeed beyond all expectations. Morlands Hall, which had previously been a NAAFI canteen and dance hall, and was situated next to the ATC squadron headquarters right in the town centre, only a stone's throw from the civic centre, was slowly but surely converted into the museum hall. In due course, the two prize exhibits, first an S.6A Schneider Trophy racing seaplane, N248, flown by Atcherley in the 1929 race and acting as a reserve aircraft in the 1931 contest, and second, a Mk 24 Spitfire, were brought into the hall and reassembled for display. A whole range of other interesting items, photographs, drawings and the like, were included in the exhibition illustrating the history of the twenty-four aircraft that R.J. designed.

Before it was moved into the hall the S.6A had to undergo extensive restoration work. After being used in 1942 in the film *The First of the Few*, it had spent many years out in the open on Southampton's Royal Pier and had been sadly neglected. Alan Jones and his team deserve the gratitude of this country for rescuing and restoring this unique aircraft.

The new hall was opened on 11 June 1976, thirty-nine years to the day after R.J.'s death, in a simple, but appropriate, ceremony. It was attended by many distinguished people from the aviation world.

A plaque in the entrance to the hall read:

> This hall, dedicated to the memory of Reginald Joseph Mitchell, CBE, FRAeS, AMICE,[17] aircraft designer, was opened on 11 June 1976 by his son Dr K.G. Mitchell, BSc, PhD, in the fortieth anniversary year of the Spitfire.

A particularly generous tribute, which was displayed in the hall, was that paid by the RAF:

> From time to time, out of the ranks of obscurity, a man little known to the public emerges to make a vital contribution to the continued existence of his country.
>
> Such a man was R.J. Mitchell, whose classic aircraft materialised at a turning point in our island history.
>
> Memories being what they are, the achievement – in this case that of the aircraft and its pilots – is often remembered before the man who made it possible.
>
> So it is fitting that there should be a memorial to a man to whom we owe so much.
>
> Today we remember him with pride and lasting gratitude.

Sadly, it was always recognised that the R.J. Mitchell Hall could only form a short-term memorial due to the temporary nature of the building itself and to the fact that Southampton City Council would in due course require the site for development.

Eventually, after much difficult negotiation by Alan Jones and his committee, Southampton City Council agreed to make available a sum of some £665,000 for the building of a new aircraft museum, on land it owned in Albert Road South, located just across the river from the old site of Supermarine. It was specified by the city council that the new museum should include not only all of the R.J. Mitchell Hall memorial exhibits but should embrace the entire history of aviation in the Solent area. It was decided that a Sandringham flying boat, acquired from the Science Museum in London, should be displayed in the new museum, which necessitated a much larger building than had previously been envisaged.

The Sandringham, which was built by Short Bros in Rochester in 1943, began its existence as a Sunderland but saw no active service in the war. It came to Southampton for the first time in 1983, ready to be moved to the Albert Road site so that the new museum could be constructed around it. With this past history of the Sandringham flying boat, the original objective of the museum, namely to embrace the history of aviation in the Solent area, had to be extended.

Eventually, after untiring effort on the part of all concerned, the 'Southampton Hall of Aviation, incorporating the Mitchell Museum' was ready to be officially opened and this ceremony was performed by Michael Montague, CBE, chairman of the English Tourist Board, on 20 September 1984. A plaque to mark this occasion reads: 'The Southampton Hall of Aviation opened on 20 September 1984 by Michael Montague, CBE, chairman of the English Tourist Board.'

In addition to the Hall of Aviation itself, new headquarters for Alan Jones's ATC squadron were constructed within the building.

The development in Southampton of a memorial to R.J. began, therefore, with the small, but very effective, R.J. Mitchell Hall, devoted exclusively to Supermarine aircraft, and then greatly expanded into the present Hall of Aviation in which Supermarine products form a major but not the sole part of the total exhibition.

About a year ago, the name of the museum was changed to 'Solent Sky'. I am sure that present and future members of Southampton City Council, and of all those hardworking enthusiasts concerned with the Solent Sky Museum, now and in the future, will always keep in mind the following question. If the Supermarine works in Woolston, with their prodigious output of world-famous aircraft during the thirty years or so of their operation, had never existed, would the possibility of having an aircraft museum of any description in Southampton ever have arisen?

17.   *The Schneider Trophy Contest fiftieth anniversary weekend, 12 and
      13 September 1981.*

As has been described earlier, the Schneider Trophy was finally won
for Britain for all time as a result of the contest held in 1931, over
a triangular course starting and finishing at Ryde, with the British
High Speed Flight being based at Calshot. With the approach of the
fiftieth anniversary of this victory, the Southampton branch of the
Royal Aeronautical Society, in conjunction with several other local
organisations, decided that some form of event to celebrate it should
be organised. A working party, with Dr Robin East as chairman and
Stephen Wolf as organising secretary, was set up to investigate what
might be done.

In the event, they organised a superb two-day weekend which was
appropriately held at Calshot Spit. This included various individual
flying displays including a Supermarine S.5 replica, a Spitfire and a
Concorde. The RAF Battle of Britain Memorial Flight and the Red
Arrows Display Team were also on the programme. There were a
number of exhibitions and the S.6A from the R.J. Mitchell Hall, rep-
licas of the Italian Macchi MC.72 and of the Sopwith Tabloid, which
won the 1914 Schneider Trophy Contest, were included in these; trade
displays, vintage cars and aircraft, and the facilities provided by the
Calshot Activities Centre were all made available to the visitors to
Calshot on the two days.

One of the highlights arranged was a reunion of the original
Schneider pilots, designers, engineers, fitters and members of the
RAF launching crews.

It gave them the opportunity to meet once more old friends and
colleagues of fifty years and more ago and was a great success.

Fortunately the weather was kind and vast crowds, totalling more
than 15,000, streamed into Calshot Spit on both days. Undoubtedly
a highly successful event, for which all those who worked so hard to
make it so deserve every congratulation.

On the evening of the first day, the 27th Mitchell Memorial Lecture
was given at the University of Southampton by Derek James, with
the title 'Schneider Trophy – Fifty Years On'. A most interesting and
appropriate lecture attended by a large audience. Following the lecture, a
special fiftieth anniversary dinner was arranged and was attended by over a
hundred people.

An excellent anniversary celebration which made all the hard work
of organising it worthwhile, and one which R.J. would have enjoyed so
much if he had been able to attend.

18. Publication by Rolls-Royce Motors Ltd of names of well-known people who have owned one of their cars.

These publications by Rolls-Royce Motors in a number of national newspapers in 1982 were in the form of an advertisement and in one of them the name of R.J. Mitchell was included.

In a letter I received in January 1986, David Preston, public relations manager of Rolls-Royce Motors Ltd, said that he had now checked the car chassis records held at their Crewe factory and was able to confirm that R.J. Mitchell owned the following Rolls-Royce/Bentley cars:

Chassis No.	Model	Year
GYL25	Rolls-Royce 20 hp	1928
GLR31	Rolls-Royce 20/25 hp	1932
B87HM	Bentley 3½ litre	1936

It is no doubt relevant that my father gave as his address for the Rolls-Royce records The Supermarine Aviation Works Ltd rather than his home address.

19. The Spitfire Society.

With a stroke of genius, the society was founded by Grp Capt. David Green at an inaugural meeting on 6 March 1984. In 1999, David received the well-deserved award of the OBE for his services to the Spitfire Society.

The primary objective of the society must, in order to have charitable status, be educational but preservation of the memory of, and adding to the history of, the Spitfire must be, David Green states, linked with the memory and life of R.J. Mitchell, and of his associates and successors. Accordingly, I felt it was appropriate that this record of the society should be included in this chapter.

As at November 2001, seventeen years since its foundation, the society flourishes with a membership remaining steady at an average of 2,300 in thirty-seven countries in the world. To cope with its widely dispersed nature, a number of regions have been formed in the UK, and representatives have also been appointed in the USA. Two journals (DCOs) are received by members each year, containing a wealth of interesting articles excellently presented, together with items of news of interest to members. Full charity status was granted by the Charities Commissioners in 1989, an honour which recognised the society's main objectives and work in the areas of historical research, education and the encouragement of interest in aeronautics and astronautics, in particular by the younger generation.

In 1996, Sir Adrian Swire was appointed president, Jeffrey Quill having indicated shortly before his death in February 1996 that he wished to retire from the presidency which he had held since the society's foundation.

In 1998, Les Colquhoun, DFC, GM, DFM, who gave distinguished services to aviation, was appointed chairman following David Green's wish to retire for health reasons, but sadly Les died on 27 April 2001.

Currently, the executive chairman of the society is Mr Harry Griffiths.

Further details of the society can be obtained from 141 Albert Road South, Southampton S014 3FR. I am a Vice-President of the Society.

20.　*Gladstone Pottery Museum commemorative bone china plate.*

This Willow Pattern plate in traditional blue colour was produced in 1985 by this working Pottery Museum in Stoke-on-Trent to commemorate Stoke's sixtieth year with the status of a city and its seventy-fifth year as a federation of the six famous Potteries towns. The traditional willow pattern has been cleverly adapted firstly to illustrate a number of important local industries and secondly to give recognition to two local men of whom the Potteries are very proud. The first is Sir Stanley Matthews, the football genius, who is represented on the plate by two goalposts and a football; the second is my father who is recognised by replacement of the two birds in the traditional willow pattern by two Spitfires.

21.　*Commemoration of the fiftieth anniversary of the first flight of R.J.'s Spitfire by the Spitfire Society, 5 March 1986.*

A very appropriate day of events on 5 March 1986 at Eastleigh Airport (now the Southampton International Airport) was organised by the chairman of the society, Grp Capt. David Green, and his colleagues. They began with the laying of a wreath by myself on the grave of my parents in South Stoneham Cemetery, adjacent to the airport.

A wreath was also laid on the grave by David Green in memory of the Supermarine workers who were killed in the air raids on the factory in September 1940. The day's events included various exhibitions and, of course, nostalgic Spitfire flypasts. The mayor of Eastleigh hosted a civic luncheon reception at the airport which was followed in the evening by a reception in the Southampton Hall of Aviation hosted by the mayor of Southampton.

Four days later, on 9 March, a moving service of thanksgiving and commemoration of the anniversary of the first flight of the Spitfire was held in St Clement Danes Church, the central church of the RAF. The service concluded with the famous 'Spitfire Prelude' by William Walton.

22.   *Plaque on the wall of R.J.'s house in Portswood, Southampton,*
      25 September 1990.

My father lived in the house, named 'Hazeldene', from 1927 until 1937, and he died in the house on 11 June 1937. He played a major part in the original design of the house in 1926. The present owners of 'Hazeldene', Professor John Norman, professor of anaesthetics at the University of Southampton, and his wife, Rowena, were very enthusiastic that a plaque, recording that my father lived there, should be produced and permanently fixed to the front wall of their house.

I had the privilege of unveiling the plaque on 25 September 1990 before a large number of personal friends and colleagues of R.J. at Supermarine. The plaque was kindly donated by Mr Robert Bathard from Southampton; he was at Dunkirk and said he wished to do this in appreciation of the debt he owed to the Spitfires and their pilots during the Dunkirk evacuation. The plaque depicts a Spitfire, round which are the words 'R.J. Mitchell Aircraft Designer lived here 1927–37'.

This most enjoyable and friendly occasion was concluded with a magnificent tea provided by Rowena. See page 289 for update.

23.   *Statue of R.J. Mitchell in the Southampton Hall of Aviation,*
      26 September 1990.

A full-sized bronze statue of R.J. was unveiled by HRH The Duke of Gloucester on 26 September 1990 before a gathering of distinguished guests from aviation and civic life. I had the pleasure of responding to the speech of HRH following the unveiling. British Aerospace generously sponsored the production of the statue.

24.   *Unveiling of a fine engraved glass window to mark the naming of*
      the R.J. Mitchell building at the Southampton Institute of Higher
      Education, 13 February 1992.

I was kindly invited by Mr David Leyland, the director of the Institute, to carry out the unveiling of the window and to officially name the building after my father. The engraved window is magnificent and beautifully produced as I stressed in the short address I gave following the ceremony.

25.   *The Spitfire prototype replica K5054, unveiled 24 April 1993.*

The idea to build this as a lasting and appropriate memorial to my father came from the late Jeffrey Quill. A committee was formed with Jeffrey as chairman, together with David Green (Spitfire Society), Alex Henshaw,

Jack Davis, Gerry Gingell and Wilf Bunting, the latter three all being ex-Supermariners. The first meeting of the committee was held on 2 May 1984 in London at which it was agreed that I should be invited to join the committee. This I did and was later to become chairman.

There were many problems to be overcome, not least that of funding. At my request, my cousin, Jim Mitchell, an accomplished artist, kindly agreed to paint, at no charge, a totally authentic picture of the prototype Spitfire taking off from Eastleigh Airport on 5 March 1936. This was universally agreed to be a first-class painting and in due course sales of prints from it raised approximately half of the total funds needed – certainly a much appreciated major contribution to the project by Jim (see page 184, illustration 48).

Over the years other people were seconded to the committee to obtain the benefit of their expertise, and one important appointment was that of Bill Williams, as project manager, in 1989. It was a long and sometimes frustrating task that the Spitfire Society had taken under its wing but eventually the society's chairman, David Green, by sheer hard work and by organising appeals, managed to raise the balance of funds required to complete the replica, identical externally to the original prototype Spitfire, and it was ready for its unveiling to the public, which took place at the RAF Museum on 24 April 1993. The unveiling was rightly carried out by the initiator of the project, Jeffrey Quill. Everyone was most impressed by the high standard of workmanship in the replica and praise and sincere thanks are due to Tony Spooner, Peter Pykett and their Aerofab expert colleagues who built it. Initially it was felt that the replica might remain permanently in the RAF Museum but subsequently it was unanimously agreed that its rightful place must be at Southampton International Airport, from where, as Eastleigh Airport, the prototype Spitfire made its first flight on 5 March 1936, watched by R.J. and a few of his senior colleagues. However, in the event, as there was no suitable building at the airport in which the replica could be housed and as there were insufficient funds available with which to pay for a completely new building, reluctantly the possibility of establishing the K5054 replica at Southampton Airport had to be abandoned.

Accordingly, the Spitfire Society decided to approach the Tangmere Military Aviation Museum Trust as to whether they might be willing to look after the replica and would be able to house it in a suitable building on display. Tangmere were delighted to take over the care of the replica. They indeed had a suitable building available and although K5054 never actually landed at Tangmere, it was, of course, a famous Spitfire squadron station in the Second World War (see Item 49).

26.   Opening of the enhanced exhibition, in memory of R.J. Mitchell, in the Southampton Hall of Aviation, by Sir Colin Marshall, then chairman of British Airways, 6 October 1993.

The costs of the enhancement of the exhibition, which centred round the hall's Mk 24 Spitfire, were generously donated by British Airways and so it was appropriate that the new exhibition should be officially opened by their chairman. Attending the ceremony were the two remaining pilots who flew the prototype Spitfire K5054, namely Jeffrey Quill and Sammy Wroath, both now sadly deceased, together with a large number of invited guests and the officers of the R.J. Mitchell Memorial Museum Ltd, including the chairman, the late Gordon Eldridge, who was responsible for all the arrangements for the event. It is of relevance that 6 October 1993 was the sixtieth anniversary of the formation of British Air Navigation by Supermarine and Southampton Docks, who together started a flying-boat service to the Channel Islands. From these early beginnings, there evolved Imperial Airways, which in turn became the forerunner of British Airways.

27.   Unveiling of a large mural in the Longton Exchange shopping centre, Stoke-on-Trent, 31 January 1995.

The mural is 15 ft by 13 ft in size and depicts Spitfires flying over the white cliffs of Dover. Unusually, and very impressively, it is formed from ceramic tiles. The mural was sponsored by the developers of the Exchange centre, I.M. Properties plc, and the unveiling ceremony was organised by David Cooper Public Relations. I was kindly invited to unveil the mural which I duly did in the presence of the lord mayor of Stoke-on-Trent, Councillor Richard Leigh, the lady mayoress and many civic and other dignitaries including Mr Mick Jones, director of I.M. Properties, David Cooper, and Mr Kenneth Potts who produced the original fine painting for the mural. In the speech I made following the unveiling, I made the point that the mural could not be in a more appropriate place since my father's childhood had been spent in nearby Normacot and, in addition, my mother was born in nearby Meir. Finally, I was presented with a painting of the mural and I.M. Properties made a much appreciated donation to the Imperial Cancer Research Fund (R.J. Mitchell Fund). Another fine honour accorded to R.J.

28.   VE Day Commemoration Cruise on the QE2, 3–10 May 1995.

I was kindly invited, with my wife, by Cunard to be their guests on this cruise in order that I could present a lecture about R.J. Very enjoyable for us but I feel that it represented a great honour for my father in that it was considered appropriate that he should be selected as one of the people connected with the 1939–45 war that passengers on the cruise might like to hear about.

I gave the lecture 'My Father, R.J. Mitchell, Designer of the Spitfire' on 7 May, one day before the fiftieth anniversary of VE Day. The lecture was followed by many questions from the large audience, which I enjoyed having. Having got it over, I could then begin to relax and thoroughly enjoy the rest of the cruise!

29. *Naming ceremony of wind tunnel at the University of Southampton, 17 May 1995.*

The Department of Aeronautics and Astronautics in the university decided that it would be, in his centenary year, a fitting commemoration of R.J.'s working years in Southampton to name its major low-speed wind tunnel facility after him. I was kindly invited to carry out the naming ceremony prior to my presentation of the R.J.M. Centenary Lecture that evening. In my short address I said that R.J. had his name attached to a whole variety of tributes and memorials but never previously to a wind tunnel! I said I was certain he would have appreciated this honour although ironically he felt, like many others in his field, that at his time wind tunnels were small and not reliable. Hence, the only thing wind tunnel-tested on the prototype Spitfire was the Farnborough-tested ducted radiator. One especially pleasing feature of the occasion was that invitations were sent to all of the twenty-six Spitfire Mitchell Scholars and over half of them were able to accept the invitation, some of them dating back to the original years when the awards were first made (see page 250).

30. *R.J. Mitchell Centenary Lecture at the University of Southampton, 17 May 1995, given by Gordon Mitchell.*

The decision to inaugurate this special lecture to commemorate the centenary of the birth of my father on 20 May 1995, was made by Sir Gordon Higginson before he retired as vice-chancellor of the University of Southampton in September 1994, and he kindly invited me to present the lecture. The chair was taken by Professor Howard Newby, the vice-chancellor of the university. The lecture was given in the main lecture theatre before a large audience, most of whom had been invited although the public were welcome to attend. Following the lecture, Professor Newby kindly hosted a dinner for a number of specially invited guests. This I particularly enjoyed since I no longer had the worry of presenting the lecture! During the dinner, one of the guests, AVM 'Johnnie' Johnson, the famous Spitfire pilot, turned to me and said, 'Your father would have been proud of you today!' This naturally gave me great pleasure. The organisation both leading up to the lecture and on the day itself was superb and I would like to record my sincere thanks to Karen Humphreys from the University Graduation/Public Lectures Office whose help throughout made it all so much easier for me. I am also greatly indebted to Sir Gordon Higginson and Professor Howard Newby for making it possible for this memorable occasion in honour of my father to be held at the University of Southampton.

31. *Honours conferred on R.J. by the Royal Mail and the Royal Mint in commemoration of the centenary of his birth on 20 May 1995.*

As my father died before the vital importance of his Spitfire could become apparent, it meant that he could not, and probably would not ever, be awarded any official honours for his invaluable creation, for the simple reason that in this country posthumous honours can be awarded solely for gallantry and not, for example, for outstanding lifetime achievement. Accordingly, to try to redress this situation to some extent, I enquired, early in 1993, whether in the light of the approach of the centenary of R.J.'s birth on 20 May 1995, the Royal Mail might be willing to consider a special stamp issue of some form to commemorate this. I then began a two-year campaign, during which I sent out over 1,000 letters seeking support for a commemorative stamp. The support I received exceeded all my expectations with everyone I contacted writing to the Royal Mail with their support. The Royal Mail were undoubtedly very impressed by all this but there were two problems. The Royal Mail normally plan and agree their yearly special stamp programmes two years ahead. Hence, when I began my campaign in 1993, the programme for 1995 had already been fixed. Therefore, my campaign should have started in 1991! Secondly, in any case, May 1995 was the fiftieth anniversary of VE Day for which the Royal Mail were committed to issuing a very special set of stamps and the addition of a stamp honouring my father was, in the circumstances, rightly out of the question. However, the Royal Mail decided to overcome these problems by honouring my father with a fine, but non-stamp, commemorative label ('label' is a philatelic term for an official issue by the Royal Mail), to be issued on 16 May 1995. A real stamp was later to be issued – see Item 44.

7 million were printed together with 3 million machine-vended stamp books, bearing on the cover, as on the commemorative label, a portrait of R.J., a Spitfire and an S.6B Schneider Trophy seaplane. My father was the first individual ever to be honoured by the issue of such a commemorative label, the second being HM The Queen, a commemorative label for whom was issued by the Royal Mail on 16 April 1996 to commemorate her seventieth birthday. I worked closely on both

R.J.'s designs with Mr Barry Robinson, the Royal Mail design director, and I was delighted with the final results.

Early in 1994, I happened to see a centenary medal produced by the Royal Mint to commemorate the 500th anniversary of the birth of Henry VIII on 28 June 1491, and I contacted the mint to enquire whether they might be willing to commission such a medal to commemorate the centenary of my father's birth. In due course, I received a letter from Mr Brian Williams, the Royal Mint director of marketing, which was encouraging although obviously much had to be discussed before a final decision could be made. Finally, it was decided that the Royal Mint would commission a special centenary medal in honour of my father, to my great delight. Two expert medal sculptors were commissioned to design the medal: Avril Vaughan to produce the portrait of R.J. on the obverse side and the late John Lobban[18] to do the reverse side, which he, in due course designed showing a Mk IIA Spitfire[19] overflying an S.6B Schneider Trophy seaplane, both sides being in relief. I worked closely with Avril and John giving a bit of help here and there and in my opinion what they ultimately produced was pure perfection – R.J. would have approved of that! The centenary medal was produced in gold proof, silver proof, in bronze and fourthly in nickel/brass which was combined with the Royal Mail commemorative label as a philatelic medalic cover.

32.   Unveiling of statue of R.J. Mitchell in Stoke-on-Trent, 21 May 1995.

Stoke-on-Trent is the city in which R.J. was born, and two weeks of special events, culminating in the unveiling of the statue, were organised to commemorate the centenary of his birth. Stoke is proud of the fact that they have two especially famous citizens. First is Sir Stanley Matthews, a statue of whom they have had in the city for some time, and the second is R.J., of whom, it was decided, they should also like to have a statue and that there was no better time to fulfil this wish than on the occasion of my father's centenary.

As the result of the untiring efforts of the chairman, Mr J.A.M. Humphreys, and members of the Reginald Mitchell Memorial Trust with support from Stoke-on-Trent City Council, the necessary funds were eventually raised and the life-size bronze statue of R.J. sculpted and sited adjacent to the City Museum in Hanley, was ready for the official unveiling. This was duly carried out on Sunday 21 May 1995 by ACM Sir Michael Knight before a large and appreciative audience, and was followed by a flypast of a Spitfire and a Hurricane.

A very fitting tribute to my father as expressed by the people of the city in which he was born.

33.   Premiere of a forty-six-minute video entitled R.J. Mitchell
      – Aircraft Designer, *7 December 1995.*

The instigator of this video was Mr Tony Edwards, chairman and chief
executive of Messier-Dowty International, with the aim that it should
serve as a tribute to R.J. The video outstandingly achieves this aim of
Tony's and I am most grateful to him for making such a fine gesture in
memory of my father. The premiere was held in the Royal Aeronautical
Society's HQ in London before a large and distinguished audience. The
video is presented by William Woollard and is produced and directed
by William Woollard and Brian Johnson. A number of experts assess
my father's achievements as an aircraft designer, while I make several
appearances in which I discuss him as a man and as a father, his illness
and death at the age of forty-two from cancer, and that he in fact died,
in spite of his Spitfire, a very frustrated man, unable to see completed
the advanced four-engined bomber he had designed in his final year of
his working life. All the shooting for the video was carried out in the
RAF Museum in Hendon which in the end was very enjoyable as well
as involving quite a lot of hard work and concentration. Shortly after
the premiere I received a letter from Jeffrey Quill referring to the speech
I made following the showing of the video. 'If I may say so, I thought
your speech was excellent and came across as very genuine and very
much from the heart.' Indeed, a much treasured letter.

*34.   Special commemoration of the sixtieth anniversary of the first flight
      of the prototype Spitfire organised by the Southampton Hall of
      Aviation, Southampton City Council and sponsored by Messier-
      Dowty Ltd, 4 and 5 March 1996.*

The event began with a reception by the mayor of Southampton,
Councillor Margaret Singerman, in the civic centre. During this
reception, I had the pleasure of presenting the mayor with one of my
father's silver centenary medals. This was followed by a dinner held
at the De Vere Grand Harbour Hotel in Southampton at which one
of the organisers, Michael Aplin, had managed to obtain and squeeze
in to the dining hall the original Schneider Trophy and the full-size
replica of the prototype Spitfire. Speeches were made by Tony Edwards
(Messier-Dowty), Alex Henshaw, Gordon Eldridge, ACM Sir William
Wratten (commander-in-chief, Strike Command), together with some
brief comments by myself.
    On the following day, a most moving service was held on the site of
the old Supermarine works on the quayside, Spitfire Court, ending in
the dedication of a memorial plaque erected on the site commemorating the Supermarine workers killed and injured in the bombing of the

Supermarine factory in September 1940. Better late than never – certainly late by some fifty years! This was followed by a superb display by Rick Roberts in a Mk IX Spitfire. Guests then returned to the Hall of Aviation to see the video (see Item 34) about R.J. and to have lunch, after which they went to Southampton Airport to see some further exciting displays by more Spitfires.

I would like to record my gratitude to all those involved for organising this fine event in memory of the Spitfire, its designer and those who lost their lives in 1940.

35.   *'Southampton Salutes the Spitfire' airshow – celebration of the*
       achievements of R.J. Mitchell, and of the sixtieth anniversary of the
       first flight of the prototype Spitfire, 5 May 1996.

This event was sponsored by thirteen organisations including British Aerospace Defence, Messier-Dowty Ltd, Southampton City Council and Southampton Hall of Aviation, the latter two organising the event. The main and unique event was a flypast by no less than thirteen Spitfires over Southampton Water, together with some twenty other aircraft of different types. Indeed, a fine tribute both to R.J. and to his Spitfire. Mr John Weston, CBE, chairman and managing director, British Aerospace Defence, wrote in the fine brochure they sponsored, 'The Spitfire represents the foundation step in the evolution and the pedigree of today's Eurofighter 2000 – which has been dubbed the Spitfire of the twenty-first century'.

36.   *Spitfire Diamond Jubilee Air Show at Duxford, 6 May 1996.*

It was very appropriate that this great occasion should be held at Duxford since it was here that the very first RAF squadron of Spitfires, the famous 19 Squadron, was formed in 1938. Twenty-one Spitfires from all over Europe descended on the airfield for the show including the Spitfire prototype replica K5054 (see Item 25) together with a variety of other famous aircraft. It was the largest public gathering of Spitfires since the 1939–45 war. The 32,000-strong crowd enjoyed a magnificent display of flying in perfect weather although many apparently never managed to reach Duxford! The occasion ended with a solo Spitfire display by Ray Hanna which was pure perfection. Ray sadly died in December 2005.

I told Ray afterwards that it made me feel very proud to see my old man's Spitfire showing what it could do in such fine hands as his.

Before the displays, I was in the line up to sign books, etc., for the public – we were at it for some 2½ hours! This interest in obtaining signatures is understandable although sometimes a signature is indecipherable and there must be the risk of forgetting who the signer was after a time! Altogether a memorable day, being made more so for me by having the privilege to be flown to Duxford from my home by David Chalmers, ex-British Airways senior pilot, in his privately owned Robin aircraft.

The next time I visited the Imperial War Museum Duxford Airfield was to attend by invitation their Spitfire Air Show on 2 May 1998. This time Frank Crosby, head of marketing, kindly agreed that I bring some copies of this book with me to sell and arranged for a table for me in their museum shop marquee to operate from. Accordingly, I took forty-five books and sold them all. Again, David Chalmers very kindly flew me up to Duxford in his Robin aircraft and again it was another of the superb shows which Duxford never fails to put on.

I think that it was probably these sales plus well over a hundred copies of my book sold to the Duxford Museum shop that prompted Peter Day, the Imperial War Museum's book buyer, to write to me, 'We regard your book as a core title, and intend to always have copies in stock'. This hands-on interest by the Imperial War Museum eventually led to their much appreciated help and support in the publication by Tempus Publishing Ltd of the Third and present Fourth Edition of this book.

37. *Battle of Britain Memorial Flight 1996 Brochure.*

This magnificently produced brochure was largely devoted to commemorating the sixtieth anniversary of the first flight of the Spitfire. It contained an Introduction by Jeffrey Quill, written shortly before he died, a comprehensive history of the Spitfire by Grp Capt. Bill Taylor, entitled 'Spitfire 60' and an article by myself under the title 'My father, R.J. Mitchell, Designer of the Spitfire', which I had been asked to contribute. On the front cover is a particularly striking picture of a Spitfire flying over Tower Bridge in London, while on the centre pages is a photograph of the flight's Lancaster dropping a million poppies over the Mall on the fiftieth anniversary of VJ Day on 8 May 1995. This photograph records a very important occasion which forms a part of the history of this country.

38. *Opening of the exhibition of the restored hull of Mk I Southampton flying boat N9899 at the RAF Museum, 24 May 1996.*

The only surviving wooden hull of a Southampton flying boat, built in 1925, was discovered in 1967 by the River Deben in Suffolk, having been used as a houseboat for thirty years. The RAF Museum acquired the hull and took it to their Cardington restoration centre. Here began the difficult and painstaking task of restoring the badly worn hull. By

1988, work on the lower hull and planing bottom had been completed and on 9 November 1988 the hull was rolled over to allow work on the upper decking of the fuselage to be commenced. This was eventually completed, together with a fine reconstruction of the tailplanes, ready to be moved into the RAF Museum for permanent display.

The Southampton is recognised as R.J.'s first outstandingly successful design and it is, accordingly, very appropriate that it should take its place in the RAF Museum alongside some of his later successes, namely the Walrus, the Stranraer and the Spitfire.

The official 'opening' ceremony took place in the museum on 24 May 1996 when I had the pleasure of seeing the finally completed and restored Southampton for the first time. I told Dr Michael Fopp, the director of the RAF Museum, that I thought they had achieved pure perfection and as such would have undoubtedly delighted my father. It was very fitting that the Museums and Galleries Commission awarded the RAF Museum their prestigious 1996 Conservation Award for this outstanding example of the conservation of a historic artefact. Present at the ceremony were AC Christopher Paul, one of the few remaining pilots who had flown a Southampton flying boat, and the family who had lived for many years in the Southampton houseboat.

39. *Unveiling of R.J.'s name on a British Regional Airways Jetstream
     41 aircraft at Southampton International Airport, 27 June 1996.*

In the words of Mr Paul Barlow, the airport's managing director, a well-deserved tribute was paid to R.J. Mitchell when a British Regional Airways Jetstream 41 aircraft was named in his honour on 27 June 1996 and I owe a great debt of gratitude to Mr Barlow for initiating and organising this fine tribute to my father. Accompanied by local dignitaries from Eastleigh and Southampton, together with other representatives closely associated with the Spitfire, I had the privilege of unveiling R.J.'s name on the aircraft. The twenty-nine people then boarded the aircraft for a flight over the Isle of Wight, piloted by Capt. Cath White and first officer Lesley Camin. Also on the flight were three children from local schools who had won a competition to design a poster depicting the airport and Jetstream 41 aircraft, celebrating the sixtieth anniversary of the Spitfire, and after the flight they unveiled the new names on three of the streets on the airport, which are 'Spitfire Loop', 'Mitchell Way' and 'Tinker Alley'. Finally, to end a memorable occasion, everyone was invited to a wartime party on the airport, complete with bunting, balloons, Spitfire cake, and strawberries and cream! It is relevant that the Jetstream 41 was built by British Aerospace, in whose 'family tree' occurs The Supermarine

Aviation Works (Vickers) Ltd, the company in which R.J. did all his work from 1917 to 1937. Accordingly, there is a link between the Jetstream 41 and R.J. Mitchell.

40. *Aircraft images alongside Reginald Mitchell Way on the Tunstall bypass, Stoke-on-Trent, 1 October 1996.*

In addition to honouring my father by naming the bypass 'Reginald Mitchell Way', three aircraft images in concrete have been built on the embankment to the bypass. When I first saw the proposals at a late stage of the plans, I assumed that the strict English definition of 'image' would apply, namely 'that which very closely resembles anything', and that the images of my father's aircraft would accordingly be very close to the actual aircraft in both shape and size. This was, however, not the artist's interpretation of 'image' and hence the length of the concrete image of the Walrus was no less than 5.6 times that of the real Walrus. Likewise the concrete, head-on view of the Spitfire has a wing span 3.5 times that of a real Spitfire. The third concrete image, a plan view of a Spitfire, is, in contrast, only 1.3 times the size of a real Spitfire. It is, in my opinion, unfortunate that these vastly different scale sizes for the three aircraft images were used since it makes a realistic comparison of a Spitfire and a Walrus impossible. Hence, the images suggest, for example, that a Spitfire is tiny compared with a Walrus, which is just not the case. Thus, in a real Spitfire and Walrus, the latter is approximately only 8 ft longer than the Spitfire, whereas the concrete image of the Walrus shows this difference in length to be some 183 ft.

However, notwithstanding these comments on the implementation of the Tunstall project, I consider that basically the project is imaginative, certainly unique and, as an added bonus, is situated close to my father's birthplace. Moreover, at the end of the day, and most importantly, it is the thought behind the project that really matters, namely the wish of the project's originators and of the people of Stoke-on-Trent to honour R. J. Mitchell, and this it does.

41. *Unveiling of a bust of R.J. Mitchell at the University of Southampton, 2 October 1996.*

Following the centenary lecture on 17 May 1995, the university generously commissioned a life-size bust of R.J. to be sculpted by Avril Vaughan, who had been responsible for the superb portrait of my father on the Royal Mint centenary medal (see Item 31). Avril said it was most desirable that she had my help in achieving the life-like representation of R.J. which was her goal and this I willingly gave her to the best of my ability. Working with Avril made me realise how very difficult it is to produce a true likeness of someone, using only photographs (and a bit of help from a close relative!). Avril did eventually achieve her goal and I was able to say to her, 'That is my father'. The bronze bust was sited in the foyer of the Department of Aeronautics and Astronautics and I was kindly invited to perform the unveiling. This I did in the presence of the vice-chancellor, Professor Howard Newby, senior members of the department, Avril Vaughan, family and friends.

The inscription on the bust pedestal reads:

R.J. Mitchell CBE AMICE FRAeS 1895–1937 by Avril Vaughan ARBS FSNAD. This bust of 'R.J.' was unveiled by his son, Dr Gordon Mitchell, on 2 October 1996. The work was commissioned by the University of Southampton with support from Tubesales UK Ltd and the Southampton branch of the Royal Aeronautical Society.

42.   *Presentation of The Spitfire Book in the Southampton Hall of Aviation, 8 May 1997*

A few weeks before he died, Jeffrey Quill, the Supermarine chief test pilot, suggested how appropriate it would be for a professionally pro-duced book to be made recording the names of all the design staff who had worked on the Spitfire from 1932 to 1945. The idea was taken up by Tony Edwards, chairman and chief executive of Messier-Dowty, and chief executive of Dowty Aerospace, who said that on behalf of the Dowty Groups, he would like to sponsor the production of the book. Accordingly, a small group of retired Supermarine employees, headed by Gerald Gingell, were formed and consisted of Pat Gingell, Harry Griffiths and Don Macdonald.[20] They had a difficult task since no offi-cial records of Supermarine staff now exist, but, eventually, based on memories of surviving colleagues, private lists and so on, they were able to compile over 300 names to be recorded in a fine, hand-illuminated, leather-bound book. At last the book was completed and was handed over to Mr Alex Henshaw, MBE, vice-president of the R.J. Mitchell Memorial Museum, before over 160 invited guests, on 8 May 1997. This was followed by the handing over of Jeffrey Quill's logbooks by his widow, Mrs Jeffrey Quill, and of his medals by his daughter, Sarah Quill, all on permanent loan to the museum. Mrs Quill died on 5 December 2000.

Following these presentations, there was a fine display by a single Spitfire in not the best of weather conditions, which in turn was fol-lowed by an excellent luncheon in the Hall of Aviation. As I said in a TV interview I made from the hall for BBC1, this occasion was something that I knew my father would have wholeheartedly supported since he always emphasised and acknowledged the invaluable help he received from his colleagues at Supermarine, and I quoted what he said on more than one occasion: 'Anything I have achieved has been as a member of a big team'. On 8 May 1997, that team was duly recognised. I was amazed, but in view of what I had said, pleased to hear later that my little piece had gone out that day on the 1 p.m., 6 p.m. and 9 p.m. news on BBC1!

43. *Issue of a Royal Mail postage stamp in honour of R.J. Mitchell, 10 June 1997.*

In December 1996, I was informed by Mr Barry Robinson, the Royal Mail design director, that they proposed to issue in June 1997 a set of five special stamps honouring renowned aircraft designers and the aircraft for which they are famous, and that one of these would depict R.J. Mitchell and his Spitfire. He then later brought the stamps for me to see and comment on. I was naturally delighted with this news and particularly so when Barry told me that the great success of the commemorative label honouring my father on the occasion of his centenary in 1995, which followed the campaign which I began in 1993 to try and persuade the Royal Mail to recognise my father in some way, had stimulated great interest in the subject of aircraft and their designers within the Royal Mail. This did much to prompt the decision to include the five aircraft designer stamps in their 1997 special issues stamp programme. These also appropriately recognised the fiftieth anniversary of Roy Chadwick, the designer of the Lancaster bomber on 10 June 1997 and they also marked the sixtieth anniversary of my father's death.

At my suggestion, the Spitfire depicted on the stamp is the Mk IIA, P7350, the oldest still flying – it took part in the Battle of Britain and now flies with the Battle of Britain Memorial Flight. I also requested that R.J.'s stamp be the 20p one in the set since, as Sir Michael Heron, chairman of the Post Office, told me, this denomination would be printed in the highest quantity, and in the event 28 million were printed. My wife and I had the pleasure of visiting Harrison Sons Ltd, in High Wycombe, to see the stamps actually being printed in six colours. Their printing machine was capable of printing no less than 60 million stamps in one working day!

My father's face is depicted in the clouds on the right of the stamp, facing his Spitfire, and occupies the whole of the right-hand side of the stamp; it is a first-class reproduction of my father. Bruce Duckworth, the artist who designed all five stamps, deserves every congratulation for the unique and excellent way in which he depicted the faces of the aircraft designers. The designers and aircraft depicted on the remaining four stamps in the set are Roy Chadwick and the Lancaster, R.E. Bishop and the Mosquito, George Carter and the Gloster Meteor, and Sidney Camm and the Hawker Hunter. The stamps received their first public showing at the International Stamp Exhibition at Wembley, 24–27 April 1997.

My father would, I am sure, have been tickled pink with his stamp, not least because he would have seen it as being artistically perfect, perfection being his middle name! At the same time, he would without doubt have wished that the stamp be seen as recognising not only him but everyone associated with the creation and production of his Spitfire, the design staff, the test pilots and last but not least, those who built it. He always saw himself as a member of a big team, but with, of course, final responsibility.

The issue of the stamps generated a great deal of publicity in the press, on TV and radio. The Royal Mail organised special publicity events at Staverton Airport on 6 June (South West Division), at the City Museum in Stoke-on-Trent on 9 June, and the major national launch at Duxford Aerodrome on 9 June, which was sponsored by British Aerospace. I was invited to all three events but due to the clash of dates could only attend those at Staverton and Duxford.

I soon lost count of the number of photographs taken, particularly at Duxford where the events included a spectacular low level flypast by the Battle of Britain Memorial Flight Lancaster in special memory of Roy Chadwick, its designer. Both events were felt to have been a great success and I was gratified to receive a letter from Mr Richard Ellis of British Aerospace two weeks later saying, 'Your contribution to the day was immense'. In addition to these events, I had the opportunity to contribute to two TV programmes, one for Central News South and the other for BBC Midlands Today.

On 10 June a very special event took place at Southampton International Airport in which I had a very personal interest since it all took place as the result of an idea that I had that originated with the unveiling of my father's name on a Jetstream 41 aircraft at Southampton International Airport on 27 June 1996 (see Item 39). The idea was basically to try and produce a special first day cover incorporating my father's stamp, which would then be flown in the R.J. Mitchell Jetstream 41 from Southampton Airport, the birthplace of the Spitfire which first flew from there on 5 March 1936. The excellent and most attractive first day cover that was eventually produced was only made possible through the expert and unsparing help of the Benham Group at Folkestone to whom I owe a great debt of gratitude.

On the morning of Tuesday 10 June, all was ready for the flight in the R.J.M. Jetstream 41. The limited edition of 1,400 covers were loaded into the aircraft and my wife and myself, with the twenty-six personal guests I was able to invite, boarded the plane. These included: Barry Robinson; Brian Janes, director of Harrison Sons Ltd, who printed the stamps; and Andrew Curd and Anne Broadhurst from the Benham Group who produced the covers. With Capt. Cath White the pilot, assisted by first officer Andy Collicot, we took off in excellent weather for a forty-minute flight at low level over Southampton and the Isle of Wight, during which time champagne was served by Stephanie Shirling-Rooke, our stewardess. Everyone agreed that this was a very special occasion, as indeed it was, and I am most grateful to all those at Southampton Airport who made it all possible. A particular word of thanks is due to Cath White who enthusiastically supported the whole project and who painstakingly signed, with me, all 1,400 of my covers!

My original idea in producing the first day cover was that all the profit from their sales should be used to help with the costs of establishing the prototype Spitfire replica at Southampton Airport. However, as in the event this proved to be impossible (see Item 25), I used the profits in the following three ways.

(1)   To make a donation of £500 to the Spitfire Society.

(2)   To cover the total costs (£625) of a leaflet I wrote about the Spitfire memorial 'window' at Southampton Airport for distribution to visitors to the memorial (see Item 46).

(3)   To make a donation of £1,775 to the Tangmere Military Aviation Museum Trust in support of a very fine memorial they were planning to establish. This consists of ten flagpoles carrying the flags of the countries from which the pilots who flew from Tangmere in the 1939–45 war came, plus one additional flagpole carrying the Supermarine flag. This was at my request as recognition of the close association of Tangmere with the Spitfire. An engraving in front of the flagpoles reads 'This memorial was kindly donated and unveiled by Lady McEvoy and Dr G. Mitchell 11-7-1999'.

44.   *A memorial for R.J. Mitchell in St Clement Danes Church in London, 17 May 1998.*

St Clement Danes in the Strand was re-built by Christopher Wren in 1682 but was completely destroyed on the night of 10 May 1941 by a hail of fire-bombs dropped from German bombers. After the war it was agreed by the Diocese of London that the RAF be allowed to restore the church and use it as its own. After much hard work the RAF were able to raise the required funds to re-build the church and in 1955 work was started on it. Three years later St Clement Danes was completed and on 19 October 1958 the re-consecration service was held in the presence of HM Queen Elizabeth II, the Duke of Edinburgh, the Archbishop of Canterbury and many other dignitaries, and thereafter became known as 'The church of the Royal Air Force'.

I was accordingly delighted when the resident chaplain, the Reverend Brian McAvoy, and subsequently the Reverend Peter Bishop, and the church trustees, agreed that it would be very appropriate for a memorial to my father to be included in St Clement Danes Church. On my visit to the Royal Mint on 5 April 1995 (Item 31) to watch the first centenary medal being struck, Mr Brian Williams, the director of marketing, kindly presented me with the two original electrotype copper plates of the obverse and reverse sides of the medal, mounted on two fine wooden plaques. These plates were produced from the plaster casts of the medal, as produced by the sculptors. After scaling down, they were then used to produce the actual dies from which the medals were struck. With the agreement of Brian Williams, it was agreed that a very fitting memorial to my father would be for me to present the two plaques to St Clement Danes and for them to be permanently fixed to the church's two medal stands. These stands are used to carry the medals of members of the RAF up to the altar during thanksgiving services held in their honour subsequent to their funeral service. The service of dedication of the two memorials to R.J. took place on 17 May in St Clement Danes Church with the then chaplain, the Reverend David Mackenzie, and the Right Reverend Frank Cocks officiating. The memorials consist of the two medal stands, together with a professional model of a Spitfire with a plaque reading –

> In memory of R.J. Mitchell, designer of the Spitfire, the original dies for the centenary medals, commissioned by the Royal Mint in his honour, are affixed to the medal-carrying stands.

Frank Cocks gave a comprehensive and moving address in honour of my father. He had not been well for some long time and it was only at the last moment that he decided he would be able to attend the service. This entailed the greatest effort on Frank's part since he was sadly to die in August, only three months after the service. I am indeed very grateful to Frank for agreeing to officiate at the service and for the great courage and regard for my father that he showed in doing so (see page 196).

45. *Purpose-built park in Normacot, Stoke-on-Trent, named after R.J. Mitchell, August 1997.*

As indicated in Chapter 1, R.J. lived in Normacot for many years until he left for Southampton in 1917. It was accordingly felt appropriate that this comprehensive newly built park should be named after him. Facilities at the park include a teenage multi-sport area and a basketball court as well as junior and toddler needs. The park was opened by the lord mayor of Stoke-on-Trent, Douglas Brown, who also unveiled a plaque on the site to R.J.. Sam Mitchell, the eldest son of Eric, my father's oldest brother, was present at the opening ceremony and said he felt it was tremendous to associate his uncle's name with something so worthwhile. I was unfortunately unable to accept the invitation to attend owing to having to go into hospital for an operation on my shoulder.

46.   *Supermarine Spitfire memorial window at Southampton*
      International Airport, 17 December 1998.

When it finally had to be concluded that it would not be possible to establish the Spitfire prototype replica at Southampton Airport (see Item 49 about Tangmere), it was decided to establish in its place at the airport an appropriate memorial to all those people that had been associated with the Spitfire in various ways.

This is in the form of a large engraved illuminated glass 'window', incorporating a reproduction of the prototype Spitfire K5054 and engraved wording illustrating those who are honoured and commemorated by the memorial. Namely, those who created, built and flight tested the Spitfire, all those who lost their lives or were injured when the Supermarine works were bombed in September 1940 and, last but not least, all those who flew the Spitfire into battle throughout the 1939–45 war.

The memorial is situated in the viewing gallery at the airport, which appropriately overlooks the place where K5054 stood before its first flight on 5 March 1936. The window was generously sponsored by BAA plc and was unveiled by their former chairman, Sir Brian Smith, on 17 December 1998.

47.   *Bust of R.J. Mitchell at the RAF Club in London. Unveiled on*
      26 February 2002.

There are on display in the club a number of busts of famous individuals associated with the RAF. In August 2001 the club decided to commission a bust of R.J. to be added to those already on display.

The bust was produced by the well-known sculptor Mr James Butler R.A., who, during the last twenty years, has been involved in a large number of commissions throughout the world. At his request, I spent several hours with Mr Butler and was able to help him with some of the finer points of the details of my father's face, to produce what I am sure will be seen as an excellent reproduction of R.J.

I had the privilege of unveiling the bust on 26 February 2002.

48.   Memorial to R.J. Mitchell at the Tangmere Military Aviation
       Museum Trust. Unveiled on 2 March 2002.

As already indicated (Item 26), it was eventually found to be financially
impossible to fund the building required to house the Spitfire prototype
replica K5054 at Southampton Airport. Accordingly, the Spitfire Society
decided to locate the replica at Tangmere, which already had a suitable
building in which to house it. Tangmere was, of course, a famous Spitfire
station in the 1939–45 war.

The trust organised a special display featuring a bust of R.J., which is
situated between the K5054 replica and a Mk V Spitfire. It depicts R.J.
sitting at a drawing board, and R.J.'s 12-bore shotgun, which I presented
to Tangmere last year, will be included in the display.

The trust kindly accorded me the privilege of performing the unveiling of the display on 2 March 2002, three days before the sixty-sixth
anniversary of the first flight of the Spitfire on 5 March 1936.

49.   Sea Wings 2000 celebration at Southampton, 3–4 June 2000.

This event was staged by Southampton City Council in celebration of
the city's historic aviation heritage. The main event took place on 4 June
on the Weston Shore, near Woolston where Supermarine was situated,
and consisted of an excellent flying display incorporating a wide range
of different aircraft, including a number of seaplanes and amphibian
aircraft, some of which landed and took off from Southampton Water
opposite the display site. To end the display and to commemorate the
sixtieth anniversary of the Battle of Britain, there was then a flypast of
thirteen Spitfires and one Hurricane – indeed a magnificent display,
greatly appreciated by the crowd of over 100,000.

On 3 June, a pilot's dinner was held in the guildhall, hosted by the city
of Southampton and The Right Worshipful the Mayor of Southampton,
Councillor Peter Wakeford. I was invited to this dinner and asked if I
would give an address of some twenty minutes following the dinner.
For this, I decided that instead of talking about my father as an aircraft
designer, as I usually did, I would pay a tribute to him as a father. I did
this by recalling the large amount of time he spent with me, taking me
to see what he was doing in his work and talking to me about my career
and so on, and all this in spite of his heavy workload and the fact that
from 1933 he knew he was probably dying from cancer. From the fine
reception I received for this personal insight of my father, I felt it was
found interesting and appropriate to the occasion.

I am most grateful to everyone involved in making possible all the fine
tributes I have described in this chapter, to a great man and a great

father, and to his Spitfire. I am sure, knowing him as I did, having lived with him for seventeen years, the only person alive today to have had this privilege, that he would have greatly appreciated the honour and recognition accorded to him in so many fine ways.

On 24 August 2004, I received a letter from Mr Sidney E. Frank, a wealthy American philanthropist, which read:

Dear Mr Mitchell,

I think your father was a fantastic inventor to design the Spitfire, and I think he was just as important as Churchill in the Battle of Britain in saving western Europe and preserving deomcracy all over the world.

In a subsequent telephone conversation, Mr Frank said he intended to do what he could to enhance the recognition and understanding of my fater's great contribution to his country and to the preservation of democracy all over the world, and he appointed Mr Abel Haddon, Senior Consultant, Bell Pottinger Communications Ltd, to oversee everything in the UK. The following four items (50–53) came about as the result of Mr Frank's much appreciated generosity.

50. *English Heritage Blue Plaque on house R.J lived in in*
Southampton. Unvieled on 8 September 2005.

The plaque reads 'R.J. Mitchell 1895–1937. designer of the Supermarine Spitfire lived here 1927–1937' and it was unveiled by me before a large audience of invited guests, which included Harry Griffiths, the last person stilla live who worked with my father. the presetn owners of the house, Professor and Mrs John Norman, provided some excellent refreshments on whatturned out to be one of the hottest days of the year See illustration 67.

51. *Detailed website about R.J. and his work.*

This was launched in February 2005 and as at December 2005 it has had over 40,000 visits. The website had my full blessing and I was able to make a significant contribution to it.

52. *Spitfire and R.J. Mitchell Exhibition accompanied by a statue of*
R.J., in the Science Museum in London.

As part of the exhibition, a real spitfire was obtained on loan from the RAF Museum and was literally taken apart so that people could see how it was constructed. It contains much else besides of personal and historic interest, including my father's actual briefcase which I was able to lend to the museum for the eighteen months duration of the exhibition, which opened on 16 August 2005.

The excellent lifelike statue was uniquely produced in Welsh slate by Stephen Kettle, to whom I was able to give some help in obtaining the desired likeness.

The statue was unveiled on 15 September 2005 by Mr Sidney frank and will remain in the museum permanently. See illustration 68.

53.   *Inclusion of R.J. Mitchell's name on the Battle of Britain*
       Monument on the Victoria Embankment in central London.

The Monument was rightly designed to honour all those airmen who took part in the Battle of Britain, and every one of their names is included in raised lettering. The Monument was unveiled by HRH The Prince of Wales on Sunday 18 September 2005, and was preceded by a most impressive Service of Thanksgiving and Rededication in Westminster Abbey, to which my daughter, Penny, and I were invited.

The organisers of the Monument eventually agreed (perhaps with a bit of pressure?) that in the light of the roles the Spitfire and the Hurricane played in the battle, the names of the two designers, R.J. Mitchell and Sidney Camm, should be added to the Monument.

54.   *Opening of the R.J. Mitchell House at Calshot Activities Centre on*
       17 October 2005.

I received an invitation to attend this occasion from Coucillor Ken Thornber CBE, the Leader of the Hampshire County Council, which I was very pleased to accept. Calshot was, of course, where the Schneider Trophy teams were based for the 1929 and 1931 races, and although I went to Calshot with my father in those two years, the last time I went there was in 1981, when celebrations of the fiftieth anniversary of the outright winning of the Trophy by Britain took place.

Calshot is now a flourishing activities centre, with many thousands of young people visiting it every year. It is to accommodate some of these visitors that the house named after my father was built. It is a magnificent building and will accommodate sixty people in almost luxury conditions.

Interestingly, the Director of the Centre is Mr Phil Quill, but he did not think he was related to Jeffrey (see Appendix 6, page 320).

20

The Role of the Spitfire in the Battle of Britain

Updated December 2005

In order that the recent new data on the subject can be fully appreciated, it is necessary first to summarise the facts previously discussed in this book. Firstly, it is relevant to repeat that it has sometimes been concluded that because there were more squadrons of Hurricanes (thirty) in the Battle of Britain than of Spitfires (nineteen), this must automatically mean that it was the former that played the major role in this great air battle. The evidence that follows strongly points to this being the wrong conclusion.

The first fact of major importance is that the Hurricane's performance was significantly inferior in speed, rate of climb and turning circle to both the Spitfire and the ME 109E German fighter in the marks used in the battle. Thus, the maximum speed of the Hurricane I was about 311 mph which compared with the 355 mph top speed of the Spitfire Mk I and that of 348 mph for the ME 109E (Quill, 1996). Unlike the Hurricane, the Spitfire could turn inside an ME 109E; in aerial combat, speed and manoeuvrability are of vital importance and this comparison shows that whereas the Hurricane was well-fitted to shoot down bombers, with their much slower speed, it was at a disadvantage when it came to attacking the German ME 109E. In complete contrast, the Spitfire had a capability at least equal to that of the ME 109E. It is of interest to mention that when the two British fighters were originally ordered, it was envisaged that their sole task would be to shoot down the enemy bombers since it was considered that with their high speed, fighter-to-fighter combat could not occur. This led to the thought that the Hurricane alone would be all that would be needed and that consequently Spitfire production should be discontinued. The long delays and difficulties initially encountered in the mass production of the Spitfire added to this line of thought.

However, as Quill (1996), Supermarine's chief test pilot, relates, Dunkirk was the first major test of the Spitfire in combat with the Luftwaffe fighters and demonstrated in unarguable fashion the Spitfire's superiority over the Hurricane, and dispelled, once and for all, any ideas that existed in the Air Ministry that the difference in fighting perform-ance between the two aircraft was marginal and of no great significance. Thus, as Quill says, at Dunkirk, Mitchell's uncompromising search for performance in his design was finally justified.

As a consequence of these vital differences between the Hurricane and the Spitfire, an important battle tactic was introduced whenever possible. This was for the Spitfire squadrons to be sent up to attack the escorting German fighters, leaving the Hurricane squadrons 'free' to attack the German bombers. That it was somewhat 'easier' to shoot down a slow-flying bomber than a fast-flying fighter goes without saying. AC Alan Deere, the famous Battle of Britain pilot who actively fought in the battle from beginning to end, and hence is well qualified to draw conclusions about the battle, writes in his book (Deere, 1959),

> On numerous occasions I witnessed the rewards reaped when enemy bombers, shorn of the majority of their fighter escort, were set upon by the defending Hurricanes which, excellent as they were, could not have coped so effectively without the intervention of the Spitfires.

New data recently published by Alcorn (1996, 2000) provides significant confirmation of the actual results of this important battle tactic. Alcorn made an in-depth study of all the available data about the battle and thereby linked confirmed German losses with the British claims of victories on a squadron basis. These data showed, firstly, that claimed victories by both Spitfire and Hurricane pilots were approximately double the true credited victories, which in the heat of battle was hardly surprising.

Number of squadrons involved		Credited aircraft shot down			Total credited aircraft shot down per squadron
		Fighters	Bombers	Total	
Spitfires	19	282	247	529	27.8
Hurricanes	30	222	434	656	21.9

Thus, of the total aircraft shot down (1,185), 44.6% were shot down by Spitfirers and 55.4% by hurricanes, but by far the greater proportion of aircraft shot down by the Hurricane pilots were the 'easier' target of bombers, (66.2%), a direct consequence of the aforementioned battle tactic. Moreover, as Deere (1959) says, it was his opinion that the Hurricane pilots could not have shot down as many bombers as they did without the protection provided by the Spitfire pilots in attacking the escorting German fighters.

In addition, the figures in the last column in the table show that the average number of aircraft shot down by each squadron of Spitfires (27.8) was very significantly higher than that of the average Hurricane Squadron (21.9), showing that the Spitfire was much more effective in action than the Hurricane.

These new data strongly reinforce what Alan Deere says in this book (Appendix 9), namely,

> There can be no doubt that victory in the Battle of Britain was made possible by the Spitfire. Although there were more Hurricanes than Spitfires in the battle, the Spitfire was the RAF's primary weapon because of its better all-round capability. The Hurricane alone could not have won this great air battle, but the Spitfire (if in sufficient numbers) could have done so because of its superior capabilities.

At the same time, it must be emphasised that these conclusions do not detract in any way from the important role the Hurricane and its pilots did indeed play in the Battle of Britain.

December 2005: I asked Michael Oakley (Editor of *The Aeroplane*) if he had ever received any criticism of Alcorn's work following its publication in *The Aeroplane*. He replied that he had not seen any major critique of Alcorn's research and considered it still stood as the definitive study.

References

Alcorn, J. (1996) *The Aeroplane*, September 1996.
Alcorn, J. (2000) *The Aeroplane*, July 2000.
Deere, A. (1959) *Nine Lives*. Hodder & Stoughton Ltd.
Quill, J. (1996) *Birth of a Legend – the Spitfire*. Quiller Press Ltd.

Appendices

I R.J. MITCHELL — AIRCRAFT DESIGNER

by Sir George Edwards, OM, CBE, FRS, FEng

All aircraft designers become identified with one particular type of aeroplane – or even one individual machine.

Chadwick – probably the most underrated of all the wartime designers – will be remembered by the Lancaster, although there were a number of smaller aircraft to his name.

On the other hand, Sidney Camm, whom I knew well, spent all his career on small aircraft, mainly fighters and fighter-bombers. On visits to my patch at Weybridge he would stand under the wings of the Valiant or VC10 or whatever and make some such remark as: 'It isn't possible! There's no way you can control a job as big as this and have any idea what your staff are up to.'

Now to come to Mitchell – who will always be remembered as the designer of the Spitfire.

In actual fact, the great range of aeroplanes he designed – Schneider Trophy racing seaplanes – small and large flying boats – land-based fighters – light aeroplanes – qualify him to be rated as the most versatile of all British designers.

There can be no doubt that the boldness of Mitchell's Schneider Trophy seaplane designs and the passion for engineering detail which they displayed, made a profound impact on aeronautical design and set the scene for successive generations of British fighters which were so decisive in saving Britain from defeat in later years. If the industry had been limited during these inter-war years to design study alone, and had not been able to translate ideas into hardware by actually building aeroplanes, it is certain that such successful fighters as the Spitfire and Hurricane would not have emerged. My personal contact with Mitchell was one occasion when he attended a Vickers meeting of designers at Weybridge. My first impact with his aeroplanes was when I was doing the tail unit of the B.9/32 prototype (which later became the Wellington).

When I needed to know the shape of the fin and rudder, Pierson, chief designer at Weybridge, said: 'Mutt Summers thinks the Stranraer rudder control is quite nice – make it like that', which I did, big top horn balance and all.

I also remember the astonishment and pain felt at Weybridge, where we regarded ourselves as the heavy brigade, when Supermarine were awarded the contract for the B.12/36 four-engined bomber. Yet the design of this aeroplane incorporated so many outstanding features that, had the prototype not been wrecked by the bombing at Woolston, it would probably have been a great aeroplane.

How then was it possible for this man to cover such a wide range of types?

I think his inventiveness was based on a solid engineering knowledge. He was equally strong on structures and aerodynamics. The single spar leading edge torsion box of the Spitfire was a sound design and in the case of the B.12/36 bomber was accompanied by very novel integral tanks, which formed part of the structure of the leading edge and carried the main fuel supply. The thin wing on the Spitfire was made possible structurally by the elliptical planform; the further refinement of the twist and camber gave it the extra performance which makes sound aeroplanes into winners.

Another feature which ran through all his designs was his understanding of the engine designers' problems and promises.

Many an aeroplane has come to an untimely halt because the airframe was unable to accept the increased performance offered by the development of the engine. Not so Mitchell's aircraft.

Joe Smith, who did so much to develop the basic Spitfire, spoke warmly of Mitchell as a humane leader of men. However brilliant the chief designer might be, he must get the best out of his team.

This Mitchell did – with an authority based on his own great technical skill and the ability to unite this with a warm humanity and a willingness at the right time to join in any fun and games.

He, like the rest of us in this business, experienced the anxiety – almost the agony – of a first flight when the result of years of blood, tears and sweat suddenly works the magic of transforming an inanimate lump of duralumin into an aeroplane in flight. Especially did he feel for the pilots who risked their lives serving him.

Almost certainly we were deprived of the best of Mitchell. He would have welcomed the challenge and opportunities provided by the jet engine and supersonics and electronics and space. There is no telling what his fertile mind would have conceived.

One thing that's for certain is that, welcome though American Lend-Lease was in the Second World War, Mitchell played a vital role in preventing us losing the war altogether. One can't ask much more of a man than that.

Sir George Edwards

Born in 1908, George Robert Edwards joined Vickers Aviation at Weybridge in 1935 at the age of twenty-seven, after studying engineering at the University of London. He worked in the experimental design and drawing offices until the outbreak of war in 1939, when he was appointed chief designer and then general manager and chief engineer, and was head of the teams responsible for the Viking, Valetta, Varsity and Viscount, and the Valiant bomber.

On being appointed managing director of Vickers-Armstrongs (Aircraft) Ltd in 1953, he continued to be responsible for the overall technical direction of the company, and for the Vanguard, VC10 and TSR2 programmes. He was awarded the MBE in 1945, the CBE in 1952 and was knighted in 1957.

In May 1961, Sir George, as executive director (aircraft) of the newly formed British Aircraft Corporation (BAC), and overall technical leader of the aircraft design teams, initiated the BAC One-Eleven short-haul jet airliner – the first product of the new corporation. Sir George then took a prominent part in the negotiations which led, in November 1962, to the Concorde supersonic airliner (with Aerospatiale of France), and subsequently played a continuing and leading role in its vast programme. He was also prominent in the Anglo-French Jaguar and Anglo-German-Italian Panavia Tornado military combat aircraft programmes.

In November 1963, Sir George was appointed chairman of BAC. He relinquished the post of managing director in November 1972 and retired from BAC in 1975 after forty years of exceptional activity and achievement in the aeronautical industry.

In 1971, Her Majesty the Queen bestowed upon Sir George the order of merit. This honour is the personal gift of the Queen, and the order is limited to twenty-four members.

2 THE SPITFIRE FROM PROTOTYPE TO MK 24

by Air Marshal Sir Humphrey Edwardes Jones, KCB, CBE, DFC, AFC

By May 1936, I had been given command of 'A' Flight of the Performance Testing Squadron of the Aircraft and Armament Experimental Establishment at Martlesham Heath (A and AEE). 'A' Flight tested all single-seater aircraft and all civil light aircraft. Normally when any prototype aircraft arrived at Martlesham it was put into a hangar and stripped of all its instruments for calibration and in most cases the flying controls were removed for measurement and balance. It would therefore be at least a week before the aircraft emerged for its first test flights. There would then be handling flights to get pilots used to the 'feel' of the aircraft which would lead on to the actual performance testing.

On 26 May I was told by Sqn Ldr Ted Hilton, my commanding officer, that the prototype Spitfire would be arriving that afternoon, that I was to fly it immediately it had been refuelled and that I was to ring up AM Sir Wilfred Freeman, the air member for research and development (AMRD) on landing to let him know what I thought about the aircraft. As the aircraft was not expected to arrive until late afternoon, Ted added that the AMRD would remain in his office until I had telephoned him.

About 4.30 p.m. 'Mutt' Summers, the firm's chief test pilot, brought K5054 in to land and about 5.30 p.m. I took off after a thorough briefing by 'Mutt'. Although normal flying activities ceased at 5 p.m. and the station closed down for the day, on this occasion a number of people of all ranks remained behind to see the first flight of an aircraft which was widely expected to be a world beater.

I flew the aircraft for about twenty minutes and found it delightful to handle with no problems in normal flight. I was very much aware of the unusual audience the flight had attracted and was therefore determined to make no mistakes in my approach and landing. In those days to use engine to assist one's approach was considered very bad flying and was known as 'rumbling'. We had a 'rumble box' in the flight office into which one had to put half-a-crown if we had been seen to 'rumble'. The proceeds went to the flight Christmas party.

Well aware of this and that all my flight were watching, I throttled back for my approach in a carefully chosen position to the south of the airfield. With the throttle closed, the Spitfire's broad nose came up to such an extent that one's forward view was obscured, but as I started my approach I spotted Sgt Bill Pegg doing 'S' turns in front of me in the Super Fury which he had been to Brooklands to fetch from Hawkers. As flying control had closed down for the day and I had no radio, I could only watch Bill to see when he landed. To gain time, I put the flaps down and continued with my approach much slowed down. As soon as I was sure the Super Fury had landed I carried on with my gliding approach, but it was not until I was on what is now known as 'finals' that I remembered that something was missing and that I had not lowered the undercarriage! I decided at first to open up and go around again, but before doing so put the undercarriage lever into 'down' and, as the wheels came down with a satisfactory clonk, decided to carry on with the landing which was easy and normal.

Immediately on arrival at my office I rang the Air Ministry and was put through to Sir Wilfred Freeman who said, 'I know you can't tell me what the aircraft does after one short flight. All I want to know is, do you consider that the novice pilots we are going to get into the RAF under the expansion scheme will be able to cope with such an advanced aircraft?' As I, a test pilot, had come very near to forgetting to lower the undercarriage, I took a deep breath and then said, 'Yes, provided they are given adequate instruction in the use of flaps and retracting undercarriages.' Both these devices were almost unknown at that time and I had only flown one aircraft with them before.

On the strength of my remarks and with encouraging figures on performance provided by the firm, 310 Spitfires were ordered by the Air Ministry on 3 June 1936, only eight days after my first flight. An order of such magnitude had never previously been given in peace time and it ensured that the Spitfire was in full use in squadrons before the war started.

The morning after my flight, my pilots kept saying such things as 'You've got a nerve, waiting until you crossed the road before lowering the undercarriage!' I never divulged to anyone, until many years after, how near I was to wrecking the only Spitfire in existence at that time.

We quickly got down to performance testing the aircraft and as flight commander, and due to the urgency the Air Ministry was showing to have the firm's figures on speeds and climb confirmed, I did most of the original tests. We found the top speed at 'full throttle height' somewhere between 16,000 and 17,000 ft, to be 349 mph, which was only 1 mph short of Mitchell's predicted speed. Climbs were highly satisfactory and I found I could hold a steady speed at full throttle at 35,000 ft, a height I had never achieved by a wide margin in any other aircraft.

After the preliminary trials had proved satisfactory, K5054 went back to Eastleigh for checks and to be polished up for the annual RAF Display at Hendon at the end of June. I collected the aircraft a few days before the display and with a following wind did the trip from Eastleigh to Hendon in exactly fifteen minutes. My instructions were to fly it round the airfield to show it off to its best advantage, but to do no aerobatics. Its beautiful shape and colouring and obvious manoeuvrability made a great impression on those present.

On my visit to Eastleigh I met R.J. Mitchell and had a long chat with him on the tarmac. He appeared to be very interested in what I had to say about the aircraft and obviously appreciated the expeditious way we had handled the preliminary trials at Martlesham, which had confirmed all his predictions for the aircraft.

Subsequently, I flew Spitfires when commanding the Fighter Operational Training Unit at Grangemouth in 1941–42, the Exeter Fighter Sector in 1942, and 323 Wing at Maison Blanche, Algiers, in 1942–43. At Algiers, I had a Spitfire Mk V allotted to me on which I had 'E.J.1' painted on the sides, and which only I flew, with one exception when AC Prince Bernard of the Netherlands borrowed it for a short handling flight. I discovered that he had not flown a Spitfire before but being a highly skilled pilot it presented no difficulties to him.

I was allowed to keep the aircraft when I became group captain fighter operations at the newly formed Mediterranean Allied Coastal Air Force in May 1943. Regrettably, when taxiing in soft sand at a temporary desert airfield at Bizerta, I got stuck and in trying to extricate the aircraft touched the propeller tips in the sand. It was considered that this might have damaged the engine internally and I could not find any technical officer who would certify the aircraft serviceable without an internal examination of the engine; as this was impossible on a temporary landing strip, to my great sorrow I was forced to abandon my pride and joy which had served me so well for the first seven months of the campaign.

The last Spitfire I flew was a Mk 24 at the Central Fighter Establishment, West Raynham, when I was group captain tactics in 1948–49. It had, I think, a Griffon twelve-cylinder engine of about double the power of the original Merlin. The aircraft was reputed to have a top speed of 440 mph. It was, however, a disappointment to fly. To balance the extra weight of the enormous engine, various adjustments had been made and these gave the aircraft a heavy and unbalanced feel, although, of course, it was perfectly controllable. I thought back to the original prototype with its ideal handling qualities and regretted what 'progress' had achieved!

AM Sir Humphrey Edwardes Jones

Sir Humphrey Edwardes Jones was granted a permanent commission in the RAF on graduation from Cambridge in 1926. After serving in various squadrons and as a flying instructor, he was posted to No 4 FTS in Egypt. Next he served three years as commander of 208 Army Co-operation Squadron in Heliopolis. On his return to England in March 1935 he went to the Aircraft and Armament Experimental Establishment at Martlesham Heath as a test pilot in command of 'A' Flight and flew the prototype Spitfire there in May 1936.

In April 1937, he was given command of 213 Squadron at Northolt, during which time he flew Hurricanes covering the Dunkirk withdrawal and was awarded the DFC. After commanding two OTU Squadrons, in 1941 he went to a Spitfire OTU with the acting rank of group captain. In February 1942, Sir Humphrey took command of the Exeter Fighter Sector and then of 323 Wing. He arrived in Algeria on 'D-Day' and took command of Maison Blanche. He was posted to the newly formed Middle Eastern Air Headquarters as group captain fighter ops in May 1943, and in the following year he re-formed 210 Group covering the western Mediterranean and later the air defence of Marseilles and the whole of Provence. Subsequently, he became SASO Middle Eastern Air Force at Casirta and then air commodore ops MAAF.

On his return to England in 1945, he was posted to the joint planning staff in the MOD and was then, in 1947, posted to the Central Flying Establishment as group captain tactics.

After two years as director of plans in the Air Ministry, in 1952 he went to 2nd TAF in Germany as SASO with the rank of air vice-marshal, returning home in 1955 to take up the post of commandant of the School of Land/Air Warfare at Old Sarum for two years. His final posting was to command 2nd TAF in Germany with the rank of air marshal during which time he was made a KCB. Sir Humphrey returned to the UK in 1961 and retired from the RAF after thirty-five years' service. Sir Humphrey died on 19 January 1987.

3 WONDERFUL YEARS

by Alan Clifton, MBE, BSc(Eng), CEng, FRAeS

In 1922 there were eight of us in the fourth year of the aeronautical engineering course at the Northampton Engineering College, now the City University, in St John's Street, Clerkenwell. We all applied for the job advertised in a daily paper for a mathematician to carry out aircraft strength calculations. No one received a reply. In the spring of 1923, while working at a patent agent's in Holborn, I was told by one of the eight, who by then was with the Royal Aircraft Establishment, that Mitchell, the chief engineer at Supermarine Aviation Works, Woolston, was looking for a technician. Thus it was that I found myself one fine Sunday morning riding down on my 1905 Triumph motorcycle for an interview with R.J. Mitchell at his house, where I also met his wife and baby son, Gordon.

A few days later I received a letter dated 24 April 1923 and signed by Mitchell, offering a salary of £3 10s a week for six months, and he also said, 'To anyone really keen on his work, every opportunity will be given for advancement'. Needless to say, I accepted. What a giant stroke of luck it turned out to be.

The firm I had joined was not large, employing perhaps 350 people, with a design team of about a dozen and a correspondingly small works staff. There was a directness about activities which was reflected in the timescale, and in the sense of everybody knowing what was going on. There was plenty of enthusiasm and, though discipline was not very strict, it is fair to say the firm got results.

At that time the inspection department was active in promoting the occasional concert, and at one of these a song was sung poking gentle fun at some of the firm's senior members, sung to the tune of *Jolly Country Lads are We*. The verse about Mitchell went:

> Number 8, number 8,
> Mitchell gets in an awful state,
> Ho my mariners, Supermariners,
> If his staff stay over late.

This song was taken in very good part by all concerned, bearing in mind that, with twelve verses, if anyone suffered, there were eleven others to laugh at.

Initially, I was housed in a small room immediately above the works lavatory – not too salubrious a location. Mitchell's office, with his typist and the filing system, was nearby. One day I was looking there for a document and I came across the large number of replies to that advertisement for a mathematician for strength calculations. R.J., as he was known to everyone, had evidently by-passed the problem of sorting out so many letters. He had himself been doing all the strength calculations, having in fact taken a prize for mathematics at evening classes during his apprenticeship to Kerr, Stuart & Co., railway locomotive builders in his native Staffordshire. He also became an associate member of the Institute of Civil Engineers, an exacting qualification.

After his apprenticeship he joined Pemberton-Billing Ltd as personal assistant to Hubert Scott-Paine, who had bought the firm from Pemberton-Billing and who soon renamed it The Supermarine Aviation Works Ltd. By 1920, at the age of twenty-five, R.J. had been made chief engineer and designer by Scott-Paine. Though theoretically well qualified, his outstanding characteristic was his practical outlook.

His first designs were noted for reliability rather than originality. Four Southampton military flying boats made a highly successful formation cruise to the Far East, incidentally using maps prepared by the famous Captain Cook for circumnavigating Australia. This led to a celebratory dinner given by the mayor and corporation of Southampton. R.J., as the guest of honour, was a modest, rather shy figure.

Winning the Schneider Trophy in 1922 with a modified Sea Lion II flying boat had been a good success. This was a Supermarine private entry flown by H.C. Biard, the firm's test pilot. However, in 1923 the US Navy, with some very clean Curtiss biplanes on floats, outclassed the further uprated Sea Lion III. Mitchell's S.4 was entered for the 1925 Schneider race as a private venture like its predecessors. Designed and built in six months, it put up a world speed record for seaplanes before being transported to the USA for the race. Throwing caution to the winds, R.J. had indeed taken a giant leap to a floatplane with cantilever wing and tail and breathtakingly clean lines, which caused a sensation when photos were released. Constructed largely of stressed skin wood with a steel tubular frame connecting fuselage and floats, it crashed in Chesapeake Bay during pre-race trials. Fortunately, Henri Biard, who was a close personal friend of R.J., was rescued without serious injury. The precise cause was not established but lack of wing stiffeners was suspected and Mitchell's next Schneider design, the S.5, had a wing braced to the floats by streamlined wires. It might be thought uncharacteristic of him to produce such a daring design as the S.4, but the Schneider race was not to be won by merely adopting well-proved features. One of his rare incursions into print is to be found in the Aeronautical Engineering Supplement to The Aeroplane of 25 December 1929 and is reproduced in full below. Re-reading this article recently, I was struck by the simple wording he used to explain technical problems and the resultant clarity of the explanations.

Racing Seaplanes and their influence on Design
by R.J. MITCHELL, AMICE, FRAeS

Quite a lot of information and experience is gained in the development of racing aircraft which is of undoubted value to the designer in all branches of aeronautical engineering and in many ways this has had a pronounced influence on the design of both military and civil types of aircraft.

During the last ten years there has been an almost constant increase of speed in our racing types. To maintain this steady increase, very definite progress has been essential year by year. It has been necessary to increase the aerodynamic efficiency, and the power-to-weight ratios of our machines, to reduce the consumption, and the frontal areas of our engines; to devise new methods of construction; and to develop the use of new materials. The results obtained in the form of speed have been a direct and absolute indication of our progress in aeronautical development.

Speed in the air must always be a measure of aerodynamic efficiency, which in turn must always be the most important consideration in all aircraft design. The special requirements of racing aircraft are very exacting. All the design requirements appear to be opposed to the production of speed. The most efficient racing machine satisfies these requirements with the smallest possible margin.

Under our present state of development the ideal racing machine must have only just sufficient excess propeller-thrust to overcome its resistance on taking off, otherwise we are sacrificing propeller efficiency under top speed conditions.

Its floats must have only just sufficient reserve buoyancy to enable it to hydroplane, take off and land reasonably safely, and to give it sufficient static stability. If these requirements are overdone we are sacrificing speed due to excess weight and excess air resistance of floats.

Tankage for petrol and oil and cooling surface for water and oil must be only just sufficient to feed and cool the engine, or further loss of speed will result.

The attainment of these happy results is sometimes assisted by the engine developing more horsepower than has been assumed in design conditions, or by the machine coming out over weight and thus working a little nearer to the limits than intended. But provided the final result is as indicated the means of attainment is of secondary consideration.

Working to very close limits demands a very accurate investigation of every detail and leads to more definite knowledge concerning the satisfaction of requirements than is obtained in the design of more conventional aircraft in which larger margins of safety can be allowed.

It will only be possible in this short article to touch very lightly on the interesting points which arise in the development of racing aircraft and the influence of some of them on the design of conventional types.

The taking-off characteristics of racing seaplanes form a very interesting subject.

Taking off is becoming one of the most difficult requirements to satisfy. As we increase speeds this difficulty increases. This appears contrary to expectations, as one would expect at first thought that taking off would become easier as we decrease our weight per horsepower, and that there would be a very large reserve on a machine with a horsepower loading of less than three pounds.

In Fig. 1 are given curves of propeller-thrust and of total resistance of machine for the S.6 seaplane, starting from rest and up to the top speed condition. It will be seen that there are very wide variations in the excess of thrust over resistance and at two points before take off this is well under 100 lbs.

One point is at the hump-resistance of the floats and the second point is just before take off. This second point is not experienced with normal types of seaplanes as they usually have plenty of reserve thrust throughout their take off if they have sufficient to get over the hump-resistance.

There are two main causes for this second point of 'stickiness'. The first is due to the special characteristics of the propeller. Starting from rest the propeller is working at angles of attack considerably larger than the stalling-angles of the sections. Its thrust per horsepower is therefore extremely low. As forward speed is gained the angles of attack are reduced

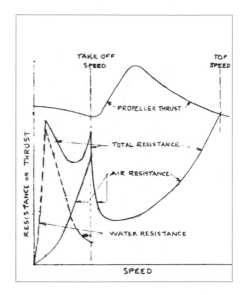

Fig. 1 Redrawn by Alan Clifton in 1985

and the blades become less stalled thus working at a higher lift coefficient. This causes a reduction in the revs per minute, and still further lowers the thrust. The stalling point of the blades occurs at about the take-off speed at which point the revs and thrust are lowest. After this there is a very rapid increase in propeller efficiency.

The second cause is due to the high taking-off speed. The water resistance of the floats remains abnormally high right up to the point of take off, when practically all the weight is taken on the wings. This is due to the very high frictional resistance at speeds of about 100 mph.

These taking-off characteristics seem to indicate that it will be necessary to use a variable pitch propeller before very much higher speeds are attained with racing aircraft, and that, as the speeds of service types increase, the variable pitch propeller will become correspondingly more important.

Very extensive progress has been made in engine design. During the past few years the weight-per-horsepower of our racing engines has been reduced by 50%, and the frontal area per horsepower has been halved. A large proportion of this progress has been passed on to standard engines used in service and civil craft.

It is quite safe to say that the engine used in this year's winning S.6 machine in the Schneider Trophy Contest would have taken at least three times as long to produce under normal processes of development had it not been for the spur of international competition. There is little doubt that this intensive engine development will have a very pronounced effect on our aircraft during the next few years.

Progress in seaplane float design during the last few years has been very largely due to the practical experience gained from the operation of our racing craft and to the intensive research work in wind channel and tank that has been found necessary to satisfy requirements. It is difficult actually to compare the efficiencies of various types of floats as they depend on a number of factors, such as water resistance, air resistance, seaworthiness and weight. The figures given in Table I, however, will serve to indicate that considerable progress has been made in float design.

Table I. Comparative weights and air resistance of floats

	Weight per 1,000 lbs weight of aircraft	*Air resistance at 100 ft a second per 1,000 lbs weight of aircraft*
S.4 (Wood)	108	3.08
(Metal)	115	3.08
S.5 (Metal)	110	2.72
S.6 (Metal)	95	2.42

It is interesting to note that a few years ago the flat-bottomed box-section type of float with a spring chassis was almost universally used. This type has now almost disappeared, and has given way to the well-known vee-bottomed and round-top-sided type developed for our racing craft.

This modern type of float requires no shock-absorbing devices in its chassis, is more seaworthy, can be built lighter and has very greatly reduced air resistance.

Flying-boat hulls have shown similar improvement in sea-worthiness, air resistance and weight.

The radiators developed in our racing craft for cooling water and oil have shown more progress than any other characteristic, and form a highly potential source of improvement in general aircraft design.

In Table II figures are given comparing our standard honeycomb radiators with the various other types of radiators which have been produced.

These figures may require a little explanation. The first of the wing-surface type radiators described in the table as the externally corrugated brass radiator is the type first used by the American racers. This type adds a considerable amount of resistance, owing to the external corrugation increasing the area of surface and thereby adding to the frictional drag. It is placed over the wing-covering of wood or metal and is about three times the weight of a corresponding honeycomb radiator.

The next development of wing-radiator is the type as used on the S.5 seaplane. This has a flat outer surface and therefore adds no direct resistance to the machine. This is still heavier, however, than the externally corrugated type owing to the necessity for covering a larger area of wing. It also is placed on top of the wing-covering of wood or metal.

Table II. Comparison of Radiator Efficiencies
Figures for Standard Honeycomb 10 x 120 mm tubes taken as 100 in each case

Constant speed taken in each case	Honeycomb		Wing surface type			
	Standard hexagonal 10x120mm	Long tube hexagonal 20x360mm	Externally corrugated brass	Externally flat brass as 'S.5'	Without interal cooling	With 12% internal cooling
Weight of radiator per hp dissipated	100	179	300	410	75	67
Resistance per hp dissipated	100	76	15	0	0	0
hp dissipated per unit of cooling surface	100	58	50	66	81	92

The next development is the type as used on the S.6 seaplane. This type is made from thin duralumin sheets formed into a double skin with a water-space of one-sixteenth of an inch between. This double skin is fixed to the spars and ribs of the wing and forms the wing covering. It is strong enough to stiffen the wing to resist torsional stresses.

The dual purpose of radiator and wing covering saves very considerable weight, and the added weight due to the radiator is very small. This type has the further advantage of placing the whole of its surface in contact with the cooling water; thus increasing its cooling efficiency per sq. ft of surface.

A further development in this type of radiator is that of internal cooling – which was used on the S.6 seaplane. Small air-intakes were placed at the wing-tips, opening in the direction of air flow, and allowing air to enter the wing. Exhaust ports were placed at the wing-roots, exhausting the air from inside the wing. A flow of air through the wing at a velocity of about 35 mph was obtained in this way, and the inside surface of the radiator covering was used for cooling purposes in addition to its external surface.

This internal cooling was responsible for an increase of about 12% in the cooling capacity of the radiators. No loss of performance could be traced to this induced air flow inside the wing.

It is not outside the bounds of possibility that by taking the air inside the wing at certain positions at the wing tip an improvement in the wing characteristics might be obtained. Further investigation on this point might be carried out with advantage.

The last column in Table II gives the comparative figures for the S.6 type of radiator, allowing for the increase due to internal cooling.

These figures show that a water-cooled engine can be cooled without adding any air-resistance to the machine, and by the addition of only 70% of the weight of a corresponding honeycomb type of radiator.

Our experiments on radiators indicate that with the development of evaporative cooling it will be possible to use metal-covered components of a machine such as wings, floats and sections of fuselage, as steam-condensers, without the addition of any internal gear – except to drain off the condensed water and return it to the engine. This would simplify cooling systems and greatly assist ease of maintenance, thereby making them more suitable for conventional types of civil aircraft.

The advantages to be gained by the 'no resistance cooling system' are indicated if the figures given for radiators are applied to an engine nacelle as used on outboard-engined machines, using the horsepowers available from standard types of water-cooled and air-cooled engines. A comparison is shown in Table III.

Table III. Comparison of standard types of water-cooled and air-cooled engines

	Lbs resistance at 100 ft/sec. per engine hp
Air-cooled engine nacelle	.12
Do. with Townend ring	.068
Water-cooled engine nacelle with radiator to cool at 140 mph	.081
Water-cooled engine nacelle without added resistance for cooling	.03

The question of interference-effects between component parts of a machine has been thoroughly investigated in our search for methods of reducing resistance on our racers.

In Table IV figures are given for the interference effects between components of the S.6 seaplane. It is indicated that if suitable precautions are taken the added resistance due to interference can be limited to that caused by struts and bracing.

Other points which can be mentioned on which our racers have supplied us with useful information are as follows:

The ventilation cooling, and heating of cockpits at high speeds.

The dissipation of heat from water and oil with various types of radiators and at high air speeds.

The effects of high centrifugal loading, as when turning, on the correct functioning of petrol systems.

The production of streamline-section bracing wires.

Problems of control at high speeds, and (last, but by no means least) the great value of close co-operation between engine and machine designers.

Table IV Percentage interference effects between the component parts of the S.6 seaplane

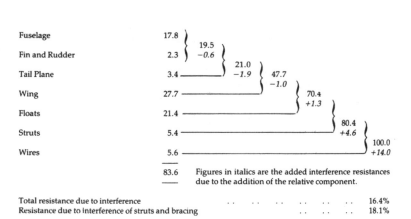

Fuselage	17.8					
		19.5				
Fin and Rudder	2.3	−0.6				
			21.0			
Tail Plane	3.4		−1.9	47.7		
				−1.0		
Wing	27.7				70.4	
					+1.3	
Floats	21.4					80.4
						+4.6
Struts	5.4					100.0
						+14.0
Wires	5.6					
	83.6	Figures in italics are the added interference resistances due to the addition of the relative component.				

Total resistance due to interference	.. ..	16.4%
Resistance due to interference of struts and bracing	.. .. ..	18.1%

R.J. was a man of sporting instincts, who played a number of competitive games: I remember joining his family one day when they were on holiday, to be promptly challenged by R.J. to a race along the beach. The Schneider Trophy fortunately enabled him in his professional work to give effect to this trait. As is well known, he came back from the S.4

debacle to win three times in a row, and win the trophy permanently for Britain, with the S.5, S.6 and S.6B.

He would visit the drawing office and study a drawing, head on hands, and mostly thinking without speaking. Occasionally he would ask a question. The chap fetched to answer would stay, with the result that gradually a number of people were gathered. On rare occasions the whole drawing might be rejected, but normally a better alternative to some feature was described to the draughtsman, and R.J. moved on to repeat the process. Survivors from that time will all say that they were wonderful years when the chief engineer would sit on the draughtsman's stool and study his drawing. The product too was wonderful as, under R.J.'s inspiration, it advanced to the frontiers of aeronautical knowledge. He himself was quite willing to listen to others and clearly had a very open mind. One of his own earliest aircraft drawings was an arrangement of the central nacelle for a quadruplane night fighter with a gun mounting and various cable control runs. This drawing showed how quickly he had adapted his railway locomotive experience to the vastly different requirements of aircraft. Incidentally, he found he could not quite get everything on the size of drawing paper he had chosen so he added a small piece of paper at the top to avoid redrawing the whole thing!

At the regular drawing office Christmas dinner he was the life and soul of the party, leading the way in much harmless fun after the meal. On one occasion when I had already had too much alcohol, R.J. persuaded me to mix my drinks with consequences that were disastrous as soon as I was in the fresh air returning to my digs. I don't think it was merely his idea of a joke. At any rate it cured me permanently of any desire to repeat the process.

On another occasion, he was to take me in his car on a business trip and when we had gone a few hundred yards he said quite casually, 'Got your case?' He obviously knew I hadn't and by making it necessary to return drew effective attention to my carelessness. He did not refrain from praise when he thought it justified and I remember a very nice letter he wrote to me from hospital praising some work for a design tender, submitted for his approval, and apologising for being away longer than he had expected (see Chapter 13, page 144).

In the early 1920s, Hubert Scott-Paine in his turn sold Supermarine to Sqn Cdr James Bird, already a director of the firm. He was a shrewd but also genial man who came back to manage Supermarine very successfully during the 1939–45 war. However, in 1928, following Mitchell's successes with the Southampton, the S.5 and several amphibian flying boats, and a number of machines sold to foreign governments, Bird sold Supermarine to Vickers, who already had an aircraft division at Brooklands Aerodrome, Weybridge. It was there that Vickers had transferred Dr Barnes Wallis after his brilliant design of the R100 airship which functioned perfectly, including flying each way across the Atlantic. Then having bought Supermarine, they wished Wallis to become Mitchell's chief assistant. There came the day when Wallis turned up at Woolston and started to interview each member of the design staff in order to understand the sort of people with whom he would be dealing. On that day R.J. did not appear. In fact, he disappeared for about ten days or so until Wallis returned to Weybridge. Subsequently, Maj. H.J. Payn, who was an excellent pilot with some technical knowledge, was transferred from Weybridge to be R.J.'s personal assistant.

Sometime about this period Dr Dornier of Germany, whose well-known flying boats had sponsons instead of wing floats, came to Woolston to meet Mitchell. Subsequently, a design for an air yacht was sold to the Hon. A.E. Guinness. He had previously bought from Supermarine, as a flying yacht, a conversion of a Danish torpedo-carrying biplane flying boat, of Mitchell's design, which had failed to fulfil its military specification, and he wanted another plane specially designed as an air yacht. The new design was a braced monoplane, lateral stability on the water being provided by sponsons, à la Dornier. With the great Depression then looming, there was a craze for cheapness and the new air yacht as built was rather square and lacked aerodynamic refinement. Like its Danish predecessor, it failed to meet its specified performance and Guinness refused to accept it. Later it was sold to a Mrs James, who flew in it to Italy where it was damaged landing on very rough seas. The air yacht broke a wing and Mrs James broke a leg but no lives were lost and the air yacht was beached, never to fly again.

Vickers' next administrative idea was to produce an aeroplane which combined the resources of the Weybridge and Supermarine aircraft works. To this end a contract was obtained to build a flying boat called the Southampton Mk X, as a potential replacement for the earlier very successful Southamptons. The hull by Supermarine was of light alloy with stainless steel bottom, while the wing and the three engine mountings were of Weybridge design. The two organisations shared considerable overweight about equally and the result was not a success. I think it was at this point agreed that each design team should follow its own bent.

The response at Supermarine was to offer to build a replacement design, instead of the last production Southampton of the earlier type, and for the same price. This proposal was accepted by the Air Ministry and a special section of the drawing office was set up under Eric Cooper to produce the drawings. There was no failure this time and R.J.'s mainly light alloy biplane was an inspired design which came out spot on the weight target. It had a better performance than contemporary British landplane bombers, and likewise flying boats, even those having twice the engine power. Called in prototype form the Southampton Mk IV, it was ordered for production as the Scapa.

When the prototype Mk IV was partly built, design work was started on a single-engined amphibian with the same name, Seagull, as an earlier

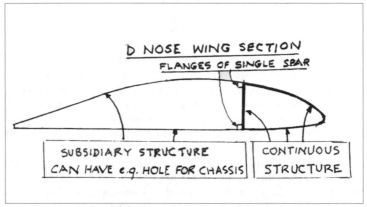

Fig. 2 D nose wing section, drawn by Alan Clifton in 1985

amphibian of which a batch had been sold to the Australian government in around 1925. The new Seagull (known as the Seagull V) had a Bristol Pegasus air-cooled engine installed as a pusher. Aimed at fleet-spotting duties, it was a bit of an ugly duckling. Light alloy hull, stainless steel wing spars, wing ribs of wood, and with fabric wing covering, its design was influenced, and the detail design supervised, by a chap called Munro who came to us from Canadian Vickers. Amphibians, of course, had to have retracting undercarriages, but until then only sufficient to get them clear of the water. I remember persuading R.J. to retract the wheels of the new Seagull into the wing by saying, 'We shall have to do it eventually, why not now?' At that time, fully retracting undercarriages were almost unknown. Although the Air Ministry's director of technical development, sitting in the prototype hull, said, 'We have no requirement for anything like this', it was in fact a great success. The Australians bought twelve to replace their earlier Seagulls and 287 were built (as the Walrus) by the firm for Royal Navy spotter reconnaissance duties. In addition, it was adopted by the RAF for Air-Sea Rescue work. When this occurred Supermarine were fully involved in Spitfire production, and although the firm retained design approval, manufacture was placed with Saunders-Roe who built some 450.

The Walrus proved extremely seaworthy and must have seemed a very beautiful sight to the many aircrews rescued from the North Sea or English Channel after they had been forced down by enemy action.

The early part of 1932 was a very busy time. Not only was the Southampton Mk IV under construction, and the design of the Seagull V under way, but in February a design was submitted to meet Fighter Specification F.7/30. This venture into the landplane fighter field was justified by the fact that the top speed of the S.6B was about twice that of current biplane fighters. An order for a prototype was received in June. In July the first flight took place of the Southampton IV which had been designed and built in eleven months. R.J.'s design for the F.7/30 looks in retrospect rather fat and draggy, and there was no visual resemblance to the S.6, indeed it reverted to the cantilever wing form of the ill-fated S.4. Harold Smith, who later became our chief structural engineer, had come to our stress office from the machine shop. He carried out some studies which showed that the single spar wing with D nose, common on gliders, was very efficient especially in relation to Royal Aircraft Establishment criteria for resisting flutter, and it was adopted by R.J. for his F.7/30 design (see Fig. 2, above). Another feature was so-called dragless cooling as on the later Schneider planes. Actually, the forward wing skin of the F.7/30 was corrugated to get enough cooling surface, so the cooling was not quite dragless. We had flown a Southampton with a pair of Rolls-Royce engines evaporatively cooled, to try out this system which Rolls-Royce were then keen on. The cooling water in the cylinder blocks was raised to boiling temperature but being under pressure did not boil until it was pumped out of the engine and the pressure released. It then turned into steam which, in the case of our F.7/30 design, was condensed in the nose portion of the D wing, the water trickling down to collector tanks in the wheel fairings, whence it was pumped back to the engine. This layout lent itself to neatly faired main wheels, which did not retract. Although he believed in the value of wind-tunnel tests on components to assess the advantage of modifications, R.J. considered that tests of small models of the complete aeroplane were not a satisfactory basis for predicting the full-scale performance, but he had had the contrary point of view rather rammed down his throat. So he used, in the tender for performance estimates, the results supplied by the Weybridge wind tunnel. The speed and ceiling of the prototype as built fell considerably short of the estimates, though above the requirements of the F.7/30 Specification. But R.J.'s first fighter, in common with a number of other firms' F.7/30 designs, was not considered appropriate for a production order.

The first flight of our F.7/30 took place in February 1934, and it was just before this, in the late summer of 1933, that unknown to us, R.J. started to suffer some pain, and soon afterwards went into a nursing home to be operated on for cancer.

The next two and a half years were very busy ones with new design proposals pouring out at an average rate of one a month. There were six amphibians, eighteen flying boats, three fighters and finally one bomber. These proposals were all submitted for consideration to meet various stated civil and military requirements. They were in many cases logical developments of our wide experience of aircraft, and R.J. applied his mind to them to criticise and finally approve each submission, though the attention he gave to each naturally varied with the importance attached to it.

He gave a great deal of thought to the next step after the F.7/30 fighter and various drawings were made and studied. The wings, which were now straight in front view, still had straight taper in plan, and the undercarriage fully retracted. It still had the Goshawk steam-cooled engine and the calculated top speed was 265 mph. The design had changed a lot by the time it got under way as a private venture with Rolls-Royce contributing to the airframe cost. It incorporated the new and more powerful Rolls-Royce PV.12 engine, liquid cooled via a ducted honeycomb radiator. This radiator system was proposed by Meredith of the Royal Aircraft Establishment and was claimed to give at top speed a small thrust instead of drag. It was really a very simple, though inefficient, form of jet engine. It was the only part of the new design to be tested in the wind tunnel. Mitchell had also moved on to a wing of elliptic plan form partly because it was a more practical shape when it came to housing the retracted undercarriage and the specified four machine guns. This shape was proposed by Beverley Shenstone, a Canadian who had joined us as aerodynamicist,[21] for climb advantages at high altitude. He also advocated the thin wing which R.J. adopted against the advice of some expert theorists. The new fighter was known as Supermarine Type 300, and at the end of 1934, shortly after the Vickers board had authorised its construction as a private venture, the Air Ministry took contractual action defined by the issue of AM Specification F.37/34 '... to cover the design and construction of an experimental high speed single-seat fighter substantially as described in Supermarine Specification No 525a...' It also specified the Rolls-Royce PV.12 engine. The Ministry also awarded a contract to Hawkers to the same basic military requirements and specifying the same PV.12 engine. As is now well known, Mitchell's plane was later named the Spitfire, and that of Hawker's Sidney Camm was named the Hurricane.

Since both planes had the same military requirements and Rolls-Royce engine, a comparison is of interest. In production, the Hurricane was ready first, and by autumn 1940 there were probably twice as many Hurricanes as Spitfires (see Chapter 20). But the Spitfire was considerably superior in performance, and it was the Spitfire that worried the German fighter pilots with their cry of 'Achtung Spitfeuer'. Without either type we should undoubtedly have lost the Battle of Britain and, we must assume, have suffered invasion. (But see page 293.)

The sporting element in this case was provided by Bill Lappin of Rolls-Royce, who bet R.J. that the prototype Spitfire would not do 350 mph. He sportingly paid up on an official measured maximum speed of 349.5 mph. This compared with the 230 mph of the Supermarine F.7/30. In June 1936, the firm received an order for 310 Spitfires. In September of that year, Mitchell's design for the B.12/36 bomber was submitted. It exploited the single spar wing with D nose of the F.7/30 and Spitfire fighters, in this case to house in the D nose the fuel and in the aft portion of the wing the required multiplicity of bombs. Its estimated performance was much better than competitive designs and two prototypes were ordered by the Air Ministry. It proved to be R.J.'s last design, for by then he knew that the operation of 1933 had provided only a respite. He died, to our great sorrow, on 11 June 1937 at the age of forty-two.

Towards the end, when he was confined to bed, he still asked for visits from some members of the firm, and all who saw him at that time testified that he showed the highest courage.

R.J. Mitchell was widely considered the greatest aeroplane designer of the period, when an age of great engineers was coming to a close, and technology in some areas was beginning to take the place of judgement. He had a very open mind and was prepared to listen to the advice of others. But when it came to deciding what form a Supermarine aircraft should take, and sometimes the form of details, he was the chief engineer and designer, and he decided. It was a responsibility he shared with no one else. Sir Henry Royce said he had the ideal temperament for a designer, 'slow to decide and quick to act'. Looking back, I would describe him as a loveable character, innovative and pre-eminently practical; a man who had that infinite capacity for taking pains which is judged the hallmark of genius.

Alan Clifton

Alan Clifton was engaged by R.J. Mitchell in 1923 to do stress calculations but other jobs were subsequently added, notably strength testing and propeller design. In 1930, he was put in charge of the technical office with a staff of about a dozen covering stressing, aerodynamics, weight estimates and the preparation of new designs, sometimes to accompany tenders. Over the years, the technical office grew much larger with the growth of technology.

In 1957, after the death of Joe Smith, who was Mitchell's successor, Alan was appointed chief designer. By this time the design office comprised about 500 people.

Before the aviation side was closed down in the late 1950s, Supermarine's final design proposal won for Vickers Aircraft a half share with English Electric in the contract for the TSR2 bomber. Alan was then transferred to Weybridge where he

*took charge of the military project design office. He retired in 1966. Alan died on
18 June 1991 at the age of ninety.*

4 R.J. MITCHELL AS SEEN THROUGH THE EYES OF AN APPRENTICE

by Jack Davis, CEng, MRAeS

I joined Supermarine as a workshop apprentice in August 1925, a week
or two before the maiden flight of the S.4 racing seaplane, built for the
Schneider Trophy race to be held in Baltimore, USA, in October. We
lads appreciated the finer points of the machine and were shattered by
the crash in America, three days before the race. The S.5 with the braced
wings received a lukewarm reception. We had already decided that all
aeroplanes should be cantilever monoplanes as were many German aircraft. In fact we carried out experiments using paper gliders of varying
wing shapes and flew them from a gallery in the erecting shop. As is
usual with young people, we thought we knew more than our superiors.
We saw Mitchell in the workshops and noticed his keen interest in the
structures. We formed the impression that some aircraft were left to his
assistants and these appeared to be less successful. This impression may
have no valid foundation but is worth recording.

As a junior draughtsman and seeing him at close quarters, it was clear
that he was a deep thinker because he spent hours alone in his office.
However, he was often seen in the drawing office accompanied by an
entourage of his senior assistants together with the chief draughtsman.
He would sit at a drawing board and take a keen interest in detail
design. During the ensuing free-for-all discussion, he would listen
carefully to the others but if someone made a suggestion which to
him seemed inane, he gave the offender a killing glare! This capacity
to absorb the principals of overall design and link it with the detailed
construction was a significant personal quality in the early days of
aircraft design, for, however brilliant the concept, it was essential to
be practicable. He did indeed show a practical approach to a marked
degree. For example, he disliked any form of construction which
failed on test without warning even if it otherwise seemed efficient.
Specimens of basic structure were tested by setting them up in the
workshop and applying a load which was gradually increased until
the structure failed. Some forms of construction held up very well
with little deflection and then failed with a bang. Others bent more
and more as the load increased before finally failing. Mitchell strongly
favoured the latter and laid emphasis on a carefully graded structure,

which behaved rather like a tapered bamboo cane when bent, as well as on its absolute strength.

He followed up the design by visiting the workshops and on one occasion picked up a rudder, decided that it was too heavy, and sent it back to the office for redesign. He was very keen on weight and during the design of the Scapa flying boat, a successor to the Southampton, he made an edict that if calculations showed that any part was more than 10% stronger than requirements, someone would be sacked! This ruling must have had good effect for the Scapa was a success and went into production. In fact later aircraft, especially the Spitfire, were noted for their low structural weight.

He was conscientious to a high degree. For instance, I was given the job of devising the mounting for a landing lamp to be fitted to a de Havilland Moth belonging to the Hampshire Aeroplane Club. It took longer than he had anticipated as without knowledge of the stress requirements, we were unwilling to drill holes in the undercarriage struts. Whilst sitting at my board, it became clear to me that he was so concerned at the time being taken on this project that he took little interest in the actual job. He knew that my time was being booked to an official contract so I presume he must have felt guilty. I found this difficult to understand since he was, after all, the 'Boss'. It was also clear that he took his own responsibilities seriously and was very aware that men's lives were in his hands. He was very upset at the loss of Kinkead in the crash of the S.5 in March 1928. He must have lived on his nerves to a high degree.

He did not seek publicity and in fact was shy in public. Capt. H.C. Biard, the test pilot of the S.4 when it crashed, told some of us of his experience at a lecture given before the Royal Aeronautical Society. Mitchell said, 'I can't go on'. So Biard said, 'Give him some firewater', As this failed to give him the necessary Dutch courage Biard said, 'Give him some more firewater', and it worked.

Through working for Mitchell during my formative years he became my mentor. I noticed he was an innovator. I may not have consciously copied him but, being of a similar nature, it gave me courage to put forward my own ideas throughout my career. Courage is the operative word, for the pioneer does not lack critics. When the top man is an innovator he will draw the best out of others.

It is instructive to examine how aircraft design progressed step by step and, as with natural evolution, some of the steps were false. No other way was possible, for very little useful published matter on the subject existed. One example is the failed S.4 racer. It was ahead of its day and a trend setter. It seemed to be the perfect design for a high-speed aircraft. But the cantilever wings were not sufficiently strong, or so it appeared. It was disliked by Henri Biard, who said he felt the wings shiver; he disliked the 'unstayed wings', as he put it. When it crashed, wing flutter was suspected. This aircraft was followed by the S.5 and S.6 with thinner, braced wings. These were successful so the new design appeared to be the logical solution. But in retrospect it seems more likely that the flutter was engendered by the large ailerons rather than inherent wing weakness. During the project stage of the Spitfire, aileron size came under special scrutiny. Mitchell said he thought that some wing failures were due to overlarge ailerons, although he did not enlarge on it. Thus the Spitfire, with the benefit of aerodynamic progress and constructed of metal, reverted to cantilever wings and became the true successor to the S.4. Many years later, whilst I was making some historical research, the similarity between the S.4 and the Spitfire wings came to light. It is most unlikely that a comparison was made during the Spitfire design stage, both shapes having evolved independently to meet the current design requirements. For high speed, the S.4 wing area could be small but for take off and alighting a larger wing area was necessary. As there was little surplus, these latter manoeuvres were so dangerous that only pilots of exceptional skill could fly the aircraft. The wing had to be as thin as possible consistent with sufficient strength. The proportion of width to span was part of the exercise. It was of wooden construction and for ease of manufacture, straight lines at the front and rear, merging into a curved wing tip, were selected. This was shaped by eye.

The requirements for the Spitfire were more diverse. The wing area was related to the weight having regard to low-level and high-altitude flying requirements, together with the need for fast climb to operational height. For ease of handling by pilots of average ability, the landing speed had to be as low as possible. The wing needed to be sufficiently thick to house the undercarriage, wheel, guns and ammunition but, at the same time, it had to be as thin as possible. These needs were met by making it very wide by the fuselage and using an elliptical form which maintained the wide wing and greater thickness where it was most needed. The elliptical shape also happens to be the best shape for aerodynamic reasons. In quantity production the manufacture was easier than might be expected thanks to the skill of the sub-contractors from the motor industry, once they had overcome the initial major problems (see Appendix 7).

Eric John Davis

Eric John Davis, popularly known as 'Jack', served an apprenticeship and studied by part-time day and evening classes at the Southampton University College. He entered the drawing office and left after two years to gain experience with the Westland and Boulton & Paul companies. Returning to Supermarine, he worked on flying boats, the Spitfire and the B.12/36 bomber. From the outbreak of the war, he worked on several Spitfire developments, and was section leader in charge of the wing of the Mk 21, followed by the wing and tail surfaces of the Seagull Air Sea Rescue 1 flying boat, ordered in April 1943 under Air Ministry Specification S.12/40. Later he became co-ordinator of design for the swept wing Swift, the twin-engined naval fighter type 508, and the Scimitar, Supermarine's last aircraft. Jack died on 4 June 1998.

5 THE MAN I WORKED WITH FOR THIRTEEN YEARS

by Ernest Mansbridge, BSc(Eng), CEng, MRAeS

On 15 September 1924, I went to the Supermarine works at Woolston, Southampton, for an interview, having applied for a job there. This was my first meeting with R.J. Mitchell, or R.J. as we all called him. After the interview he showed me his current interest, the Sparrow biplane being prepared for the Light Aeroplane Contest at Lympne. Ten days later I was told I had got the job and joined Supermarine, becoming the third member of the newly formed technical office and initially working with Alan Clifton on stressing.

Although R.J. is best known for the Spitfire, it should not be forgotten that he also led in other aircraft fields. The Southampton flying boat and the subsequent Scapa and Stranraer were leaders in their class, as indeed were the S.5, S.6 and S.6B seaplanes and the Seagull V amphibian which later achieved fame as the Walrus.

Mitchell was a quiet man, broad shouldered and fair haired. With any problem his method was to call in the leaders of the various groups involved and get them arguing amongst themselves. He would listen carefully making sure that everyone said what he thought and at the end would perhaps give a decision or go home to sleep on it. Sometimes, I am sure, he had reached a decision beforehand, but he listened closely to see if there was any point that he had overlooked.

When he was beginning to think about designing a fighter, he got 'Mutt' Summers, the Vickers chief test pilot, to lay on a visit one day to the Aeroplane and Armament Experimental Establishment at Martlesham Heath. I accompanied him and we spent the day discussing, with the RAF test pilots, the merits and shortcomings of the current fighters in the service. These discussions had a marked effect on our thinking in the months ahead.

R.J. had a good sense of humour and was always ready to see the funny side of things and react accordingly. One occasion may be related as a good example of this characteristic he frequently displayed. The Rolls-Royce team used to visit Woolston for discussions on the S.6 engines and produced power curves, showing engine horsepower against revolutions per minute, for our meetings. The points we wished to have would invariably be off the curve and so it had to be bent and extended to go through the points we wanted. One day, sometime later, R.J. noticed that I was using a flexible rubber French curve. Having ascertained that I could get a replacement, he sent my flexible curve off to Rolls-Royce expressing the hope that it would help them to produce more satisfactory power curves!

All in all, an inspiring and inspired leader.

Ernest Mansbridge

After leaving grammar school, Ernest Mansbridge went to the East London (now Queen Mary's) College where he obtained his BSc(Eng) degree. He obtained a job at Supermarine in 1924 where he joined the technical office working with Alan Clifton on stressing. Later he worked with Oliver Simmonds on aerodynamics; when Simmonds left in 1929, he became directly responsible to Mitchell for aerodynamics, performance, weights and flight testing. Subsequently, flight testing and performance estimation became his predominant occupation and in this capacity he played an essential role in the testing of the prototype Spitfire and its subsequent development and production.

Ernest continued to work with Supermarine and their successors until he retired in 1966. Ernest died on 2 June 1996, aged ninety-four.

6 A CHIEF TEST PILOT'S APPRECIATION OF R.J. MITCHELL

by Jeffrey Quill, OBE, AFC, FRAeS

My association and, I hope I may say, friendship with R.J. Mitchell was confined to the short period between the beginning of 1936, when I joined Vickers (Aviation) Ltd as a test pilot, and June of 1937 when he died.

By 1931, R.J. Mitchell, although still under forty years old, had achieved immense stature and prestige in the aeronautical world through his successful series of racing seaplane designs. By 1931 these had won the international Schneider Trophy on three successive occasions, thus winning the trophy outright for Britain as well as setting up several world speed records. These seaplanes, all extremely advanced designs, were the Supermarine S.4, S.5, S.6 and S.6B.

When I joined Vickers (Aviation) Ltd in January 1936 as a test pilot, I had served five years in the RAF. Apart from my training, my RAF service had been entirely in Fighting Area (the predecessor of Fighter Command) so I was very much a fighter pilot by training, by inclination and by temperament.

Obviously we had all studied the history of the Schneider Trophy races and, as a schoolboy, I witnessed the 1929 and 1931 contests over the Solent. The pilots who flew those aircraft were our youthful heroes, but the name of R.J. Mitchell was already held in awe and respect in the RAF as the presiding genius who had designed the aircraft, ranking with the great Sir Henry Royce who had designed the Rolls-Royce engines of the S.6 and S.6B.

My job at Vickers (who by then owned the Supermarine works) was assistant to the then chief test pilot, Capt. J. 'Mutt' Summers. 'Mutt' held this appointment not only in Vickers (Aviation) at Weybridge but also in Supermarine at Southampton. My first visit to Supermarine, made in company with 'Mutt', must have been some time in January 1936, and I remember the keen interest with which I looked forward to meeting the great R.J. Mitchell.

At that time all minds at Supermarine were pre-occupied with the completion of the prototype fighter being built at Woolston to the Air Ministry Specification No F.37/34. This aircraft was generally referred to at that time as 'Mitchell's fighter'; the name 'Spitfire' was not adopted until a little while after the aircraft began flying in March 1936 and, incidentally, Mitchell was not altogether pleased with the choice of that name when it was made.

My first recollections of R.J. are of a quiet, sandy-haired and fresh-complexioned man who seemed to do a good deal more listening than talking. During the three-month period before we started to fly the prototype, I attended various meetings and discussions at which R.J. was present. He was held in some awe by his staff who obviously had the highest respect for him and his technical authority.

R.J. had undergone a major operation about two years earlier and, unknown to any of us, had a serious physical disability to cope with, as is described in Chapter 18. On occasions he could be somewhat choleric, and it was obvious that he did not suffer fools gladly. Nevertheless, beneath it all he was a very kind-hearted and considerate man, and this became increasingly apparent the more one got to know him.

·I was privileged to do a great deal of the early flying on the Spitfire prototype K5054. This aircraft was based at the aerodrome at Eastleigh and Mitchell's office was, of course, in the main works at Woolston. R.J. was always informed by telephone when K5054 was airborne, and usually he would get into his old Rolls-Royce car and head for the aerodrome, with the result that by the time I came back to land he would be waiting on the tarmac. He would walk over to the aircraft and listen in to the informal 'de-briefing' sessions which used to follow each flight. The principal links between the test pilot and the design organisation at that time were Ernest Mansbridge and Alf Faddy, and R.J. would join our discussions and listen to everything, often without comment.

Very often, if there were no 'snags', the aircraft would be refuelled and immediately prepared for a further flight, and some of my most happy memories of R.J. are when he would often invite me to sit with him in his car – just the two of us – while this was going on, and he would ask questions about the progress of the flying and would talk on all manner of aeronautical subjects. I used to question him about the Schneider seaplanes and about the four-engined bomber he was then designing.

From these, all too brief, talks with R.J. in the relaxed atmosphere of the airfield and away from his office, I began to appreciate his enormous common sense, his quiet humour, and the balance and crystal clarity of his judgement in all things. He seemed to take the mystery out of even the most complex subjects.

I was not a trained engineer, only a pilot, and I felt very much inhibited in communicating with the many highly qualified engineers and technicians with whom I found myself working in my new capacity as test pilot. R.J. (by now recognised as one of the greatest aircraft designers of all time) completely removed these inhibitions for me. I began to realise that however erudite or complex the processes by which engineers and designers conducted their work, the basic objectives which they sought, and the conclusions which they reached, were nevertheless capable of being expressed in clear and straightforward terms intelligible to all. Half the business of being a development test pilot in those days was establishing a thorough rapport and position of mutual confidence with the designers and engineers on the ground. Above all, this meant clear and effective communication.

Any humble success which I may have achieved in this respect during my subsequent career as a test pilot was certainly very largely due to the lessons I learned from the example of R.J. Mitchell. As I wrote in my book, *Spitfire – A Test Pilot's Story*, published in 1983:

> He [Mitchell] made me see that the most valuable contribution which I could make was to concentrate upon becoming a better and better pilot and try to absorb a natural understanding of the problems of engineers and designers by maintaining close personal contacts with them and doing my best to interpret pilots' problems to them, and vice versa.

My sadly brief association with this great man, when I was so young and inexperienced, is a memory which I have always treasured and will continue to do so to the end of my life. I shall never forget the acute sense of loss which we all felt when he died.

I have often been asked whether in those early days of the flying of K5054 we were aware that we had a worldbeater? In answering such a question one must be careful to avoid the influence of hindsight, but I think it fair to answer it thus:

Whilst we were all very conscious of the threat of war with Germany, none of us could possibly have foreseen at that time that we would eventually produce more than 20,000 Spitfires in a large number of variants, and that it would become the most famous fighter in the world.

I think we regarded the Spitfire primarily as our runner in the competition for the RAF order with Sidney Camm's Hurricane, which had made its first flight some four months ahead of us. The Hurricane was designed largely for ease of production, and Hawkers had earned a great reputation in building Harts and Furys for the RAF, as well as for several important overseas customers. We, at Supermarine, were trying to break into the fighter market for the first time, and I think we all realised that we should need to have something very good indeed in order to beat the Hurricane.

I think we were all confident that in performance the Spitfire had a substantial edge over the Hurricane, and that this would clearly emerge when the aircraft went for its official trials at Martlesham Heath.

We knew also that we had a more efficient, modern and higher technology structure than the Hurricane, but that it was undoubtedly less suitable than the Hurricane for quantity production. We also knew that we had an aircraft which was challenging and exciting to fly – indeed a real pilot's aeroplane – but I had some misgivings as to its suitability in some respects for everyday squadron pilots, and feared that it might be criticised on this score (as indeed it was). At that time the RAF fighter squadrons were equipped exclusively with biplanes, aerodromes were of grass and small in size, and the only recent service experience of monoplanes had been with the Schneider seaplanes, which were highly specialised and had handpicked and very expert pilots. In short, there was a certain neurosis in some quarters about high-performance monoplanes.

All in all, therefore, whilst we felt that we had a superb and exciting aeroplane, most of us felt that some 'practical considerations' and some well-entrenched prejudices might go severely against it, vis a vis the Hurricane. In any case that was my feeling in the matter.

In the event, orders were placed for both aircraft later in 1936, although the initial order for the Hurricane was more than double that for the Spitfire. Perhaps it is fair to comment here that this reflected the relative importance then attached to the 'practical considerations' on the one hand and the Spitfire's superior performance capabilities on the other.

Later, when the shooting started, and fighter-to-fighter combat developed on a large scale, while the problems of producing and operating the Spitfire seemed not so daunting, these priorities were quickly reversed. Combat performance became paramount, and the Spitfire's potential for continued development brought it to the dominant position which history has recorded.

Jeffrey Quill

Jeffrey Quill was born just before the First World War. He was commissioned in the RAF in 1931 and later served in a fighter squadron followed by service in the Meteorological Flight. In 1936 he was appointed assistant experimental test pilot to Vickers (Aviation) Ltd, under Capt. 'Mutt' Summers, the then chief test pilot at Weybridge and Supermarine. Although Jeffrey Quill test flew a wide range of aircraft, he is best known for his work on the Spitfire. He played a prominent part in the testing of the prototype in 1936 and 1937 and was subsequently responsible as chief test pilot at Supermarine for the extensive development flight testing of that famous aircraft throughout its long and distinguished career. During the Battle of Britain, he served in 65 Fighter Squadron on Spitfires, and later in the war served in the Fleet Air Arm to study the problems of Seafires operating from aircraft carriers. After the war, Jeffrey remained with Vickers and was a director of Sepecat concerned with the Jaguar programme. He was also marketing director of Panavia, the Anglo-German-Italian consortium company responsible for the Tornado programme. After retirement, Jeffrey continued to be much involved in various 'Spitfire activities', and was president of the Spitfire Society from when it was founded in 1984. Jeffrey died on 20 February 1996.

7 MY EXPERIENCES WITH THE SPITFIRE AT SUPERMARINE AND CASTLE BROMWICH, 1939 TO 1946

by Alex Henshaw, MBE

The first time I had the opportunity to climb inside the cockpit of a Spitfire was on 15 February 1939. As I landed my Mew Gull G-AEXF on Waltham Airfield in Lincolnshire, I was awaited by a small group of dignitaries taking me to a civic ceremony and I carefully taxied to park alongside this magnificent fighter.

The school holiday and many other accolades to be handed out in that particular day were for my little Mew's flight to Cape Town and back, so I wondered why a Spitfire from Fighter Command should also have been sent over to greet me.

My ego was quickly deflated, however, when Roger Frogley, in helping me out of the Mew Gull cockpit, said that the Spitfire had got lost flying from Hornchurch and that the pilot had 'cooked' his engine on the ground and now awaited a service crew.

Before I was able to leave the airfield, press photographers insisted that I give them a 'shot' climbing on to the Spitfire and sitting in the cockpit with the Mew Gull in the background.

Whatever my thoughts might have been on that brief occasion, I do not now remember. Of one thing I am quite sure. As a non-professional pilot, this was about as close as ever I would have got to a fighting aircraft but for the war due to erupt in but a few months' time. Nor would I in my wildest dreams ever have envisaged that I would then commence an association with the famous firm of Supermarine that would last over six years and that during that time I would get to know the Spitfire in fair weather and foul, in daytime and night, better than any other aircraft in my lifetime.

As I peered through the bullet-proof windscreen and lined up the imaginary gunsight, the cockpit struck me as being spacious and workmanlike but the enormous shining black pump-handle for the undercarriage re-traction completely spoilt what I thought at the time was a compact instrument and operational layout. Ironically, it struck me as I examined every detail that I knew more about its arch rival the ME 109 than I did about our own Spitfire.

During the decade preceding the Second World War, Britons and Germans cultivated a very happy and harmonious relationship, particularly in aviation circles. The British often in a carefree, naïve and sometimes indiscreet manner, the Germans always ebullient, full of bonhomie and a disarming charm. I had formed many friendships there during those idyllic years. I enjoyed being taken to see the energetic gliding activities by one of the leading exponents of that art at the time, Fraulein Lisle Bach. Another highlight that I remember so well was the invitation to dine on the massive airship the Hindenburg on its return flight from the USA. There were also numerous weekends at exciting, colourful and extremely noisy airshows, but the real climax for me was undoubtedly the last two years of that momentous decade. For some reason, the real purpose of which I am not sure, the Germans, both civilian and military, took a great interest in my Mew Gull. The engrossment, for this is what it amounted to, started with my winning the King's Cup and culminated with my record flight to Cape Town and back in 1939; and yet in a few months we would be at each other's throats.

So many doors suddenly opened to me that I could have spent much more time in Germany with civilian and Luftwaffe friends than I could have afforded.

A close associate in the British Intelligence Service was aware of this and pointed out how useful my visits could be to them.

In August 1939, I was invited by the president of the Berlin Aero Club to stay with him after the Frankfurt Air Show. German hospitality was legendary and it was perhaps fortunate that I did not then drink alcohol.

Before I left for Zlin in Czechoslovakia I was fortunate enough to be given the chance to visit a first-line Luftwaffe fighter squadron.

The ME 109s were lined up with great precision and looked very formidable indeed. Somewhat crude and basic in finish, they also lacked the artistic symmetry of the Spitfire and although not so graceful and pleasing to watch in flight, one could not fail to be aware of the lethal potentiality and the extremely confident and sometimes arrogant demeanour of the young pilots. The commandant was extremely friendly and charming as he proudly marched down the long line of fighters expressing a frankness that was almost embarrassing.

There had been rumours that the ME 109 was fitted with a central cannon which fired through the propeller shaft. When I discussed the armament, no mention was made of the cannon other than to extol the extraordinary firepower which, as was made very clear to me, could shoot any other aircraft out of the sky. I did not pursue the matter but certainly the machines which I examined were not fitted with cannon nor was any other weapon fired centrally. Before I finally left Germany, I was informed by an excited pressman that the countdown for the invasion of Poland had already begun. Like most experienced pilots of my age, with the atmosphere of a very dubious peace with Germany now removed, my sole objective was to get involved in the fight.

Not receiving an early reply to my application to join the RAF, I accepted another offer from Vickers-Armstrongs[22] and in less than two weeks from the outbreak of war, I found myself joining 'Mutt' Summers and Maurice Hare as a test pilot at the company's works in Weybridge.

A glowing picture had been painted of the important and demanding work to be done and of the exceptional qualities that were required for flight trials on the new high-altitude pressure-sealed bomber being designed to outrange existing enemy fighters and also the heavy workload on testing the production Wellingtons.

Perhaps because I had never before worked for a large public company and had only ever been involved with my own commercial interests, it soon became apparent that I had made a serious mistake in accepting the appointment.

In less than a month I had become so despondent with many of the facets of the firm that I decided to hand in my resignation to Trevor Westbrook, the general manager.

Just prior to my decision to resign I had been offered the job of forming a special duty flight. This was the brainchild of an old flying acquaintance, Sidney Cotton, whom I often used to meet in Europe playing the same sort of 'game' as myself. As a result of a collection of some almost unobtainable photographs, which he had astutely presented to the air minister, Sir Kingsley-Wood, he was able to obtain his support for the project. I had also met the minister and was confident of the far-reaching potentiality of a flight of picked pilots with carefully chosen and prepared aircraft.

I had made up my mind to accept the offer and was about to lift the phone finalising the details with Cotton when in walked a young man in flying gear. Jeffrey Quill had heard 'grapevine' talk of my resignation and had flown over to Weybridge from Southampton to see me. I told him I was thoroughly fed up at Weybridge; Jeffrey replied that that was unfortunate and later made it quite clear that he would like me to join the Supermarine group if I would like to do so. The mental picture of that first meeting with Jeffrey remains, after forty-six years, as clear as crystal. In the frame of mind I had reached during those traumatic days at Weybridge, I felt that no one would be able to persuade me to stay a day longer. I knew something of Jeffrey Quill's reputation, as no doubt he did of mine, but our paths had not crossed until that moment. I do not know what he thought of me but the views that I formed of him have not changed in all the years we have known each other. I trusted him immediately and there is no doubt in my mind that but for his visit to Weybridge at that particular moment, I would not be writing this contribution on my experiences with the Spitfire.

I drove to Southampton on 7 November 1939, my twenty-seventh birthday, and celebrated the occasion with my first flight in a Spitfire. Although this was the first time I had ever visited the renowned Supermarine works, I had always taken a great interest in what they were able to produce, particularly the spectacular Schneider Trophy racing seaplanes.

My subsequent work with Jeffrey Quill and George Pickering more than confirmed my previous assumptions about Supermarine. A small but dedicated group accustomed to working under pressure with limited resources, to turn out a finished job in which all would take pride. As a child in 1922, I remember my father praising a man called Mitchell for what he was doing in aviation. Much of this I did not, of course, understand at the time but I do recollect that in the Schneider Trophy Race of that year the Italians were confident of winning the trophy outright, having won the races of 1920 and 1921. They had the finest aeronautical engineers, and, moreover, the resources and financial help from a willing government. In Supermarine's case, no outside help was forthcoming. As a last resort Supermarine undertook the responsibility and risks themselves, and the race was won by their Sea Lion II, piloted by Henri Biard, at an average speed of 145.7 mph.

All this had a great impact upon me as a child and from then on I became an ardent admirer of R.J. Mitchell, who, unfortunately, I never actually met.

Mitchell's aeronautical talents and originality of mind as a designer perhaps first began to show real genius when in 1925 the Supermarine team produced a remarkably advanced racing seaplane, the S.4. It was a complete breakaway from orthodox constructional procedures in having an unbraced cantilever mid-wing as is described in other chapters.

In 1927, I closely followed the development of the new S.5 racing aircraft produced by Supermarine, which were a development of the S.4.

As a young boy I persuaded my father to allow me to drive my mother's Austin Seven from Lincolnshire all the way to Southsea where I watched with awe the RAF pilots practising for the race which was to take place later that year in Venice and which Britain subsequently won. Although I was not fifteen years old at the time, I have little doubt that the experience determined my own aims in life from then on.

Much has been said about the Spitfire evolving from the Schneider Trophy designs and there can be no doubt that the team which Mitchell built up over these years had accumulated a vast amount of knowledge in their particular fields with the complexities of design, stressing and construction involved in high-speed flying.

It was my good fortune to work with this team of Mitchell's and to get to know many of them well in the six years or so that I was associated with Supermarine. It was only to be expected that I should meet and work with some members more than others. The most prominent of these was Joe Smith, who had taken over as chief designer after the death of Mitchell. Joe was a splendid chief with a likeable approach to problems, as was Alan Clifton – his right-hand man, who eventually took over the design office when Joe was taken ill. Ernest Mansbridge was more in evidence than anyone as it was from his office that the performance figures submitted by the pilots were subjected to analysis. There were, of course, many others with whom I came into continual contact and it is regrettable, to say the least, that so few of these backroom men, who quietly and unobtrusively contributed so much, are still alive to share the limelight. At the time I was so contentedly engrossed in the work of this small factory and what it had achieved that I began to appreciate what it meant to spend a lifetime always struggling and striving towards what appeared at times to be an unobtainable goal. The challenge was always in front of you and for a while I regretted not making this branch of flying my career.

It is a measure of the calibre of Mitchell that not only did he create at the end of his short lifespan such outstanding aircraft as the Spitfire and the less glamorous, but nevertheless important, Walrus amphibian but that he collected together a small team who were so well qualified and able to continue after his death on the lines he had so firmly established. This in itself must be a tribute to the respect and loyalty that such men had for R.J. that they wished to continue where he left off rather than to seek employment elsewhere. This bond which had been welded may be demonstrated by the fact that not only did Mitchell's Spitfire start the war as our first-line fighter but remained as such throughout the long conflict. Also that in spite of its many guises and improvements in performance and armament it remained basically the same aircraft that Mitchell had conceived all those years before.

This remarkable team was more than adequately served in the air by two men of unusual ability and experience, whom I have already mentioned. The first and older of them was George Pickering. He had been with Supermarine since 1934 when Mitchell, conscious of the calibre of his work as an RAF officer, engaged him as senior test pilot, initially for flying boats and the Seagull V amphibian (later known as the Walrus).

When the Spitfire came into production, he also participated in the prototype and experimental trials. Certainly he taught me the art of mixing 'sailing' with flying and I shall never forget my flights with him in very rough seas with the Walrus and Sea Otter. On his tragic death in an accident involving an Army vehicle, the aviation industry lost a very conscientious and competent test pilot, while Jeffrey and I lost a loyal friend. Jeffrey Quill at the age of twenty-three was an outstanding RAF officer who had already built up an enviable reputation for bad weather flying in the Meteorological Flight. Later, when he joined Vickers-Armstrongs, he became recognised as one of the finest demonstration and aerobatic pilots in the world.

For my part, I had never had any pretentions of becoming a test pilot or indeed any inclination to do so until this time. I was an amateur civilian joining a select group of professionals and service personnel. However, perhaps the experience I had so far acquired in racing, long-distance record breaking and other overseas flights would stand me in good stead. Certainly I would think that the heavy responsibility of planning, financing, preparing, tuning and modifying my own aircraft with limited resources would not be a bad foundation from which to start. It was without question a challenge in that I now found myself measuring up to a unique band of designers and producers of the best flying boats and fighter aircraft, which were flown by test pilots at the top of their trade.

I always considered myself very fortunate that what success I had achieved in peacetime had also given me the opportunity and privilege of meeting most, if not all, of the outstanding pilots of various nationalities. Airmanship, of course, covers a wide field and takes in many aspects of success in the air. Most of those whom I did meet were of the highest calibre and ability but such was the publicity emanating from certain flights that there were those whose reputation would not bear close scrutiny. Although on the basis of this evaluation a test pilot may be in the highest category, it would not necessarily make him an outstanding airman. Nevertheless, if I had to choose the pilot making the greatest contribution within the field as a whole, I would have no doubts in naming Jeffrey Quill.

The value of a test pilot's contribution to the design and development of an aircraft during the pre-war years varied with each individual and the company concerned.

In the years I served Vickers-Armstrongs, I came to appreciate more than ever before the significant role that Jeffrey Quill had played through this vital period. If Mitchell were alive today I am sure he would be the first to recognise this fact.

The first virtue a pilot undertaking this work must have is integrity. All pilots at some time or another are faced with problems that they cannot easily resolve. This may in most cases be due to some inherent fault in the design but a compounding factor may also be the pilot's own shortcomings. It has to be a courageous and truthful man who can expound his inner feeling with the boffins from the design office. It helps if the pilot has outstanding abilities in flying an aircraft but he must also understand thoroughly the work in progress and adapt his mind and body to approach it with the means of obtaining the desired answers. He must also be articulate and lucid enough to ensure that those in the design office are left in no doubt as to what is really taking place in the air, and have a probing analytical type of mind so that each exercise may be examined in depth. An excellent grasp of engineering principles and a retentive mind will also help.

Jeffrey Quill had all these qualities and I also remember him, during a lull in the flight office, drawing a 'cut-away' sketch of the Merlin automatic boost control – I knew precisely how the unit worked but to draw it in detail was another matter.

Of all the test pilots who did such sterling work I know of no one who took such pride in their profession or could have made a better contribution to the Mitchell team than Jeffrey Quill. I am sure that many were more than aware of the serious loss when his flying career was stopped so prematurely with illness in 1947.

Strange as it may seem today, the Spitfire was not accepted with alacrity. No one would doubt its speed and handling qualities but many doubted its armament potentiality and had grave doubts about the feasibility of mass producing such an advanced aircraft. This ominous doubt was reinforced to some extent by the huge Nuffield factory at Castle Bromwich, specifically built to turn out fighters and bombers on a prodigious scale. The frustrating problems and difficulties encountered at this factory, in spite of modern equipment and a vast workforce, seemed insuperable. It all came to crisis point when France collapsed and the mighty German blitz swept us to the Channel ports.

Our backs were now to the wall – we needed weapons of every description but most of all we needed fighter aircraft.

One can only speculate upon what might have happened had Nuffield remained in charge of this vital source of supply. It was fortuitous that the dynamic, ruthless and astute Lord Beaverbrook came into power at this time as minister of aircraft production. Ruthless he may have been but it is very doubtful whether anyone else was really alive to the situation that faced us or had the ability and guts to handle an industry under such conditions.

Aware that the very survival of the free world could depend only upon our own efforts and with the war daily taking a more depressing and ominous turn, heads had to roll and Beaverbrook was certainly the man to chop them off.

He trapped Nuffield into a situation where his resignation was irrevocable. He then called in Supermarine, the only aircraft company which could possibly alleviate what was rapidly becoming a national scandal.

From the time I had arrived in Southampton in November 1939, until May the following year, the Nuffield progress with the Spitfire Mk II was pitiful. Therefore, when Supermarine were handed this headless giant on a plate, it represented a somewhat frightening challenge of immense proportions. It did not help matters when feelings between the two organisations became strained and not exactly harmonious.

There is no doubt in my mind that but for the intervention of Lord Beaverbrook and the handing over of the Nuffield factory administration to Vickers-Armstrongs and the Supermarine organisation, many of whom were sent up to Castle Bromwich, we might well have been invaded before a single aircraft had flown from the factory.

Jeffrey was instrumental in recommending my appointment in charge of the Castle Bromwich flight programme, under which, by June 1940, only ten Spitfires had been produced. It was a great compliment to me and represented not only great responsibility but also an enormous challenge. In spite of these feelings, I had been extremely happy working with George and Jeffrey. I felt that I was fitting into a day-to-day routine with members of the whole organisation and was reasonably content that my contribution, however small, was at least worth while. Hence, notwithstanding the importance of the Castle Bromwich appointment, I decided to turn it down.

Later, on one of our mad drives from Eastleigh to Castle Bromwich in the early hours of the morning to flight-test the second or third Spitfire, I discussed the matter with my wife. Suddenly, she expounded firmly that perhaps I ought to reconsider my personal viewpoint and accept the offer of transfer to the 'Black Country'. So, as I always listen to my wife's advice, I decided after much heart searching, to do just that.

My thoughts and reflections on those early months at Castle Bromwich recall the desperate straits into which we had been driven.

For a while it seemed that those warnings of the difficulties of Spitfire production on a large scale would prove to be right. It was a nightmare from top to bottom, from the man or woman on the shop floor to the managing director at the top. There were many sleepless nights during that first summer of the war. Lord Beaverbrook, no respecter of persons, would think nothing of telephoning Sir Alex Dunbar in the middle of the night telling him to get his finger out and find out what was going on.

In retrospect, I have always felt that not enough credit has ever been given to those members of the Supermarine group who came up to the Midlands and worked themselves to a standstill. With an expertise and knowledge unknown to those who had previously only produced cars, somehow or other they got the Spitfires on to the airfield for final inspection and flight-trials. With constant bombing at night and the inevitable loss of life and material damage, the problems of co-ordinating the production and final assembly with an inexperienced workforce, no matter how enthusiastic, were immense.

When Mitchell designed the Spitfire, thoughts of its large-scale production probably never entered his head. I often wonder what he would have said when this apparently sleeping monster at Castle Bromwich was eventually trained to turn out 320 Spitfires every month – not the straightforward Mk I, but later marks, more advanced in performance and with armaments to match.

Another tribute to Mitchell's genius lies in the famous Spitfire wing. At the time he decided to incorporate the legendary elliptic-shaped wing, which his aerodynamicist Beverley Shenstone had been working on, not a great deal was known, by today's standards, of the flying characteristics or the strength and load factors that might be required when the aircraft was fully equipped for battle. Certainly Supermarine was more fortunate than most aircraft constructors in that they had had more experience in this field, particularly with a mono wing at high speed.

One has to remember that at the time Mitchell was sitting at the drawing board, all our first-line fighters were biplanes. I had flown quite a number of monoplanes before I took to the air in a Spitfire. The high-wing and strutted variety I found to be pleasant and easy to fly. The low-wing types offered a better speed performance but those which I had flown were less predictable and sometimes disconcerting in their behaviour, although there were undoubtedly some whose flying characteristics were beyond reproach.

I found, in general, that whilst most of the monoplanes of that period were quite docile, the angle of attack and the relative position of the empennage played a great part in the control response, particularly on landing. But as I have said, they could be very unpredictable. One light monoplane in which I flew a great deal could be landed engine off with remarkable precision and docility right up to the point of touch-down in the calm air of morning or evening – do the same approach technique in the turbulence of a hot day and it would prove to be a real Jekyll and Hyde, with embarrassing results. I mention all this only to emphasise the excellent, almost incredible, aerodynamic behaviour of the Spitfire wing through a speed range never before conceived.

After the desperation of those early months, slowly but surely Castle Bromwich matured and grew up. So much so that it quickly became the show-place of fighter aircraft production in this country. Over the years, literally hundreds of visitors were received from Allied and neutral countries. Some were political, some military, but many missions and delegations were purely propaganda or window dressing. All, however, were heavily supported by a strong security guard and by the press with the usual photographers.

They came when our prospects of success were grim indeed and we had to impress them with our ability and determination to help win a war others had thought we had already lost.

It was part of my duty to demonstrate just what this pretty little Spitfire fighter could do. Naturally, with thousands of such flights spread over the years I came to know the business fairly well. It did not take a great deal to make the majority who came to watch jump out of their seats with enthusiasm, but occasionally there were others who were more than sceptical and less than complimentary. One such mission was a Russian delegation headed by one of their chief test pilots. On these somewhat rare occasions, I would take a Mk II or Mk V from the line of Spitfires on the tarmac and take off from where the group was situated. As the wheels of the machine left the ground, the aircraft would be pulled up smoothly but firmly into a vertical climb. Revs would be at maximum and engine at full power. At the top of the climb the Spitfire could then be pulled over to complete the top half of a loop followed by a half-roll to continue on the climb. To the ordinary onlooker this was a simple straightforward manoeuvre of no importance. To the professional expert, he would realise that to go into a vertical climb and with no excess speed in hand, the half loop and roll had to be made at 20 mph or so below the aircraft's normal engine off stalling speed, and that ailerons, rudder and elevator, together with maximum engine power and torque, would all have to play their part. Without sensitivity, harmony and complete authority with all these controls, such a manoeuvre could only end in disaster. I have never flown any monoplane that could execute an exercise to these limits so well as the early mark Spitfires and I was quite sure that the Russian pilot watching would have much food for thought. To ensure that the Russians would not leave us with the conviction that the Spitfire was some old ineffectual cow, the flight would end with a double-flick roll that could be controlled to a split second. During that period in wartime conditions, flying-control restrictions did not exist and I was able to use Castle Bromwich airfield as I wished. This unique situation, free from any other aircraft intervention, permitted a display to take place at extremely low altitude in front of an audience whose knowledgeable members could see clearly all that was taking place either with a fighter or with a bomber.

As Mitchell sat at the drawing board considering all the complexities of performance, strength and handling qualities of this delightful-looking shape that was to be flown by an average pilot at speeds from the stall to beyond 500 mph, and at the same time, carry machine guns or cannon with sudden and often violent use of the controls, he would I am sure have been proud and very satisfied by the acclaim given by leading pilots of all nationalities who were lucky enough to fly his brainchild, some excellent examples of which are included in this book.

Credit must also go to those around him with their own problems in calculating, stressing and determining the choice, for example, of wing spar and skin gauge. The anxiety of mass production must have been far from their minds at that period and I must confess to some sympathy with those who said that such a wing could not be produced in large quantities with unskilled labour. When one reflects that this cantilever wing, shaped in its elliptic form by hand and then, as detailed drawings were prepared, the incorporation of such refinements as two degree plus incidence at the root and tapering out to minus half a degree at the tip, is to appreciate the depth of knowledge Supermarine had acquired even in those early days. To do this with a fixed undercarriage and no guns inboard would have been formidable enough but to have designed such a thin section wing with a stress factor of over twelve and at the same time have space for retractable chassis and to carry guns, cannons and cameras, was nothing short of miraculous.

As test pilots, our job was to test production aircraft within their design limitations. The normal dive restriction on early model Spitfires was 470 ias (indicated air speed), whereas on the Mk 21 and comparable Seafires it was raised to 520 ias.

The dive at 470 was nearly always clean and smooth and did not approach terminal velocity. Only on one occasion did I reach the maximum diving speed possible and that was for a specific purpose. This happened during the early part of the war when a machine was taken to 30,000 ft, given a full throttle level speed run before rolling over into the inverted position for a vertical dive at full power and maximum revs before pulling out with comfortable ground clearance. Up until that time the power of the Merlin was insufficient to permit the aircraft to attain a speed that might encounter compressibility problems. Later with the Mk 21 and Mk 22 the dive was not always as smooth and straightforward as we had come to expect. Depending upon height and conditions, there were lateral responses which at the time were puzzling and the design office ruled a reduction in the dive speed to 500 ias. Although we were unaware of it, we were touching an area of aerodynamics not previously experienced and which would reveal itself more fully as the faster jet aircraft came into prominence.

Nevertheless, the RAF carried out a series of diving trials and in 1943 pushed a Spitfire Mk IX to an indicated Mach 0.92. Again in 1946 a reading of 0.90 was obtained and these are thought to be the highest Mach numbers ever achieved by any aircraft with a reciprocating engine anywhere in the world.

The legend of the Spitfire will remain and become immortal.

The defence of our country in 1940 will forever rank in the pages of history with other momentous occasions when our nation was in mortal danger. Without the Spitfire and the Hurricane few would doubt that the war might well have been lost almost before it began.

Future generations will not lose sight of these salient facts and will continue their appreciation of two outstanding fighters and the courageous young men who flew them. They may not realise, however, just what separated the Spitfire from the Hurricane, apart from the superior overall performance of the former, in the conflict that raged over southern England during that memorable summer of 1940.

A psychological factor in victory is not always recognised until the fight is over. An intangible weapon, it is none the less most formidable. It is not easy to analyse exactly when the Luftwaffe began admitting to themselves the apprehension and fear many of their pilots felt when confronted with a tight, disciplined and well-directed formation of Spitfires whose pilots were more than a match for them. The true extent of this overall impact on the German forces will never be known, but notwithstanding the enormous part that the Hurricane, with greater numbers, played in the Battle of Britain, without the Spitfire there can be little doubt that the Luftwaffe would have won the battle (see Chapter 20).

Our nation will forever owe R.J. Mitchell a debt that can never be repaid, but to all of those who know and care, R.J. and his incomparable Spitfire will never be forgotten.

Alex Henshaw

Alex Henshaw has been a private aircraft owner in Lincolnshire, where he was taught to fly, since April 1932.

In 1933, he was the youngest pilot ever to win the Siddeley Trophy in the King's Cup Race of that year with a Pobjoy Comper Swift flying a Leopard Moth, he was amongst the leaders in several races in the following year.

During the King's Cup Race of 1935, Alex crashed into the Irish Sea with a Miles Hawk due to a broken crankshaft. On the last day of that year he parachuted from an Arrow Active when it burst into flames whilst executing extreme aerobatics.

In 1936, in a Leopard Moth, he won the London to Isle of Man race in appalling conditions and was also winner of the Midlands Contact Race.

In 1937, he acquired the famous Mew Gull G-AEXF in which he subsequently had a large number of major international race successes.

After much work and many modifications on the Mew Gull, he won the King's Cup Race of 1938 at the fastest speed ever recorded and was also successful in a number of other important international races, in all of which he put up the fastest speed.

In February 1939, in his Mew Gull, Alex broke all records to the Cape and back in the astonishing time of thirty-nine hours outward and achieving the same time for the return flight. This record is still intact today and has been recognised by such celebrities as AC Clouston as the greatest solo flight in the history of aviation.

Henshaw was awarded the Britannia Trophy for the most outstanding flight by a British subject. War broke out soon after this flight and Henshaw joined Vickers-Armstrongs as a test pilot at Eastleigh with George Pickering and Jeffrey Quill.

When the enormous fighter and bomber factory came into production at Castle Bromwich, Henshaw was appointed chief test pilot.

In 1940 he married Barbara Countess de Chateaubrun and after the war returned to Lincolnshire to develop his family commercial interests having previously spent two years in South Africa as a director of Miles Aircraft S.A.

In 1944, Alex was awarded the MBE for his sterling work in test-flying Spitfires, Lancasters and Wellingtons during the war, during which he made over 37,000 sorties.

In 1953 he was awarded the Queen's Commendation for Bravery for saving lives during the East Coast Sea disaster.

Alex now lives in Suffolk and, although semi-retired, is still chairman of a large family group of companies covering a wide field of activity. He is also still involved in various 'Spitfire activities' and is one of the inaugural vice-presidents of the Spitfire Society, which was founded in 1984. His wife, Barbara, sadly died on 5 November 1996.

8 MEMORIES OF THE 1931 SCHNEIDER
TROPHY CONTEST

by Group Captain Leonard Snaith, CB, AFC

Perhaps I can best contribute in perpetuating the memory of R.J. Mitchell by describing my personal memories of the Schneider Trophy Contest of 1931, in which I was a member of the High Speed Team, and which resulted in the Supermarine S.6B designed by Mitchell winning the trophy outright for Great Britain.

The 1929 win generated great enthusiasm in the RAF, and when nominations for the 1931 team were called for, I was one of the large number of hopefuls. However, it was not until December 1930 that anything happened, because Britain's finances were somewhat shaky at the time and the government of the day decided against staging the contest. There was great disappointment at this but fortunately there was one dedicated enthusiast in the country, Lady Houston, who generously came forward and offered £100,000 towards the cost. The press made the most of Lady Houston's magnificent offer which so rallied public opinion that the government finally gave its approval to entering a team and staging the contest.

Approval, however, was not obtained until early in 1931, consequently there wasn't enough time to design and construct an entirely new type of aircraft. It was decided therefore to base the design of the new aircraft on the S.6, the winner of the 1929 contest, and the Rolls-Royce company promised to extract another 400 hp from their 1929 engine. Although they had only a few short months for the development, Rolls-Royce carried out their promise handsomely and increased the horsepower from 1,900 to 2,350, albeit with a 'life' of one hour only. This short 'life' was only accomplished one month before race day, and then only after many previous failures on the test bench.

At the same time an order was placed with The Supermarine Aviation Works for the supply of two new aircraft to be known as S.6Bs, and to modify the two old S.6s, after which they would be known as S.6As. The same developed engines were to be installed in the S.6As as in the S.6Bs. Mitchell rose to the occasion. The success of the S.5 in 1927 and the S.6 in 1929 were due largely to his brilliant work, and he was again to succeed with the S.6B, as will be described later. The whole world today knows of his ultimate success, the Spitfire, and there can be no doubt that he was one of the world's greatest aircraft designers. He was a most likeable man and it was a great loss to his many friends as well as the whole aviation world, when he died at the early age of forty-two in 1937.

Meanwhile, Sqn Ldr Orlebar was appointed team captain as he was in 1929, and he and the pilots from whom he would select his race-team assembled at Felixstowe. The selected team was as follows: Sqn Ldr Orlebar, Flt Lt Boothman, Lt Brinton (RN), Flt Lt Dry (engineering officer), Flt Lt Hope, Flg Off Leach, Flt Lt Long, Flg Off Snaith and Flt Lt Stainforth.

Stainforth, a member of the 1929 team, was the most experienced high-speed pilot. Boothman and Long were also fairly old hands. They were already based at Felixstowe as also was Hope who had had a few trips. Brinton, Leach and myself were newcomers.

Brinton, a Naval officer, had of course flown float-planes, but Leach and myself had had no such experience and so we were sent off first in a Fairey IIIF float-plane and then a 'Flycatcher', also a float-plane.

Then came the great day, 24 April, when the three of us flew the Gloster IV for the first time – and what a thrill that was; to take off, fly twice as fast as ever before, and then land the old racer – perhaps not beautifully, but at least successfully.

Shortly after this, however, came bitter disappointment for Brinton and Leach. They were dropped from the team, because it became obvious that our meagre resources in aircraft were insufficient to train more than one new pilot in the limited time available. I think I was kept on only because I had had considerably more general flying experience.

We went to Calshot in May and almost the first person we met there was Mitchell, or 'Mitch' as we soon found ourselves calling him. His firm of Supermarine was only a few miles away and he took full advantage of this. There was rarely a day when he failed to visit us. Sometimes in the evenings he came to the mess and, after dinner joined us in games, and there we discovered his guilty secret – he was lousy at shove-ha'penny.

In retrospect, I think he was trying to sum up our individual characters. This was perhaps just another pointer to his own character in that he was utterly committed to the job in hand and neglected no detail which might affect it.

He always seemed to have time to talk to members of the team. On one occasion when he and I were talking quietly on our own I asked him if he thought our speeds could ever be exceeded and I will never forget his reply. He just said simply, 'Oh yes, it's only a matter of horsepower and frontal area.'

On arrival at Calshot the only thing that then mattered was to get ready for the race in September. The aircraft immediately available to us were one Gloster IV and two Supermarine S.5s. These 1927 veterans were invaluable for our early training. Naturally enough some of their old joints creaked a bit and occasionally gave us a problem or two. The following remarks regarding a flight in the Gloster IV will illustrate what I mean – I quote them from my old logbook:

'Extraordinary flight. Took about two miles to get off. Eventually rocked it off. At intervals of about eight seconds propeller felt as though it fluttered badly and the whole aircraft shuddered.' Need I add, I was down again in seven minutes. Here's another entry, about S.5 N219: 'Serious trim-up behaviour at low air speeds. During the floating period before touch down, had to push the stick forward until it was at the full extent of its travel by the time the floats touched the water.'

Sometimes their vagaries helped. At first I wore rubber shoes and on one occasion, whilst flying a Gloster IV, the back part of the left shoe came off my foot and interfered with my use of the rudder bar. However, I managed to shed the shoe altogether. Whilst doing so I was able to control the rudder with the right foot only, because (and luckily for me) the old Gloster was carrying left rudder. You may not be surprised to know that my logbook includes the remark, 'I was a bit perturbed – and overshot badly on landing.'

Two S.6As arrived in July and the two S.6Bs in August. Let us look at an S.6B in more detail. It was a wire-braced monoplane with cantilever tail unit. The wing surfaces – top and bottom – were water radiators, as also were the tops and sides of the floats. Oil coolers were fitted to the sides of the fuselage, and also along the centre-line underneath. The oil tank was in the fin. The whole aircraft was virtually a flying radiator.

With the exception of a 3.5-gal. header tank, all the fuel tanks were housed in the floats. The port capacity was 48 gal. and the starboard 110 gal. The consequent difference in weight helped to counteract the effect of engine torque.

Fuel was pumped up from the floats through the float-struts to the header tank, which fed the carburettors. The header tank contained enough fuel to feed the engine for the duration of a turn when the centrifugal force exerted was sufficient to break down the suction-feed from float-tanks to pump. The only noticeable difference between the S.6Bs and the S.6As was in the lengths of the floats: the S.6Bs were 24 ft and the S.6As 22 ft.

Flying was only possible when weather conditions were very good. The most suitable conditions were a combination of good visibility, a gentle wind and short, sharp choppy water with no 'white horses'. This condition of the water gave the best turbulence behind the float step. The two conditions we had to avoid were, firstly, a flat calm, because it was not conducive to generating turbulence behind the float step; moreover, a flat calm is often associated with a mirrored surface which makes it extremely difficult to judge height above water. Secondly, a swell had to be avoided at all costs, because it was impossible to counteract porpoising in such conditions.

Our aircraft were rather slow compared with the jet aircraft we see today, as the fastest could reach a speed of only about 400 mph in normal level flight, but they were very much faster than anything we or anyone else had ever flown at that time.

Apart from adjusting our ideas in relation to speed there were other factors to be taken into consideration. For instance, we had only fixed-pitch airscrews, as variable-pitch propellers had not yet been invented. It will be appreciated that a coarse, fixed-pitch airscrew, designed to give optimum performance at 400 mph, will not do much more than churn up the air at 4 mph and, in addition, will have a terrific torque reaction. As a matter of fact, the airscrews specially designed for the S.6As and S.6Bs never got us off the water. I remember Sqn Ldr Orlebar testing the first one. When he opened the throttle to take off, he found it quite impossible to control the swing. He described the aircraft's behaviour as 'like a cat chasing its own tail'. As a result we had to fall back on the 1929 S.6 airscrews. To illustrate the limitations of the airscrews then available to us, let me describe the most difficult manoeuvre of all, namely, the take off.

The effect of torque was our first concern, especially in the S.6As and S.6Bs. As engine power was increased, so the left float was forced deeper into the water, and this, coupled with forward movement, dragged the aircraft round to the left. So the start of the take off had to be at least 45 degrees to the right of the wind, and full right rudder had to be applied and held. If all the preliminaries had been co-ordinated nicely, the aircraft accelerated to a speed at which the air-flow over the rudder was just sufficient for directional control by the time the aircraft had been dragged round into the wind.

But there was more to it than that. The noses of the floats tended to dig into the water and produced, if unchecked, a porpoising movement, which was more spectacular than efficient. This particular problem was resolved by holding the stick hard back throughout the whole of the take off. Kept in this position, the porpoising could be held in check.

Then there was the final unsticking, which was the most critical phase in the whole take-off operation. When the aircraft eventually unstuck it did so quite suddenly. It leapt off the water and into the air at a pronounced angle and in a partially stalled condition. It was virtually hanging on its airscrew. The attitude was so pronounced that it was the hardest thing in the world to resist the impulse to push the stick forward, but it had to be resisted. If we failed in this respect, the aircraft fell back into the water and we ran into really serious trouble, as will be seen later. The whole manoeuvre was complicated because we often had to take off 'blind', our goggles having misted up or become covered in spray. Incidentally, immediately after take off acceleration was slow, because we were starting from a near-stall speed and, in consequence, the airscrew was at minimum efficiency. The landing also had to be watched carefully, since as there were no flaps and the aircraft was exceptionally 'clean', deceleration was very slow. On the other hand, the wing loading was high and the stall critical, consequently the only safe way to tackle the landing was to accept a very long 'hold off' just above the water. One also had to be quite sure beforehand that the alighting path was clear of obstacles, because one travelled a long way before coming to rest. It was impossible to see straight ahead, because the nose of the aircraft (which was quite high, even in level flight) kept getting higher, in relation to the water level, as the speed dropped and as the angle of attack increased, so that the heels of the floats touched the water first.

After touchdown, the rudder had to be applied coarsely in order to keep straight; one could be caught out, even in this last stage, as indeed George Stainforth was on one occasion. In correcting a swing to the left, his right heel jammed between the rudder bar and the slide. Not being able to release his foot immediately, the aircraft swung round to the right and finally cartwheeled completely over and sank, slowly, to the bottom of the Solent. Fortunately not so George, who came up rapidly and quite unhurt.

My first attempt at taking off an S.6A was a ghastly failure. I think I stuck to the formula, namely 45 degrees out of wind, full right rudder, stick right back. Nonetheless, porpoising started so I closed the throttle and stopped. Then I remembered what I had found on the S.5, namely that I could, with advantage, let the stick go forward just a little, and so I tried this out on the S.6A. How wrong I was! I found myself porpoising all over the Solent in a most terrific way without getting airborne. I kept on with this deplorable exhibition until high-speed motorboats came out from Calshot and stopped me.

I shall never forget what happened afterwards. Besides being wet through with spray, and being inexpressibly miserable at having failed my first big test, I had the awkward task of having to explain to Orlebar, my team captain, what I had done. To my astonishment he just laughed at me for a minute and then all he said was, 'Child' – his personal nickname for me – 'Child, you shouldn't have done that.' What a leader! No wonder everybody had a special regard for him.

Notwithstanding his forbearance, or maybe because of it, I felt that I might be dropped from the team. However, a few days later, I was given another chance and, sticking to the strictly laid-down drill, got off all right this time. It is interesting to recall the observations I made after that first flight of mine in an S.6A:

> Three-quarters of take off satisfactory, then lost sight of ship ahead. In looking for it, goggles got covered in spray. Actually got off fairly well – but almost blind. Had to throttle back shortly after take off owing to rising water temperature – slightly tail heavy – tightened up in turns. Left wing low – holding it up very tiring. Landing OK but very short to avoid running into the wash of a ship ahead.

You will have gathered that we were confronted with the difficult problem of rigging our aircraft to fly accurately over a much larger speed-range than ever before. Eventually Mitchell got over this difficulty by having duralumin strips approximately 1 in. wide fitted to the control surfaces. These strips, while adequately stiff under air loads, were easy to bend with suitable tools and relieved the pilot of any permanent control bias, when deflected in the appropriate direction. There was also some longitudinal instability to cope with, but this was overcome to some extent by placing lead ballast in the nose of the floats. In regard to temperature control, it should be appreciated that, although the entire surfaces of the wings and the tops and sides of the floats were covered with radiators, their capacity for cooling was not quite adequate. Allowable time for flying at top speed was therefore governed by maximum permissible water temperature.

Concern in regard to running into the 'wash' from a ship was very much in our minds, since it was this disturbance which caused Freddie Hope's accident when landing an S.6A. He hit a ship's wash and was bounced into the air about 30 ft. The aircraft cartwheeled back into the water, but to our relief Freddie was soon to be seen and swimming strongly. He had, however, burst an eardrum which put him out of the team. Surprisingly, the aircraft was not a 'write-off' and Supermarine managed to rebuild it and make it available again to us by August.

Freddie Hope's accident created a vacancy in the team and Jeremy Brinton was brought back to take his place, but this proved to be a sad move because he was killed shortly afterwards in trying for the first time to take off in an S.6A. I was sitting in a motor boat nearby, and saw everything. Jeremy was obviously caught out by the attitude of the aircraft when it leapt off the water. He probably pushed the stick forward impulsively to rectify this attitude and the aircraft came down again, bounced to a height from which it was impossible to recover, and dived straight into the water.

As the weeks went by, the public became increasingly interested in our activities, and we had numerous visitors. Amongst our special visitors were Lady Houston and Sir Henry Royce. Lady Houston was undoubtedly a great character; but for her foresight and bold intervention, Britain might well not now have permanent possession of the Schneider Trophy. Sir Henry was, of course, already a legendary figure. In talking to him one was left in no doubt as to why the name 'Rolls-Royce' had, for so long, been synonymous with perfection. Sir Henry seemed to know everything about our problems and of course we did have problems.

One of them, possibly the most vital one, was as follows. Sqn Ldr Orlebar was up testing an S.6A and seemed to be flying along quite comfortably, when suddenly, right over Calshot Castle, the engine stopped, and he landed miles away from base. What had actually happened was that the rudder had started to flutter badly and he was unable to hold the controls. It was not until the speed had dropped to under 200 mph that the flutter stopped. But by then he was down to about 50 ft. Fortunately, however, he had plenty of sea-room and he managed to land successfully. When the aircraft was towed back to base, the fuselage plates were found to be buckled just in front of the tail-plane. With this evidence in front of us a lot of hard thinking had to be done. Flying was stopped and scientific experts from far and near came to discuss the flutter problem. Our office, usually a quiet place, was for once the noisiest place on the station. Of course, 'Mitch' was there but he hardly opened his mouth, just sitting quietly in a corner. But I think it was he who eventually solved the problem, and that was to mass balance the rudder and elevator by attaching a bob-weight to a lever projecting from the leading edge spar of the control surface thus obtaining the required balance. The basic cause of flutter having been established, the same action was taken in respect of the ailerons.

The flutter modifications were not completed until the end of June and, the July weather having been indifferent, nearly all of the S.6 flying was carried out during the last six weeks before the day of the race. During this period we did a good deal of experimental work on turns, the object of which was to determine a good compromise between a sharp turn which gets round a corner quickly, but loses speed rapidly in doing so, and a wide turn which drops the minimum amount of speed, but takes longer to do. We tackled this problem by carrying out a succession of tests. At the conclusion of the tests it was established that the minimum time lost in a turn was achieved by accepting a load of 4G. Incidentally, we had to cope with the 'black-out' problem, and we began to realise that to prevent, or at least, delay it, one had to be prepared for it. When anticipating a turn I contracted my diaphragm just as I would if somebody tried to punch me in that area and the medical experts said I was probably right in doing so because, roughly speaking, it is the flow of blood from the eyes which is responsible for 'black-out', and in contracting the diaphragm, one restricted this flow.

During the last fortnight before race day, it was decided that Stainforth should go for the world absolute speed record, while Boothman, Long and myself would be the race pilots. However, shortly after this came the news that we had been fearing; after serious accidents and technical troubles, both the French and Italian teams found themselves unable to compete. This was a bitter disappointment for them and for us also, particularly as it was then decided that only one of our aircraft should fly over the course. The plan of action was altered as follows:

Boothman was to fly an S.6B and go all out for a high speed, keeping however within water temperature limits. If he failed, then the next to try would be myself in the one remaining S.6A, to fly strictly on the water-temperature gauge. No chances to be taken with overheating. Speed to be considered as of less importance than finishing the course. This restriction was because prolonged full power was impossible in the S.6A, with its shorter floats and consequent limited cooling area. If I got round all right, then Long, in the second S.6B, would make a second attempt at a high speed. If I failed, he would go off with instructions similar to mine.

The final week before the race was very hectic. First we had to practice a full fuel load take off and landing. In our earlier practice trips, we had carried only sufficient fuel for a 20–25 minute trip, whereas the full race course would take about fifty minutes. In addition, due to a change in the rules for this contest, the race proper had to be preceded by a take off and immediate full load landing. Naturally the take off took longer – forty seconds in my case as against thirty the time before – and for my part, I confessed to a feeling of relief when I eventually 'unstuck'. Then came the landing. The light-load approach speed was 130 mph, but since the wing loading was at the maximum, I came in at about 160. This meant that we had to take extra care. But all went well with each of us – John Boothman on the Sunday, Frank Long on the Monday, and myself on the Tuesday.

But Monday was specially exciting for me as on that day I took off in S.6B 1595 towards the Isle of Wight and was over land at a quite low altitude when the engine cut out. Fortunately it came on again, but kept cutting in and out. After about the sixth cut the engine failed to come on again. However, by this time I was over the water once more and I managed to get down all right off Ryde, right in the middle of a crowd of sailing boats, all of which I missed but more by luck than judgement. On examination later it was discovered that some new fuel mixture we had been testing had choked up all the fuel filters (see Chapter 11). My forced landing occurred in the same aircraft with which we retained the trophy only six days afterwards. From all this it will be appreciated that the British team also had troubles and problems and that we got ready only just in time.

During that last week Boothman, Long and myself also got in two trips of twice round the Schneider Course in the old S.5s, and one last flight in our S.6s to test our newly installed race engines.

At last we came to the day – Saturday 12 September – and what a day! It was quite unsuitable for any sort of flying. It was raining, blowing hard, and the sea was very rough, and so the fly-over was postponed until the following day.

Sunday 13 September, was much better and we were all ready with our aircraft. The event took place before a vast crowd of people on both the Hampshire and Isle of Wight beaches. By midday, Boothman, Long and myself were alongside the pontoons from which our aircraft were to be launched and, just after 1 p.m., John Boothman set off for the sea-worthiness tests. He made a perfect take off, and then, in accordance with the new rules, did a short circuit and landing, which was also perfect. His second take off was equally good and he went off in fine style for the seven-lap Schneider Course, whilst Long and I waited, need I add, in some suspense. Our state of mind wasn't improved when it became apparent that lap by lap his speed was gradually dropping. The explanation for this was that after about one and a half laps, the water temperature started to rise above the maximum allowed for, and so the throttle had to be eased back slightly for the remainder of the contest.

John Boothman made a recording early in 1932 of his impressions of the race and this is reproduced in full in Chapter 11.

Despite his temperature troubles, John Boothman had completed his flight of 350 km at the new course record of 340 mph. Boothman's fine performance meant, of course, that neither Long nor myself were required to do any flying for the race. One could not help having mixed feelings, on the one hand great relief and pleasure that Boothman had done everything necessary to win the race for us, and on the other hand a natural feeling of disappointment that I was not going to have the opportunity to demonstrate what I could myself do.

The proceedings of the day didn't end with the winning of the trophy. By 5 p.m. the second S.6B had been prepared for an attack on the absolute speed record which is flown over a 3-km course. The pilot was George Stainforth who, although the arrangements were somewhat hurried, was able to raise the record to 379 mph. But the success story didn't end there. Later in the month, with a specially boosted engine, and by superb flying, George Stainforth achieved the magnificent speed of 407.5 mph. A new world record.

Thus ended a year of outstanding achievement in British aviation and one which highlighted the enormous influence of the Schneider Trophy Contests in increasing the speed of racing seaplanes. Its influence on the design of normal aircraft, although it was not immediately apparent, proved to be of the greatest importance and Mitchell was to demonstrate only too clearly that the large amount of time and money spent on the development of the Schneider aircraft was unquestionably fully justified as a powerful stimulant and aid to aeronautical development.

As a postscript, in 1984, I was very pleased to be invited to attend a revival of the Schneider Trophy Races to be flown over a course similar to that used for the 1931 contest. The race was sponsored by the Digital Equipment Co. Ltd, the world's second-largest computer manufacturers. It took place on 24 June 1984 with sixty-two aircraft competing. The Digital Schneider Trophy Race differed from the 'real' Schneider Contests in that it was a handicap event, the aim of the handicappers being to try and get all the competitors to cross the finishing line off

Ryde Pier more or less together! The race was won by Paul Moorhead in a Beagle Pup 150 at an average speed of 134 mph which compares with the average speed of 340 mph at which Boothman won the 1931 contest.

I had the great pleasure and honour of starting the Digital Schneider Race, flagging off the first competitor to start from Bembridge Airport in the Isle of Wight. The race brought back many happy memories of the time fifty-three years ago when I was personally involved in the 1931 contest as I have described. It also served to honour and to pay a distinguished further tribute to Mitchell, both in the extensive official publicity surrounding the event in which his vital role in the Schneider Contests was highlighted, and in the comments made about him by Mr Geoffrey Shingles, managing director of Digital Equipment Co. Ltd, in his speech at the formal dinner held in Bembridge on the evening before the race. Mitchell's son, Gordon, who was a guest at the dinner must, I am sure, have felt very proud that his father was still remembered with such high regard all those many years after one of his aircraft won the Schneider Trophy outright for Britain.

Grp Capt. Leonard Snaith

Grp Capt. Leonard Somerville Snaith was born in 1902 and educated at Carlisle Cathedral School, which he left at the age of fifteen to join the RFC during the First World War. In 1923, he gained his wings and was capped for the RAF rugby side. In 1926, he won the Duke of York's Landing Cup and was presented to HM King George V. He was commissioned in 1927 and joined the High Speed Flight in 1930 in preparation for the 1931 Schneider Trophy Race.

Subsequent to that Grp Capt. Snaith was involved in over a hundred catapult launchings from worships including HMS Ark Royal and various experimental rough-water landing techniques. In 1933, he was awarded the AFC and in 1934 was posted to squadron service in Iraq as adjutant of 70 Squadron and later the command of 83 Squadron at Turnhouse and Scampton. During and just after the war he served in the UK, Egypt, Italy, Palestine and Aden with a term in the US test flying on behalf of the British government. In 1948 he became commandant of the Empire Test Pilot School and later commanding officer experimental flying at the Royal Aircraft Establishment, Farnborough, in 1950, retiring in 1952 at which time he became a companion of the Bath. From 1952 to 1968 he worked at the Royal Aircraft Establishment, Bedford, in the civil service at which time he was also president of the local RAF Association and sometime vice-chairman of the Bedfordshire Territorial Army Association. He was appointed deputy lieutenant of Bedfordshire in 1961. Leonard Snaith died on 6 September 1985 shortly after completing his contribution to this book.

9 TRIBUTES FROM A FEW OF THE MANY WHO FLEW THE SPITFIRE INTO BATTLE

Air Commodore Alan Deere, DSO, OBE, DFC

I am greatly honoured to be invited to make a small contribution to this book about R.J. Mitchell. In the world of aircraft design the name Mitchell is synonymous with that of the Spitfire, the outstanding fighter aircraft in the Second World War.

There can be no doubt that victory in the Battle of Britain was made possible by the Spitfire. Although there were more Hurricanes than Spitfires in the battle, the Spitfire was the RAF's primary weapon because of its better all-round capability. The Hurricane alone could not have won this great air battle, but the Spitfire could have done so.

The outstanding characteristics of this great little fighter were many. Of course, it had its shortcomings but these were few, and far outweighed by its attributes of versatility and toughness. These became more apparent as a changing battle scene witnessed a transition from a purely defensive role in the United Kingdom to one of offence in the form of ground attack and dive-bombing in all theatres of war.

To me, the Spitfire was more than just a fighter aircraft, it was a constant companion and partner throughout five years of war in which, as a team in combat, it played the dominant role. That I am alive today to pen these few words is not so much due to my much-publicised luck as to the durability of this supreme fighter.

R.J. Mitchell is a man to whom we Spitfire pilots owe so much.

AC Alan Deere

Alan Deere was born in Auckland, New Zealand, on 12 December 1917 and joined the RAF when he was nineteen. As a Spitfire pilot, he was in action right from the beginning of the war. He took part in the air cover given during the evacuation of Dunkirk and was in the thick of the action throughout the Battle of Britain; in 1943, he became wing leader of the famous Biggin Hill Wing. He retired from the RAF in 1967 after thirty years' service. His final 'score' in air combat was 21.5 destroyed, nine probables and nineteen damaged. Alan died on 21 September 1995.

Air Vice-Marshal 'Johnnie' Johnson, CB, CBE, DSO, DFC, DL

Recently I have been in touch with fighter pilots from all over the world about writing brief autobiographies to raise funds for the Douglas Bader Foundation, of which I am a trustee. One of the questions we asked was: 'Please mention all fighters flown in combat and select the particular type preferred above all others', and here are some of their replies:

> It [the Spitfire] was always a delight to fly, was supremely responsive to the controls at all speeds in all attitudes of flight and, with all of this, a very stable gun platform.
>
> 'Dutch' Hugo
> South Africa

> I only flew Spitfires in combat. No mean fate. I grew to envy the Mustang's great range, however.
>
> Rod Smith
> Canada

> I flew most of the various marks of Spitfires, but I felt sort of invincible in the Spitfire Mk IXB. It was a beautiful aeroplane and I was very happy to fly and fight with her.
>
> Larry Robillard
> Canada

> The Spitfire was an incredible, immortal combat vehicle.
>
> Danforth Browne
> USA

> I preferred the Spitfire to other fighters because it had few vices. It was fast, very manoeuvrable and had a high rate of climb.
>
> Pat Jamieson
> New Zealand

> I flew a Spitfire for the first time in March 1939. It was a thrill I shall never forget. The versatility and the deceptive toughness of this fighter made it, I think, without question the outstanding fighter aircraft of the Second World War.
>
> Al Deere
> New Zealand

> The aircraft was part of you and, when frightened, either in testing or in combat, I think one used to talk to one's Spitfire, and you may be equally sure that it used to answer.
>
> Paddy Bathropp

Because I lost my second and third logbooks, I do not know exactly how many hours I flew a Spitfire altogether, but it must have been about 2,000, of which at least half must have been on operations. The Spitfire never let me down.

                                                                    'Cocky' Dundas

I said in my autobiography that my only regret about this great fighter was its lack of range; I wrote:

> How we longed for a wing of Spitfires which would fly to Berlin and back, for fighter pilots of every nationality thought the Spitfire Mk IX was the best close-in fighter of them all; but our radius of action remained the same as before and we had to confine our activities to short-range operations while the Americans fought those great daylight battles single-handed.

The Spitfire Mk IX could indeed have played its part in the great daylight battles all over Germany, but the chief of the Air Staff at that time, Portal, firmly believed that a long-range fighter could not possibly have the same performance as a defensive fighter and turned down the proposals to develop the full offensive potential of the Spitfire.

The Spitfire was a beautiful fighter and these comments about its long-range offensive qualities do not in the least detract from Mitchell's wonderful design.

AVM 'Johnnie' Johnson

'Johnnie' Johnson was the top-scoring RAF fighter pilot of the Second World War. He was born at Barrow-on-Soar in Leicestershire in 1915.

Shortly before the war, he joined the RAFVR and by August 1940 had joined 19 Squadron at Duxford. From there he was posted to 616 (South Yorkshire) Squadron of the Auxiliary Airforce at Kenley on a day when they lost more than half their pilot strength and were pulled out of the front line. The squadron was reformed at Coltishall and although 'Johnnie' Johnson participated in the Battle of Britain he did not claim any victories. In the spring of 1941, 616 Squadron moved to Tangmere where 'Johnnie' frequently flew number two to Douglas Bader. During the summer of 1941, Johnson destroyed at least six enemy aircraft whilst carrying out fighter sweeps, low-level flights over France and bomber escort duties. In September 1941 he was awarded the DFC and promoted to flight commander.

In the summer of 1942, 616 Squadron, re-equipped with the pressurised Spitfire Mk VI, returned to Kenley but 'Johnnie' was shortly afterwards posted to command 610 (County of Chester) Squadron, Auxiliary Air Force at Coltishall. After supporting the combined operation against Dieppe in August 1942, 'Johnnie' was promoted to wing commander leading the Canadian Wing at Kenley with his tally of victories rising to eight.

By September 1943, his score had reached twenty-four and he was awarded the DSO and Bar and the American DFC.

In March 1944, 'Johnnie' Johnson was posted to lead 144 Canadian Wing, based at Tangmere. Flying Spitfire Mk IXs, they were engaged in dive bombing and strafing attacks across France in the lead up to D-Day. Subsequently he was appointed leader of 127 (Canadian) Wing and was engaged in the pursuit of the retreating German Army, protected by a formidable screen of FW 190s and Messerschmitts. Just before the end of the war, 'Johnnie' was given command of 125 Wing at Eindhoven and promoted to group captain.

By the end of the war, 'Johnnie' Johnson had been credited with thirty-eight enemy aircraft destroyed and continued his career with the RAF including Officer Commanding Cottismore, SASO No 3 Bomber Group Mildenhall and AOC Air Forces Middle East, Aden. He retired from the RAF at his own request in 1965 aged forty-nine and subsequently published his autobiography and a treatise on the history of air fighting.

In 1969 he formed the 'Johnnie' Johnson Housing Trust which provides more than 2,500 flats for elderly and disabled people; he was chief executive of the trust which today has a portfolio of property worth many million pounds.

'Johnnie' was one of the inaugural vice-presidents of the Spitfire Society which was founded in 1984. 'Johnnie' died on 30 January 2001 aged eighty-five. This was understandably widely reported both in this country and overseas.

Wing Commander Bob Stanford-Tuck, DSO, DFC, RAF (ret'd)

My first flight in a Spitfire was at Duxford on 2 January 1939. The aircraft was owned by 19 Squadron and I had been attached to them for a few days, as my squadron at Hornchurch was to be re-equipped with Spitfires very shortly. Naturally I was delighted about this, as rumours of war were strong and if we had to go to war it was better to go in this aircraft rather than in our comfortable, but old, Gladiators. My stay with 19 Squadron started a long and fascinating association with this superb aircraft, and after my last flight in a Spitfire in 1948, I had notched up just over 1,000 hours flying on them.

This wonderful aircraft, which came into being out of the brilliant brain of R.J. Mitchell, seemed to be capable of almost endless development and improvement, and this was applied to it with tremendous advantage to all those who flew her. The Spitfire was a true thoroughbred and both the aircraft and its creator, Mitchell, will remain in aviation history for ever.

Finally, all these years later, it is only fitting that I should salute Mitchell and his tireless design team for bequeathing to this country the Spitfire in our moment of such great need.

Wg Cdr Bob Stanford-Tuck

Bob Stanford-Tuck was born in 1916; he obtained a short service commission in the RAF in 1935. In May 1940, he became flight commander of 92 Squadron (Spitfires) and was in the thick of the Dunkirk evacuation and the subsequent Battle of Britain. Following being in command of 257 Squadron (Hurricanes), he was promoted to wing commander to lead the Duxford Wing and then in December 1941 went to Biggin Hill to lead the Spitfire Wing there.

Bob was shot down in January 1942 and spent three years as a prisoner of war until he escaped via Poland and the advancing Russian Army in January 1945. His final score of confirmed victories of German aircraft destroyed was twenty-nine. He finally retired from the RAF in 1950 after twenty-five years' service; later, he had a public relations appointment with the RAF Museum at Hendon. Bob died on 5 May 1987.

Flight Lieutenant Denis Sweeting, DFC

It was halfway through my first tour of operations in 1942 that our squadron changed from Hurricanes to Spitfires.

My first view of the Spitfires, as they were delivered, impressed upon me the clean and beautiful lines of the aircraft which had been clearly designed to slip through the air rather than to bulldoze its way through with sheer power.

Although the taxiing was more difficult than the Hurricane because of worse forward visibility, due to the long flat-topped nose, and there was more swing on take off, once in the air the lightness of the Spitfire's controls was remarkable. The slightest pressure of hand or foot was answered immediately. The balloon shaped hood made all-round visibility so much better and must have saved the lives of many pilots.

Somehow, sitting in the cockpit flying the Spitfire, I always felt I was in partnership, something I never felt with any other aircraft. Although I had many nerve-racking experiences in the Spitfire, I never lost my admiration of it and today if I see one fly over I still experience a thrill of delight coupled with great nostalgia; the last forty plus years slip away and I am back in the cockpit high up in the clear blue sky flying over the Channel towards France.

Flt Lt Denis Sweeting had what can only be described as a miraculous escape from a Spitfire in an uncontrolled terminal velocity dive at some 650 mph.

Denis Sweeting recalls what happened:

Early in the morning of 10 September 1942 I took off on a scramble and when airborne was directed to climb to 30,000 ft over Scapa Flow. We entered 10/10ths cloud at about 5,000 ft climbing flat out. At 15,000 ft still in cloud my no 2 lost me and I continued on my own. At about 20,000 ft I was having difficulty following the instruments and the last thing I remember was seeing the altimeter showing 24,000 ft and still in thick cloud.

My next memory was hearing the engine roaring away and vision came back to me just like waking from a dream. The cloud cleared and I realised the aircraft was diving vertically at full boost. For a moment I was not sure whether I was dreaming or whether it was really happening, then I could see the ground coming up fast and I can remember sighting a small village and a church with a spire. Still partially dazed with an unreal feeling, I groped around the cockpit to pull the control column back and shut the throttle. I pulled back on the control column with all my strength and blacked out. I kept heaving back and suddenly there was a tremendous explosion and everything was quiet and black.

At first I thought the aircraft had hit the ground and that I was dead! The thought then occurred to me that I might have been thrown out of the Spitfire. In the blackness, I moved my legs about but couldn't feel anything around me. Remembering from the parachute instructions I had been given that when in difficulties, the way to find the D-ring on the rip cord was to walk the fingers of your right hand around the waist strap until the handle could be felt, I did this in complete blackness getting hold of the handle and pulling. Immediately I felt the jerk of the parachute opening and could feel myself floating down. As I could still not see anything, I thought I had gone blind. I began to feel very hot and I passed out again.

The next awakening was hearing voices and running feet; I was lying on the ground still in complete blackness. There was considerable pain in both shoulders and I couldn't move my arms but I found I could move both legs.

The voices came nearer and I heard in a broad Scottish accent, 'He'll no be alive after all that'. I called out to them, 'No, I'm all right'. When they came up they covered me with their coats and some bracken and said an ambulance was coming. I lay there in great pain for what seemed ages. They asked what had happened and I said that I had no idea.

When one remarked, 'The war's over for you, you'll not fight again.' I replied, 'Oh yes I will. I'll be all right next week.' They did not answer, which was not surprising considering the picture I must have presented: my trousers, shoes and socks had been torn off and my legs were covered in blood, both my shoulders were dislocated, my face was blue where it was not covered in blood and my eyes were full of blood.

I asked if the parachute was still on me and when told it was, I instructed them on how to undo and take it away. Not surprisingly, they were reluctant to touch me but succeeded in getting it off.

Apparently I was lying in a rough peat field some way from the road and my Spitfire had gone in about half a mile away.

At last, the Army ambulance men arrived with a stretcher and gave me a shot of morphine. They then carried me for what seemed miles across the ground and over ditches. Every time they jerked the stretcher the pain was excruciating. It was a most agonising journey.

I was taken to a sickbay, sewn up and cleaned up and my shoulders put back with some difficulty. The doctor told me my pulse rate was 160 and that the cords of the parachute had got caught around my neck and had been strangling me, accounting for my period of unconsciousness after the parachute opened.

I was still unable to see the following day when the CO visited me. We pieced together what had happened. In the rush to take off, the oxygen cylinder had not been turned on and although I had turned the oxygen on in the cockpit, once the gas in the pipes had gone, no more came through. Concentrating on the instruments in cloud I had not looked again at the oxygen gauge.

Having passed out through lack of oxygen at 24,000 ft and fallen forward, the control column was pushed forward so that the aircraft then dived at full throttle for nearly 20,000 ft until I recovered consciousness emerging from the cloud base. The speed of the Spitfire must have been its terminal velocity of about 650 mph. From such a dive, time and care was required to pull it out but in my semi-conscious state, I had attempted to do so far too violently, putting such strain on the wings that they were both torn off, one slicing off the tail section. The fuselage with me in it had done a bunt.

The negative G to which I was subjected was so great that the seat straps ripped out and I was ejected through the canopy tearing off my clothing and cutting me. Miraculously the parachute stayed on me. When I pulled the rip cord I was most likely turning head over heels in the air, accounting for the cords catching around my neck. When hitting the ground in the strong wind that was blowing, my shoulders must have been dislocated as I was dragged by the parachute over the rough ground. The negative G had caused the blood vessels in my eyes to rupture and that was why I was unable to see. In fact, it was three days before my sight was fully returned and for weeks afterwards the whites of my eyes were blood red.

Flt Lt Denis Sweeting

Denis Sweeting joined the RAF in May 1940; following completion of flying training, which amounted to a total of less than 100 hours, and which included just ten hours on Hurricanes (!), he was posted in March 1941 to 79 Hurricane Squadron in South Wales, on convoy patrols. He next went to 504 Squadron which changed from Hurricanes to Spitfires early in 1942. In June of that year, he was posted to Malta but as a result of his ship being sunk off Liverpool, went to 167 Spitfire Squadron instead. Denis finished his first operational tour in

February 1943; after several months as an air gunnery instructor, he was posted to 198 Typhoon Squadron at the end of 1943. The following June he was awarded the DFC and became a flight commander. He completed his second tour in early 1945 and went as an instructor to the Fighter Leaders School at Tangmere, finally leaving the RAF in April 1946.

During his career in the RAF, Denis flew a total of around 300 hours on Spitfires.

10 A SPITFIRE WING LEADER LOOKS BACK

by Group Captain W.G. Duncan Smith, DSO, DFC, AE, RAF (ret'd)

It was on a sunny afternoon in March 1939, while reclining in a deck-chair on the lawn of the Woodley Flying Club, near Reading, that I first saw R.J. Mitchell's beautiful creation – the Spitfire – close enough to note every detail. A smiling pilot clad in overalls stained by oil and showing signs of sweat, stepped down from the wing and waved in my direction. Since I did not recognise him, I looked round and saw a pretty girl, fair hair blowing across her brow, waving back. The pilot walked through the gate in the lawn fence and joined her at a table neatly laid for tea. I strolled over and walked round the Spitfire noting the long line of engine in front of the tiny cockpit, the rounded wing shape housing the eight machine guns; the silence broken at intervals by the mysterious hissing and tapping noises made by a Rolls-Royce Merlin engine, cooling down.

At the time I was a RAFVR pilot under training at No 8 EFTS based on Woodley, flying Miles Hawks. I suppose it was the rape of Austria and the crisis over Czechoslovakia that made me realise war with Germany was inevitable and I had better do something about it. I never discovered who the Spitfire pilot was that March day but I am thankful I got such a close look at the Spitfire because it changed my life. I became determined to fly this wonderful machine with its exciting lines and matchless speed. Presently, I watched as the pilot, having finished his tea party, kissed his girlfriend before climbing into the cockpit with a large grin and a wave of his hand. Soon he was taxiing to the far end of the airfield before turning into wind and taking off – the roar from the Merlin unforgettable. This was life, I thought... flying a Spitfire and having tea with a pretty girl... what could be better?

After frustration and disappointment over many months of training, some of it useless, I found myself one evening in the summer of 1940 at a Spitfire Operational Training Unit rather excited at the thought that at long last I would be flying a Spitfire for the first time the following morning. This great goal was duly achieved without incident.

Hawarden near Chester wasn't exactly a holiday camp but the spirit of the hour prevailed and the excitement of knowing that in a matter of days the lucky ones amongst us would be on our way to an operational front line Spitfire squadron and action against the enemy, made up for all the heart-searching that had haunted me over the previous months. I nearly fluffed it because on the return from my last flight – a battle climb to 30,000 ft – having completed the exercise, as I came in to land I collided in mid-air with a ferry command Avro Anson and crashed. Lucky for me I was nearly out of fuel so the Spitfire didn't go up in flames when we hit the ground. Apart from cuts to my face, head and legs, I got away with it and after a stern rebuke from the CO next morning, I was on my way to join 611 (AAF) Squadron at RAF Digby in Lincolnshire. The ruggedness of the Spitfire and beginner's luck had seen me through.

611 Squadron were equipped with Mk I Spitfires, some with pump-handle operated landing gear and others with recently modified gear which was hydraulic operated. The engines were Rolls-Royce Merlin IIs rated at 1050 hp. The aircraft was a joy to fly and its armament of eight Brownings and splendid handling qualities gave me a confidence in the Spitfire that stayed with me through operational experiences spanning eleven different marks. One has, of course, to include the various types of Rolls-Royce engines that powered Spitfires over a period of many years. Reliable to an extent that was fantastically excellent, never did I ever think I would be let down by engine or airframe. One could stretch both to the very edge of disaster and yet feel fully confident in the operating ability of both. My Mk I aircraft, X4253, stayed with me till we were re-equipped with Mk IIs in the early part of 1941. It had been a happy partnership with morale-lifting successes and not a few frightening occasions in combat against superior numbers of Messerschmitts, alone and under attack, but in a crisis, my Spitfire rose to the occasion and never let me down.

I remember a particular occasion when the squadron was heavily engaged over Dunkirk by twenty ME 109s. I became separated from the rest of the squadron after attacking and probably destroying an enemy, dodging and splitting the attentions of three ME 109s on my tail. Discretion, I thought, was the better part of valour so, spiralling down with a succession of aileron turns to zero feet, I ducked over the coast and escaped by skimming the wavetops with every pound of boost Messrs Rolls-Royce could give me till I sighted North Foreland and the snow-sprinkled fields of Kent beyond. X4253 got me home safely without a murmur though I cannot say the same for myself. Out of breath and exhausted, I could not resist the urge to give the engine cowling a loving pat followed by a breathless 'thank you' as I tottered towards our dispersal hut to fight another day.

I have to say that at this time the daylight operations, consisting of escorts to day bombers targeted on German-occupied French industrial installations, road, rail and river/canal communications, military head-quarters, camp sites, airfields, ports and other important targets, were being stepped up. As high-altitude fighters, Spitfire squadrons usually flew at heights above 20,000 ft. We had also to maintain, of course, our defensive operations, defending selected areas in the south and south-east of England. All this activity meant we were in constant engagement with German fighters.

I stayed with 611 Sqn till August 1941 when to my delight I was appointed flight commander of 'B' Flight 603 (AAF) Squadron, also based at Hornchurch. I think the most important changes in new equipment available for our Spitfires during 1940/41 were: more powerful engines; introduction of VHF radio, thus getting rid of the old and inefficient TR9 radios; and, not least, the addition of 20-mm Hispano cannon armament. As mentioned, we briefly flew the very attractive Mk IIs with Rotol propellers (excellent for take off and climb) and easily the best aircraft for aerobatics in its day (Merlin XIIs). Soon we got the Spitfire Mk Va (Rolls-Royce Merlin XLV, eight machine guns) which was quickly fol-lowed by the Mk Vb which had the same engine but now fitted with 20-mm cannon armament. Immediately we noticed the difference with our 20-mm armament because when a shell hit the enemy aircraft things happened in dramatic form. I remember my first Mk Vb clearly because it was an aircraft presented by the motor industry and named 'Crispin of Leicester'. She flew beautifully and I christened my two cannons with a pint of beer, 'Anne' on the port side and 'Briggy' on the starboard. Named after two quite splendid and lovely WAAF officers at Hornchurch, their names were written on the sides of the cannon muzzles and I'm pleased to say quite a few Messerschmitts bit the dust from 'Anne and Briggy'!

It was during a big 'circus' operation when 611 Squadron were top cover at 28,000 ft to twenty-four Blenheim bombers targeted on Bethune that I was first able to fire my cannons. Suddenly we were attacked by twenty ME 109s, very surprising to say the least considering the altitude, anyway, I was able to latch on to four enemy aircraft and got behind one flying wide and opened fire with everything I had – two cannons and four machine guns. The muffled boom-boom from the Hispanos was a welcome new sound but the vivid orange flash from a cannon shell as it exploded against the enemy aircraft's cockpit canopy, even more startling! Closing, I fired a second burst but my Spitfire pitched and yawed away from my line of sight so that in a split second my aim was thrown off balance and I became frustrated as the ME 109 rolled on to its back diving steeply, pouring grey smoke from a hit in the cooling system. As I recovered my surprise at seeing the enemy dive away (I felt sure the pilot was dead), I realised one of my cannons had stopped firing, thus twisting my aircraft sideways from the recoil of the live cannon. We had to put up with this sort of snag during the early days till we sorted out stoppage problems. Eventually the guns proved most reliable and effective. On the other hand, as the pilot of 'Crispin of Leicester', I began to receive, from kind ladies in that remarkable city, woollen socks, mufflers, fruit cakes and love letters, not to mention a surprise package one day containing a long scarf in the blue and white colours of Leicester City Football Club, with, wait for it... a delightful proposal of marriage! The months that followed hold vivid memories of one combat after another. The summer passed into the loveliness of autumn when we were surprised one day by running into some of the first, unpublicised FW 190 radial-engined fighters. These aircraft were to prove, in the coming months, a thorn in Fighter Command's side and too good in combat against the older, slower Spitfires of the time.

After a five weeks' spell in hospital at the end of 1941, I returned to the fray in March 1942 in command of 64 Squadron at Hornchurch. My first brush with FW 190s, however, was encouraging and very instructive since I shot down one off Le Touquet as he was trying to escape. It seemed the Spitfire was still treated with respect and, dare I say it, with a degree of fear. Out of the blue one day I was informed that 64 Squadron had been selected by the commander-in-chief, ACM Sir Sholto Douglas, to be the first squadron to be equipped with the new and astonishing Spitfire Mk IX. I had flown the new aircraft with its Merlin 61 engine specially developed for high altitude and much improved performance at all altitudes. It had impressed me no end and I felt my squadron would be able to operate against the FW 190 with great success. I was to be proved right. But I must pay a special tribute to Jeffrey Quill, Supermarine's chief test pilot, for all his hard work based on operational and personal know-how against the German fighters and also to Ronnie Harker, Rolls-Royce's test pilot for his dedication in flight testing the new Merlin 61 engine. They were a great team. The engine power had now been increased to 1565 hp and the top speed to over 400 mph.

The weeks that followed were exciting and, after completing the conversion programme with no snags and no accidents, we carried out the first offensive sweep over France on 28 July 1942. We saw no Germans and returned rather disgusted with the fighting qualities of the Luftwaffe but, on 30 July, we engaged FW 190s and ME 109s and shot down five enemy fighters also probably destroying one and damaging two. Our combat performance over the Luftwaffe that day was so potent it was obvious thereafter that the Germans treated us with respect, believing a new Spitfire had joined the ring.

Since it was extremely difficult to separate Mk IXs from others or positively identify them, then all Spitfires would have to be treated as the new version by the Luftwaffe.

Further successes followed; the escorting of the American Flying Fortresses over France on their first daylight mission – 17 August 1942 – followed two days later with the combined operation raid on Dieppe. My squadron flew four sorties in support of the landings that day including escorting the flying forts to Abeville aerodrome where they bombed with devastating accuracy. We destroyed five enemy aircraft, damaging four; I shot down two Dornier bombers but got shot down myself in the process, baling out into the Somme Estuary from my precious Mk IX. Some time later the Navy picked me up, dried me out and handed me a large glass of whisky.

In September, I was posted to take over command of the North Weald Wing and in December, I was taken off operational flying and appointed to the staff at HQ Fighter Command in charge of the tactics branch. After an interesting time which included setting up the Fighter Command School of Tactics at RAF Chalmy Down in April 1943, which later developed into the Central Fighter Establishment, the Mecca of air fighting for all Allied air forces, I was posted to Malta in command of the Luqa Spitfire Wing in May. The squadrons, 126 and 1435, were equipped with Mk Vbs and Mk IXs and following the invasion of Sicily, I was transferred as Wg Cdr (Flying) to 244 Wing Desert Air Force (Mk VIIIs and IXs). The enemy fighters at this time put up stiff opposition and many hard fought dog-fights went the distance. We also had the Italians to cope with in their Macchi 202s, 205s and the Reggiane 2000/5, an extremely potent aircraft with a wing shape not unlike the Spitfire. The 2000/5 fitted with the German-built DB605 engine was a very fast aircraft and thank goodness only about twenty of them were built before the Italian surrender. It had a maximum speed of 447 mph at 24,000 ft and reached 20,000 ft in 5 1/2 minutes! Not bad – not at all bad. Italian pilots, too, were very good flyers but they tended to show off rather than get stuck in and when they did, lost heart for the fight and either ran away or got shot down. On the day, the Spitfire was more than a match for any of these aircraft.

On 2 September, the day before Gen. Montgomery invaded Italy, I was flying on an armed recce when, near Catanzaro, east of the Lipardi Islands, on changing over from drop tank to mains, the steel cable (Bowden type) snapped somewhere inside the casing and I was left high and dry and unable to use my main fuel supply. I was able to glide some twenty miles from my height of 28,000 ft in my Mk VIII before taking to my parachute into the sea off Cape Vaticano. To cut a long story short, I was in the sea for some six hours swimming in my Mae West. My dinghy had sunk on hitting the sea, carried away in a stiff breeze by the billowing parachute after release. Eventually I was picked up by a Walrus by sheer luck, and as I was helped aboard rather the worse for wear, we were strafed by a gaggle of ME 109s, Macchi 205s and a

Reggiane. A bullet from one of them pierced my Mae West grazing my neck and spinning me away from the Walrus as cannon shells hit the amphibian aircraft, holing the main petrol tank and hull, so that by the time I was dragged aboard the main cabin was awash. The pilot, Flg Off Dick Eccles, a South African with whom I still keep in touch, expertly handled the Walrus in the rough sea taking off across the swell and breaking waves; later a hairy but relatively orthodox landing at Milazzo. The aircraft was so badly damaged it became a write-off. It says much for Supermarine's products that even rough treatment of that order couldn't dispose of us!

Since we needed an airfield on the Italian mainland quickly, I was ordered to join the 1st Airborne Division in north Africa and land with them by sea at Taranto with the task of getting the airfield, Grotaglie, into operational order to receive one of my Spitfire squadrons plus two Kittyhawk squadrons. This so that the 8th Army could call on air support in its drive to join up with the American and British forces at the Salerno beach-head. It turned out to be quite an interesting and exciting experience and forty-eight hours later the three squadrons flew into Grotaglie.

I remained with 244 Wing till November when I was appointed to command 324 Wing RAF (Spitfire Mks VIII and IX) based at Naples operating in support of the American 5th Army. I remained in command of 324 Wing till 30 March 1945. During this period, we covered front-line operations during the Cassino siege and the Anzio landings. At this time, German air strikes increased and we were continually in action up to and beyond Rome. In the period to June my wing destroyed over eighty enemy aircraft with half as many again probably destroyed and damaged. My Mk VIII played her part and I led the wing personally as often as I could.

In August, 324 Wing received orders to proceed to Corsica where we were assigned to provide air cover for the invasion of the south of France by the American 7th Army, supported by French divisions. Apart from the air superiority function, we also attacked Radar sites, and German transports along the roads leading up the Rhone Valley. We shot down about eight enemy aircraft and had very successful pickings along the roads and in the mountains. After landing and setting up the wing on a prepared air strip near Frejus, we moved on to Sisteron near Grenoble and on 7 September based ourselves on the main aerodrome of Lyons. Regretfully, from our point of view, we were recalled to Florence, and converted to the fighter-bomber role, later moving back under the control of Desert Air Force, basing ourselves at Rimini. I found it strange to fly the sleek and beautiful Spitfire with a 500-lb bomb hanging between the wheels but, let me say at once, the Spitfire did her job magnificently and proved a deadly accurate launching pad for dive-bombing. Unlike many other fighter-bombers, the Spitfire, once the bomb was released, became a fighter aircraft again and, as we all know, was immediately superior to any other fighter within the Allied or enemy camp. The Germans feared the Spitfire more than any of its contemporaries, even the Rolls-Royce–engined North American Mustangs (Mks III and IV). These aircraft were very fast but very un-American, since they had been built to a British specification, designed by a German holding American citizenship, and flown for the first time by a British (RAF) pilot, Sqn Ldr Teddy Donaldson as he was then (1941). He recommended to the Air Ministry that the Mustang was, in his opinion, the only worthwhile fighter aircraft the Americans had to offer at that time.

The following is rather off the record but might be interesting. Because of the difficulty being experienced by the 8th Army in the 'river battles', while fighting northward, we had to find a way to 'winkle' out Germans dug deep into the banks of these rivers (Sangro, Senio, Rapido and others). It was a nightmarish problem since low-level attacks by strafing Kittyhawks, Mustangs and Spitfires seemed to have no effect. One morning, Sqn Ldr Perry, my armaments officer, suggested we use a Spitfire's 45-gal. drop-tank filled with Napalm (used by the flame-throwing tanks) as a lethal anti-personnel weapon by dropping it at zero feet. Nobody, as far as I remember, had tried anything like it before. I asked him how he thought it should be armed. His reply: 'A hand grenade, so that when the pilot pulls the release lever to drop the torpedo-shaped tank, the pin on the grenade will also be removed'.

'Not much time,' I said, 'before it detonates, would you say?'

'Yes,' he replied, 'the pilot will have to fly very low and accurately.'

I asked, 'Who will fly such a silly idea of yours?'

Perry looked at me and smiled, 'I cannot think of anyone, sir, more qualified to do the job than yourself!' And so it went ahead. I flew the first experimental sortie and the idea worked perfectly after some modification. Later it was tried operationally with outstanding success.

I returned to England in August 1945 and was posted to the staff college as a student. The years rolled by but I kept in flying practice and I was delighted when in June 1949 I was alerted to take command of 60 Squadron based in Singapore, Far East Air Force. Equipped with Mk XVIIIs (Rolls-Royce Griffon 65 engine) the squadron was based on a temporary basis at RNAS Sembabwang when I took over before moving later to RAF Tengah. On the evening of 10 July, after Tommy Broughton had officially handed over command to me, he suggested I lead the squadron the following morning at dawn on an offensive strike operation, deep into the Malayan jungles, to bomb and rocket a Communist insurgent camp. Though I had flown the Mk XII Spitfire (Griffon 111 engine) at Worthy Down in 1942, I hadn't even seen a Mk XVIII. Armed with a 500-lb bomb and six 60-lb rockets mounted under the wings, I took off from Sembabwang's 1,200-yard strip (pierced steel plank thirty yards wide) with my heart in my mouth. All's well that ends well, however. The time that Spitfires were finally to be retired from combat duty had come. I led the very last offensive strike carried out by Spitfires of the RAF, on 1 January 1951; the target a Communist hutted camp in the Kota Tinggi area. We did not know the historical significance of the occasion at the time. Soon we were re-equipped with jet-engined de Havilland Vampires, and the Spitfire had passed into history. I felt the going very much and somehow I had not been able to imagine a day when there would not be a Spitfire in service with the RAF somewhere. I was never able to strike the same rapport with the jet aircraft I flew in the years that followed both in England and the USA. The Spitfire was a unique aeroplane and when R.J. Mitchell turned a vision into reality he saved mankind from slavery.

In conclusion, I think we all have to thank the great Mitchell and his dedicated team of designers, engineers and test pilots who together were responsible for giving life to the Spitfire – without doubt in my book the greatest and most successful fighter aircraft the world has ever known. In particular, a special tribute has to go to the test pilots, particularly to Jeffrey Quill, without whose expert professional knowledge, flying skill and dedication, the remarkable lifespan of the Spitfire might have been rather less remarkable. Finally we must pay tribute to all the operational pilots who, having been given a thoroughbred, never had to look back in passing the winning post. Ronnie Harker, chief test pilot of Rolls-Royce Ltd, and Jeffrey Quill arranged a presentation to 60 Squadron of a beautiful silver model Spitfire in commemoration of this famous aircraft's final exit from operational flying. On the base of the silver model are inscribed the opening words of the Nunc Dimittis, 'Lord, now lettest thou thy servant depart in peace.'

Grp Capt. Duncan Smith

Duncan Smith (popularly called 'Smithy') joined the RAFVR in 1935 and converted to Spitfires in September 1940 before joining 611 (County of Lancaster) Squadron in October 1940. In November 1940, the squadron moved to Rochford to counter daylight attacks by ME 109s upon south-east airfields. He flew as a squadron pilot and later as flight commander of 603 Squadron throughout 1941, providing fighter escorts to bombing missions, and after sick leave following hospitalisation with double pneumonia, applied pressure to return to action. He was put in command of 64 Squadron (the first to have Mk IX Spitfires) and in August 1942 took part in the operation against Dieppe in the course of which he was shot down for the first time. 'Smithy' was then promoted to lead the North Weald Wing and then in December 1942 was posted to HQ Fighter Command.

In May 1943, 'Smithy' was sent to Malta in command of the Luqa Spitfire Wing and took part in the Allied invasion of Sicily. By November 1943 he had been promoted to group captain in command of 324 Wing RAF based at Naples and later in Corsica supporting the US 5th and 7th Armies. After providing support to the 8th Army's crossing of the Po Valley, 'Smithy' returned to England in August 1945 and continued in the RAF until retirement in 1960 after twenty-two years of active service, including a final Spitfire period from 1949 to 1952 with Griffon engined Mk XVIIIs in command of 60 Fighter Squadron in Malaya.

Grp Capt. Duncan Smith's final 'score' in air combat was nineteen destroyed with a further twenty-two probably destroyed and damaged.

Duncan was one of the inaugural vice-presidents of the Spitfire Society, which was founded in 1984. Duncan died on 11 December 1996.

II THE ROYAL NAVY CALLED THEM SEAFIRES

by Capt. George Baldwin, CBE, DSC, RN (Ret'd)

In the early summer of 1938, I had settled on a plan to apply for an officer cadet course at the RAF College at Cranwell. However, by the autumn when I had left school, war now seemed imminent and everything was in a state of flux – I had been greatly influenced by the occasional sight of a Spitfire flashing across the sky above the RAF station at Henlow where my father was serving as an engineer officer, but now the urgency was to start a training course as soon as possible and Cranwell seemed too far in the future. What incredible beauty those Spitfires possessed and what speed they had compared with other current aircraft! To fly one would be the ultimate experience for a technically minded young man.

At that time the Royal Navy was expanding its Air Arm very rapidly and planning to introduce new aircraft; they needed aircrew recruits urgently and were offering early courses. The thought of going to sea and qualifying as a pilot suddenly appealed to me and I put in my application, but not without a very deep feeling of disappointment that I was probably throwing away my chance to fly the Spitfire.

Fate, however, plays strange tricks. In 1941, after completing my training and an operational tour in a Skua Dive-Bomber Squadron, I was appointed to the Naval Air Fighting Development Unit which soon moved from Yeovilton to Duxford to be close to its sister trials squadron in the RAF. In this arena, pilots were encouraged to fly every type of aircraft in order to broaden their experience, and on 17 July, I managed to 'borrow' a Spitfire Mk IIA from a front-line squadron CO in exchange for a trip in our Sea Gladiator – this was quite a deal for both of us but I was certain that I had come off best!

At about this time the decision had been taken in the Admiralty that the Spitfire would be adopted for operations in aircraft carriers in the Fleet Air Defence role and a number of the older marks of Spitfire were transferred from the RAF for trials and training. In May 1942 we received some of these superb aircraft into the NAFDU and I was able to continue my initiation, while in the following month I received the splendid news that I was to be posted as senior pilot to the first operational Seafire Squadron (807) when it formed up the following month.

Seafires were fundamentally Spitfires with the minimum modifica-tions to enable them to be operated from an aircraft carrier's deck; a dorsal arrester hook and four spools for catapult launches were the pri-mary items, together with the necessary airframe strengthening to absorb the extra loads imposed by rapid acceleration and deceleration. Different marks of Merlin engine were also fitted to give the Seafire additional performance at low altitude where there was a particular need for very rapid reaction to the approach of low-flying enemy reconnaissance and torpedo aircraft, and bombers flying at medium heights. In 1944, folding wings were introduced – a major modification which greatly facili-tated the stowage of large numbers of aircraft below in the hangars, but which, alas, also degraded performance through the considerable extra weight. The mechanism for the fold, which was operated manually, was of excellent design and was established without any noticeable change in the beautiful double curve outline of the wing form; best of all, the aerodynamic excellence of the wing was completely unimpaired. Later in the war when Griffon engines replaced the Merlins, other more major alterations took place in many different parts of the airframe and are too numerous to mention here. It is fair to say, however, that these aircraft could no longer be considered to be 'sisters' of the original Spitfire; more likely 'cousins', perhaps.

Luck stayed with me until the end of the war as I had the good fortune to remain with the Seafire throughout, and the saddest moment of all occurred in November 1945 when we returned to the UK from the Far East and our beloved aircraft were taken from us and hidden away in an MU for storage. 'Spitfire' reappeared in my logbook in the following year, however, when I had a few flights in the Mk IX (a very popular variant which I had flown whilst on temporary attachment to 244 Wing in Italy in 1944) and then in 1947 I was in the Service Trials Unit and back with the Seafire. In that year the Griffon engine variants were in service, the Mk 17 becoming the standard, although we began trials on the Mks 45, 46 and 47 in the following year. This was a period of very rapid change and between the years 1946 and 1953 the Seafires Mks 17 and 47, the Hawker Sea Fury, the Supermarine Attacker and the Hawker Sea Hawk were all introduced into single-seat front-line fighter service in the Navy. The Seafire Mk 47 lasted longer than most piston-engine types, ending its service career in 1833 RNVR Air Squadron in 1954 while the Mk 17 was withdrawn as a fighter trainer from 764 Squadron at about the same time.

Looking back on all my flying in the various marks of Spitfire and Seafire (fifteen in all), I can truthfully say that I enjoyed virtually every minute of it, and I believe that the majority of other experienced pilots would say the same. The pure joy of being in sole control of such a superbly designed and built aircraft gave one a special confidence in the ability of both the machine and the occupant to survive almost any hazard that could be encountered both in operations and in general flying. The most exhilarating experience for me was to carry out aerobatics on a fine day around and about tall cumulus clouds and, again, I think most other pilots would agree.

With regard to carrier operations, there is no doubt that the earlier, lighter Seafires were tricky to deck-land, especially in the escort carriers which could only make 14–17 knots – in these ships, when there was no natural wind, to stall the aircraft into the arrester wires within a distance of some 100 ft was difficult since a full stall occurred at a very low speed and a slightly fast approach could mean floating over the wires and damaging the aircraft in the barrier. The wing-form of the Seafire was as close to perfect as design and technology of the day could make it and this meant a stall in earlier marks of as low as 55–60 knots. Furthermore, the very perfection of the wing made it sensitive to the slightest variation in construction, rigging or servicing, and errors in these fields could induce an increase in stalling speed of as much as 8 knots. Such a 'rogue' aircraft in a squadron, showing different stall characteristics from all the others, constituted an unacceptable deck-landing hazard. This was not because it was necessarily any more difficult to put down on the deck – it was dangerous because an unsuspecting pilot, not realising the aircraft he was flying had an abnormally high stalling speed, might get into trouble on the landing approach to the flight-deck through allowing his speed to drop too close to the stall. Fortunately, 'rogues' were rare and in most cases their faults were rectified without too much difficulty. Conversely, of course, a major naval advantage was gained in the low wing-loading since it meant that take off from the deck could be made freely with a full military load and without resort to any rocket or catapult assistance.

During the war, as the Seafire was developed to carry more and more operational payload, and as the wing-form remained the same, stalling speed increased and the stall became more positive and more predictable

– deck-landing thus became progressively easier. In the period when wing-tips were removed to increase rate-of-roll in the Seafire Mk LIIC (and concurrently in the Spitfire Mk VI), there was a further increase in stalling speed and crispness of the stall, and the Mk LIIC produced much better deck accident statistics. It should be pointed out, however, that the stall speed was still extraordinarily low for the type of aircraft and that in later marks the tips were replaced to regain high-altitude manoeuvrability.

Wartime Seafires were operated in the main by three air wings each comprised of three naval air squadrons; at one time I had the privilege of leading No 4 Wing in the Mediterranean with 120 Seafires operating from four escort carriers and later in the Indian Ocean with ninety aircraft in three ships. Earlier, however, squadrons were embarked individually and were operated as high-performance fighters in the Air Defence of Shipping role. They were thus employed during the invasions of north Africa, Sicily and Italy. As the German and Italian Air Forces became less active from 1943 onwards, the Seafire, like other fighters, took on increasing Army support tasks and began to carry bombs, rockets and recce. cameras. In addition, the wing which operated from Lee-on-Solent performed a major role for the D–Day landings in providing gunfire spotting in addition to fighter protection around the beaches. The wing which was employed for the south of France invasion were 'Jacks of all Trades', flying all types of Army support missions. This role was repeated in operations to drive the Germans out of the Aegean and the Japanese out of South-East Asia, although the latter was curtailed by the sudden surrender of Japan. In the British Pacific Fleet the Seafires flew, more predominently, fighter sorties and destroyed many Japanese aircraft in the air and on the ground in support of the American drive from Okinawa and all the way to the Japanese mainland itself.

The Seafire could not be said to have had a spectacular success in the Second World War, mainly because of the fact that it started life as a lightly constructed, high-performance airfield fighter. No aircraft in this category could be expected to stand up for long in the rough and heavy treatment it would be bound to suffer in carrier deck landings. In the air, of course, it performed admirably but did not possess the endurance desirable in a naval fighter flying long air defence patrols. By the end of the war many of the disadvantages had been overcome and all the lessons learned were put to good advantage in the Mks 17 and 47. The Seafire, nevertheless, was much beloved by all of its pilots and it undoubtedly made a great contribution to the war and to the development of air fighting in the Royal Navy.

Mitchell produced a most timely and brilliant design in the Spitfire and we owe him a great debt for his contribution to British aviation progress. In the Spitfire series, he gave us the ultimate in the combination of beauty, operational effectiveness and sheer joy of flying for those who had the privilege and good fortune to fly his masterpiece.

George Baldwin

In December 1938, George Baldwin joined the Royal Navy's Air Branch and after flying training, was appointed to 801 Naval Air Squadron (Skua Fighter/ Dive Bombers). He spent 1941–42 in the Naval Air Fighting Development Unit and was then posted as senior pilot to 807 Naval Air Squadron (Seafires Mks IIC and LIIC). In 1943, George took over command of 807 Squadron and then in 1944 commanded No 4 Naval Fighter Wing until the end of the war (Seafires Mks LIIC and LIII). In 1946, he carried out the Empire Test Pilot's Course, then spent two years in the RN Service Trials Unit followed by two years as naval liaison officer with RAF Central Fighter Establishment. In 1951–52, he was commanding officer of 800 Naval Air Squadron (Supermarine Attackers).

After a year as commander (air) at the RNAS Ford, he was appointed in 1955 as staff officer (air), British Navy staff in Washington DC, USA. During 1959–60, he was deputy director of the Gunnery Division (Air Weapons) in the Admiralty and then in 1964–66, director, Naval Air Warfare, MOD. George Baldwin commanded the RN Air Station at Lossiemouth in 1961–62 and then the RNAS at Yeovilton from 1966 to his retirement in 1968.

12 SENIOR MEMBERS OF MITCHELL'S TEAM AT SUPERMARINE IN OR AROUND 1936 (IN ALPHABETICAL ORDER)

Arthur Black	Chief Metallurgist and Rig Tester
Alan Clifton	Head of Technical Office of the Design Department
Jack Davis	Senior Design Draughtsman
Wilfred Elliott	Works Manager
Alfred Faddy	In charge of detail design of the Spitfire with an influence on its layout
Eric Lovell-Cooper	Senior Draughtsman – had charge of the detail design of the Scapa flying boat
Ernest Mansbridge	Performance Estimates and Flight Test Observation
Maj. H.J. Payn	Mitchell's Personal Assistant
Jack Rice	Head of Electrical Design

Ken Scales	Firm's Inspector in charge of Spitfire construction
Beverley Shenstone	Chief Aerodynamicist
Arthur Shirvall	Hydrodynamic hull design and Tank Testing: future Project Design
Harold Smith	Senior Stressman; later Chief Structural Engineer
Joe Smith	Chief Draughtsman (Chief Designer following Mitchell's death)
H.O. Sommer	In charge of Propeller Design and all Strength Tests
Trevor Westbrook	Works Superintendent

Test Pilots

Capt. 'Mutt' Summers	Chief Test Pilot (Vickers Aviation Ltd)
George Pickering	
Jeffrey Quill	Chief Test Pilot (Supermarine)

Inspection Department

Mr Macfarlane	Chief Inspector
Charlie Johns	Deputy Chief Inspector

13 FAMILY TREE OF R.J. MITCHELL

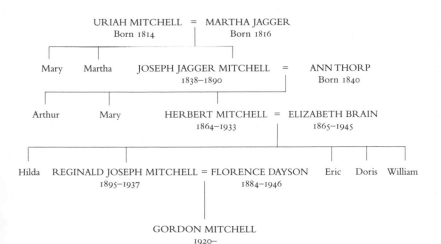

URIAH MITCHELL	was a millwright working in a woollen factory. He lived near Holmfirth, North Yorkshire.
JOSEPH JAGGER MITCHELL	was a mule spinner working in a woollen factory. He lived near Holmfirth, North Yorkshire.
HERBERT MITCHELL	was born in Holmfirth and lived in Normacot, Stoke-on-Trent, initially as a school master. He later became a master printer and founded the firm of Wood, Mitchell & Co., which still operates.
REGINALD JOSEPH MITCHELL	was born in Stoke-on-Trent and lived there until 1917 when he started work at The Supermarine Aviation Works in Southampton.

14 NUMBER OF SPITFIRES AND SEAFIRES EXISTING AS AT DECEMBER 2005

These total approximately 210, of which some fifty are airworthy, AR 501 depicted in the painting by Mark Postlethwaite (above) being one of the Spitfires currently still flying regularly. Full details of airworthy Spitfires can be found in an article by Peter R. Arnold in *Flypast*, February 2002.

15 TEST FLIGHT RECORD NO. N/300/1 OF F.37/34 FIGHTER[23] 4 K5054

Flight No.	1	2	3	4
Date (1936)	5 March	6 March	10 March	14 March
Time of flight (hrs)	16.35	15.25	17.05	13.30
Time in air (mins)	8	23	31	50

Most of the test results reported by Summers were rated as favourable, thus –

Taxying	Chassis was quite smooth in operation with no tendency for the machine to swing during the run on the ground. [Chassis = Undercarriage].
Ailerons	These are powerful and quite light to operate.
Elevators	These are very effective and light and are in harmony with the ailerons.
Rudder	Very effective but considered to be on the light side as it would be possible to apply full rudder at top speed. Requires a reduction of the rudder balance.
Trimming flaps	Quite ample to compete with the different conditions of flight. This also applies to the rudder trimming flap.
Wing flaps	These are very effective although there is a very slight change of trim when applied, giving a nose down tendency, but this can be easily trimmed out on the elevators.
Wheel brakes	It was noticed that after the flaps had been operated twice from the air supply reservoir, there was no air left to operate the brakes on landing. Suggests there is a need to install a separate air supply reservoir for the brakes.
Stability	Stable laterally and directionally up to a speed of 260 mph.
Pitching	No pitching tests were carried out.
Cockpit	Very comfortable and all controls accessible and very well laid out.
Sliding hood over pilot	Requires modification as possible for lock to become unfastened in flight allowing the hood to come out of its runner when slid backwards. Also, at high speed, it is practically impossible to open.
Retractable chassis operation in the air	Very light to operate but at present in an emergency, such as a fracture occurring in any of the hydraulic pipe lines, it would not be possible to get the chassis into the down position. It is suggested that an emergency system should, therefore, be installed.
Flying	The handling qualities of this machine are remarkably good.

Notes

	Page	
1	60	*Journal of the Royal Aeronautical Society*, 58, 311–328 (1954).
2	129	*Vickers: A History* (1962).
3	142	*Vickers: A History* (1962).
4	151	*Supermarine Aircraft since 1914* (1981).
5	154	*Vickers: A History* (1962).
6	157	The lecture was reported in full in the Journal of the Royal Aeronautical Society, 58, 311–328 (1954).
7	191	Brig.-Gen. W.B. Caddell was a special director of the Supermarine company with responsibility for sales.
8	192	Archibald Jamieson was chairman of Vickers Ltd – later Sir Archibald Jamieson.
9	204	*Vickers: A History* (1962).
10	207	*Nine Lives* (1959).
11	209	*Journal of the Royal Aeronautical Society*, 58, 311–328 (1954).
12	214	*Nine Lives* (1959).
13	233	*Journal of the Royal Aeronautical Society*, 58, 311–328 (1954).

14	238	*Journal of the Royal Aeronautical Society*, 58, 311–328 (1954).
15	264	Patrick Lindsay died in January 1986.
16	264	Edna Bianchi died in April 1997.
17	266	AMICE should have come before FRAeS.
18	276	John died on 20 October 1996 after a long illness.
19	276	P7350, the oldest airworthy Spitfire in the world.
20	282	Mac, who joined Supermarine in 1924, died on 14 December 1999.
21	314	Shenstone later became chief engineer of BEA and BOAC.
22	326	The two Vickers aircraft companies had been made a part of Vickers-Armstrongs in 1938.
23	368	Not given the name Spitfire when first flight tests carried out.

Illustrations

Photographs courtesy of Gordon Mitchell unless otherwise stated.

afterwards. Stainforth is on R.J.'s right

34. The 1931 Schneider Trophy RAF High Speed Flight with Lady Houston, on her yacht, *Liberty*, 1931. R.J. Mitchell on the right standing (Martin Boothman)

35. Schneider Trophy Dinner given by the mayor of Southampton, Councillor Cross, in honour of R.J. Mitchell at the South Western Hotel on 7 October 1931. From the left: R.J. Mitchell, Councillor Cross, Mrs R.J. Mitchell

36. Supermarine Walrus during take-off. This aircraft gave sterling service in the Navy and the RAF during the 1939–45 war (Flight)

37. Fine cutaway drawing of a Stranraer flying boat by M.A. Barnes (Aeroplane)

38. Lady McLean (wife of the chairman of Vickers Aviation and Supermarine) with Mrs R.J. Mitchell on holiday in Austria, *c.*1934

39. R.J. Mitchell's pilot's licence (photo by RAF Museum)

40. R.J. Mitchell's logbook (photo by RAF Museum)

41. Statement of expenditure on K5054 at 29 February 1936. See note 'Flew 5 Mar '36' at lower right. Entry following 'Not yet flown' is '£15,000 approx.' The original document is now lodged in the Vickers Archives at the Cambridge University Library (reproduced by permission of Vickers plc)

42. HM King Edward VIII inspects the prototype Spitfire at Martlesham. R.J. Mitchell is standing next to the propeller

43. The prototype Spitfire K5054 at Eastleigh, 11 May 1936

44. The prototype Spitfire

45. After the first flight of K5054. From the left: 'Mutt' Summers, 'Agony' Payn, R.J. Mitchell, S. Scott-Hall, Jeffrey Quill

46. Artist's impression of Mitchell's last design – the B.12/36 four-engined bomber (Cliff Machin)

47. Pass for R.J. Mitchell to enter the Royal Aircraft Establishment, the Aeroplane and Armament Experimental Establishment, and the Marine Aircraft Experimental Establishment

48. First flight of the prototype Spitfire K5054, painted by Jim Mitchell, R.J.'s nephew

49. Mitchell embarking for Vienna, 29 April 1937, assisted by Mr Gingell from Supermarine

50. A few of the floral tributes

51. R.J. with his wife in their garden, shortly before his death

52. Three Battle of Britain Mk I Spitfires from 19 Squadron, Duxford (Imperial War Museum)

53. Two 610 Squadron Mk Ia Spitfires. This photograph is one of the few available of Spitfires in action during the Battle of

Index

TEMPUS – REVEALING HISTORY

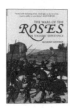
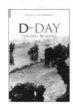

The Wars of the Roses
The Soldiers' Experience
ANTHONY GOODMAN
'Sheds light on the lot of the common soldier as never before' *Alison Weir*
£25
0 7524 1784 3

D-Day: The First 72 Hours
WILLIAM F. BUCKINGHAM
'A compelling narrative'
The Observer
£9.99
0 7524 2842 X

English Battlefields
500 Battlefields that Shaped English History
MICHAEL RAYNER
'A painstaking survey of English battlefields... a first-rate book' *Richard Holmes*
£25
0 7524 2978 7

Trafalgar Captain Durham of the Defiance: The
Man who refused to Miss Trafalgar
HILARY RUBINSTEIN
'A sparkling biography of Nelson's luckiest captain' *Andrew Lambert*
£17.99
0 7524 3435 7

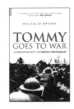

Battle of the Atlantic
MARC MILNER
'The most comprehensive short survey of the U-boat battles' *Sir John Keegan*
£12.99
0 7524 3332 6

Okinawa 1945 The Stalingrad of the Pacific
GEORGE FEIFER
'A great book... Feifer's account of the three sides and their experiences far surpasses most books about war' *Stephen Ambrose*
£17.99
0 7524 3324 5

Gallipoli 1915
TIM TRAVERS
'The most important new history of Gallipoli for forty years... groundbreaking' *Hew Strachan*
£13.99
0 7524 2972 8

Tommy Goes To War
MALCOLM BROWN
'A remarkably vivid and frank account of the British soldier in the trenches'
Max Arthur
£12.99
0 7524 2980 9

If you are interested in purchasing other books published by Tempus, or in case you have difficulty finding any Tempus books in your local bookshop, you can also place orders directly through our website

www.tempus-publishing.com

TEMPUS – REVEALING HISTORY

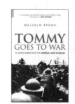

Quacks
Fakers and Charlatans in Medicine
ROY PORTER
'A delightful book'
The Daily Telegraph
12.99
0 7524 2590 0

The Tudors
RICHARD REX
'Up-to-date, readable and reliable. The best introduction to England's most important dynasty'
David Starkey
9.99
0 7524 3333 4

The Kings & Queens of England
MARK ORMROD
'Of the numerous books on the kings and queens of England, this is the best'
Alison Weir
9.99
0 7524 2598 6

The Covent Garden Ladies
Pimp General Jack & the Extraordinary Story of Harris's List
HALLIE RUBENHOLD
'Has all the atmosphere and edge of a good novel… magnificent'
Frances Wilson
20
0 7524 2850 0

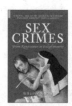

Private 12768
Memoir of a Tommy
JOHN JACKSON
'Unique… a beautifully written, strikingly honest account of a young man's experience of combat' *Saul David*
9.99
0 7524 3531 0

Sex Crimes
From Renaissance to Enlightenment
W.M. NAPHY
'Wonderfully scandalous'
Diarmaid MacCulloch
10.99
0 7524 2977 9

Ace of Spies The True Story of Sidney Reilly
ANDREW COOK
'The most definitive biography of the spying ace yet written… both a compelling narrative and a myth-shattering *tour de force*'
Simon Sebag Montefiore
£12.99
0 7524 2959 0

Tommy Goes To War
MALCOLM BROWN
'A remarkably vivid and frank account of the British soldier in the trenches'
Max Arthur
12.99
0 7524 2980 4

If you are interested in purchasing other books published by Tempus, or in case you have difficulty finding any Tempus books in your local bookshop, you can also place orders directly through our website

www.tempus-publishing.com